MARRIAGE UNBOUND

STATE LAW, POWER, AND INEQUALITY IN CONTEMPORARY CHINA

Ke Li

STANFORD UNIVERSITY PRESS

Stanford, California

Stanford University Press
Stanford, California

©2022 by the Board of Trustees of the Leland Stanford Junior
University. All rights reserved.

Printed in the United States of America on acid-free, archival-quality
paper

Library of Congress Cataloging-in-Publication Data

Names: Li, Ke (Sociologist), author.
Title: Marriage unbound : state law, power, and inequality in
contemporary China / Ke Li.
Description: Stanford, California : Stanford University Press, 2022. |
Includes bibliographical references and index.
Identifiers: LCCN 2021051792 (print) | LCCN 2021051793 (ebook)
| ISBN 9781503613140 (cloth) | ISBN 9781503632011 (paperback) |
ISBN 9781503632028 (ebook)
Subjects: LCSH: Divorce—Law and legislation—China. | Divorce—
China. | Sex discrimination against women—China.
Classification: LCC KNQ558 .L55 2022 (print) | LCC KNQ558 (ebook)
| DDC 346.5101/6—dc23/eng/20220427
LC record available at https://lccn.loc.gov/2021051792
LC ebook record available at https://lccn.loc.gov/2021051793

Cover art: Eric Bedford, Stony Brook University

MARRIAGE
UNBOUND

For Yu Jiayao

Contents

Abbreviations

CCP	Chinese Communist Party
HRS	Household Responsibility System
MOJ	Ministry of Justice
PRC	People's Republic of China
SPC	Supreme People's Court

Figures and Tables

TABLES

Acknowledgments

In summer 2006, I took a trip to visit my extended family in Weifeng, a county about a four-hour's drive south of Chengdu, the capital of Sichuan Province in southwest China. During that trip, I began hearing stories of marital disputes and divorce suits in the countryside. My first conversation was with a peasant who had served for decades as a barefoot doctor, one among the millions in rural China, providing basic health care to community members, albeit with limited training and resources. Owing to that experience, he had come to know about country folks' troubles at home. Sitting in his small clinic in a remote village, I listened to the doctor—someone with vivid memories of the 1980s and 1990s when divorce was a rare occurrence in most parts of the country—recalling one household after another torn apart because of how desperately a wife, a sister, or a daughter-in-law tried to break free from her conjugal family in the village. Over the next decade or so, many in Weifeng opened their doors, as well as their hearts, to me. Some invited me into their homes and places of work, some trusted me with their innermost thoughts and feelings, and others were courageous enough to reveal the dark side of the official justice system in rural China. This book would not have been possible without the honesty, kindness, and generosity provided by the women and men I met in Weifeng.

In a decade or so, many at Indiana University, Bloomington, offered inspiration, encouragement, and unwavering support. Philip Parnell introduced me to the Law and Society scholarship. Ethan Michelson sparked my interest in the sociology of law. Thomas F. Gieryn showed me the beauty of social theory. Brian Steensland profoundly shaped my thinking about culture and power. Sara L. Friedman piqued my curiosity about the interplay of gender and politics, and taught me the importance of intellectual integrity, perseverance, and patience with research. Brian Powell offered invaluable advice on career development and teaching. I would not have gone this far without their mentoring.

My field research in China from 2006 to 2011 was funded by the following organizations: the Office of the Vice President for International Affairs, Indiana University; the Department of Sociology, Indiana University; the Association for Asian Studies; the National Science Foundation; the Social Science Research Council; and the Chiang Ching-kuo Foundation for International Scholarly Exchange. The China Times Cultural Foundation in 2012 offered me an award and funding so I could turn my findings into publications. Since I joined the City University of New York (CUNY) in 2017, the Research Foundation of CUNY has funded my research in three consecutive years, allowing me to conduct a follow-up study of divorce litigation in Weifeng and to cover other expenses. Between 2018 and 2019, the American Council of Learned Societies and the John Jay College of Criminal Justice invested in my work; the former provided a postdoctoral fellowship and the latter offered me a scholar incentive leave. Thanks to their support, I took a two-semester leave from teaching to fully immerse myself in book writing. The next year, I attended the Faculty Fellowship Publication Program sponsored by the Office of the Dean for Recruitment and Diversity at CUNY. Through this program, I became part of a university-wide research network, a crucial experience that helped me branch out professionally and intellectually. I am grateful to all these institutions and entities for their interest in and support for my scholarship.

In the past four years, colleagues at CUNY have strengthened the book ahead through their close readings of various chapters. Many thanks to Michael Yarborough, Nicholas Rush Smith, Marcus Johnson, James Rodriguez, Lina P. Newton, Diana B. Greenwald, Huang Paoyi, Jennifer Laird, Liza Steele, and Liu Min. I learned so much from these colleagues who shared with me their sharp insights, critical thought, and research experiences as historians, sociologists, and political scientists. I am also grateful to Elisabeth Gitter, Alice Pease, and Wayne Svoboda. At a time when I was new to CUNY, the aforementioned colleagues keenly facilitated my efforts to navigate the university in hopes of making my first foray into nonfiction writing. Later, Frederick Kaufmann, Tim Harper, and Jeffrey Heiman welcomed me into their classes, knowing that I was a newbie to creative writing; their teaching enabled and emboldened my experimentation with feature writing in this book. Moreover, administrators at the John Jay College, especially Li Yi, James Cauthen, Andrew Sidman, Anthony Carpi, Amrish Sugrim-Singh, and Susy G. Mendes Cullen, stepped in at critical moments. Their leadership and collegiality ensured that I could complete this book in a timely manner.

My deepest appreciation also goes to colleagues elsewhere, whose wisdom, knowledge, and generosity made research and writing at once humane and intellectually stimulating. Deborah S. Davis time and again reminded me of the importance of modesty, open-mindedness, and continuous learning. Rachel E. Stern encouraged me to stay true to what I believed in as a researcher and a writer, a piece of advice I have taken to heart. Carl Minzner challenged me on multiple fronts to think long and hard about the links between citizens' intimate lives and national politics. Xiao Suowei helped my field research in China and subsequently shared her monograph with me long before I could find a copy in the United States. Hae Yeon Choo was unfailingly generous in her endeavors to support and nurture the younger generation of scholars, especially women of color. These colleagues, in one way or another, offer a model of scholarly excellence.

Over time, I have become indebted to colleagues in anthropology, sociology, political science, and the law, who took time to read and comment on my work. These colleagues include William P. Alford, Karen J. Alter, Lynette Chua, Rachel Cichowski, Donald C. Clarke, Matthew Erie, Susan Finder, Fu Hualing, Mary Gallagher, Margaret Hanson, He Xin, Hu Xiaoqian, Danielle Kane, Margaret Lewis, Li Ling, Benjamin L. Liebman, Liu Qian, Liu Sida, Lü Qinghu, Alyx Mark, Mou Yu, Michael Palmer, Poulami Roychowdhury, Caroline L. Silva, Narendra Subramanian, Wang Di, Wang Guojun, Wang Juan, Timothy Webster, Lynn T. White III, Margaret Y. K. Woo, Zhan Yang, and Zhang Taisu. Also on my mind are individuals who assisted my data collection and writing. Yang Qinxin for three years worked as a research assistant, tirelessly gathering news articles and other materials online and elsewhere; my gratitude to him is immense. Agnieszka Rec carefully copyedited the manuscript. Michelle M. Lipinski, Kate Wahl, and Marcela Cristina Maxfield at Stanford University Press offered crucial editorial guidance.

Finally, a few words to those in my life: I dedicate this book to Yu Jiayao, my mother, who has taught me that authority is not something merely to be complied with but to be questioned and examined critically. The book cover is based on a graphic generated by Eric Bedford, whose friendship and perceptivity has enriched my life like no others. Péter Szigeti has remained a steady source of compassion, comfort, and humor. This book would have pained me even more without his constant reminder—outside my work, there is a whole world right there.

MARRIAGE
UNBOUND

Introduction

MINUTES PAST NINE IN THE MORNING, on May 10, 2010 , Hou Yuemei, a migrant worker in her late thirties, pulled herself out of a shuttle bus. Her face paled, her back aching, legs sore, her stomach twisting from car sickness. Days of travel—from eastern, coastal China to the western inland, from Yuemei's workplace in Jiangsu to her native soil in Sichuan— had sapped her strength. But, instead of slowing down, she quickened her pace. Before long, she headed into a dark corridor of an office building, just a few blocks away from the bus station. Inside that corridor was Yuemei's destination—the Qinchuan People's Tribunal, where she was about to make her first court appearance.

Exactly 215 days earlier, Yuemei fled home after her husband had attacked her, once again leaving bruises all over her body. Amid that assault, she grabbed a kitchen knife to defend herself, an instinctive reaction that saved her life. Only after that did the man back off. Days later, with the help of a coworker, Yuemei escaped Fujian, the place where the couple had been eking out a living as migrant workers, and boarded a bus to Jiangsu, a province hundreds of miles away, similarly awash with cash-paying jobs for migrants hailing from the countryside.

For the next few months, Yuemei lived in secrecy and fear, constantly watching her back. The bruises covering her body faded away, but the invisible scars hardly healed. She frequently woke up from night terrors. "The moment I fall asleep, I dream about him beating me repeatedly," said Yuemei.

Working a factory job in Nanjing, the capital city of Jiangsu, Yuemei saved every penny she could. By the spring of 2010 , she had finally amassed enough cash to hire a legal worker to help with her divorce suit. She was ready to press her case inside a courtroom, hoping to cut ties with a violent, abusive man.

That same May, another migrant woman, Miao Shuihua, was contemplating a similar decision. Unlike Yuemei, who journeyed to remote places like Fujian and Jiangsu to search for off-farm employment, Shuihua stayed in rural Sichuan close to her family and her infant son. Although her parents lent a hand from time to time, the responsibility of child-rearing squarely fell on Shuihua's shoulders.

Barely thirty, Shuihua had spent the past six years earning minimum wages as a menial laborer in the nearby county seat. Doing so, she hoped, could help balance her family's income and expenditure on the one hand and care for both the young and the elderly on the other. That hope rarely materialized, though. The gap between her paycheck and the family's various expenses kept growing. Putting food on the table, paying utility bills, refilling a prescription, getting milk powder and diapers … all the little things that allowed her to raise a family seemed more and more taxing by the day.

Shuihua's husband, whom she described as "an honest man" with a quick temper, scarcely eased her burden. Plowing farmland day in, day out, the man "just couldn't feed or clothe his family," Shuihua said. While wrestling with a strained marriage, Shuihua constantly thought about her son. What would happen to him if her marriage could not survive? Could she retain child custody after divorce? Would her husband, a peasant man about to turn forty, let go of his only child, a healthy boy destined to become the sole heir of his family? With these questions in mind, Shuihua sued her husband, later in 2010, expecting the court to mete out fair rulings over divorce and child custody.[1]

All happy families are alike, they say, and every unhappy family is unhappy in its own way. Yet Yuemei and Shuihua, two ordinary Chinese women, entangled in conjugal strife for different reasons, share important commonalities. Both have partaken in the massive rural-to-urban migration that has transformed Chinese family, marriage, and gender relationships. They are part of China's ever-expanding floating population (流动人口), in other words. This population has grown to 288 million over four decades, primarily comprising rural residents relocating from the countryside to work in rapidly growing metropolitan areas. By the end of 2018, nearly 95 million rural women have headed for various urban destinations for employment.[2] Today, women of rural origin can be found in virtually every labor-intensive industry, running the gamut from manufacturing to construction, from transportation to the service sector, including hotels, restaurants, housekeeping, and caregiving.

Both Yuemei and Shuihua initiated legal action by taking their husbands to court. Their endeavors point to an increasingly salient trend: dissolving marriage inside a courtroom, a rare occurrence in China for most of the twentieth century, has become far more common today. The court system, in 2018 alone, processed 1.37 million divorce suits, a sixfold increase since the late 1970s. Among those seeking judicial remedies for marital discord, women have consistently outnumbered men. Over 70 percent of divorce suits nationwide were initiated by wives as opposed to by husbands, according to the Supreme People's Court (SPC), the highest court in the country.[3] To put it another way, Yuemei's and Shuihua's courtroom experiences bear witness to the Chinese judiciary's response to the rise of legal mobilization and rights contention among women.

Examining responses of this kind is critical, not only because family and marriage have evolved due to vast social and economic transformation in society —but also because the Chinese state has reconfigured its interventions in citizens' intimate lives. In 2001, the National People's Congress, China's highest legislative body, amended the Marriage Law. In the area of divorce, the revised law introduced significant changes by codifying concrete grounds for divorce and by establishing measures aimed to penalize blameworthy conduct, such as infidelity, spousal abuse, and abandonment. In subsequent decades, top decision-makers brought into effect a series of legislative and regulatory changes, including the first national law against domestic violence.

The state's attempts to revamp its governing tool kit to insert official influences into citizens' intimate relationships, together with women's participation in labor migration and their growing willingness to contest rights inside courtrooms, I believe, beg several questions of great significance. First, how has women's integration into the urban labor force affected marriage, family life, and gender relationships in Chinese society? Among those mired in marital discontent, who manages to enter the official justice system? What happens inside? How does the system handle conjugal disputes and conflicts? In what ways does the system redress inequality and injustice? Or, in what ways does it reproduce and reinforce male dominance in the family and society at large? Finally, how could a study of women's legal mobilization forge new ground for our understanding of law, politics, and inequality in an authoritarian state?

To address these questions, this book follows a group of Chinese women seeking judicial remedies for conjugal grievances and disputes. Using data from multiple sources—participant observations, in-depth interviews, judicial statistics, government publications, and news articles—I show how these women wrestle with government officials and village leaders on the front line of dispute management; how they interact with legal professionals who operate as market players and make a living by serving clients; how they struggle to convey their grievances and rights claims to judges at the grassroots level; and, in the end, how the local government, the legal profession, and the court system far too often fail to protect women's rights and interests. In this way, the book ahead untangles the processes, mechanisms, and power dynamics at play both within and without courtrooms that shape women's experiences in disputation and in litigation.

In what follows, I first identify the audiences intended for this book and outline a view of legality at its heart. Then I detail the methodologies and data sources that have laid the empirical foundation of my analysis. What follows is a discussion of why and how this book experiments with a particular style of writing. This experimentation, I hope, serves at once stylistic and epistemological purposes. Finally, a road map is included so that readers can forge their own paths forward.

A VIEW OF LEGALITY SENSITIVE TO HISTORY, CULTURE, AND POWER

In writing this book, I have kept two audiences in mind. The first consists of political scientists, sociologists, and China scholars whose research centers on law, legal professions, and courts in authoritarian contexts—or what is known as *authoritarian legality*. In building a dialogue with this audience, I argue that the time is ripe to reorient our inquiry, steering away from a functionalist, utilitarian approach to legality and toward a historically charged, culturalist perspective. To hammer out the alternative perspective, I commit half of the book (especially chapters 3 and 4) to exploring the complex interplay of culture and the state—the first theoretical objective motivating my research.

The other audience on my mind pertains to sociolegal researchers who consider dispute resolution their key intellectual interest. (To avoid repetition, I use the following terms interchangeably throughout this book: *disputation, dispute resolution, conflict resolution, dispute management,* and *conflict management.*) To those colleagues, my argument is set against an individualistic, behavioristic view of disputation. By constructing a power-centered framework, we can more effectively unpack the linkage between legality and inequality in politically repressive settings and per-haps elsewhere, I suggest. Accordingly, I devote the latter half of the book (chapters 5, 6, and 7) to reconceiving the notion of *dispute resolution*—the second theoretical objective, which completes the arc of my analysis.

Together, in pursuing these two objectives, I promote a view of legality that is sensitive to history, culture, and power. To fully engender this view, chapter 1 presents an elaborate account as to how this book engages two scholarly communities, in part by critiquing well-established approaches in extant literature and in part by charting the alternative course I have treaded in my own work. Moreover, chapter 1 lays out theoretical arguments stemming from my empirical findings, thus delineating law and politics, culture and the state, and power and inequality—the key param-eters shaping the contour of the book. Readers keen on theory building may find that chapter particularly pertinent. Otherwise, the following paragraphs, in a few broad strokes, might just suffice to foreshadow conceptually the chapters ahead.

Central to this book is the inquiry of how an authoritarian regime, like the People's Republic of China (PRC), has configured and reconfigured law, legal professions, and courts, as ruling elites calibrate and recalibrate a cultural repertoire of statecraft. To frame my query this way, in effect, is to bring history to center stage. Indeed, taking women's experiences in disputation as a point of departure, I trace and analyze a number of legal developments in contemporary China. In doing so, this book maps the historical trajectories along which the PRC—once a revolutionary regime, then a socialist one, and today post-socialist—has continually streamlined its governing methodologies, techniques, and tactics in the context of dispute management and beyond. And it reveals that, with time, state actors have unlearned certain ruling methodologies applied in the Maoist era; remodeled techniques and tactics inherited from the socialist period; and, what's more, selectively appropriated governing experience from liberal democracies. State actors, in that sense, have cultivated a repertoire of statecraft of diverse origins. In historicizing Chinese women's struggles with marital grievances and disputes, I connect the dots between an authoritarian regime's past and ongoing efforts to refine its governance.

In addressing the query above, I also strive to bring culture into the limelight. Here, the term *culture* refers to a system of symbols, meanings, and practices—a system that is often contradictory, contested, loosely integrated, subject to change, weakly bounded, but nonetheless operates with its own autonomy, distinct from and irreducible to other features of social life.[4] My use of this term has been informed and inspired by sociologist Ann Swidler's theory of culture in action. The central problematic for cultural analysts, Swidler contends, is not necessarily to parse the content of culture but rather to uncover how social actors use cultural materials. In her own words, the key task is to analyze "the varied ways people use diverse cultural materials, appropriating some and using them to build a life, holding others in reserve, and keeping still others permanently at a distance."[5]

Note that Swidler invokes this practice-oriented conception of culture to explore how ordinary people employ cultural materials, such as moral visions, images, vocabularies, meanings, skills, habits, and strategies of action, in everyday life. In this book, I apply a similarly practice-oriented approach to unveil how the PRC's ruling elites appropriate cultural resources—including political ideologies, orthodox norms, mainstream values, discursive frames, cognitive categories, policy instruments, and institutional memories and practices—from divergent origins. In this manner, they regularly engage in cultural appropriation, a sphere of activities through which political elites extract cultural materials from multiple sources, repackage preexisting institutional practices and arrangements to pursue new goals, and, frequently, wind up imbricating inherited and borrowed governing experience into the fabric of their ruling.[6]

By centering culture, I set my work apart from many others in the studies of authoritarian legality, which often treat culture as ephemeral at best and utterly irrelevant at worst. While formulating a cultural-ist view of law and courts in a nondemocratic context, I place a heavy emphasis on how the PRC's rulers calibrate and recalibrate their ruling methodologies, techniques, and tactics by tapping into diverse cultural resources, including, but not limited to, the country's (real or imagined) roots in Confucianism, the Maoist past, socialist legacies, and foreign influences. In this process, the PRC's decision-makers have assembled and reassembled institutional practices of various stripes in hopes that they could craft more or less novel solutions to emerging problems in ruling. As the remainder of the book illustrates, decision-makers of the reform era have demonstrated remarkable audacity, ingenuity, and efficacy in cultural appropriation.

The upshot? Legality, in the form of lawmaking and law-applying, has become an integral part of the PRC's repertoire of statecraft, thereby enabling state actors to select (or deselect) legal methods to tackle dispute management in one way or another. While stressing the enabling effects of cultural appropriation, this book does not lose sight of the downside of such a phenomenon. Culture can enable political elites by endowing them with a wide range of resources and assets. Under different cir-cumstances, though, culture can also turn into liabilities and troubles, complicating and constraining political elites' problem-solving efforts. Drawing on insights from cultural sociologists, and particularly from Pierre Bourdieu, Ann Swidler, and John L. Campbell, chapter 1 further spells out how culture can operate in practice like a double-edged sword, sometimes facilitating and sometimes hampering the PRC's attempts at harnessing law. By illuminating at once the enabling and the constrain-ing effects of cultural appropriation, this book sets out to remedy the widespread indifference to culture, a persistent problem in the literature on authoritarian legality.

Finally, to bring forward a view of legality sensitive to power, I break free from an entrenched research tradition in sociolegal studies. Over the past four decades, sociolegal scholars have repeatedly treated conflict resolution as corollaries of individual behaviors. This view is particularly salient in the so-called *dispute pyramid model*, which posits that conflict resolution is either initiated, prolonged, and resolved by individual actions (e.g., searching for help of a third party, staking out claims, and seeking the intervention of authorities in community or in government), or it is suppressed, suspended, and terminated by individuals' inaction (e.g., swallowing grievances, avoiding conflicts, and opting out of recourse to formal laws).[7] In privileging the question of what individuals do (or fail to do) in the genesis, evolution, and resolution of disputes and conflicts, this model leaves researchers with little analytical leverage to dissect the institutional practices at the root of injustice and inequality in China and elsewhere.

To shift scholarly attention from individual behaviors to institutional practices, I turn to sociologists Steven Lukes and John Gaventa for their insights about power and powerlessness. This book, accordingly, reconceptualizes dispute resolution in terms of interconnected power relations. Taking divorce litigation as a window, I specify the workings of three distinct types of power—*agenda-setting power, consciousness-formation power*, and *formal decision-making power*—all of which undergird institutional practices inside courtrooms and surrounding rural communities. As the book ahead reveals, when the three powers are all stacked against women, gender inequality is bound to emerge and deepen in the course of dispute resolution. In the end, rather than serving as the weapon of the weak, legal mobilization and litigation wind up reinforcing and reproducing inequality between the average woman and man. In this regard, chapter 1 features a full-blown critique of the individualistic, behaviorist approach to dispute resolution and provides a detailed account of a power-centered framework as an alternative perspective.

ETHNOGRAPHY, HISTORIOGRAPHY, AND DATA SOURCES

Methodologically, this book stems from years of arduous efforts to coalesce ethnography and historiography. Applying the former, I have documented and analyzed present-day social phenomena—notably those at the individual and interpersonal level. Engaging in the latter, I have examined historical developments—at the organizational and institutional level. The combination of these two methodologies, in turn, offers certain epistemological rewards. To begin with, it allows me to travel back and forth between the present and certain bygone eras, between one social space and another, between the mundane and the microscopic on one side and far-reaching social, economic, and political changes in Chinese society on the other.

Such time and space travel proves instrumental for my attempts at solving empirical puzzles. Here is one telling example: inside courtrooms, I saw judges frequently turn away divorce petitioners and dispose of their cases via a procedure called *withdrawal* (撤诉). Why did judges routinely invoke this procedure, notwithstanding reluctance and resistance on the part of petitioners, who often had gone to great lengths to bring grievances and rights claims to the courts? Interviews and on-site observations did not yield a satisfying answer. After that, I decided to journey into the past, into the PRC's long, winding history of stipulating procedural rules and norms necessary for civil litigation. Delving into archival research, I stumbled on important findings. Thanks to methodical examination of legislative and statistical records, I unearthed the process whereby withdrawal, as a civil procedure and then as a mode of case disposition, had become institutionalized in Chinese courts. Along the way, I discovered what had incentivized judges to favor this mode, whose interests were best served, and whose rights were abrogated (chapter 5 details these findings). Suffice to say that connecting the dots between ethnographic findings and revelations from archival materials profoundly deepened my knowledge of law and politics.

Two waves of data collection, stretching from 2006 to 2011, and then from 2017 to 2020, have made it possible to weave ethnographic and historical analyses into the texture of book writing. The 2006–2011 period was particularly critical, as it laid the foundation for my efforts to fuse two distinct methodologies. During that period, I spent a total of twenty months conducting fieldwork in Weifeng, a county with a large agricultural population in Sichuan Province in southwest China. Inside Weifeng, my research activities mainly revolved around two rural townships: Guxiao and Xiqing.[8]

My choice of these two places as the main research sites was guided by my familiarity with the local communities. With the help of extended family members scattered in Guxiao, Xiqing, and the adjacent townships, I managed to build ties with key players in the field—village cadres, government officials, legal workers, lawyers, and, most crucially, judges and court clerks. In the summer of 2006, 2007, and 2008, I conducted three rounds of preliminary research in Weifeng; in each summer, I spent weeks gaining hands-on research experiences by observing court proceedings, by interviewing divorce litigants and their counsel, and by talking to individuals knowledgeable about popular grievances in rural communities. I also paid visits to various state bureaucracies in charge of dispute management at the grassroots level. These activities helped me secure access to the key institutions involved in my research and paved the way for a full-scale ethnographic study, carried out between January 2010 and May 2011, a seventeen-month period that formed the bulk of my field research.

I also chose Guxiao and Xiqing because they epitomized rural backwaters in western inland China. In these two townships, senior residents still harbored fond memories of the 1980s and 1990s—a time when farming brought peasants stable income. The port along the Min River infused rural communities with cargo, cash, and energy, and state-owned enterprises were burgeoning, supplying the locals with a sense of pride and prosperity. The younger generation, however, could hardly hide their disappointment at the new millennium. The first decade of the twenty-first century bore testimony to the townships' decline as a result of economic underdevelopment, ecological deterioration, and rising labor out-migration. By the end of 2010, the annual per capita income for rural residents throughout Weifeng barely reached 5,000 yuan. That was the equivalent of $800 a year.

Supporting largely agricultural populations, Guxiao and Xiqing accommodated approximately 25,000 and 48,000 residents around 2010. Since the turn of the century, the townships had experienced a rapid exodus of labor; thousands of residents had traveled far and near, searching for off-farm employment. In recent years, residents developed a palpable sense that their marriages had become more vulnerable, as one household after another saw their wives, daughters, sisters, and other female family members dip their toes in labor migration and then in divorce. Indeed, that divorce was notably on the rise among country folks was the perennial talk of the town.

It was against this backdrop that I assembled four research samples. The first comprises a large number of observations I carried out at two legal workers' offices, one located in Guxiao and the other in Xiqing. As primary providers of legal services in the local communities, the offices regularly handled contractual disputes, labor disputes, personal injuries, debts, and divorces among villagers. To assess the legal profession's role in disputation and in litigation, I visited the offices five times a week for nine months. Each time, I spent at least six hours cataloging legal workers' daily routines. This is to say, when they engaged in small talk with coworkers, I quietly noted insider stories, rumors, hearsay—basically any information flowing through the grapevine. When they exchanged chitchat with village cadres and government officials, I eavesdropped endlessly, more than I ever thought I could. When villagers knocked on the door, seeking out professional advice, I was there to jot down the legal workers' reactions to contention and strife in rural communities. When clients turned up, I had my eyes glued to their face-to-face interactions with those practicing law in the countryside.

When the moment finally came for legal workers to represent their clients inside courtrooms, I followed them around like a shadow. Over twenty months or so, my footsteps fell in five of the six People's Tribunals (人民法庭) under the jurisdiction of Weifeng. Every time I stepped into a courthouse, I scanned its interior with my eyes, made mental notes of human interactions, and built memory lanes for the different divorce suits I was tracking. I also documented casual conversations, mediation sessions, and formal trials. On numerous occasions, I talked to litigants, their family members, counsel, judges, and court clerks. On many evenings, I racked my brain to extract as much remembrance on paper as possible. Immersing myself in fieldwork, I treated everything and anything that came my way as a potential source of data. Ultimately, I spent upward of one thousand hours recording six legal workers' day-to-day operation at the offices and inside courtrooms.

The second sample consists of one hundred and fifteen in-depth interviews. The bulk of the interviews involves wives and husbands who were so deeply enmeshed in conjugal strife that they approached the legal workers' offices for help. Taking the offices as key sites to recruit respondents, I conducted sixty semi-structured or unstructured interviews with thirty-two wives, and twenty interviews with sixteen husbands.[9] At the time, some of the respondents had already initiated divorce litigation, and others were mulling over marital dissolution. In each case, I tried hard to track the progression of a marital dispute and to hold interviews at multiple points in time. Thus, I wound up with eighty interviews, concerning forty-eight respondents on the verge of divorce.

Additionally, I approached thirty-five individuals whose daily routines revolved around village affairs, dispute management, or divorce litigation. Among these individuals, some were local political elites (e.g., village cadres and government officials); some were court insiders (e.g., judges and clerks); and others were professionals—legal workers and lawyers—seeking to keep their business afloat by trading legal know-how for fees. My interactions with those groups led to another thirty-five interviews. Together, the interview sample enabled my analysis of legal mobilization, rights contention, and litigation from diverse vantage points.

The third component of my field research pertains to a sample of divorce case records. During my stay in Weifeng, I reviewed all the case records maintained by the Guxiao Legal Workers' Office. Between 2003 and 2011, the office handled over two hundred divorce-related disputes and lawsuits. This in turn generated more than three thousand pages of documents, including divorce petitions, minutes of meetings between petitioners and their counsel, witness testimonies, other forms of evidence, mediation agreements, and court judgments. Sifting through these records and arranging them in order, I formed a sample of one hundred and ninety-eight divorce suits. Owing to this sample, I came to discern stark gender disparities in litigation outcomes—particularly outcomes concerning domestic violence, division of marital property, and allocation of child custody.

Finally, the fourth sample incorporates various government records retrieved from multiple state agencies other than the court system. During the twenty-month field research, I visited the Justice Bureau (司法局), the Women's Federation (妇女联合会), the Housing Management Office (房屋

管理所), and the Weifeng Archives—basically, county-level state bureaucracies. I also found my way to myriad state authorities at the township level—the Justice Office (司法所), the Office of Justice and Mediation (司法调解办), the Office of Letters and Visits and the Masses (信访与群众办公室), the Office of Comprehensive Management of Public Security (综治办), and the Center for Integrated Mediation for Disputes and Conflicts (矛盾纠纷大调解中心), to name a few examples. Furthermore, I gained access to seven Villagers' Committees (村民委员会), the governing body at the village level. Everywhere I went, I amassed official documents; some were available to the public, including county annals (县志), court annals (人民法院志), and brochures and flyers promoting state laws and policies; and others were strictly internal materials, intended for official use only. In collecting and reviewing thousands of pages of government records, I explored how state actors—apart from judges and clerks— tackled marital disputes, as well as other types of popular grievances and rights contention in the countryside. These records, in totality, offered a rare glimpse into the local state's diverse approaches to governance and to dispute management.

* * *

If the 2006–2011 period could be described as formative, laying the groundwork for the book, the next five or six years should be characterized as ruminative. While turning ethnographic findings into a dissertation and two journal articles, I grappled with the limits of my fieldwork—conducted in one place, during one period. By the end of 2017, I was convinced that ethnography alone would not suffice. It was time to branch out, methodologically and theoretically. Right then and there, I began to delve deeper and deeper into historiography.

Several online databases provided the means for my travel back in time. The first one, PKUlaw (北大法宝), has been my go-to website whenever I need to parse law on the books. Between 2017 and 2020, I combed through approximately five hundred national laws, departmental regulations, judicial interpretations, and policy directives, covering the entire history of the PRC over seven decades. On a side note: throughout the book, I cite over one hundred legislative, regulatory, and judicial documents, mostly in the notes. Readers can easily find the sources of my citations in case they need such information for their scholarship.

Where PKUlaw offered a frontal view of law on the books, the second database, China National Knowledge Infrastructure (中国知网), supplied invaluable opportunities to probe into law in action and law on the ground. Using this database, I downloaded hundreds of pages of yearbooks and magazine articles published by the Ministry of Justice (MOJ), the Ministry of Civil Affairs, the National Bureau of Statistics, and so on. These publications—together with two waves of massive data release carried out by the SPC, first in 2000 and then in 2018—proved to be a treasure trove, containing in-depth, minute, and yet rarely used records, spanning from 1949 to 2016.[10] In the references, I detail the yearbooks, magazines, and judicial statistics appearing in various chapters ahead.

Finally, with the help of a research assistant, I used an online database (人民日报图文数据库) to assemble media coverage, published by the *People's Daily*, the flagship newspaper of the Chinese Communist Party (CCP) since 1946. In three years, I collected and examined nearly 1,200 news articles, exploring subjects ranging from folk disputes (民间纠纷) to marital regulations, from Township Legal Services (乡镇法律服务) to state-sponsored legal aid. Using media coverage as a weathercock, I traced shifting priorities and trends in state actors' policymaking and lawmaking.

The combination of media data, government publications, and national legislation helped me piece together the images state actors strove to project in official discourse, in symbolic performance, and in public imagination of statehood. It also facilitated my inquiries into the actual practices state actors partook in with regard to lawmaking, policy wrangling, and institution building. For that reason, these records are of enormous value to sociologists and political scientists interested in untangling not only state images but also state practices. Similarly, they provide a precious window through which sociolegal researchers can gauge potential gaps between rights promised on paper and right infringements in practice.

A cynic might contend otherwise, readily dismissing official bookkeeping on the grounds that authoritarian regimes like the PRC have always had a hand in data manipulation. Researchers should therefore shun such data sources altogether. This view is unwise, in my opinion. In retrospect, I find my experience in exhuming government records rather rewarding, though at times fraught with anxieties. Such records often contain an ocean of information otherwise unreachable to institutional outsiders and especially to researchers based in the West. The experience is also fraught, because from time to time I must question the veracity of the evidence in front of me by cross-referencing it with other sources.

All that said, here is what I come to believe: there is no such thing as a perfect crime in data distortion. The more systematically and expansively state authorities engage in creating, amplifying, and rooting disinformation, the more traces they could leave behind. The more trace evidence we researchers muster, the more we engage in data triangulation by cross-checking findings from multiple sources—interviews, observations, archival inquiries, and analyses of media coverage—the closer we inch toward truths, thus rendering ourselves less susceptible to disinformation and misinformation.

In sum, the archival research I conducted in 2017–2020 set the stage for me to situate previous fieldwork in larger historical and social contexts. Now, I am ready to transform ethnographic findings, derived from one time-space, into the continuation of certain histories and into the extension of large-scale social or political processes that have been unfolding in contemporary China. In combining the two methodologies, I also provide a thoughtful response to the challenges ethnographers and historical sociologists have long contemplated. Indeed, from Clifford Geertz to James C. Scott, from Michael Burawoy to more recent practitioners, ethnographers have mulled over the question of how to extend the temporal or spatial bounds of field research.[11] Similarly, historical sociologists have chewed over the use of comparative case studies as a remedy for otherwise time- or space-bounded scholarly inquiries.[12] Recognizing these methodological ruminations, this book strives to breach the geographic and temporal boundaries researchers typically face. It does so by placing ethnographic findings side by side with revelations from archival inquiries in virtually every chapter. Underscoring the connections between the present and the past, between the interpersonal and the institutional, this book, I hope, transcends certain analytical cleavages like the micro versus the macro, the quotidian versus the monumental, social history from below versus history of great men. Finally, to further expand the frontiers in merging ethnography and historiography, I have incorporated comparative evidence into the book. In chapter 3, I present a "positive" case—the revitalization of people's mediation (人民调解) in the twenty-first century—to illustrate how culture enables state actors. In chapter 4, I switch to dissect a "negative" case—the downfall of legal workers in the new millennium—to demonstrate how culture constrains state actors. Applying a comparative scheme like this, I articulate the complex interplay of culture and the state—as part of my larger endeavors to advance theory building.

EXPERIMENTING WITH FEATURE WRITING

If theory and methodology constitute the supportive bottom points of a triangle, I consider writing the vertex, ultimately giving shape to a piece of scholarship. To fuse ethnography and historiography, and to crystalize this fusion on paper, I have developed certain prose suitable for the intended methodological synthesis. Bearing that goal in mind, I studied writing at the CUNY Graduate School of Journalism and then in the Department of English at the John Jay College of Criminal Justice. This experience, from 2018 to 2019, opened my eyes to a genre journalists call feature writing or long-form journalism.

Throughout the book, I try out certain literary techniques borrowed from journalists. Chapter 2, for example, opens with the story of a migrant woman named Li Zhiqing taking a homebound trip to divorce her husband amid the Chinese New Year. Readers may find that story reads like a profile in a magazine. It does, because I have taken to heart a rule of thumb in feature writing: *show, don't tell.* Additionally, I have applied several other techniques in that chapter as well as the subsequent ones. The first technique is to sprinkle the prose with granular details—clothing, footwear, gestures, manners, facial expressions, body language, and home interior—to exhibit individuals' socioeconomic status and character. The second is to conduct scene-by-scene narration—namely, to build the arc of a story by moving the narrative from one place to another, say, from a bus station in the throes of *chunyun* (春运), otherwise known as the Spring Festival travel rush, to a living room in a house of hill people. Third, to present dialogue at length; that is, to re-create conversations I witnessed firsthand by using quotations captured by a digital recorder or by drawing on detailed field notes. Last but not least, to alternate strategically between narratives and expositions, using the former to spur readers into a journey over time or across space and deploying the latter to expound contexts, histories, and other background information.[13]

Incorporating these techniques into my work, I hope to foster a style of writing capable of conveying experiential knowledge. As with most social scientists, I care enormously about conceptual knowledge. Much of the book, in fact, revolves around conceptual matters. For example, chapters 3 and 4 place a heavy emphasis on historical processes, chapter 5 on mechanisms of power, chapter 6 on dynamics between power and resistance, and chapter 7 on litigation outcomes and gendered patterns. Put in different words, at the core of each chapter stand somewhat abstract constructs—processes, mechanisms, dynamics, outcomes, and patterns.

The story of Li Zhiqing seeking divorce, however, touches on none of those abstract ideas. Rather, I am drawn into storytelling because I have longed to capture people's lived experiences. To do so, it occurs to me, is to translate concrete, specific life experiences into descriptive writing. Take poverty as an example. To write about destitution as embodied experiences is, in a way, to pen the imagery of penury, along with its jarring smell, touch, and shrillness; to detail how it gets under one's skin, festers, and mutates into a bitter taste, an unshakable desire, a fixation dominating the psyche; and to spell out how it comes to sculpt the ways one relates to herself and to others.

No amount of conceptualization or theorization could communicate those mundane, physical, or affective experiences, which, in their totality, constitute experiential knowledge—a body of knowledge we ethnographers can and should create. To me, that has always been the unique appeal of ethnography. By turning to colleagues in journalism, by selectively adopting their skills and techniques in reportage, I intend to call out a duality taken for granted in much of academic writing—"the old antithesis of style versus content" in Susan Sontag's language.[14] If style is never something merely "decorative" or "accessory," if content and form of writing are indeed inseparable, as Sontag insists, here is the basic question we ought to address: What kind of writing allows researchers and ethnographers in particular to carry experiential knowledge?

To look for an answer, and to preserve the fusion of ethnography and historiography on the page, I have experimented with feature writing almost from the beginning to the end of the book. Certain epistemological rewards have, I think, emerged from this experimentation. Rather than separating the present from the past, the micro from the macro, as many typically do in academic writing, this book preserves the nexus between present and past happenings, between a storm in a teacup and sweeping sociopolitical and economic changes on a national scale. Which is to say, feature writing gives me a skill set to transport readers—in just a few pages—from one time-space to another, from a migrant woman's struggles to exit a bitter marriage to China's decades-long social transformation. Instead of leaving readers to ponder how to see a world in a grain of sand, or a heaven in a wildflower, I have striven to lay bare the points of connections.[15]

This is not to suggest that I have it all figured out. My attempts to blend feature writing into a scholarly work are characteristically experimental. Only readers can decide on what works and what does not in this book. Here is the bottom line: I hope a book like mine will prompt ethnographers to converse with one another, to raise more questions, and to put more thoughts into the craft of writing. As far as I can tell, much ink has been spilled on ethnography as a one-of-a-kind research methodology. Much has been said about how to jot down observations, how to prepare field notes, how to conduct interviews, how to move from data collection to coding and to analytical memorandums, and so on. Yet there is hardly enough reflection on ethnography as the practice of writing. What kind of workflow writers need; which style, tone, or voice works for journal articles versus monographs; what literary devices are useful and why; how narratives can be structured to bolster expositions; what counts as good or effective prose and, finally, what criteria should be applied to assess scholarly writing—all these questions are still dangling in sociology and beyond. A lively conversation on these matters is still hard to find anywhere in the social sciences.[16] It is time to start that conversation.

ROAD MAP

Three principles help me organize the book: spatiality, temporality, and theoretical pursuits. From the angle of spatiality, I divide the book into two halves. Chapters 2, 3, and 4 explore the humming outside world surrounding the grassroots court system in rural China. Chapters 5, 6, and 7, conversely, dive into the Chinese judiciary, into judges' offices, mediation rooms, and courthouse hallways, where formal and informal decision-making transpires, leaving some contented and many others disheartened by their brush with the law.

Temporality is another important organizing principle. This is particularly the case for the three middle chapters, where I recount historic events in chronological order. More specifically, chapter 3 chronicles how the PRC has recalibrated its methodologies, techniques, and tactics for dispute management over time. Chapter 4 extends this historization by revisiting the process whereby the state has engineered the rise of a legal services industry, setting two groups of law practitioners—lawyers and legal workers—on different trajectories, one upward and the other downward. After that, chapter 5 details the steps the PRC has taken to alter divorce laws on paper and in practice over seven decades.

Moreover, the book is structured in a way to facilitate the advancement of two theoretical objectives. Chapters 3 and 4 are geared toward the first objective—to explore the complex interplay of culture and the state. To that end, the former centers on how culture capacitates state actors, whereas the latter specifies how culture, under certain circumstances, can incapacitate state agents. The latter half of the book extends this culturalist, historically charged analysis of authoritarian legality. It does so by establishing that cultural appropriation—something of a blessing for the regime—often turns into a curse for ordinary citizens. I unfold this analysis by addressing the second objective—to revamp the notion of dispute resolution. Chapters 5, 6, and 7, accordingly, bring into focus *agenda-setting power*, *decision-making power*, and *consciousness-formation power*, the key components forming a new conceptual framework. Making plain the workings of these powers in divorce litigation, I illustrate that, decades of top-down legal reforms notwithstanding, judges and legal professionals routinely fail women on multiple fronts, trampling on their spousal, custodial, property, and land rights. Below is a more detailed outline, which highlights both the empirical contents and the analytical thrust of each chapter.

Chapter 1, as indicated above, identifies this book's intended audiences and outlines key theoretical takeaways. The next chapter puts a human face on divorce. Drawing on the experiences of the women at the center of the book, chapter 2 brings to the fore the links between marital instability and labor migration in contemporary China. It shows that participation in labor migration opens up new space for women to reimagine and rearrange selfhood, intimacy, and marriage, on the one hand, and exposes them to unwanted speculations, suspicion, and scrutiny from their husbands and in-laws, on the other. Rural-to-urban migration, which is, in and of itself, a product of China's decades-long socioeconomic and demographic transformation, has greatly complicated the intimate lives of the average woman and man.

Chapter 3 opens with a pivotal shift in the history of the PRC: the institution of marriage—once a key vehicle for nation-state building—nowadays carries less political weight than before. Today, women and men, in search of public intervention in marriage and family life, have few options other than taking their grievances and claims to the courts. In that sense, marital and familial discontent, once a thoroughly political matter, has been judicialized. As the chapter segues from the past to the present, it takes history as a window onto the PRC's shifting governance, into an authoritarian regime's former and current efforts to cultivate a repertoire of statecraft.

Analytically speaking, this chapter takes the first step toward articulating the complex interplay of culture and the state. Invoking Ann Swidler's metaphor of culture as a tool kit,[17] I argue that the PRC has managed in recent decades to appropriate diverse cultural resources, either from its own past or from liberal democracies. Emerging from such appropriation is an expanded governing toolbox wherein judicial devices, practices, and mechanisms coexist with quasi- or extrajudicial components. Moreover, state actors' mobilization of one part of the toolbox in one scenario can be more or less insulated from their deployment of other parts in other situations. The PRC's laborious efforts to expand and diversify its governing methodologies have enabled state actors to line up cultural materials in varying configurations to solve different kinds of problems.

Chapter 4 further builds the argument that the reform-era PRC ought to be parsed as a case of an authoritarian regime continually refining its repertoire of statecraft by extracting cultural resources from divergent origins. In recent decades, legality has become an integral part of that repertoire. That said, state actors' attempts at cultivating and deploying legal techniques, tactics, and personnel—as if they were a set of open-ended devices and could be assembled and reassembled to pursue all goals—do not always deliver. They do not always succeed, because the Chinese state is often too fragmented to devise highly consistent, coherent, or integrated schemes to instrumentalize legality.

To concretize these theoretical arguments, this chapter presents a case study of the rise and fall of legal workers to empirically demonstrate the constraining effects of cultural appropriation. Marking the key moments in the PRC's development of a legal services industry, it reveals how legal workers rose to prominence in the socialist era and then fell from favor in the new millennium. That top decision-makers have struggled to transform this group of law practitioners and that they have botched attempts to capitalize on a socialist legacy testifies powerfully to the state's limits in cultural appropriation. These limits, it proves, have enormous implications for ordinary citizens. The downfall of legal workers in the new century, I point out, has disproportionately impacted on the have-nots than the haves, afflicting rural residents more than those residing in urban areas. Today, women, however miserable in marriage and family life, can hardly access official justice unless they find ways to afford legal mobilization.

Chapter 5 provides a close-to-the-ground view of the power the court system exercises in divorce litigation. This power, it turns out, has a long and tortuous history. Connecting present-day court practices to those in the past, this chapter dissects the mechanisms of power judges have employed to restrain marital dissolution among citizens. Three mechanisms stand out: turning divorce petitioners away through a procedure called *withdrawal*; adjudicating against divorce; and stalling marital dissolution by imposing cooling-off periods on litigants.

Theoretically, this chapter joins the previous one in a united endeavor to recast the notion of dispute resolution. It shows that, to curb divorce, judges have combined *formal decision-making power* and *agenda-setting power* in the day-to-day practice of law. By expounding the workings of these two power relations, I argue that while much has changed, much has remained the same inside Chinese courts. Unlike their predecessors in the Maoist or the socialist era, judges nowadays rarely fall back on highly oppressive or intrusive measures to interfere in citizens' intimate lives. Much has changed in that sense. On the other hand, in the reform era, while many other state bureaucracies progressively retreat from citizens' domestic lives, the courts have nonetheless entrenched their role of defending the state's vision of marriage as a public institution, central to the cohesion of the Chinese nation-state.

Chapter 6 exposes a paradox inside the grassroots court system: mediation, as an integral part of divorce law practices inside the People's Court, has long remained impervious to formal, institutional scrutiny, and, paradoxically, permeable to informal, outside influences. This paradox often turns mediation into a seedbed, where court insiders (such as judges and clerks) and court regulars (like lawyers and legal workers) may collude to deny women crucial rights on the books. Consequently, divorcing women can suffer from the collusion among an unsympathetic court system, a co-opted legal profession, and an indifferent conjugal community. At times, women do push back the frontiers of insubordination. But they do so not onstage but off, usually outside of the court system, thereby engaging in what James C. Scott terms the *hidden transcript of resistance*.[18] In that sense, this chapter sheds new light on the intricate dynamics between power and resistance.

Chapter 7 completes the second theoretical pursuit of the book by zooming in on *formal decision-making power* and *consciousness-formation power*. Focusing on judges' routine decision-making, I show that divorce litigation oftentimes winds up reproducing gender inequality in the family and in rural communities. Most of the women in this book eventually walked away from their divorce suits with little or no

marital property, child support, or any remedies for blameworthy conduct, like domestic violence and spousal abandonment. Their husbands,
by stark contrast, managed to retain child custody and family property;
those responsible for wrongdoings—adultery, spousal abuse, and marital
rape—invariably emerged unscathed from their encounters with the law.

The latter half of the chapter switches to examine consciousness-
formation power by solving an empirical puzzle: why some issues, such as
the allocation of child custody and the division of marital property, were
vehemently disputed by women, while other matters like landholding remained unquestioned and unchallenged in divorce litigation? Confronting
this puzzle head-on, this chapter uncovers that the most insidious exercise
of power over the disempowered is, it turns out, the one that can "keep
issues from arising, grievances from being voiced, and interests from being recognized," as John Gaventa once noted.[19] Finally, in the epilogue,
I reflect on how future research can further explore authoritarian legality, state interventions in citizens' intimate lives, and rights contention
in China.

Audiences, Theoretical Objectives, and Arguments

WHO WOULD BE INTERESTED in the marital disputes of China's floating population? Who would deem courtroom battles over divorce pertinent and significant? Why should anyone make time for a monograph on law, legal professions, and courts in contemporary China? Bearing these questions in mind, I devote this chapter to explicating how marital disputes and divorce litigation, seemingly prosaic, serve as strategic research sites to tackle important theoretical issues that concern political scientists, sociologists, sociolegal researchers, and China scholars.

Accordingly, this chapter first engages researchers who study authoritarian legality—namely, law, legal professions, and courts in authoritarian contexts. Keeping that audience in sight, I argue that it is time to pivot, shifting away from a functionalist, utilitarian approach to legality and toward a historically charged, culturalist perspective. To hammer out this alternative approach, this chapter unpacks the intricate interplay of culture and the state—the first theoretical objective at the heart of the book.

In the latter half of the chapter, I bring forward the second theoretical objective—to reconceptualize the notion of dispute resolution. And I do so in hopes of engaging sociolegal researchers who view conflict resolution as their central intellectual interest. To these colleagues, my argument is stacked against an individualistic, behavioristic view of disputation. By formulating a power-centered framework, we can more effectively untangle the nexus between legality and inequality in China and perhaps elsewhere, I argue. In advancing these two objectives, in promoting a view of legality sensitive to history, culture, and power, the book ahead forges a new path in the studies of law, legal mobilization, and rights contention in an authoritarian state.

AUTHORITARIAN LEGALITY,
CULTURE, AND THE STATE

To many in political science and in sociology, this is a book, first and foremost, about authoritarian legality. Be that as it may, it departs from extant studies in several fundamental ways. Substantively, the book offers no account of constitutional judicial review. It barely engages chief justices or constitutional courts at the pinnacle of state power. And it hardly speaks to the judicialization of politics in nondemocratic contexts.[1] Rather, this is a study of judges, legal professionals, government officials, and community leaders wrestling with a mundane, outwardly apolitical phenomenon—women seeking out official remedies for marital grievances and disputes.

Analytically, this book sets itself apart from prior studies of authoritarian legality. It does so in part by laying aside a research question that has galvanized political scientists and sociolegal scholars in recent decades: Why authoritarian regimes, like the People's Republic of China (PRC), choose to buttress law, legal professions, and courts. This question has animated many in academia, giving rise to a large number of monographs, edited books, and journal and review articles—a critical mass of scholarship.[2] This book makes no attempt to address that "why" question. I do not pursue this inquiry, because I do not share researchers' bent on a functionalist, utilitarian view of legality in China and beyond. Instead, I tread a different path. Before more is said about the alternative path, I shall elaborate on my reservations with the extant scholarship.

The first reservation centers on the role of the scholarship in magnifying and entrenching a functionalist explanation for the genesis, evolution, and reproduction of institutions, including judicial institutions in China and elsewhere.[3] To explicate why some authoritarian rulers enhance law and empower courts—a move seemingly counterintuitive, given their thirst for unfettered power—researchers arrive at a decision. That is, to address the "why" question, many contend, is to probe what "functions" or "functional purposes" legality serves in authoritarian states. The said functions include, but are not limited to, the following: law and courts are frequently deployed to "(1) exercise state power vis-à-vis opposition, (2) advance administrative discipline within state institutions, (3) maintain cohesion among various factions within the ruling coalition, (4) facilitate market transitions, (5) contain majoritarian institutions through authoritarian enclaves, (6) delegate controversial reforms, and (7) bolster regime legitimacy."[4]

Among the researchers espousing this view, few expressly acknowledge a potential problem in their causal inference. This is regrettable, for the problem has been around for a long time, perhaps as old as functionalism itself. James Mahoney, a professor of political science and sociology, pinpoints the crux of the matter, "scholars who employ this kind of functional explanation often assume that the initial origins of an institution can be explained teleologically by the beneficial effects the institution brings to a system after it is created."[5] Put differently, the said functions of legality—that is, the ensuing *effects* of law and courts on an overall political system—may or may not be the actual *causes* that spurred autocrats to erect, sustain, or strengthen such entities at earlier moments in history.

In terms of research practices, this means that, while conducting a functional analysis, scholars should remain judicious, empirically and conceptually, by staving off the equation of the effects with the causes of authoritarian legality. It also means that, epistemologically and methodologically, researchers should restore temporal sequence to their analysis of why and how autocrats come to elevate the stature of law and courts, as opposed to bracketing off temporality from causal inference.[6] Unfortunately, not all researchers demonstrate such sound judgment. Not all build a research design that is truly diachronic rather than synchronic. Instead, working backward from identifiable institutional effects to impute preferences, motivations, and goals to state actors involved in the genesis or evolution of that institution—a practice political scientists Jack Knight and Kathleen Thelen regard as "one of the most significant mistakes" in institutional analysis—has become a standard, unquestioned, and almost unavoidable approach in the studies of authoritarian legality.[7]

My second reservation concerns an assumption buried deeply in the literature. While casting law and courts as a cat's-paw for autocrats, researchers embrace a utilitarian—and some may call it an instrumentalist—view of legality to varying degrees. Accompanying this view is, at times, a scholarly characterization of autocrats—remarkably rational and calculating, equipped with a vision so clear and panoramic, as if these actors were invariably cognizant of their needs, wants, and self-interest. Aided by this vision, regimes like the PRC, it is said, have established well-calibrated models of law enforcement to "make bargains and commitments to elite supporters of the regime" and to "manage principal-agent problems between levels of government, to cultivate mass support, and to exploit and reshape social cleavages."[8] In short, the assumption goes like this: autocrats know very well how to leverage law and courts to maximum advantage.

In this account of authoritarian legality, there is little room to question political elites' foresight, rationality, or coordination within the body politic. The state, seen in this light, is all but a well-oiled, high-capacity juggernaut, capable of turning almost everyone into its lackeys. This unbridled utilitarian view of legality contains two pitfalls, I believe.[9] One, it hardly considers that social actors—ruling elites included—do not have unbounded rationality, much less prescience or omniscience. Rather, they have limited capacities to collect and process information and use it to make well-informed decisions.[10] In attempts at harnessing legality, authoritarian rulers, more often than not, do not begin with a crystal clear, all-seeing vision, and, at times of great uncertainty, may not even have a clear sense of what their self-interest or goals could be.

Furthermore, even if autocrats have worked out core regime interests and long-term goals, they may still struggle to align their preferences and strategies of action; some may still have to wrestle with segmentation and fragmentation within the state apparatus. After all, authoritarian rulers do not inhabit an undivided, autonomous kingdom these days. Nor do they operate like "a single, centrally motivated actor performing in an integrated manner to rule a clearly defined territory." In practice, the PRC, as well as other authoritarian regimes, often acts like "a heap of loosely connected parts or fragments," like many other modern states.[11] This suggests that autocrats have their abilities constrained in efforts to compose and orchestrate concerted—let alone holistic or forward-looking—schemes to instrumentalize law, the legal services industry, and judicial institutions. An unchecked utilitarian view of legality, when coupled with insufficient attention to the cracks, fissures, and fault lines within the body politic, can lead researchers to overstate regimes' capacities to modulate legality.

Lastly, I take issue with the extant literature because it has yet to reckon with the constitutive roles of culture in (re)molding legal developments in politically repressive settings. To explain why autocrats prefer well-functioning legal institutions, researchers frequently operate under a functionalist or utilitarian premise, or some combination of the two. The functionalist premise, as indicated earlier, posits that an institution is created and reproduced because it serves certain "purposes" for a political system. The utilitarian premise, on the other hand, maintains that an institution is generated and sustained as a result of decision-makers' rational cost-benefit assessments.[12] Either way, researchers cast authoritarian rulers as goal-oriented and interest-driven, which is largely unproblematic. What is problematic, though, is that many stop there. Few take additional steps to parse the ways culture has configured these rulers' efforts to interpret and materialize their interests, preferences, or priorities in legal developments.

This disinterest in culture is lamentable, considering some of the most significant theoretical developments in institutional analysis since the early 1990s. With the rise of the so-named New Institutionalism in sociology, and particularly in organizational sociology, more researchers shifted from emphasizing the explanatory *logic of instrumentality* to exploring the *logic of appropriateness* in the studies of modern organizations, such as the state, the market, and corporations.[13] Accordingly, many came to grapple with a possibility: social actors are not invariably driven by instrumental rationality, with their action being governed by cost-benefit analysis; rather, even goal-oriented, interest-driven actors must forge perceptions and action by mobilizing cultural resources from historically specific repertoires inherited from their predecessors, thereby rendering themselves susceptible to the clout of culture.[14] Political elites in nondemocratic settings are no exception in this regard. The New Institutionalism, in distancing itself from rational choice theories and structural functionalism, places decidedly greater emphasis on culture and especially on normative and cognitive ideas. Thus, researchers who identify themselves as organizational institutionalists strive to articulate the processes and mechanisms whereby culture leaves its unique imprint on actors and action.

By the mid-1990s, sociologists Mark C. Suchman and Lauren B. Edelman had called for a greater intellectual exchange between the New

Institutionalism and the Law and Society tradition.[15] This exchange, conducted properly, could lead scholars to dissect more purposely and effectively the moral, discursive, symbolic, and other cultural dimensions of institutional environments, which loom large in shaping at once actors and action.

This call, alas, has fallen on deaf ears for the most part. In fact, even researchers who explicitly apply the sociological literature on organizational ecology seem to throw culture out the window in an instant. For example, in a study of the Chinese judiciary's susceptibility to external influences, researchers readily identify the administrative, political, social, and economical dimensions of the courts' embeddedness in a larger institutional environment.[16] Yet nowhere in this analysis do the researchers give serious consideration to a key insight of the New Institutionalism; namely, culture persists as a constituent, irreducible aspect of organizational life and, thus, ought to be reckoned with in its own right. In the end, treating culture as "merely froth on the tides of society," to use the words of William H. Sewell Jr., becomes the rule rather than the exception in the literature on authoritarian legality.[17]

***

Stepping away from the extant scholarship, I draw two lessons, one theoretical and the other methodological. Regarding the former, culture matters, and we have a stake in recognizing its distinct place in the analysis of authoritarian legality. As for the latter, we ought to take history, temporal sequence, and timing more seriously in studies of law and courts in China and elsewhere. This in turn leads to my decision to fuse two methodologies, ethnography and historiography, as indicated earlier. This methodological endeavor, I hope, can render my analysis receptive to historical continuities and discontinuities in legal developments in the PRC.

Taking these lessons to heart, I map out a historically charged, culturalist analysis of law, legal professions, and courts in this book. More specifically, I trace and analyze legal developments in contemporary China by charting the historical trajectories through which the PRC—once a revolutionary regime, then a socialist one, and today a post-socialist state—has cultivated and deployed a cultural repertoire of statecraft. To view legality through this lens, analytically speaking, is to make a fundamental shift. Rather than questioning what purposes legality serves, I ask instead how authoritarian rulers build and rebuild law, legal professions, and courts over time as they calibrate and recalibrate a cultural repertoire of statecraft. In actualizing this inquiry, this book forcefully brings culture back into the analysis of authoritarian legality. Along this line, I advance several arguments.

(1) Culture is of paramount importance to authoritarian rulers.

To frame legality as part of a regime's repertoire of statecraft is, in a sense, to conjure up an image of law, the legal services industry, and judicial institutions as potential elements comprising a governing tool kit on the part of ruling elites. This image, I should note, emanates from sociologist Ann Swidler's theory of culture in action. Likening culture to a tool kit, Swidler contends that culture matters because it furnishes social actors with a wide variety of resources, worldviews, moral visions, cognitive schemas, symbols, meanings, skills, habits, and strategies of action, to name a few.[18]

In a similar vein, culture is of paramount importance to authoritarian rulers, I argue. It is crucial, for culture equips these rulers with a toolbox for governing. Inside the toolbox, there could be miscellaneous pieces and items, including political ideologies, orthodox norms, mainstream values, official discourses, narratives, rhetoric, symbolic boundaries, cognitive categories, policy instruments, and, in particular, institutional memories, principles, and practices. All of these provide building blocks for ruling elites to organize their perceptions and action.

Culture can enable authoritarian rulers. But so can it constrain them, limiting their options, and, under certain circumstances, even incapacitate their action. This is an argument I present later in this chapter. Here, I quickly note that culture does not serve autocrats in a straightforward fashion.

(2) Understanding ruling elites' bravado, ingenuity,
and agility in cultural appropriation holds the key for
political scientists and sociologists to make sense of regime
resilience and state capacities.

As a cultural analyst, Swidler celebrates human agency, practicality, and creativity in social actors' use of a cultural tool kit to solve everyday problems. In a similar fashion, anthropologist Sally Engle Merry draws attention to political actors' ability to appropriate cultural materials—and particularly legal ideals, practices, and institutional arrangements—from one social group, one geographic context, or one historical period and to reassemble and reapply those materials in another space, in relation to a different group, and at some other times. Depicting this phenomenon as *cultural appropriation*, Merry brings into view political elites' agency, flexibility, and ingenuity in transposing, blending, and layering diverse cultural influences in legal developments.[19]

Inspired by Swidler's theory of culture in action, and also informed by Merry's study of law and cultural appropriation, I come to discern similar inclinations on the part of the PRC's ruling elites. Indeed, decision-makers of the reform era, in a few decades, have demonstrated striking alacrity, agility, and inventiveness in attempts at mobilizing cultural resources in varying configurations to tackle challenges and difficulties in governing. And their strategies abound when it comes to cultural appropriation.

Today, the PRC's decision-makers have imbricated the old with the new, the inherited with the borrowed, ruling experience. Government officials on the front line of dispute management, for instance, have re-vitalized people's mediation (人民调解), an institution that originated in Maoist China, and have established arbitration, administrative adjudi-cation (行政裁决), administrative reconsideration (行政复议), and other quasi-judicial mechanisms for conflict resolution. Similarly, inside Chinese courts, a keen observer can spot notable traces of the PRC's past side by side with legal transplants adopted from Western countries. Take divorce litigation as an example. To settle marital disputes, judges nowadays continue to rely heavily on mediation, an institutional practice with deep roots in the revolutionary past of the Chinese Communist Party (CCP) (for more details, see chapter 6). The same group of judges has also been instructed to issue personal safety protective orders (人身安全保护令) as a new measure to protect victims of domestic violence, a measure adopted from countries that have entrenched due process and rule of law.[20]

In the table below, I highlight the strategies top decision-makers em-ploy to appropriate cultural resources—and institutional principles and practices, in particular—either from the PRC's own past or from foreign

TABLE 1.1 Strategies of cultural appropriation employed by the PRC's ruling elites

Strategy	Definition	Empirical Examples	Level of Innovation
Diffusion	Craft novel solutions by adopting and enacting institutional principles and practices originating elsewhere	In the 2015 Anti-Domestic Violence Law, the National People's Congress codified personal safety protective order as a new measure to protect victims of domestic violence. This measure was nowhere to be found in the PRC's Maoist or socialist past; rather, it was adopted from Western countries (see chapter 5).	High
Translation	Craft solutions by combining locally available institutional principles and practices with new elements originating elsewhere	In the early 2000s, the Supreme People's Court (SPC) and the Ministry of Justice (MOJ) refashioned people's mediation, an institution originated in the Maoist era, by rendering part of it more lawlike and leaving another part no more susceptible to legal rules and norms than before. In doing so, the SPC and the MOJ sought to remodel this institution for a new purpose: stability maintenance (see chapter 3).	Relatively high
Bricolage	Craft solutions by reconfiguring locally available institutional principles and practices	The SPC converted a preexisting practice—judges' use of withdrawal as an expedient procedure to dispose of civil suits—into a formal metric to measure judicial actors' efficacy in maintaining a harmonious socialist society (see chapter 5). The SPC turned a widespread, informal practice—judges' routine rejection of first-time divorce petitions—into a formal, procedural requirement called *divorce cooling-off period* (离婚冷静期), in hopes of further curbing divorces (see chapter 5).	Relatively low
Path dependence	Draw on institutional principles and practices that have become locked in as a result of a sequence of feedback loops	The court system relied for decades on Township Legal Services (乡镇法律服务) to meet popular needs for legal assistance, although lawmakers fell short of recognizing legal workers' role as counsel in civil and administrative litigation (see chapter 4).	Low

countries. Four strategies stand out: diffusion, translation, bricolage, and path dependence.[21] Deploying these strategies, ruling elites have sought various initiatives and goals, including shielding women from domestic violence, curbing divorces, ensuring popular access to official justice, promoting a harmonious socialist society (社会主义和谐社会), and conducting stability maintenance (维稳). By foreshadowing these strategies, together with the corresponding empirical examples discussed in later chapters, I underscore ruling elites' inclination and capacity to extract and repackage cultural materials from sundry origins in hopes of crafting somewhat novel solutions to emerging problems in ruling. Once capacity as such comes to light, it becomes clear that in the PRC, the functional purposes legality serves are contextually contingent and historically specific, with much more variability and fluidity than the literature on authoritarian legality recognizes .

In short, I find Swidler's and Merry's works helpful on several fronts for my study of law and courts in China. Swidler claims that culture affects action, not only by supplying actors with ultimate ends (e.g., values, interests, and goals) but by endowing them with vital means (e.g., resources, options, and capabilities); that culture, as a tool kit, is mobilized piecemeal, without the logical coherence of a singular theory; that actors, rather than punctiliously following general rules, norms, or unified worldviews, employ cultural resources flexibly and locally around core concerns. And these theoretical insights, as the book ahead reveals, have found potent empirical manifestations in the reform-era PRC. Similarly, Merry's arguments that ruling elites often engage in cultural appropriation by selectively adopting legal ideals and practices from other social groups (and/or contexts) and that such appropriation, as concrete historical processes, are fraught with competing cultural logics, power relations, and popular resistance certainly ring true in the Chinese context. For that reason, understanding the PRC's bravado, ingenuity, and agility in cultural appropriation, I argue, holds the key for social scientists to make sense of regime resilience and state capacities.[22] Indeed, with a rigorous comparative analysis of how some but not other regimes have strategically appropriated governing experience from their own past and/or from liberal democracies, political scientists and sociologists may develop new conceptual frames to expound why communist regimes have faltered worldwide and some have disintegrated, and yet the PRC has survived.

(3) Unpacking the cultural logic behind state-sponsored legal developments is crucial for scholars seeking to build a firm grasp of ongoing legal reforms in China.

A perspective sensitive to culture can facilitate researchers to advance studies of legal reforms in contemporary China. Over the past two decades, China scholars have debated whether the PRC, in the new millennium, has been on a trajectory against or toward law. On one side of the debate are researchers holding a rather bleak view of the country's ongoing legal reforms. The PRC, since the mid-2000s, has backpedaled from previous reforms, sliding more and more into unbridled authoritarianism, some insist. In this view, the state's increasing recourse to mediation and other extrajudicial forms of conflict resolution serves as evidence, indicative of a "top-down authoritarian political reaction to growing levels of social protest and conflict" in Chinese society.[23]

On the other side of the debate are scholars narrating a very different story: the PRC's ruling elites have elevated the symbolic as well as the instrumental standing of law and courts. In fact, under Xi Jinping's watch, the regime has empowered the courts against other state and party entities and has further strengthened legal professionalism. This state-sponsored legalism, as others have noted, has gone so far as to hand over more authority to the judiciary so that it can scrutinize and penalize illegal administrative activities, thereby making it more effective in checking governmental abuse and overreach.[24] Unable or unwilling to reconcile these two competing and somewhat conflicting assessments, some in China studies come to the conclusion that the PRC, over the past four decades, has been "torn between a strong preoccupation with [political] stability and a desire to promote law-based governance." In short, it has been caught up in a "paradox" in ruling.[25]

At the heart of the debate, it dawns on me, is a binary cultural logic that pits legality against extralegality, casting one as the antithesis of the other. This is not entirely unexpected. From Claude Lévi-Strauss to Roman Jakobson, from Émile Durkheim to Mary Douglas, many in the social sciences have long maintained that we live in a world symboli- cally, cognitively, ideologically, and/or institutionally organized around binary oppositions, such as the sacred versus the profane, the pure versus the polluted, the deserving versus the undeserving, democratic versus counter-democratic, American versus un-American, and so on.[26] Together, these binary codes anchor a semiotic system through which actors—and scholars included—orient themselves, arrange their understandings, and relate to others. In recent years, this binary logic has made deep inroads into the literature on authoritarian legality. For example, to capture how regimes like Myanmar and the PRC deviate from the endearing political ideal, the so-termed *rule of law*, scholars have developed several opposi- tional concepts, such as *un-rule of law*, *thin rule of law*, *law and order*, and *order maintenance paradigm*, all of which are constructed in sharp contrast to the rule of law.[27]

Here is the remaining empirical question, though. While the literature is drenched in this binary logic, treating legal and extralegal forms of governance as unresolvable antinomies, do the PRC's decision-makers subscribe to the same logic? More plainly, do autocrats themselves view legality and extralegality, judicial and extrajudicial forms of dispute man- agement, as antithetical to each other or not? If not, what cultural logic do they uphold?

This book presents evidence in detail, suggesting that the semiotic system depicted above is a world apart from the one the PRC has been constructing in the reform era. Notwithstanding official rhetoric, which claims such aspirations as "comprehensively promoting law-based gover- nance" (全面依法治国), in practice, top decision-makers hardly set extrale- gality at odds with legality. Nor do they view their practice of enhancing extrajudicial forms of conflict resolution as diametrically opposed to of- ficial decisions to consolidate the judiciary. Rather, two decades into the twenty-first century, the PRC has fortified judicial, quasi-judicial, and ex- trajudicial institutions—by and large at once—in attempts to deploy them to tackle different kinds of social problems. In this fashion, the regime has cultivated a multipronged system with officially designated difficult, hot-button disputes (难点、热点纠纷), such as widespread discontent with land-taking and demolition, labor relations, and medical malpractice, routinely channeled into quasi-judicial and extrajudicial bureaucracies for the sake of social stability, and mundane, frequent disputes (常见性、多发性纠纷), including marital disputes and torts, thrust into judicial space in the name of the socialist rule of law. Under Xi Jinping's watch, these measures taken together have been branded as efforts to diversify conflict resolution (多元化纠纷解决) (see chapter 3 for details).

The cultural logic behind these developments, I argue, is hardly a binary one, congruent with an ideology that polarizes legality and extra-legality. On this matter, the PRC's ruling elites have been rather up-front about their stance: what they envision is a socialist rule of law combined with Chinese characteristics. In a similarly up-front manner, Deng Xiaoping, the grand architect behind the Reform and Opening-Up (改革开放), laid out his practical logic: "It doesn't matter whether a cat is black or white, as long as it catches mice," and, to get China where he wants it to be, the proper approach is to "cross the river by groping the stepping-stones" (摸着石头过河).[28]

What Deng Xiaoping conveyed—the cat theory (猫论) and the theory of groping (摸论), as party cadres came to call them later—is a kind of pragmatism and a candid acknowledgment that, in moving China forward, top decision-makers did not set out with a ready-made road map in mind. Rather, they had limited foresight and knowledge, and thus there must be a strong emphasis on trial and error, constant policy experimentation, and active learning, based on experiences rather than on theories or ideologies. While accentuating pragmatism, urgent need for learning and experimentation, and boldness to forge ahead in reforming, Deng Xiaoping was nevertheless clear about his bottom line: only one organization could carry China through fundamental transformation—the CCP. This is to say, decision-makers' boldness, experimentation, and innovation can be boundless, except that they should not undercut the Party's political dominance.[29]

In prescribing his cat theory and theory of groping, Deng Xiaoping articulated what cultural analysts like Pierre Bourdieu and Ann Swidler would call *a logic of practice*. This logic is not anchored in the universal features of human minds (as Claude Lévi-Strauss once claimed); nor is it filtered through collective census (as Émile Durkheim and Talcott Parsons maintained).[30] Needless to say, it has little to do with the canon of rule of law. Rather, this logic arises out of political elites' practices, and not least institutional practices. This logic—unlike the kind studied by logicians or jurists—is rooted in hands-on experiences, in trial and error, and in practical wisdom. It can "organize all thoughts, perceptions, and actions by means of a few generative principles, which are closely interrelated and constitute a practically integrated whole," according to Bourdieu. It can achieve coherence, precisely because "it ignores the niceties of formal logic" and downplays rigor "for the sake of simplicity and generality." And, most crucially for Bourdieu, this logic of practice—or *practical logic* as a shorthand—is driven by urgency and therefore would "never cease to sacrifice the concern for coherence to the pursuit of efficiency."[31] At the risk of grossly oversimplifying Bourdieu's theory of culture and practice, one might as well compare his notion of practical logic to a particular outlook, modus operandi, and rule of thumb; when combined, they may guide ruling elites to find their ways out of the woods.

Unpacking this practical logic, I believe, is crucial, if China scholars intend to develop a solid grasp of the PRC's apparently inconsistent and incoherent legal developments in the twenty-first century. Rather than fixating on the question of whether China is moving toward or away from law, closer or further away from a more or less canonized version of rule of law, we should meticulously examine under what circumstances state actors select legal methodologies to address challenges in ruling and in what instances they deselect legal measures and prefer nonlegal, extralegal, or even illegal techniques and tactics. We should investigate what incentivizes the regime to favor legality in one scenario and to disfavor it in another, and what rationale stands behind this selection. Furthermore, we ought to scrutinize what parameters ruling elites erect around state-sponsored legalism, how they delimit citizens' rights and entitlements, and how they parole the boundaries between what is officially deemed legal and what is regarded as illegal or extralegal. And we must unpack the strategies autocrats employ to carve out social, political, or geographic spaces in which lawfulness, rights, and entitlements are suspended in the name of law, social stability, or economic development. Ultimately, by studying the ways in which state actors use law, by analyzing what cultural logic informs such uses, we can better fathom the PRC's shifting stance toward Chinese law.

> *(4) Culture can enable state actors. And so can it constrain and*
> *even incapacitate state actors' attempts at harnessing legality.*

The lack of concern for culture is not just limited to the scholarship on authoritarian legality, I must point out. The question of how culture sways the state in one way or another has received little attention in sociology and in political science. This is particularly the case in the studies of state formation, in which culture as an independent, detectable causal force rarely registers with researchers. Rather, many brush culture aside altogether. Or they take note of various cultural elements vis-à-vis the state, but only do so at the empirical level; culture evaporates at the theoretical level. Or they view culture as ultimately determined by material factors, thus merely a derivative of structural conditions. Or they subscribe to a view of culture as a somewhat direct expression of political or economic power, therefore barely an agentic player in the game. Or they treat culture as chiefly a product of the state or as part of the "state effects," as some call it.[32] Much less conceivable in terms of causal flows is the other way around. "The strands of causality running from culture to the state have been ignored, marginalized, or declared illegitimate objects of investigation," sociologist George Steinmetz maintains.[33]

Recognizing this gap in the literature, this book painstakingly analyzes the ways culture impinges on the state. In the case of the PRC, culture has left striking marks on the regime's legal developments over the past decades. As mentioned before, to explicate how culture has capacitated the PRC's ruling elites, I draw on Ann Swidler's and Sally Engle Merry's works (see chapter 3 for empirical examples along this line). Now, to specify how culture can constrain authoritarian rulers, restricting their options and incapacitating their action, I turn to a group of institutionalists and most notably sociologist John L. Campbell for their insights.

These institutionalists—some belong to the camp of organizational institutionalism, and others consider themselves proponents of historical institutionalism—are united on one front: they all reject assumptions of cultural homogeneity as an analytical starting point.[34] Rather, they stress that culture is plural, contradictory, contested, loosely integrated, and subject to change and that it is crucial to recognize the constitutive roles of culture in molding institutional changes and reproduction. This recognition, in turn, leads Campbell and others to unearth how cultural heterogeneity, fluidity, and multivalence could present unique challenges to political elites. Among others, these elites must grapple with the challenge of properly aligning the normative, cognitive, schematic, discursive, and other cultural dimensions of policy formation in relation to their constituents.[35] When elites fall short of coordinating these dimensions, or when they fail to confront entrenched cultural influences in policymaking at multiple fronts, they may find themselves in disarray, incapable of moving in one direction or another.[36]

What further compounds this challenge is that political elites inhabit a state, often too segmented, too divided, to harmonize their preferences and interests. In this regard, decision-makers in authoritarian contexts are no exception. The combination of cultural heterogeneity and state fragmentation, as this book shows at length, gravely complicates authoritarian rulers' attempts at exploiting legality. Indeed, to leverage law, the legal services industry, or courts to maximum advantage, an authoritarian regime must coordinate its decision-makers in multiple bureaucracies, structured vertically or horizontally within the state apparatus on the one hand, and foster a certain degree of cultural coherence by lining up the normative, cognitive, discursive, and other cultural dimensions of policy formation and implementation on the other. This is a tall order to fill.

Later in the book, I present one concrete example to illustrate how the PRC, on the cusp of the new millennium, failed to rise to the challenge, resulting in state actors producing policy decisions that could hardly be characterized as functional or well calibrated (see chapter 4). Where the literature on authoritarian legality insists that regime behavior results from "rational and shrewd political calculation,"[37] I show that miscalculation occurs frequently on the part of the PRC's ruling elites. It happens, not because those elites are irrational or insufficiently calculating but because they cannot escape the reign of culture. To understand how authoritarian rulers become stuck in policy wrangling and how they end up issuing regulations and policies inconsistent with their interests, we must heed the complex interplay of culture and the state, I argue. In one instance, culture can furnish state actors with manifold resources, assets, and options. In another scenario, precisely because culture is plural, multidimensional, and subject to reinterpretation and contestation, state actors may find themselves in a quagmire, unable or unwilling to align the various pieces and items in their cultural toolbox.

What's more, the PRC's pragmatism in cultural appropriation, together with its emphasis on constant policy experimentation—epitomized by Deng Xiaoping's cat theory and theory of groping—can expose the regime to additional risks and hazards. Behind Deng Xiaoping's pragmatism is an assumption: the CCP, with its audacity, active learning, and tireless trial and error, would sooner or later tame all cats, black and white alike, making them catch mice for the master. Whether this assumption holds water is debatable, awaiting empirical investigation. For the time being, I remain skeptical.

After all, not all cultural resources readily lend themselves to state actors' appropriation. Which is to say, cultural appropriation cannot be conducted effectively without actors' meticulous efforts to nurture a certain degree of *internal coherence* among the moral, cognitive, schematic, and other cultural components or dimensions within a political system. Nor can it be done meaningfully in the absence of actors' endeavors to interweave the semiotic and the non-semiotic aspects of society, thereby maintaining a somewhat *external congruity* with social structures.[38] True, few cultural analysts nowadays would contend that, absent internal coherence or external congruity, a society or a political system would fall apart.[39] Having said that, I must add: no institution can sustain infinite cultural incoherence or endless incongruity between the semiotic and the non-semiotic, while remaining functional or legitimate. In any case, the health of an institution, as the New Institutionalism suggests, hinges on its ability to produce and reproduce patterned and somewhat stabilized perceptions, meanings, routines, and behaviors among its members.[40] Thus, it is conceivable that when an institution is repeatedly bombarded by competing and conflicting norms, rules, values, and expectations, its capacity to regularize members' outlook, conduct, and interactions will suffer, and so will its legitimacy in the eyes of members or nonmembers.

In other words, as the PRC strives to imbricate statecraft of almost all stripes, enacting ruling methodologies inherited from its revolutionary and socialist past, and at the same time deploying governing techniques and tactics adopted from liberal democracies; as it dives further into cultural appropriation, treating legality and extralegality as if they were so malleable and mixable that they could be used to pursue all goals, the regime opens itself to contradictions (among various cultural elements and dimensions) and incongruities (between culture and social structures).

Indeed, this book reveals the extent to which the Chinese judiciary, as an institution, has plunged itself into contradictions, inconsistency, and incoherence, thereby potentially undercutting its own workings and legitimacy. Again, take divorce litigation as an example. Time after time, judges have been told to safeguard citizens' rights to marry freely and to dissolve marriages freely, for the PRC's top legislature has long enshrined individual freedoms as such. Moreover, judges have been instructed to enforce national laws to protect women from domestic violence. On the other hand, the same group of judges, according to the CCP and the Supreme People's Court, shall contribute to a "harmonious socialist society"—by turning away divorce petitioners, by stalling marital dissolution among citizens, by mediating disputes between husband and wife, even if the former is responsible for the latter's victimization, and, last but not least, by upholding the PRC's vision of marriage as a cornerstone, central to the cohesion of the Chinese nation-state. Suffice to say, there are considerable tensions and contradictions among those expectations. As the remainder of the book illustrates, while judges find ways to stay above the fray amid the foregoing contradictions, women—who make up the bulk of divorce petitioners—come to shoulder the negative repercussions stemming from institutional insiders' wrestling with authoritarian legality. In the end, among these women, few find their courtroom experiences fair, equitable, or empowering. Many walk away from divorce litigation with their faith in law in tatters.

DISPUTE RESOLUTION, POWER, AND INEQUALITY

In tracing the historical trajectories along which the PRC has built and rebuilt law, legal professions, and courts over time, this book brings into the open the complex dynamics between culture and the state—the first theoretical objective central to my research. Now, I turn to the second objective in hopes of revamping the notion of dispute resolution. To do so, in effect, is to engage sociolegal scholars who take conflict resolution as their key research interest and also to further expose the dark side of authoritarian legality. To that end, adopting well-established approaches in the existing literature will not suffice, I argue. Instead, an alternative is needed, one that can cast light on power and its imprint on ordinary people's experiences in disputation—and to do so without falling into the traps of methodological individualism. Let me explain why I find the extant approaches inadequate before more is said about this alternative perspective.

The first approach, known as the dispute pyramid model, entered the spotlight in the early 1980s. Over time, it has entrenched a particular set of views in the minds of many sociolegal researchers. To begin with, disputes are social constructs, rather than objects found in the world. Disputation constitutes a process, usually comprising multiple, distinct stages, such as perceiving certain experiences as injurious, naming and blaming the responsible parties, staking out claims, and seeking out interventions and remedies. The driving force behind this process, in general, is the disgruntled person. His needs and wants, perceptions, and particularly behaviors, thus, warrant close scholarly attention. The institutions in charge of conflict resolution—be they formal or informal, public or private—are simply out there, to be approached and utilized by the disgruntled. These institutions may compete with one another on the grounds of justice, efficiency, or availability. But ultimately, it is the disputant's decision to pick and choose among these institutions.[41]

I appreciate this model's emphasis on a constructivist, processual view of disputes, as it paves the way for researchers to analyze dispute management in terms of a social process, unfolding over time and across space, with part of it transpiring in everyday life, and another part potentially in formal institutional settings, say, inside courtrooms. Having said that, I must mark the limits of this model. Dispute management, in this view, is either initiated, prolonged, and resolved by individual actions (e.g., searching for the help of a third party, or inserting grievances and claims into formal or informal forums for dispute resolution) or is suppressed, suspended, and terminated by individuals' inaction (e.g., swallowing grievances, avoiding conflicts, or opting out external intervention). In treating dispute management as chiefly a corollary to individual behaviors, this model leaves researchers with little analytical leverage to probe the day-to-day operation of the institutions responsible for conflict resolution. Unsurprisingly, the state—a key player with enormous clout in molding the landscape of legal mobilization and rights contention—simply fades into the background. At most, it is just part of the larger social contexts against which disputes and conflicts occur.

While the dispute pyramid model is inadequate owing to its fixation on individual behaviors, the second approach in the literature—legal endogeneity theory, as some call it—features a different set of problems for the analysis of judicial decision-making. Rather than taking individual action and inaction as a point of departure, legal endogeneity theory underscores the significance of overlapping institutional environments, shared cultural meanings, and the cyclical relations between formal lawmaking and social norm–making. From this angle, proponents of the theory contend that organizations like Walmart have exerted tremendous influences on formal laws. They have done so in part by configuring the meanings of key concepts at the core of civil rights legislation—discrimination, equal employment opportunity (EEO), and compliance, to name a few examples.

From the 1960s to the turn of the century, American judges at both district and circuit court levels have increasingly deferred to work organizations in lawsuits filed by employees against employers, the theory suggests. Such judicial deference to the corporate world congeals into reality, mainly as a result of judges' practice of inferring nondiscrimination—and hence compliance with EEO law—from the mere presence of symbolic structures organizations have established at the workplace. Whether these structures—anti-harassment policies, grievance procedures, employee handbooks, and affirmative action and diversity offices, say—prevent discrimination or sexual harassment is often immaterial in judicial decision-making. Stated differently, as work organizations find ways to decouple their actual practices from symbolic structures, as corporate lawyers, human resources professionals, and managers come to define the terms like *compliance*, *EEO*, and *nondiscrimination*, judges and legislators have uncritically accepted their interpretation of formal laws.[42]

To sociolegal scholars, there is much to admire in the way legal endogeneity theory untangles the interplay of law and society. That said, I find this approach to dispute resolution utterly unconvincing on one aspect: its inattention to power, politics, and the state. Empirically speaking, proponents of the theory make it clear that political elites, on multiple fronts and levels, fall short of delivering the legal ideals sparked by the civil rights movement. Top legislators, for example, left EEO law ambiguous on key fronts. Title VII of the 1964 Civil Rights Act, the landmark legislation, did not specify the meaning of the term *discrimination*. Nor did it clarify the types of evidence courts should consider in order to determine whether discrimination occurred in the workplace.[43] Similarly, chief justices sitting on the Supreme Court made it harder, not easier, for ordinary people to hold their employers accountable. Although nothing in Title VII or in other civil rights statutes explicitly discussed intent to discriminate, the Supreme Court insisted on the necessity of a plaintiff proving the state of mind of a discriminating employer. Following *McDonnell Douglas Corporation v. Green* (1973), subsequent cases placed greater emphasis on the requirement that a plaintiff must prove discriminatory intent so as to establish claims of disparate treatment, where an employee is treated unfavorably by an employer, because of that person's membership in a protected class.[44] Finally, judges in district and circuit courts repeatedly dismissed evidence indicative of the inadequacy of the symbolic structures adopted by corporate employers.[45] In sum, political elites have been deeply and systemically implicated in blunting the sharp edges of EEO law—at the expense of the less powerful in the organizational world, especially of individual employees with low socioeconomic and minority statuses.

These findings, however, did not lead proponents to theorize the roles of power struggles in mediating the interactions between law and society. Instead, to explain why judges at both trial and appellate courts, time and again, sided with employers as opposed to employees, legal endogeneity theory readily falls back on social psychology—that is, "judges are likely to be unaware of the extent to which organizations decouple formal structures from core activities or infuse managerial interests and objectives into the interpretation and implementation of formal policies and procedures," proponents of the theory claim. Also, "they [judges] are equally unlikely to be aware of empirical research questioning the efficacy of structures that appear fair and rational." Moreover, "it is likely that judges are susceptible to the illusion of fairness" and thereby "tend to assume that non-discrimination is the norm among rational employers and, conversely, that discrimination is an aberrant condition that exists only when employers or managers do something wrong, unprofessional, or irrational."[46] In short, as one book reviewer puts it, "judges...are duped by fake equal-opportunity programs."[47] Half a century has elapsed since Title VII was put in place. Yet, to explain why the U.S. judiciary repeatedly rallies behind the powerful in the corporate world, proponents of legal endogeneity theory still lay blame on judges' naïveté, ignorance, and cognitive limits.

This explanation for judicial decision-making is hardly convincing or compelling. While legal endogeneity theory draws attention to judges' susceptibility to the organizational world, it scarcely acknowledges the power play in this very environment. In emphasizing the significance of shared cultural scripts between judicial and corporate actors, this theory barely recognizes that "dominant cultural norms emerge out of concrete political conflicts, in which different groups fight over which norms will prevail," to use political scientist Kathleen Thelen's words.[48] Stated differently, seemingly "shared" cultural meanings, all too often, arise from power struggles among competing social groups. Proponents' indifference to power struggles, in the end, leads to a big drawback: legal endogeneity theory fails to reckon with a reality—judicial decision-making is all but a sphere of activities, shot through with willful action, power relations, and overt or covert resistance launched by the disempowered. Seen from this angle, the U.S. judiciary is far more than a mere conglomerate of somewhat open political arenas waiting to be the captives of influential social groups. Rather, judges and other institutional insiders take active measures to shape the landscape of conflict resolution.

* * *

After taking stock of the well-established approaches in the literature, I proceed to reconceive the notion of dispute resolution. To achieve this goal,

I place power, especially state and professional power, at the center of my study of divorce litigation. Behind this decision is an intellectual commitment: rather than privileging individual behaviors and decisions, rather than taking a powerless approach to law and society, a new conceptual framework should bring to the fore institutional practices, especially those undergirded by entrenched power relations within and surrounding the official justice system.

In reckoning with this commitment, I argue that, just like other political systems, the official justice system does not simply respond to existing disputes and conflicts in society. Rather, institutional insiders, such as legislators, judges, and government officials in charge of dispute management, can mobilize material and cultural resources to preclude the aggrieved from inserting their grievances and claims into formal decision-making arenas. Moreover, they can prevent grievances, disputes, and rights contention from arising in the first place, thereby (re)producing a deceptive façade of harmony between those in dominant positions and subordinate groups. This effect of "harmony"—or, more accurately speaking, compliance on the part of subordinate groups—can be induced and reinforced by altering group members' perceptions of reality, as well as their ability to imagine alternative lines of action. Stated otherwise, how disputation unfolds, which trajectory it takes, and what outcomes it eventually produces hinge on not just individual choices and behaviors but, more fundamentally, on institutional practices and particularly those configured by deep-seated power relations.

Drawing on Steven Lukes's and John Gaventa's works on power and powerlessness, this book reframes disputation in terms of *interconnected power relations*.[49] And divorce litigation, I believe, provides a window into the workings of three distinct types of power:

> (1) *Formal decision-making power, which determines who prevails over the resolution of manifest conflicts.*

In this book, formal decision-making power—or what Lukes and Gaventa term the *first dimension of power*—is manifested mainly as the authority judges exercise in deliberating who gets to divorce, who does not, and who receives what at the end of a marriage (see chapter 7 for an account of how judges exercise this type of power).[50] The operation of this power carries certain costs and risks, though. It consumes enormous judicial resources and time. Besides, in wielding this power, judges expose themselves to internal and external scrutiny. Wives and husbands, when dissatisfied, can take trial courts' decisions to appellate courts or to other state bureaucracies, an outcome few on the bench would welcome. This partly explains why Chinese judges, from the mid-1970s onward, have increasingly resorted to the second type of power to dispose of divorce suits.

(2) Agenda-setting power, which delimits the scope of official decision-making by excluding certain issues and/or participants from entering formal deliberation.

In the context of divorce litigation, the legal profession regularly exerts the second type of power. It does so typically at an early stage in the process of disputation. In meeting with clients to discuss divorce suits, law practitioners often (re)shape wives' and husbands' perceptions of marital discontent, remake or unmake their claims upon divorce, and, most crucially, channel some but not other concerns into formal court proceedings. By doing so, they transform certain grievances and rights claims into contested issues—division of marital property and allocation of child custody being the primary examples—and pave the way for such matters to subsequently enter judicial decision-making processes. On the other hand, law practitioners frequently turn women's complaints of domestic violence into nonissues, thus forcing them out of formal decision-making arenas. Consequently, these complaints fall through the cracks long before they can even reach the courthouse. By asserting their influences on clients at early stages of legal mobilization, the legal profession becomes instrumental in predetermining the outcomes of litigation (see chapter 4 for more details).

Note that judges also apply *agenda-setting power*. They do so by shutting divorce petitioners out of court proceedings via a procedure called *withdrawal* (撤诉). This procedure allows judges to close divorce cases without making any rulings on substantive issues like marital dissolution, property division, and child custody, thereby shielding themselves from the legal and political fallout that can follow formal decision-making. Indeed, since the mid-1970s, the Chinese judiciary has increasingly applied this procedure to turn away divorce petitioners and other litigants (see chapter 5). This trend attests poignantly to what Lukes and Gaventa describe as the *second dimension of power*—that is, power is exercised not only upon participants within the formal decision-making arena but also toward the exclusion of prospective participants and issues altogether.[51]

(3) Consciousness-formation power, which, through ideological indoctrination, acculturation, and other processes, instills consent and compliance in subordinate groups.

It must be emphasized that state actors, including legislators, judges, government officials, and village cadres, have been systemically implicated in eviscerating women's rights on certain fronts. And this is done, in no small measure, by animating *consciousness-formation power*. To unveil this power, later in the book, I analyze why women vehemently contest their spousal, property, and custodial rights upon divorce, but often remain silent on their lawful entitlement to landholding. By solving this empirical puzzle, the book uncovers how the third type of power comes into effect, shaping the conceivable, as well as the inconceivable, in citizens' legal mobilization.

Consciousness-formation power, it turns out, would not become operative without the PRC's decades-long lawmaking and policymaking geared toward institutionalizing a reform-era rural land regime. In that process, decision-makers have implemented countless laws, policies, and official measures that entrench—rather than uproot—men's dominance in land use and management. Contesting rights to landholding in this milieu proves not just legally and politically unactionable but rather unspeakable and unthinkable to many women. By connecting the dots between ruling elites' willful action to buttress patriarchy in rural China, on the one hand, and women's powerlessness and quiescence in divorce litigation, on the other, this book decidedly holds state authorities as opposed to divorcing women accountable for the absence of rights contention in certain areas—a phenomenon some refer to as *nonevents* or *nonparticipation* in the studies of political mobilization. To better understand this phenomenon, we must be attuned to what Lukes and Gaventa call the *third dimension of power*. Understanding this phenomenon is critical, for it directs us toward a meticulous inquiry into the ways power induces a profound sense of powerlessness, acquiescence, and compliance on the part of subordinate groups.[52]

To sum up, by illuminating the workings of three types of power, this book advances sociolegal studies along several lines. First, it shifts the thrust of the analysis from examining individual behaviors to problematizing institutional practices, thereby jettisoning an individualistic account of disputation. Next, in demonstrating how the PRC's ruling elites have made it difficult for women to contest the status quo, I avoid blaming the disempowered for their complicity in the reproduction of inequality and injustice—a fallacy that has persisted, despite repeated scholarly attempts to demystify obedience and compliance. Moreover, a power-centered framework brings into view *issues*, *events*, and *manifest conflicts*; what's more, it also minds *nonissues*, *nonevents*, and *latent contention* in the course of legal mobilization. A careful study of these nonissues, nonevents, and latent disputes, I argue, allows researchers to unearth how power manifests itself by keeping issues from arising, events from materializing, grievances from being voiced, and interests from being recognized. This is critical if we intend to capture the mechanisms whereby a sense of powerlessness is instilled in the minds of subordinate group members.

Finally, demarcating the key arenas where power concentrates—for example, courtrooms, legal workers' offices, and government agencies in control of dispute management—opens new analytical space for the study of what James C. Scott describes as the *hidden transcript of resistance*. If power tends to revolve around formal institutional settings, it is conceivable that subordinate groups may display genuine or feigned compliance within those settings. Group members, however, may develop strategies of disobedience and defiance in secluded settings (e.g., places outside the purview of the court system), hence (re)producing the hidden transcript to push back the frontiers of insubordination. Indeed, in chapter 6, I present concrete evidence, showing that women, under the right circumstances, do affront patriarchy. And they do so often in the underbelly of state law. By cultivating a power-centered approach, I hope to provide sociolegal researchers with an innovative framework to illuminate the fluid nexus between power and resistance.

CHAPTER 2

Marriage on the Move

A BUS TO A BRAVE NEW WORLD

The Weifeng bus station was on the verge of explosion. Too overwhelmed to check luggage rolling in, several security guards stood still, stone-faced, while travelers raced to secure spots in the long lines outside the ticket office. As they inched toward the glass window of the office, many shouted their destinations: Baishan, Chenluo, Guxiao, Qinchuan, Shipan, Xiqing…

Inside the station, the waiting room was small and run-down, crammed with passengers anxiously awaiting their ride. Some forgot to hold back on drinking and snacking. Before long, they found themselves itching, fidgeting, cursing in another line meandering outside the public restroom. The odor of urine, mixed with the smell of tobacco smoke and instant noodles, permeated the enclosed space.

Too broke to afford air-conditioning in summer or heating in winter, the bus station nevertheless served as a main travel hub in Weifeng, a county perched along the Min River crisscrossing the Sichuan Basin in southwest China. Connecting the county seat and two dozen towns in the surrounding region, the station was a lifeline for the locals.

At that moment, the station was in the thick of *chunyun* (春运), or the Spring Festival travel rush as some call it, which usually begins two weeks before the Chinese New Year and lasts about forty days. In 2018 alone, over 382 million Chinese traveled by train during *chunyun*.[1] Notwithstanding their diverse pathways, they were united in one goal: family reunion. Overlapping this tradition is another convention, hardly noticeable outside the country's court system: the Chinese New Year is known to judges as the peak season for divorce. This is the time of the year when hundreds of thousands of migrant workers finally pause backbreaking toil, arrange return trips to the countryside, and rejoin their families. Some, however, would seize the opportunity to approach a court—and petition for divorce.

Dissolving marriages inside a courtroom, a rarity in China for most of the twentieth century, has become far more common today. In 2018, the court system processed 1.37 million divorce suits nationwide, a six-fold increase from the late 1970s.[2] The steady rise of divorce litigation in recent years has been more notable among the floating population—a gargantuan group of rural residents migrating to cities and towns to search for cash-paying jobs. The size of the group has swollen to 288 million by the end of 2018.[3]

Li Zhiqing, a migrant worker in her late thirties, was among those journeying east, west, north, or south—to seek a divorce around the Chinese New Year. Despite the gloomy purpose of the trip, she managed to look pretty, with her hair permed, carefully combed, and pulled back into a ponytail, and her face embellished by a pair of flower-shaped, gold dangle earrings. To complete the look, she put on shiny black leather, high-heel boots, not the most comfortable footwear for long-distance travel.

No singular narrative can adequately capture the struggles of women like Zhiqing in labor migration or in family life constantly on the move. That said, this chapter strives to convey part of the nexus of women's experiences in migration and in marriage. As Zhiqing's story illustrates later in this chapter, rural women's participation in the urban workforce often extends their day-to-day interactions with men outside the home. Many, over time, have acquainted themselves with male coworkers, be-friended migrant men from other regions, and built new relationships outside marriage. Along the way, Zhiqing and others have come to reassess their aspirations and desires as women, wives, and daughters-in-law, thus setting off a strenuous expedition in search of a new self and a new life. Labor migration, in that sense, offers women not only much-needed financial independence but fresh opportunities to reimagine and reconfigure selfhood, intimacy, and marriage.

To rural men, their wives' employment in faraway metropolises signals unprecedented challenges to matrimony formed in accordance with a patriarchal tradition. Some, out of anxiety, jealousy, and disorientation, take extreme measures to preserve that tradition—only to quicken the collapse of their intimate lives. These micro-level individual changes, when occurring at a large scale over an extended period, amount to a quiet revolution, the kind that revolutionary party elites in the Maoist era never envisioned (see chapter 3 for an account of the PRC's family revolution in the early 1950s).

Tracing Zhiqing's steps in the course of marriage, labor migration, divorce, and postdivorce crisis, this chapter foregrounds the desires—and the perils—looming behind this quiet revolution. And I do so by underscoring the vantage point of women who aspire to rise above their rural origin; who yearn for financial security, human dignity, and social inclusion; and who seek to blend in a brave new world that looks modern, sleek, and free—from afar. The story of Zhiqing thus entails recounting a journey, starting from her teenage years in an impoverished village to her marriage into a better-off family, from her miseries in domestic life to the daily grind of work in the urban labor force, from her evasion of conjugal troubles to the ultimate showdown of facing her husband inside a courtroom. This is a story of entrapment and escape, of promises and betrayals. And, above all, it is a story about the pursuit of individual freedom and the hefty price that must be paid for it. In writing a story like this one, I hope to put a human face on divorce litigation. Moreover, I intend to unpack the linkage between labor migration and marital instability in contemporary China. As rural women gain novel opportunities to expand individual freedom outside the home, they are often subject to suspicion, scrutiny, and obstruction imposed by their husbands. Labor migration greatly complicates women's intimate lives, to say the least.

* * *

Inside the bus station, Zhiqing finally got a ticket. At last, she could sit down for a moment to gather her thoughts. A lot more must be done before she could set foot in a courthouse, pleading for a divorce. For that reason, there would be none of the usual seasonal activities—no holiday shopping, no mahjong games, no trips to temples to pray for the Lunar New Year, and certainly no time for sentimental feelings over homecoming. Instead, she had to quickly gather the paperwork needed for her divorce petition. As Zhiqing mapped out her plan for the next few days, her thoughts floated back toward the past.

Born in a village outside a small town called Nanshan, Zhiqing came from an area the locals call *po*. The Chinese character *po* (坡) means hills. In the local vernacular, it is often paired with another word, *ba* (坝), which refers to flatlands. The sharp contrast between these two did not register with me until I went on a trip to visit Zhiqing and her family one foggy winter morning.

After a bumpy two-hour ride that cut through Weifeng and then penetrated the inland of the neighboring county of Chuanyu, Zhiqing and I landed in her hometown, Nanshan. With forest covering nearly 70 percent of its jurisdiction, Chuanyu is touted as China's capital of bamboo. That idyllic title, however, did not match my first impression: for decades, Zhiqing's hometown had seen one generation after another leave for cities for off-farm employment. So desolate had it become that it looked like a ghost town. Seeing the look on my face, Zhiqing assured me, "We'll be home soon."

Over the next two hours, Zhiqing kept repeating the same reassurance. As we walked away from the town, the roads became rockier and the farmhouses fewer and farther between. Each time I spotted a house, it raised my hopes, but disappointment followed shortly. It was always someone else's home. Around noon, we at last reached our destination: a brick farmhouse sitting atop the hill, overlooking sprawling woods (see figure 2.1).

The scenery around the house was breathtaking. The house's interior, however, quietly bespoke another reality. The ceiling had never been covered, the walls never plastered, the floor never tiled. The color of cement, dark and gray, blurred the boundaries between the four sides of the room, creating a sense of visual oneness. As my eyes got used to the dimly lit living room, more details appeared: widening cracks were spreading everywhere, from the ceiling overhead to the floor underfoot; a strange smell enveloped the space and hung in the air, immovable.

Before I could take another look at the furnishings, Zhiqing invited me to join her parents in the kitchen for a chat. Over a stone stove, Zhiqing's mother was cooking, frying vegetables, while boiling feed for pigs. Here, basic home appliances—a gas stove, rice cooker, electric kettle, refrigerator, or microwave—were nowhere to be seen (see figure 2.2).

FIGURE 2.1 The farmhouse Zhiqing's parents lived in. Photographed by the author in 2010.

FIGURE 2.2 Zhiqing helping her mother in the kitchen. Photographed by the author in 2010.

In Nanshan and the adjacent areas, hill people like Zhiqing's folks harbored no grudge against air pollution, traffic congestion, or rising housing costs. Their biggest concern was abject poverty and had been for a long time. In this region, families had long struggled to make ends meet. Absent modern irrigation, transportation, or access to the latest farming technology, none of the following was feasible: planting rice, growing fruits, developing animal farms, running small businesses, or turning gorgeous scenery into tourist attractions. This bleak prospect is precisely what a family of *po* stands for in the local vernacular.

That impoverished family background did not stop Zhiqing from curating a good look. Tall and sturdy, she was about five foot six, a bit unusual for a thirtysomething born in Nanshan—not all the children in that small town had been fed well in the 1970s as Zhiqing and her generation grew up. Destitution, however, did not stymie Zhiqing's pursuit of beauty and fashion.

"Women from the countryside are generally hardworking," said Zhiqing. "But few are into clothing or style."

Zhiqing clearly considered herself as an exception. "Rain or shine. No matter. I was always out there, mowing pigweed, plowing the land, so I could save enough to buy new clothing," said Zhiqing. "I took a liking to clothing, early on."

That fondness for fashion did not impress Zhiqing's in-laws. Three years into her marriage, she had not produced a son. And that was sinful, according to the patrilineal tradition, captured in a popular saying, "Among the violations of filial piety, the worst is one's failure to produce an heir."

Zhiqing's inability to produce an heir made her a pariah in her conjugal family. "I had to put up with the trash talk from my mother-in-law. All the time."

To appease her in-laws, Zhiqing and her husband adopted a one-year-old girl, an attempt to little avail.

When Zhiqing finally gave birth to a healthy boy five years later, her mother-in-law lost no time spreading rumors in the village, taking credit for the birth of an heir in her family. "Thanks to her countless prayers, Buddha took pity on me by giving me a son," Zhiqing remembered.

"Didn't you talk to your husband and ask him to intervene?" I asked a question and then another one: "Didn't he do something? Anything?"

"I complained to him, hundreds of times, thousands of times. Nothing ever changes in that household."

In the end, even Zhiqing herself could not tell who pushed her away from her marriage: the mean-spirited mother-in-law who badgered her constantly or the husband who remained willfully blind to her pains. "I might as well run to the city to make a living there," Zhiqing decided.[4]

* * *

If demography is indeed destiny, as the sociologist Auguste Comte once claimed, this destiny has taken a unique path in contemporary China, swiftly producing some of the most gigantic cities in the world. By the end of 2018, Shanghai, a coastal city in east China, boasted a population of 25.5 million, followed by Beijing (19.6 million), Chongqing (14.8 million), Tianjin (13.2 million), Guangzhou (12.6 million), Shenzhen (11.9 million), Chengdu (8.8 million), Nanjing (8.2 million), and Wuhan (8.1 million).[5] By 2025, China will feature 221 cities that accommodate over a million inhabitants. The most populous country on the globe, by 2050, will add another 255 million residents to metropolitan areas.[6] Unstoppable urbanization is the future. And that future would not be possible without a great many Chinese women making the long march from the countryside to these rapidly expanding metropolises.

The past preceding that future can be traced back to 1955, the year the People's Republic of China (PRC) instituted hukou (户口) nationwide.[7] Hukou, also referred to as the household registration system, required each couple to register their newborn at a police station of a particular locale, usually at the child's birthplace. Then the police would place the newborn in one of the two categories, agricultural or nonagricultural population, depending on the parents' hukou status. If the child were fortunate enough to be born in a city, say, Chengdu, the capital of Sichuan Province, she or he would be most likely to come of age as a city dweller, with access to state-sponsored benefits, such as guaranteed food supplies, health care, education, housing, lifelong employment, and a retirement pension. And a child whose birthplace happened to be Weifeng, a county about one hundred miles south of Chengdu, would grow up as a rural *hukou* holder, tending to farmland day in and day out, receiving much less state support throughout life.

The implications of the *hukou* system, in other words, were far-reaching at both the individual and collective level. As an officially designated status, *hukou* was essential to the ordinary citizen's material well-being, social status, and self-identification. Without it, "one cannot establish eligibility for food, clothing or shelter, obtain employment, go to school, marry or enlist in the army," Judith Banister, a demographer, observed in the 1980s.[8] At the collective level, *hukou* divided the Chinese population into two tribes, one privileged to breed future generations of urbanites and the other obliged to reproduce the peasantry. In so doing, *hukou*, as a bedrock institution in the PRC's plans for creating socialist citizenry, was meant to "maintain social order, protect citizens' rights and interests, and serve the construction of socialism," the National People's Congress, the highest legislative body in the land, declared.[9]

Between the mid-1950s and the 1980s, the central and local governments put in place myriad regulations and policies to entrench the *hukou* system, making it exceedingly difficult for peasants to alter their standing in the eyes of the state. For women and men born in villages, upgrading their status to urban *hukou* holders, thus obtaining expanded access to state-sponsored benefits under normal circumstances was a bit like hitting the jackpot—easy to dream about, but rarely achievable. What's more, the central government was adamant for decades in curbing rural-to-urban migration, which in turn led to low levels of population movements in the Chinese territories.

By the mid-1980s, official restrictions on internal migration appeared increasingly unsustainable. Agricultural reforms initiated by the central government in the late 1970s revamped the ways labor and income were distributed in rural China, incentivized peasants to improve farming, and, in the years that followed, unleashed millions of surplus rural laborers. The enactment of the Open Door policies—part of official endeavors to integrate the Chinese economy into the global one—started drawing in foreign investments. As more foreign investors brought their manufacturing facilities to China, a global factory came into being, and the demand for cheap labor rose sharply. Finally, the emergence of a domestic service sector craved new blood for its labor force as well. Together, the combination of agricultural reforms, the influx of foreign investments, and the development of a service-oriented economy prompted the central government to rework the *hukou* system.[10]

A turning point came in 1984. The State Council, the PRC's central government, issued a notice that year, which eased the official ban on rural-to-urban migration. A provisional regulation released by the Ministry of Public Security followed the next year, allowing peasants to obtain temporary residence permits to stay in cities and towns.[11] Before long, these policy changes ushered in an unprecedented era of internal migration. Within a few years, about 25 million migrants of rural origin began working in urban settings. That figure jumped to 80 million in 1995. Now, two decades into the twenty-first century, migrant workers have totaled 288 million.[12]

Note that rural women did not start out as front-runners of the newly emerged population movements. Men did and have continued to make up the bulk of the massive rural-to-urban move. Despite that, female participation in labor migration has been robust in the new millennium. A series of survey reports, compiled by the National Bureau of Statistics, estimate that women have consistently comprised about one-third of the migrating population. Which is to say, approximately 95 million women have joined the journey from the countryside to various urban destinations over the course of a decade or so.[13] These women, no longer tied to farmland like their mothers and grandmothers, have shed blood, sweat, and tears in cranking out products like iPhones, IKEA furniture, Prada bags, Nike sports shoes, Victoria's Secret lingerie, and car parts going into Buick Envisions, Ford Focuses, and Cadillac CT6 plug-in hybrids.[14] Today, women of rural origin can be found in construction, manufacturing, transportation, and the service sector—all labor-intensive industries.

* * *

It took Zhiqing years to realize the impact of labor migration on her marriage and family life. In the 1990s, when Zhiqing and her peers came of age, two criteria dominated matchmaking in villages. The first one, *chaifang shuibian* (柴方水便), could be translated as follows: convenience in gathering firewood and easy access to drinking water. As far as hill people were concerned, natural advantages like proximity of home to drinking water were a big plus for the families of *ba* to attract brides from the households of *po*. As for the second criterion, it pertained to a young man's prospect of inheriting his parents' property and landholding.

Zhiqing felt lucky. Her husband-to-be met both criteria. Back then, marrying a man from a *ba* family, who happened to be the sole heir of his parents, was as good as mate selection could get. Besides, Zhiqing and her husband had eyes for each other. "He had other dates, but only fell hard for me," said Zhiqing. "We never told each other things like 'I like you' or 'I love you.' What we had [back there] was lots of singing and dancing."

That lovey-dovey feeling for her husband did not last. To flee her mother-in-law's reign of terror, Zhiqing started looking for employment outside her conjugal village. Within a few years, she had dabbled in various odd jobs in several cities, working on assembly lines, washing dishes in smelly diners, trading medicinal herbs, selling small goods—basically, grabbing every earning opportunity she could. All along the way she wrestled with loneliness, meager pay, harsh work environments, not to mention brazen discrimination and biases against migrant workers of rural origin. Her husband, on the other hand, remained unsympathetic. Whenever Zhiqing called him, he dived immediately into a harangue about cash, debts, and household expenses. "He wouldn't take the initiative to contact me," Zhiqing recalled. "But when he did, all he could talk about over the phone was like 'how many debts the family has owed' and 'how urgently I should bring home cash.'" Where Zhiqing yearned for emotional connection and support, her husband stood aloof, unwilling or unable to recognize her needs and wants.

The husband's inability to capitalize on off-farm employment drove another wedge between the couple. After a short period of trial and error as a migrant laborer, he went back to the village and refused to give it another try. Growing ginger "suited" him better, Zhiqing quoted her husband as saying, with more than a whiff of sarcasm in her tone. The man she once desired, the husband she used to depend on, no longer seemed desirable or dependable.

Then Zhiqing met someone else.

"He is understanding," "he is sweet-natured," and he found "better ways to make a living." That was Zhiqing's description of the new guy, who later became her longtime boyfriend. Unlike the husband, the boyfriend had turned migration into a life-altering opportunity. Hailing from a dirt-poor village, he recast himself as a skilled construction worker and managed to purchase an apartment in a city, thereby putting down some roots in one of China's fast-developing metropolitan areas.

The boyfriend's extended families, likewise, exemplified a trajectory some would describe as a rags-to-riches story. One cousin, who had barely graduated from elementary school, headed a county-level state bureau. Another relative served as a hospital president. "Did I mention someone else in his family, working somewhere, as a high school principal?" Zhiqing tried hard not to gloat by keeping a matter-of-fact tone. "You can't purchase this nobility with money." Zhiqing enunciated the word *nobility* (高贵) as if the concept were entirely foreign to me.

Out of curiosity, I asked what she meant.

"Well, everywhere you go, you are respected. People would mention your name like 'this is so-and-so.'"[15]

What should I make of Zhiqing's emphasis on nobility as a trait that renders men, especially those of rural origin, attractive and desirable? In what ways could her experience—falling out of love with her husband and getting swept away by another man—inform us of the socioeconomic and cultural changes Chinese society has undergone in recent decades?

With these questions in mind, I reached out to Xiao Suowei, a Berkeley-trained sociologist and a professor at Beijing Normal University, whose book, *Desire and Dignity: Class, Gender and Intimacy in Transitional China*, came out in 2018. Spending a decade researching extramarital intimacy in China, Dr. Xiao had a lot to say about this controversial topic.

As China grows richer, economic inequalities among its population have deepened. The symbolic meaning of wealth, over time, has also shifted in the context of intimate relationships. "How much a man earns, in what ways he amasses wealth, and through what channels he converts material resources into a dignified life have come to define his *suzhi*," said Dr. Xiao.

Nowadays, the term *suzhi* (素质) increasingly marks a set of presumably innate, as well as nurtured, human qualities in a popular discourse of masculinity in contemporary China. Within this discourse, a "high-*suzhi*" man, it is said, is willing and ready to spend money for his girlfriend or wife. A "low-quality" guy, by contrast, is much less inclined to do so due to moral or educational deficiency. Put differently, men with deep pockets stand a better chance of being viewed by others as decent and reliable and harboring a strong sense of familial responsibility, whereas those stuck in poverty tend to come off as petty, shady, and morally irresponsible toward their significant others. While *suzhi* defines men's desirability and popularity in the eyes of women, it renders both gender groups susceptible to old patriarchal rules, as well as newly emerged cultural norms and values.

Citing a popular saying, "A woman is loved by a man insofar as she controls his purse strings," Dr. Xiao highlighted an emergent reality in today's gender relationships: the country's old patriarchy has been grafted onto a consumer culture that has arisen in China in recent decades, and the talk of *suzhi* obscures rather than illumes the strange fusion of the two.[16] Dr. Xiao's research, together with recent studies of popular discourses surrounding *suzhi*, casts new light on the complexities behind extramarital intimacy in Chinese society.[17] Compared to college-educated, professional women holding urban *hukou*, migrant women of rural origin could be particularly vulnerable to the fusion of the old patriarchy and the new consumer culture. This vulnerability, I must point out, stems from the fact that migrant women generally face greater barriers to social inclusion—let alone upward mobility—than those with college degrees and urban *hukou*. The combination of entrenched discrimination against rural *hukou* holders, atrocious working conditions, spotty protections for labor rights, and renewed stereotypes about peasants as boorish and uncultured has profoundly limited migrant women's quest for financial security, a sense of belonging, and human dignity. When their desires for prosperity, inclusion, and, ultimately, a dignified life cannot be met in a public space, like the workplace, some have to pin their hopes on the private domain by cultivating an intimate relationship with a man of certain resources and social status.

For that reason, there is a real danger in treating extramarital affairs as little more than a form of individual transgression, which often functions as a convenient explanation for the dramatic rise of divorce in reform-era China. This explanation is downright flawed, for it omits the workings of social and political institutions in shaping individual choices in life. Examples of those institutions include, but are not limited to, a state that has time after time refrained from confronting patriarchy head-on; a market economy that has deepened gender inequalities in pay and in career development; and a consumer culture going all out to convert old female submission into new moneyed expressions of love, fidelity, and family responsibility.

* * *

Back in Weifeng, Zhiqing's elaborate planning paid off. Weeks before the Chinese New Year, a judge confirmed the date for court proceedings. Finally, Zhiqing would face her husband in front of a judge. This courtroom encounter would be the first face-to-face interaction between the two in the six years since the last time Zhiqing visited her conjugal family in the village. It would also determine the fate of their marriage.

On the day the hearing was scheduled, I arrived at the courthouse early in the morning. Inside the mediation room—a tiny office stuffed with slogans, such as "Harmony is gold," "Conciliation yields beautiful memories," "Reconciliation gives parents and children peace of mind"—I saw Zhang Yuanjun, Zhiqing's husband of fourteen years.

The man was not much to look at: a rugged face, unkempt hair, gnarled hands, dirt stuck under every fingernail. For years, he had supported his family by growing ginger, although many in his village no longer cared about it, due to its low profitability. Unapologetic and unashamed, Yuanjun felt no need to justify his chosen lifestyle. Something of a straight shooter, he made no secret of his views and feelings.

"Give me fifty thousand yuan, and I'll sign divorce papers." Shortly after the mediation session began, Yuanjun dropped the announcement.

"You know the law. And so do I," Yuanjun told the judge.

Judge Zhou, who presided over the divorce case, was mute for a moment. He then mumbled, "Well, if you two reach agreements, we—"

"You tell her to make the payment," said Yuanjun. "I'll sign the papers right away."

"Her family members may offer you money [upon divorce]. But we can't order them to do so." Judge Zhou took the opportunity to spell out some legal technicalities.

"You can't guarantee the payment? Well, I won't settle," said Yuanjun. He then offered an alternative, "Get the money ready. Bring it to my place or have it deposited into my bank account. After that, I'll give you my signature."

Upon hearing her husband's demand, Zhiqing began fidgeting in her seat, flashing an annoyed grimace. Before she could utter anything, Yuanjun interposed. This time, he turned to face his wife.

"You were gone for years," Yuanjun said. "Did you cook for the kids? Wash their clothes? Take care of anything? Pay their tuition? Buy them books?"

Judge Zhou tried to weigh in. "Regarding monetary compensation, you two can discuss it—"

"You didn't bring home bread or butter. You didn't provide for us. You didn't care for the kids," Yuanjun cut in again. "You were gone for six, seven years."

Zhiqing sat there, emotionless. She made no attempt to dispute her husband's claims or to explain her extended absence from family life. There was no apology, no pleading, no repentance, only silence hanging in the air.

To chime in, Judge Zhou turned to Zhiqing: "Your husband no longer trusts you—"

"When you get the money ready, I'll sign the papers. Otherwise, don't hold your breath," Yuanjun again interrupted the judge.

"What about signing a [payment] agreement with him?" Judge Zhou asked Zhiqing.

"You might as well give me a child," Zhiqing murmured.

"The kids have no feelings for you." Enraged by his wife's suggestion, Yuanjun plunged into an angry outburst. "You *think* they'd let you raise them." His voice shivered. "They'd rather stay home with their father. The bottom line is that I'll feed them."

Both Zhiqing and the judge tried to say something. Neither of them succeeded.

"The kids know better. Only their father will take care of them," Yuanjun insisted. "You were gone, completely out of the picture."

Time and again, Yuanjun accused his wife of abandoning her family, a moral debt that could be offset only by making a one-time cash payment of fifty thousand yuan.

Time and again, Zhiqing stressed that she could not afford such a divorce settlement.

The judge went back and forth, seeking to close the gap between the two sides. The first round of mediation failed to achieve that goal. After a brief recess, Judge Zhou conducted another round of mediation, which fell flat in short order. Out of options, he held a trial, in which both the defendant and the plaintiff agreed on marital dissolution. What remained in dispute, however, was the amount of cash payment the former demanded from the latter. Toward the end, Yuanjun made a concession: "Thirty thousand yuan! Whenever you are ready to pay, I'll sign the papers."

That concession made little difference to Zhiqing. It was still far beyond what she could afford. Eventually, Judge Zhou had to halt the trial, asking the couple to return for another court hearing in two weeks.[18]

* * *

An unexpected phone call, on a late Friday night, brought Zhiqing back into my view, nearly eleven months after she and I had said goodbye outside the Weifeng bus station, following the court's ruling in favor of her divorce petition, an official decision that legally terminated her marriage of fourteen years, setting her free from a relationship marred by bitter resentment toward her in-laws at the beginning, plenty of the silent treatment in the middle, and prolonged periods of no contact toward the end. At long last, Zhiqing was liberated, I thought.

Yet when Zhiqing resurfaced eleven months later, she did not sound liberated. Her voice went up and down at the other end of the phone, trying to recap the latest episode in her life.

Why not get together and talk more during the weekend, I suggested.

"All right," said Zhiqing.

At a teahouse that offered unlimited refills, I saw Zhiqing again. Hard to tell what she had been up to lately. The fashionable look I remembered from the first time I met her—the flower-shaped earrings, slim leggings, shiny leather boots, and other details so imprinted in my memory as if I saw them yesterday—was gone. Looking pretty was perhaps the last thing on her mind now.

"My daughter called me recently," said Zhiqing. "If I have time, I should go home more often. Have dinner with her. My ex told her to put it that way."

"That's thoughtful, isn't it?" I replied.

"Once divorced, everything about me goes back to 'fine' in his eyes."

So, this was a conversation about the ex-husband and his flaws, I gathered, without saying it out loud.

It took me the next ten minutes or so to find out why Zhiqing had suddenly contacted me. The boyfriend she had been living with for the past eight years; the man with whom she had raised a son born out of wedlock; the man she had expected to depend on for the rest of her life; the one she married soon after gathering divorce papers was having an affair with someone he had met during labor migration. Zhiqing's marriage was teetering, again.[19]

LABOR MIGRATION AND MARITAL INSTABILITY
New aspirations and desires

Zhiqing's experiences, at certain aspects, are all too familiar to researchers studying Chinese marriage and family. The reform era (1978–present) has seen a dramatic surge of divorce in the country, a pattern well-documented in official records. A quick survey of these records reveals the extent to which Chinese marriage, as a social institution, has been destabilized. Between 1978 and 2018, the number of marriages dissolved by courts annually has risen fourfold, climbing up from 114,865 to 648,600. Meanwhile, the volume of divorces granted by local governments every year has soared from 170,449 to 3,804,682, a twenty-one-fold increase in four decades (see figure 2.3).

Various factors have contributed to the rise of divorce in the reform era. Among others, a regulatory change must be noted. The State Council,

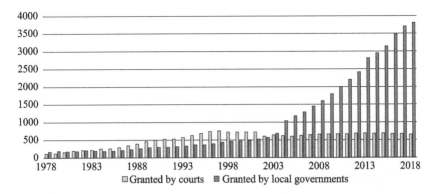

FIGURE 2.3 Number of divorces (in thousands) granted by courts and by local governments in China, 1978–2018

SOURCES: *China Civil Affairs' Statistical Yearbook* (2001–2019); *China Law Yearbook* (2000, 2002); *Historical Statistical Books of the People's Courts, 1949–2016 (The First Volume on Civil Litigation, 1950–2004).*

NOTE: Chinese couples can dissolve their marriages by either registering uncontested divorces with local governments or by filing petitions for marital dissolution at local courts to seek judicial remedies for contested divorces.

in 2003, revised Regulations on Marriage Registration (婚姻登记条例), which eliminated the power of state actors, such as village cadres (in rural areas) and employers (in urban settings), to block citizens' pursuit of divorce.[20] From then on, wives and husbands, miserable in conjugal life, can legally dissolve their marriages by registering divorce agreements with local governments. Seeking divorce, free from the state's interference, at last became a real choice for wives and husbands (chapters 3 and 5 provide elaborate accounts of how local governments and the court system have altered their interventions in citizens' intimate lives in the history of the PRC).

Scholars generally recognize the broad trend: Chinese marriage has become more dissolvable than ever before. But few have explicitly addressed the question of how women's participation in labor migration might give rise to conjugal tensions, discord, and even disputes. This is not surprising, though. For a good part of the twentieth century, demographers, economists, and sociologists treated women's rising labor force participation, by and large, as an economic phenomenon, with implications mainly manifest at the workplace or in the labor market. When they did heed the interplay between female employment and marital instability, many settled with an instrumentalist view—that is, integration into the paid labor force was instrumental for women's attempts to exit unhappy marriages, as employment came to equip them with financial means and job skills.[21] This view is limited, I must stress, in that it offers few clues about how women's labor market experiences might have (re)shaped their understanding of the meanings of selfhood, intimacy, and family. A similar problem stands out among anthropologists, sociologists, and geographers who, on the cusp of the new century, started examining Chinese women's experiences in labor migration. Many turned their critical gaze to rural women's day-to-day struggles in the urban workforce. Rarely did they look beyond the factory floor, assembly lines, massive dormitories, or the rapidly expanding service sector to assess migrant women's lived experiences outside the workplace.[22]

In recent years, more researchers have shifted their attention to women's and men's sexuality, desires, and identity (re)formation during migration.[23] In this chapter, I join these researchers by illustrating how women themselves connect the dots between migration and intimate lives. Agreeing with Max Weber and Clifford Geertz that humans are social beings "suspended in the webs of significance" they themselves have spun, I focus on cultural meanings—especially those women attach to their aspirations, desires, and fancies.[24] To put it another way, unlike researchers assessing the "utility" of marriage or the "functions" of female employment from their own perch, I place women's perspectives front and center.

To that end, I draw on findings from sixty in-depth interviews with thirty-two women of rural origin.[25] Through these interviews, I realized that Zhiqing's experience was neither random nor incidental. In fact, eight out of the thirty-two women divulged that, prior to divorce, they had formed long-term, intimate relationships with other men, and two gave birth to children born outside formal wedlock. Apart from Zhiqing, Du Huiying and Wu Manli (the latter also appears in chapter 6), both in their late twenties, were particularly vocal about their involvement in extramarital intimacy.

Manli and Huiying, just like Zhiqing, saw problems in their marriages long before their entry into migration. Divorce, nevertheless, did not register as a viable alternative back then. While making their first forays into glittering metropolises, both women encountered difficulties and challenges—low pay, long work hours, literally toxic work environments, social isolation, origin- and gender-based discrimination, to name a few examples. At a moment when Manli felt like a zombie, churning out the same product day after day, a migrant man brought a beam of light into darkness. To explain how the two kicked off a romantic relationship, Manli walked me through their initial encounter. "Back there, we had a mutual friend who borrowed my phone to call him. He called back later. That's how we began chatting. After all, I was lonely," Manli revealed. Shortly after, it occurred to her how different this man was from the one she had married. When asked about the exact differences between the former and the latter, Manli explained, "He is mature" and "thoughtful"; "if you were feeling blue, he would comfort you, and, if you got mad at him, he would call and talk to you until you feel all right." Manli's husband, by contrast, fiddled around, "drowning himself in gambling," "spending money on nobody but himself," "with no plan to save [for the future]." Plus, he hardly ever lifted a finger to help with the housework.

In our conversations, Huiying similarly brought back certain memories, some joyful and others agonizing. Years ago, when she ran into trouble in her business—transporting and selling farm-raised ducks—a street vendor helped her. And he comforted her, "It's tough for a woman to manage a business like this." Huiying's face lightened up, as she recounted that remark, a soft grin, like a pebble falling into a pond, setting in motion concentric waves that spread out on the water. Before I realized it, I was smiling with Huiying. I was not surprised to learn that the man had become Huiying's boyfriend and the father of her son (before she could file a petition for divorce). At a time of enormous hardship and countless challenges, a brief encounter with another man, one who demonstrates empathy, understanding, and appreciation for hard work, often marks the beginning of a new relationship outside the home.

After having spent more years as migrants, Huiying and Manli gradually adjusted the lens through which they assessed manhood and gender relationships. Speaking of her husband, Huiying picked phrases such as "lazy," "opiniated," "pompous," "lacking in education and skills." She described her boyfriend as "hardworking" and "down-to-earth," on the other hand. A similar contrast is central to Manli's characterization of her husband and of the man she dated. In her account, her husband was "self-indulgent and indolent," whereas her boyfriend, once a peasant, pulled himself up by launching a profitable business as an internet café owner.

These contrasts hark back to the distinctions Zhiqing made in her decision to leave her husband and to marry another man. Journeying from villages to faraway cities, some men falter and bail out eventually, and others soldier on to survive and even thrive. Comparing and contrasting the former (oftentimes one's husband) with the latter (the current partner) is a recurring theme in divorcing women's narratives. These comparisons, I must emphasize, do not merely speak to how women view men's characters, personalities, or socioeconomic standing. Rather, they embody two distinctive lifestyles, one marked by human bondage and the other by individual freedom and growth.

In her own language, Manli sums up the differences between the two lifestyles. "I didn't want to stay in the countryside. Back there, I had no money at my disposal, and the in-laws kept an eye on me all the time." Manli took a deep breath, as if she needed more air for stepping into that past. "I had no say or freedom."

Months after her divorce, I found Manli at an internet café on the outskirts of Chengdu, a city about one hundred miles north of the household she previously married into. After years of preparation, Manli and her boyfriend started a business supplying teenage boys with a haven so they could bathe in the unending thrill of online gaming. Setting up the business, Manli had a hand in every decision from picking the right location to budgeting, from paying taxes to dealing with local regulations for small business owners. Along the way, she learned to use a computer, write emails, and master other skills as needed. Manli and her boyfriend were not just partners in life; they were partners in business. In this way, she gained a great amount of freedom, respect, and personal growth she had long fancied. When asked about her plan for remarriage, Manli—unlike Zhiqing—harbored little illusion about her future husband. Rather than searching for a man of abundant resources or a certain social status, she expressed greater interest in building her career in business management.

In this regard, she had become "much more confident these days," Manli told me.[26]

Heightened anxiety and disorientation

As women of rural origin embark on an expedition beyond the horizon, their significant others must adapt to new living arrangements. Men in the countryside, however, do not always find such arrangements bearable. The fact that their wives are perennially out of sight, without the constraints of family life in the village, is in and of itself disquieting for some. Out of anxiety, jealousy, and perhaps profound disorientation, they may resort to extreme measures to cling on to conjugal relationships increasingly susceptible to new aspirations and desires. Indeed, throughout the interviews, I heard the women over and over lamenting their husbands' distrust, suspicions, and flat-out accusations of infidelity. Ten of the thirty-two women expressly complained about their husbands' attempts to scrutinize, constrain, or block their contact with other men, although much of it involved routine interactions with the opposite sex at the workplace and beyond. When suspicions and accusations morph into ridicule, humiliation, emotional, physical, and/or sexual abuse, efforts to hold on to one's wife often end up pushing her away and even decimating the marriage.

Yuan Yue, a migrant woman in her late thirties, shut fast much bitterness inside her chest. Years ago, she started working as a cook in Chengdu. Her dream job was to run her own restaurant in a city forever fixated on refined cuisine. Yue's husband, Fang Bin, did not share that aspiration. Nor did he support his wife's pursuit of a career in food service. Rather, he was skeptical of her dream from day one. Skepticism, slowly, grew prying eyes, ears, feelers. This metamorphosis became ugly and uglier over time.

"He didn't want me to make any friends. Even when I hung out with female friends, he complained. As though he didn't want me to meet anyone out there," Yue said, recalling her husband's reactions to her work outside the village. Outgoing and sociable, she ignored those reactions and went on to build a social circle of her own, dining out with coworkers, playing mahjong with friends at teahouses, going on excursions into nature, and so on. In her recollection, her friends were "full of fun" and "candid"; her husband, by contrast, was "dull" and "fussy," almost granny-like. When it came to the issue of socializing with one's peers, the two could not be further apart. Nothing good could come out of those social activities, and that was Bin's conclusion.

Time went by. The friction between the two grew more heated, flashing hotter each time a conflict arose. Yue remembered one incident in particular. Waiting outside her restaurant to give her a ride, Bin spotted his wife chatting with a waiter almost a decade her junior. "You know what he said to me afterward?" Yue asked rhetorically, her voice prickling with disbelief and disgust. Later that day, Bin confronted his wife, railing against her wooing of "a baby-faced lad" (小白脸), the expression purposely insulting in Chinese in that it invokes the image of an old woman indulging herself in exploitative relationships with young men. That accusation, unsurprisingly, did not sit well with Yue. It scarred the couple's relationship, and the wounds it left behind never healed.

When friction escalated into skirmishes, skirmishes into battles, and battles into ruthless ravage, the marriage reached its breaking point. Stalking his wife all day long, Bin finally "caught" her being alone with another man, drinking tea, at a teahouse. Although Yue and her friend repeatedly explained the nature of their relationship, Bin remained convinced that his wife was cheating on him. Shortly after, he summoned Yue's parents and other relatives, went up on his toes in rage, and exposed his wife's "adultery" in front of her own folks. These acts, however one might read them, amounted to public shaming and condemnation. "He [the husband] drove me into a corner," said Yue. "How could I possibly live with him after that?" Eventually, Yue sued her husband for a divorce. A court ruling put an end to their seventeen-year relationship in 2011.[27]

The current study, unfortunately, does not allow me to separate two scenarios, though. Here is the first scenario: a migrant woman forms an extramarital relationship first, which in turn triggers her husband's distrust, conjugal discord, and disputes, and then the eventual divorce. The second scenario involves a somewhat different sequence of events. It starts with a husband projecting his fears and frustrations onto a wife serving in the urban labor force. Extended ill-treatment then leads to the wife's attempts to seek out another man's attention, respect, and emotional support, followed by heightened conjugal tensions, conflicts, and marital dissolution in the end. Absent a prospective, longitudinal research design, I cannot ascertain which of the two scenarios happened to the women in the book.

Moreover, as a female researcher, I experienced persistent difficulties in obtaining divorcing men's consent to interviews. Among the thirty-two women I interviewed—that is, thirty-two cases of marital disputes—I managed to talk to both the wife and the husband in only four cases. Additionally, I recruited and interviewed another twelve rural men on the verge of marital dissolution (in these cases, unfortunately, I was unable to get ahold of the wife for various reasons). Together, I interviewed sixteen husbands. The gender disparity in my sample—thirty-two wives and only sixteen husbands—means that my analysis heavily relied on women's narratives, but not enough on men's accounts. Notwithstanding the limitations, I did hear several husbands speaking about extramarital intimacy.

Lei Mingliang, a thirty-seven-year-old migrant worker, was among the few men pulling the curtains aside so I could peek through a window onto a domestic corner otherwise unlit. On the day I met with him, he was awaiting counsel to further discuss his case. His wife, Yin Chen, had filed a lawsuit against him, demanding a divorce. Candid about his own missteps, Mingliang admitted to being unfaithful to his wife a few times. But that was not why his marriage was falling apart, he insisted. The "real" cause was rather his wife's affairs with another man.

As the interview unfolded, I listened in anguish as Mingliang stitched together a year-by-year narration, fraught with his struggles to grapple with the wife's muffled frustrations, suppressed anger, and soundless despair. She had been drifting away, inch by inch. But where the blame lay was somehow beyond her husband. Upon discovering his wife's affairs, Mingliang was all at sea, unable to form an understanding or a course of action. "I spent just a few years in school, with little education. I don't know how to handle this sort of things [his wife's infidelity]," Mingliang told me.

Desperate and confused, he made a request to his wife. "I asked her if I could check her phone record or if I could answer her calls," Mingliang remembered. "Of course, she should have privacy, and we all should. But this matter [infidelity] is beyond privacy." Mingliang cast his eyes down.

"Anyway, I just can't handle a situation like this." Nevertheless, he was determined to save his marriage.

Later, during an interview with Yin Chen, I learned the depth of her emotional suffering and the causes: Mingliang's infidelity, together with other vices—gambling and heavy drinking—plunged one dagger after another into her heart until it bled no more. All the suffering, on both sides, however, brought few heart-to-heart conversations between the two. Neither party seemed to know how to communicate with each other in a supposedly intimate relationship. Their marriage of twelve years eventually came to an end in 2010.[28]

CONCLUSION

Drawing on interview findings, this chapter unravels the linkage between labor migration and marital instability. As Zhiqing's, Manli's, and Huiying's experiences illustrate, women of rural origin, upon entry into the urban workforce, often find themselves in a world full of potential and constraints, at once titillating and disheartening. On the one hand, new aspirations, desires, and fancies make their ways over time into women's married lives, prompting many to grapple with the meanings of wealth, intimacy, and matrimony. Yearning for financial security, emotional satisfaction, and individual freedom could drive some to break away from unhappy relationships.

On the other hand, while labor migration opens space for new imaginations, it nevertheless offers migrant women limited structural opportunities to actualize their longing and yearning. Over the years, study after study has identified formidable barriers keeping migrant workers from being fully integrated into the urban labor force, let alone achieving upward social mobility.[29] This grim reality is hardly unfamiliar to women on the move. In the interviews, I heard one woman after another contemplating her eventual plan to return to the countryside. Few anticipated permanent settlement in cities and towns. Acutely aware of their economic and social vulnerability, migrant women have continued to deem marriage and family a crucial safety net. Some, in the long run, would have to turn to a man and a conjugal family for support.

A related note: whereas Zhiqing pinned her hopes on another husband, only to realize how quickly that strategy could tank, Manli questioned remarriage as *the* solution. Given the choice between becoming another man's dependent and searching for her own foothold in the world and perhaps fostering a new kind of intimacy, Manli clearly preferred the latter. Sobering up through the experiences of migrant life, some women may tread a path their mother, grandmother, and great-grandmother never could.

At first glance, rural men like Lei Mingliang and Fang Bin could not be more different from each other. Facing real or imagined betrayals on the part of the wife, one became stuck in his paralysis, and the other progressively descended into a dark abyss, dragging himself and his spouse into endless paranoia, torment, and emotional suffering. Looking beyond the apparent dissimilarity, I see much commonality between these two men. Exposure to a metropolitan world may stir up novel needs and wants and generate fresh opportunities for both women and men to reassess their intimate lives. Yet, all too often, that exposure falls short of upgrading husbands' and wives' cultural toolboxes in identifying and addressing (preexisting or emerging) conjugal problems.

Sifting through interview notes and transcripts, I kept looking for signs, indicative of migrant women's and men's efforts to improve such a cultural toolbox. Instead, what I saw, again and again, were wives' and husbands' frustrated, blocked, or derailed attempts to grasp marital strife, to verbalize discontent, and to find common ground at home. The consumer culture that has arisen in China, as sociologist Xiao Suowei has noted, dictates that women and men consume more stuff, fancy personal wealth and social status, and attach new meanings to intimacy and marriage. In many cases, it has yet to render men and women better life partners.

CHAPTER 3

Disputation as a State Enterprise

LONG DAY'S JOURNEY INTO NIGHT

"I have to badger the government"

It all started with a simple request, a request so pedestrian that Han Donglin later struggled to recount how the trouble began, how it escalated within minutes—and how it eventually landed her in a courtroom.

It was late afternoon. Donglin had been washing clothes in the kitchen. Her son, eleven years old, would be home any minute, and dinner had been ready by then. The thought of her son coming home, starving, pushed Donglin to act fast. Just then, someone opened the front door. Cartwheeling across the floor and racing to her side was the schoolboy, not looking for food but begging to take his pocket money to a comic bookstore.

"Why don't you ask your dad about that?" Donglin suggested.

That request must have riled Xia Tian, Donglin's husband. He stomped in and out of the kitchen, ranting and raving, trashing his wife's parenting style.

Donglin froze. Fixing her gaze on the fabric between her fingers, she tried to keep her mind on cooking.

In his early forties, Xia Tian was short, barely five foot three, but muscular and bulky, with a build hinting at years of physical labor. Donglin had learned the hard way not to confront him when he was angry.

As the cursing and yelling dragged on, Donglin began edging toward the dining area in an adjoining room. While letting herself out of the kitchen, she might have rubbed her shoulder against her husband's. Her memory got fuzzy after that point...What she remembered afterward was the repeated punches to her face, the blood pouring from one eye, and the coldness of the cement beneath her body lying still on the ground.[1]

It is unknown how many times throughout her sixteen-year relationship with Xia Tian Donglin was left with a swollen cheek, a bruised body, or a broken spirit. This time was somehow different. Soon after the assault, Donglin approached one state authority after another on a spirited quest to bring public intervention into her strained domestic life.

In spotlighting Donglin's bitter struggles to seek official attention to her marriage, this chapter underscores a pivotal shift in the history of the People's Republic of China (PRC)—that is, marriage used to be a key vehicle for nation-state building—its integrity and soundness were of paramount importance for the nascent PRC to carry the country from a backward, feudal past into a modern, socialist future. Once socialism was firmly established, marriage proved instrumental for official endeavors to build a socialist civilization. When the new millennium finally dawned, controlling marriage had become far less useful as a form of direct political governance, prompting state bureaucracies to look further away from citizens' intimate lives. Nowadays, women like Donglin, in need of public intervention in marriage and family life, have few options beyond taking their grievances and claims to the courts. In that sense, marital and familial discontent, once a thoroughly political matter, has been judicialized in the PRC today.

To unpack this historical shift is, on the surface, to take stock of how and why the state has continued to adjust its relation to the institution of marriage. At a closer look, this unpacking entails a methodical examination of how the PRC, over time, has calibrated and recalibrated governing methodologies, and not least its techniques and tactics for dispute management. As the pages ahead illustrate, from the early 1950s onward, the PRC has had a vested interest in tackling the so-called folk disputes (民间纠纷).[2] This official catchphrase, which literally means disputes among citizens, has borne witness to the Chinese state's decades-long attempts at penetrating and containing society. It also attests to the PRC's past and current efforts to refine its governance. This refinement is achieved, I argue, partly by unlearning certain ruling methodologies applied in the Maoist era, partly by remodeling techniques and tactics inherited from the socialist period, and partly by selectively appropriating governing experience from foreign countries, including liberal democracies.

What emerges from these official endeavors, I must note, is anything but a state's retreat from society (although the PRC, in the new century, has further downscaled direct interference in citizens' intimate lives).

Instead, two decades into the twenty-first century, the Chinese state has not only widened official intervention in folk disputes but expanded its toolbox for conflict resolution. Through this expansion—diversification of conflict resolution (多元化纠纷解决), as it came to be known in official language—state actors, from the commanding heights to those in the trenches, have sought to consolidate both legal and nonlegal methods for dispute management. These methods include, but are not limited to, litigation, mediation, arbitration, letters and visits (信访), and other administrative measures. In simultaneously strengthening these methods, the PRC aims to sort popular grievances, funnel citizens' demands into divergent state institutions, and, ultimately, dissipate prevailing contention in society. Together, these efforts have engendered a triage-esque system, so to speak. Within the system, citizens' grievances and claims are gauged in terms of their potential to subvert the political status quo. Accordingly, officially designated difficult, hot-button disputes, such as widespread discontent with land expropriation, environmental pollution, and labor relations, are routinely channeled into extrajudicial and quasi-judicial bureaucracies for the sake of social stability. Meanwhile, mundane, frequent disputes, including marital strife and torts, are thrust into judicial space in the name of the socialist rule of law. As Donglin's experience of seeking help reveals, the rise of this triage-esque system has profound implications for citizens. Many would have to navigate an increasingly complicated terrain of dispute management, a terrain fraught with intricate politics accompanying the state's continued penetration into society.

Analytically speaking, in writing the chapter, I seek to engage two scholarly communities. To sociolegal scholars, this chapter represents a decisive departure from extant theoretical orientations in the studies of dispute management. As detailed in chapter 1, one orientation—associated with the dispute pyramid model—centers on individuals, with a heavy emphasis on their action or inaction in the face of grievances and contention. Disputation, in this view, constitutes a somewhat linear progression prompted by individual behaviors (e.g., perceiving certain experiences as injurious, blaming the responsible parties, seeking redress, or swallowing grievances and opting out of remedies). In this highly individualistic and behavioristic view, the state has virtually no ontological standing, let alone theoretical significance.[3] The other orientation—illustrated by legal endogeneity theory—places society (work organizations in particular) at center stage of dispute management. Cast in this light, the state, as well as the court system, is little more than a conglomerate of somewhat open political arenas, right there, waiting to be the captives of influential social groups.[4] In short, the two deem the state either irrelevant or secondary in the genesis, transformation, and resolution of disputes and conflicts, a view this chapter sets out to counter. And it does so by demonstrating that over the course of seven decades, the Chinese state has remained a driving force in shaping and reshaping the landscape of dispute-making and dispute-resolving. War makes states, and, in turn, states make war, Charles Tilly once claimed (in his study of nation-state formation in Western Europe).[5] In the PRC, a similarly circular relation stands—namely, the state dictates the terms of dispute resolution, and dispute resolution compels the state to continually attune its governance to changing circumstances at home and abroad.

To China scholars, this chapter constitutes a counternarrative. Far too often the reform-era PRC is portrayed as a regime "torn between a strong preoccupation with stability and a desire to promote law-based governance."[6] Political stability and the rule of law, in this rendition, signify two distinct political ideals, two separate models of governance. Caught in the middle, the PRC in the past decades has oscillated between the two, with one administration, one party elite, or one head of the country's highest court leaning more toward one ideal or model rather than the other, or vice versa, researchers contend. Driven by similarly binary thinking, China scholars have debated whether the PRC, in the new millennium, has been on a trajectory against or toward law, a debate only reenergized after Xi Jinping's rise to the pinnacle of state power in 2012.[7]

However persuasive and pervasive, this binary thinking does not stand up to a thorough historical scrutiny. Rather than viewing political stability and law as a paradox in ruling, the PRC, I argue, has come to treat the two as part and parcel of the same toolbox for governing. The methodologies, techniques, and tactics in the toolbox—whether they originate from the revolutionary past of the Chinese Communist Party (CCP), grow out of communist ideology, get nourished by the principles of liberal democracy, or are refurbished with the scientific impress of technocracy—can be and have been mobilized piecemeal, without logical coherence of a singular theory of statehood. The past two decades, in other words, did not witness China shifting against or toward law categorically. Rather, the PRC has been weaving legality into the fabric of governance by juxtaposing it with—not pitting it against—extralegal practices, institutions, and ruling methods. Put simply, if the PRC must be a case of some sort, to use common parlance in the social sciences, it might as well be examined as a case of an authoritarian regime continually cultivating a cultural repertoire of mixed statecraft. This cultivation, of course, is not without its limits or consequences, intended or otherwise, a theme this chapter and the ensuing one explore.

* * *

Donglin was once pleased with her marriage. The youngest of five children from a rural household, she grew up with a visceral understanding of hardship, the kind peasants must endure to raise a big family. Marrying Xia Tian, who held a job at a state-owned enterprise, came as a relief. She would not repeat the life her parents had lived.

Her contentment with her marriage did not last long. Months after Donglin gave birth to their son, Xia Tian was badly injured in a car accident. Signs of sequelae soon surfaced in his postsurgical recovery—agitation, combativeness, and depression, to name a few symptoms potentially associated with traumatic brain injuries. The man Donglin once counted on faded away day by day.

Xia Tian's mental health improved little over time. Worse, violent outbursts punctuated his daily interactions with family members. As verbal and physical violence became the defining feature of their relationship, their marriage seemed increasingly unsalvageable. Following yet another beating—the one described at the beginning of this chapter—whatever options had existed narrowed to one. Donglin knew she had to get help.

The first door she knocked on belonged to the Residents' Committee (居民委员会), a nominally grassroots mass organization that governs itself (基层群众性自治组织), but, in actuality, possessing close ties with the local state. After much hustling, Donglin got a phone number from the committee. "They told me to call this number, the one for the office of some party secretary. I did. The guy at the other end of the phone line directed me to contact this [Residents'] Committee, instead." Donglin paused a second to bring down her voice. "I said to the guy, 'You don't want to deal with this matter. All right!' Then I dialed the police's number."

Within hours, a police officer accompanied by a local government official turned up at Donglin's doorstep. Upon seeing her wounds, the two immediately arranged for a vehicle to send her to a nearby hospital. The moment the medical examination was over, Donglin rushed to the police station, bringing along evidence, including a doctor's diagnosis and photos of her injuries.

"There, I was told, 'It's just soft-tissue injury.' So they couldn't do much," said Donglin.

No further action could be pursued because she suffered "just soft-tissue injury?" I asked.

"That's right." Donglin confirmed.

A few days into her attempts to find help, local authorities' reactions left Donglin at a loss. A neighbor then made a suggestion, "Why don't you approach the Women's Federation? Aren't they committed to standing by women like you?"

The All-China Women's Federation (中华全国妇女联合会), according to its website, is a "mass organization that unites Chinese women of all ethnic groups, from all walks of life, and strives for their liberation and development." In reality, it is a government-staffed and -funded entity, with numerous branches scattered across the country. To seek its support, Donglin had to travel to the county seat, for the federation had no local offices below the county level.

The next morning, Donglin headed for the county seat, determined to take her marital problems to authorities at a higher level. In mid-September, Weifeng, a county perched along the Min River in southern Sichuan Basin, baked in the heat of an Indian summer. The barometer stood high; the sky was glowing, the sun ruthless, the air oppressive. By the time Donglin found the Women's Federation in a gated work-unit compound, she was drenched in sweat.

Nicknamed the natal family of all Chinese women, the federation did not exactly welcome Donglin's homecoming. A staff member promptly sent Donglin off to the Legal Aid Center (法律援助中心), affiliated with the county-level Justice Bureau (司法局), a government body in charge of local legal affairs. "The Women's Federation urged me to look for the help of a lawyer there," Donglin told me.

"That was it?" I had to ask.

Donglin nodded.

So the journey dragged on. On a narrow, tree-lined street, Donglin spotted a sparsely furnished office occupying a storefront in a three-story building. Here at last was the Legal Aid Center.

Inside the center, Donglin finally received some useful suggestions. She could sue her husband for a divorce, for instance. The center would then help her secure professional assistance for divorce litigation, free of charge, as long as Donglin could verify her standing as a low-income resident of Weifeng. "The staff [at the center] was like 'How would I know your family struggles with hardship? You must show me proof,'" Donglin recalled.

Apparently, neither her status as a woman nor her experiences of domestic violence registered with the center. The request for proof of financial hardship sent Donglin into another round of bureaucratic jujitsu with the authorities in her neighborhood. Her dogged efforts paid off eventually. Months later, with papers issued by the Residents' Committee, Donglin convinced the center of her need for legal aid.

The Xiqing People's Tribunal, later that year, granted Donglin a divorce and custody of her son, but left her with no marital property on the grounds that Xia Tian was incapable of providing alimony and child support owing to his mental disability. From September 7, 2010, the day Donglin was assaulted by her husband, to the moment a judge dissolved her marriage on November 25 that same year, it had taken Donglin seventy-nine days to obtain a "solution" to her problems. Yet Donglin's struggles did not end there.

About a week after her divorce trial, I visited Donglin in the tumble-down rental she had moved into. Free of an abusive spouse, she could barely bring herself to savor this newfound "freedom." The judge rejected her claims on housing, a family-run business—the small teahouse where she had been employed—and other conjugal property. Going back to the apartment where she used to live or maintaining her income at the teahouse was no longer possible.

Divorced and divested of all her marital property, Donglin was having a hard time envisioning a future for herself and her son. Her new hope was to enroll in the minimum living standard guarantee program—that is, essentially to get on state welfare. To do so, she had to go back to the local authorities. "I have no housing, nothing. And I must raise my son. What am I supposed to do?" Donglin asked. "I have to badger the government." All over again.[8]

One of the feistiest women I have met in a decade of research on divorce litigation, Donglin nevertheless could not make government officials heed her conjugal predicaments. Approaching one state agency after another, at multiple levels of government, only led to one aching realization: few in the officialdom cared about women like her, stuck in strife at home, thus in need of public intervention. For Donglin and many other women across the country, one of the few conceivable solutions is to find one's way to the court, ask for a divorce, and foot the bill for litigation. This judicial "solution," as the remainder of the book shows, carries serious limits and pitfalls. Women hailing from the countryside often end up losing the bulk of their rights as wives, mothers, property owners, and land users.

"Divorce is a matter of the law"

Ever since I had learned Donglin's difficulties in seeking official attention to her marriage, I wanted to meet with state actors on the front line of dispute management. A contact of mine, also from Donglin's town, suggested that I talk to Fan Yongpin. Few would be more knowledgeable about divorce, village affairs, and conflict resolution than he was, the contact insisted.

When I found Fan Yongpin in his office, he had just steeped tea, sending the aromas of recently dried jasmine and tea leaves, the specialty of his village, wafting around the room. Over two decades, Fan Yongpin had served as a village cadre in various roles, first as a production team leader and later the party secretary, heading the Villagers'

Committee (村民委员会). In explaining his routines as the party secretary, Fan Yongpin launched into a speech. The Villagers' Committee was a "mass organization of self-government at the grassroots level, in which villagers administer their own affairs, educate themselves, and serve their own needs," Fan Yongpin told me, summoning a line from the law verbatim.[9]

Around our second or perhaps third cup of tea, Fan Yongpin waded into a more relaxed conversational mode. The members of the committee, it turned out, were all on the local state's payroll. Fan Yongpin, for example, got paid about 8,000 yuan a year, an amount he deemed "too little." The per capita income for villagers in Weifeng was, however, only 4,937 yuan around 2010, according to the county government. That was less than $800 a year.

More to the point, cadres like Fan Yongpin hold sway over village life on multiple fronts. A seven-page internal memorandum listed a total of twenty-four targets and responsibilities (目标责任) the township government had delegated to cadres who ran village affairs on a daily basis—building grassroots organizations, developing local economy, maintaining social stability, and managing social affairs, such as family planning, health insurance, and environmental improvement, to name only the most important duties. Cadres, in other words, wield immense power in shaping village life from womb to tomb.

What kind of sway have cadres exerted in fellow villagers' marriage and family life? This question brought back Fan Yongpin's memories of serving as an accountant (村文书) on the Villagers' Committee, a position he held for fifteen years. For decades, villagers had to seek his approval whenever they needed the committee's stamp on their papers. Fan Yongpin's access to the stamp made him the most authoritative figure in a village of more than seven hundred households. Young women and men could not apply for marriage certificates without stamped letters issued by the committee, verifying their age and marital status. Absent a similar letter, those miserable in marriage could not register their divorces with the local government.

"But the system in our country has changed," Fan Yongpin told me. Nowadays, villagers no longer need the committee's approval for their marriages or divorces. "These days, we cadres have little grip on such affairs."

When I asked whether cadres still mediated villagers' marital and family disputes, a function Villagers' Committees had long served, Fan Yongpin nodded, but quickly added a qualification. "Today, divorce is a matter of the law, the Marriage Law, whereas other disputes are still within the government's reach."[10]

Fan Yongpin never explained what "other disputes" he was referring to. Intrigued by his attempt at separating the law and the government's "reach" in dispute management, I decided to approach more state agents to probe their stance on this matter. This intention to dig deeper brought me in subsequent months to another six Villagers' Committees, five government offices at the township level, and four at the county level, an expedition that culminated in a face-to-face conversation with the former head of the Political Legal Committee (政法委员会) in Weifeng, the party organ in charge of the judiciary, the police, the procuracy, the justice bureau, and the armed forces.

After conducting eighteen in-depth interviews with village-, township-, and county-level state actors and combing through hundreds of pages of internal government documents, I could not stop mulling over Donglin's experiences in disputation. Why did Donglin, in search of a remedy for her marital grievances, land in a courtroom, while many others, besieged in disputes over land-taking, labor rights, medical malpractice, and so on, find their complaints and demands flowing into the Justice Office (司法所), the Office of Justice and Mediation (司法调解办), the Office of Letters and Visits and the Masses (信访与群众办公室), the Office of Comprehensive Management of Public Security (综治办), the Center for Integrated Mediation for Disputes and Conflicts (矛盾纠纷大调解中心)— all essentially extrajudicial state bureaucracies? Why do the aggrieved find themselves under the purview of different institutions—some judicial, some quasi-judicial, and others extrajudicial? How did this terrain of dispute management come into being in the PRC?

To address these questions, the remainder of the chapter chronicles how the PRC has deployed drastically different methodologies for its interventions into folk disputes during the post-1949 Maoist era, the socialist period, and the new century. In the Maoist era, the dominant mode of state intervention was mass campaign. In the socialist period, mass campaign gave way to people's mediation (人民调解). Then, a decade into the twenty-first century, top decision-makers arrived at a novel realization: rather than privileging one mode over others, the PRC must institute a multipronged system, comprising litigation, mediation, arbitration, letters and visits, and other official measures, all of which serve to dispel popular contention, preempt social unrest, and safeguard citizens' rights in some but not other domains. Disgruntled wives and husbands, throughout all the three periods, thus find themselves standing in awe of a leviathan, too mighty to be ignored. Toward the end, this chapter sums up the broader implications for our understanding of the interplay of law and politics in an authoritarian context.

DISPUTATION AND STATE-(RE)MAKING
Mass campaigns in the post-1949 Maoist era

On March 17, 1949, the *People's Daily*, the CCP's flagship publication, featured a short article pronouncing a recent decision by the North China People's Government (华北人民政府), the predecessor of the PRC's central government. "The key to folk disputes is mediation," the article title read tersely. Reflecting on the CCP's governing experience in the Liberated Zone (解放区)—the territories the Party controlled during the Republican era in the late 1940s—the article exhorted party cadres to properly handle popular disputes in society. To that effect, all civil disputes and minor criminal cases must be mediated by "impartial individuals," including disputing parties' kin, village leaders, and government officials.[11] The 1949 decision, although far from earth-shattering on its face, thrust the concept of folk disputes into the national spotlight. This concept, in the decades to come, would prove to be a remarkably resilient cultural category reverberating across official discourse, policymaking, and lawmaking.[12] Its meanings would continue to evolve as the PRC braved new challenges and difficulties in ruling. The aggrieved, in turn, would face the state's shifting methodologies in governance. Their experiences in disputation, political participation, and legal mobilization would vary from one historical moment to the next.

Months after the 1949 decision, Mao Zedong delivered that triumphant speech, atop Tiananmen Gate, proclaiming the establishment of the PRC. The nascent PRC did not wait long to promulgate its first national law. In May 1950, the Marriage Law debuted on the national stage, placing the PRC side by side with modern sovereigns that inaugurated their reign with marital regulations—colonial Virginia, revolutionary France, the breakaway republic of Texas, and the Soviet Union, to name a few famous examples.[13] Within just twenty-seven articles, the law vowed to accomplish a mission of historic proportions: to rid the populace of the feudal marriage system.[14] Manifest in entrenched practices, such as polygamy, concubinage, arranged marriage, and sales of women and girls as brides, this system had bedeviled China for centuries, plunging its people into cultural backwardness and the country into prolonged political disunity. To set China free from its backward past, and to transform it into a strong, unified, socialist nation-state, the PRC must first revolutionize Chinese marriage, liberate women and men from feudal beliefs and practices, and create awakened citizenry, marriage reformers within the Party declared.[15]

Within two and a half years, the new law brought nearly three million marital and family disputes to courts nationwide, of which 80 percent were divorce petitions.[16] The vast majority of those petitions were initiated not by men but by women, from varying walks of life—well-read intellectuals, office clerks, factory workers, and tailors in Beijing, Shanghai, and other urban centers, as well as peasant women in remote villages in Yunnan, Guizhou, Sichuan, Shanxi, and Fujian Provinces. Indeed, the law's power was felt palpably by Han Chinese, who made up the bulk of the country's population, and so did it reverberate in the inner ears of ethnic minorities, including Yi, Lisu, Dai, Hui, and Hui'an.[17] So fast did the tremor of the law travel that almost no group or region was left untouched by the end of 1953. This was all the more remarkable considering the context in which the consequences of the new law were unfolding. The PRC's judiciary at the time was barely fledging, a well-trained legal profession was nonexistent, and formal rules and procedures necessary for civil litigation were almost unheard of among party cadres. In a country where divorce was historically rare and stigmatizing, where the judicial infrastructure was in its infancy, how did the first national law achieve such sweeping effects within just a few years?

Scholarship on the 1950 Marriage Law, although divided about its long-term impact, converges on one point: the law violently jolted millions of Chinese families and did so mainly through mass campaigns (群众运动). One researcher defines such campaigns as follows: "a government-sponsored effort to storm and eventually overwhelm strong but vulnerable barriers to the progress of socialism through intensive mass mobilization of active commitment."[18] Put more plainly, mass campaign is a type of political movement, with a number of intrinsic elements: a strong commitment to revolutionary change; centralized ideological control; extensive propaganda work; and a point-to-surface approach in policy implementation, intended to broaden the reach of a campaign from model sites to the rest of the country. In some instances, ad hoc committees were formed at the national level to spearhead a campaign by coordinating multiple government agencies, by dispatching work teams to diverse sites to supervise local officials, and by recruiting mass activists at the grassroots level.[19]

Moreover, mass campaigns in the early 1950s carried two crucial features: intensive, large-scale mobilization of the general population and a public display of coercion and moral rightness, often conveyed through political theatrics. Recounting a public accusation meeting (控诉会) in Heilongjiang Province in 1951, political scientist Julia C. Strauss vividly describes how campaign organizers placed the "enemies" of the revolution in front of fourteen thousand pairs of eyes. Representatives of the masses were invited to mount the stage and speak bitterness inflicted by counterrevolutionaries. Harsh criminal sentences soon followed. In the end, death penalty was executed amid deafening outbursts from the crowd, "Thanks to the Chinese Communist Party," "Thanks to Chairman Mao," "Thanks to the People's Government!" As an integral part of mass campaigns, political rituals such as public confession meetings, show trials, struggle sessions, and speaking-bitterness sessions, were used to deliberately engage the emotions of the public, whip up hatred against designated campaign targets, and assert the Party's absolute confidence in its moral correctness, all of which, Strauss contends, was geared toward mobilizing the masses into positive support for the new regime.[20]

Judging by the existing accounts of the 1950 Marriage Law, its implementation in the early years of the PRC carried all the hallmarks of the quintessential, Maoist-style mass campaigns. The CCP's official discourse certainly insisted so. The *People's Daily*, for example, devoted much front-page coverage to the primacy of mass campaigns in disseminating, popularizing, and enforcing the law. One article, published on February 1, 1953, captured the gist of the message from the top leadership in a crisp headline, "Launching a Vigorous Mass Campaign to Administer the Marriage Law."

Scholarly works on this period are awash with granular details about the mass campaigns. Historian Kay Ann Johnson's work is a case in point, which delineates how step-by-step, top-down, national campaigns injected the new law into ordinary people's lives, leaving some to marvel at its emancipatory power and many others to deplore their fate on the wrong side of the regime's revolutionary ambitions. Moreover, Johnson walks readers through the young PRC's organizational and operational assemblage of the campaigns countrywide—with the National Committee for the Thorough Implementation of the Marriage Law at the top, municipal and district campaign committees and bureaus in the middle, and numerous checkup work teams on the ground. Accompanying this top-down structure was a point-to-surface approach, first testing the law in thousands of selected villages and counties and then fanning out the experimentation to the other parts of the country.[21]

During this period, cultural workers, including playwrights, artists, journalists, and editors, carried out elaborate propaganda—under the thumb of censors—to ensure centralized ideological control over campaign materials. Party cadres everywhere received training, so they could identify and combat feudal beliefs and practices among the masses. Judges and local government officials, under enormous political pressure, dished out divorces upon women's request, lest they violate the law and become enemies of the regime. Willingly or not, ordinary people participated in nightly classes, mass meetings, and speaking-bitterness sessions to be educated about the new law.[22]

From 1950 to 1953, as the entire country slipped into a frenzied crusade against the feudal family system, ordinary women and men saw their family lives being politicized beyond their control. A marital dispute in Shanghai, in 1953, illustrates how local officials handled domestic friction at the peak of the Marriage Law campaigns. At the time, Jin Xiangsheng, a fifty-four-year-old factory worker, maintained a household with one wife and one concubine. After a spat at home, Jin stormed out. Jin's wife, upset, went to the township government, asking officials to educate her husband. The timing could not have been worse for Jin. The township government was just about to convene a mass meeting to teach residents about the recent legislation. Within days, one authority after another knocked on Jin's door. First was a Marriage Law instructor, then a police officer, and eventually the township chief, all demanding that Jin rectify his conduct at home. Shortly thereafter, Jin was told that a confession session would be staged, and his wife, son, and daughter-in-law would publicly denounce his old feudal way of life. By that point it was abundantly clear to Jin what might be awaiting him. So he urged his family to attend the confession session: "You should all come participate…Accuse me and let yourselves live!" Days after that, Jin took his own life.[23]

Similar examples pervade scholarly accounts of the early 1950s, showing in detail how ordinary people were sucked into the vortex of the Marriage Law campaigns, their family lives being cracked wide open, vulnerable to the new regime's intervention, one that frequently turned abrasive and abusive. Many, almost overnight, woke up and found themselves engulfed by a revolutionary divide. As far as the young PRC was concerned, they were either the incarnation of the old, traditional, feudal China, culturally backward, politically degenerate, and thus needing to be purged, or they were among the oppressed, waiting to be emancipated and awakened so they could join the new, modern, socialist nation-state then in the making. While a great many women embraced the law, their husbands and in-laws were at the mercy of zealous campaign organizers. Some of the men were beaten or jailed, and more than a few turned to suicide to escape a revolution they had never signed up for.[24] In short, the PRC—a revolutionary regime at the time, resolved to dismantle an older society—developed myriad governing techniques and tactics (see table 3.1 for a summary). It did so in no small part by inserting an iron fist into citizens' intimate lives. In the decades to follow, as the PRC moved away from that revolutionary

TABLE 3.1 State interventions in marital and family disputes in China, 1950–2018

	The Post-1949 Maoist Era (1950 to the late 1970s)	Socialist Era (the late 1970s to the early 2000s)	New Century (the early 2000s to the present)
Dominant mode	Mass campaign	People's mediation	Litigation
Key events	1950 Marriage Law 1951 and 1953 Marriage Law campaigns	(1954 Regulation on People's Mediation) * 1980 revision of the Marriage Law 1989 Pro-Democracy Student Movement	2001 revision of the Marriage Law 2003 revision of the Regulations on Marriage Registration
Guiding principle	Rid the populace of the feudal family system	Maintain a family system conducive to the construction of a Socialist Material and Spiritual Civilization	Protect individual rights, but also defend marriage as a bedrock institution, buttressing a harmonious socialist society
Ruling methodologies, techniques, and tactics	A top-down approach, establishing ad hoc committees at the national level, leaving regional government agencies in the middle, and dispatching checkup work teams to local sites Centralized ideological control and extensive propaganda A point-to-surface process of policy implementation and refinement Large-scale mobilization of the general population A blend of coercion and moral appeal, achieved through political theatrics	Decentralized, routinized surveillance, monitoring, and interventions conducted by party cadres embedded in the workplace, schools, and communities Use of a mix of material and symbolic rewards to induce compliance and conciliation on the part of citizens Application of state laws and policies, also invocation of traditional norms, such as human relations (人情) and moral right and wrong (道理), to mediate disputes and conflicts	Setting high standards on paper (e.g., gender equality on all fronts) Individualized, piecemeal enforcement of the Marriage Law and other family-related laws (citizens foot the bill for legal mobilization) Specialized interventions conducted by judges and legal professionals Reinventions of certain Maoist legacies (e.g., the centrality of judicial mediation in divorce law practices inside courtrooms)

NOTE: People's mediation has its roots in the Maoist era. It was a 1954 regulation, issued by the Administration Council, that brought this institution into being. But it did not achieve predominance on the landscape of conflict resolution until the early 1980s.

past, it would alter methodologies for dispute management, downplaying some ruling experience and striving to retool other skills and methods.

PEOPLE'S MEDIATION IN THE SOCIALIST ERA

By the mid-1950s, the Marriage Law campaigns had died down. Throughout the country, authorities continued to promote the law, but increasingly with an eye to family harmony. Divorce became harder to obtain year by year. (Chapter 5 provides a detailed account of how the courts in the remainder of the 1950s and 1960s altered their divorce law practices, making marital dissolution exceedingly difficult for the general population.) Remaining dormant for three years, the concept of folk disputes reemerged into the national limelight in 1954. That year, it appeared in a regulation issued by the Administration Council (政务院), the predecessor of the State Council. In explaining the import of the regulation, the *People's Daily* proclaimed, "Folk disputes over land, housing, irrigation, marriage, and debts, if not handled properly or promptly, would hurt the unity of the people, hinder their production work, and may even trigger armed confrontation and homicide...But it would be unrealistic to expect courts or district and township governments to resolve all these disputes."[25]

The realistic solution, at that time, was to institute a mass organization (群众性组织) to address popular grievances, thereby freeing courts and local governments for more important tasks. This organization came to be termed the people's mediation committee (人民调解委员会). Its primary goal, according to the 1954 regulation, was to manage folk disputes—defined as regular civil disputes and minor criminal cases—by means of mediation conducted by representatives of the masses who maintained a clear "political outlook," "impartiality," and "enthusiasm."[26] Later that year, the Ministry of Justice (MOJ) explained the modus operandi of such committees, stressing that people's mediators (人民调解员) ought to "follow government policies and laws" and to rely on "democracy," "persuasion," and "voluntariness" to settle differences between disputing parties.[27] In other words, once the Marriage Law campaigns started to atrophy, the PRC's central government revived its earlier rhetoric of mediation and conciliation. And this shift was not just rhetorical. It rather marked the beginning of an ending in the PRC's interventions in folk disputes. The regime's departure from the quintessential, Maoist-style mass campaigns as a dominant methodology with which the state inserted its influences into society would not be completed until 1980, four years after Mao's death.

Within a year of enacting the 1954 regulation, reports surfaced, insisting that more than 70 percent of counties and districts nationwide had instituted people's mediation, with over a million mediators in service.[28] The veracity of such estimates may be debatable, but one thing is certain. Party leadership was firmly behind the idea of enlisting mass activists to deal with prevailing disputes, especially those concerning marriage, eldercare, farmland, and debts. Liu Shaoqi, the then chairman of the PRC, championed people's mediation, calling it the "first line of defense" in the administration of justice.[29] Dong Biwu, the head of the Supreme People's Court (SPC), made a similar point, saying, "People's mediation...provides a good organizational form to resolve regular disputes among the masses, and it does so by swiftly settling civil cases, lowering the costs of disputation, and consolidating the ties between party cadres and the masses."[30]

Official praise of people's mediation carried over into the mid-1960s.[31] Up until 1964, the then SPC president, Xie Juezai, like his predecessor, applauded mediators' contributions in restoring harmony among the masses.[32] What happened after that remains less clear. People's mediation, according to some official accounts, languished as the country descended into a decade of political tumult known as the Cultural Revolution (1966–1976). Scholars, on the other hand, summon somewhat different memories. Stanley Lubman, for example, recalls his visits to mediators in Beijing and Shanghai, in 1973, when the country was in the throes of mass upheaval. Other scholars similarly maintain that mediators carried on their work throughout the 1960s and 1970s in both rural and urban areas. No evidence could be found to indicate an official call to halt this form of dispute resolution either before or during the Cultural Revolution.[33]

Following Mao's death, Deng Xiaoping took over the reins of party leadership, in 1977. One year later, the CCP's Third Plenary Session of the Eleventh Central Committee officially ushered China from the Maoist era into the Reform and Opening-Up period. People's mediation, within a few years, was elevated to an unprecedented political standing. A sequence of events led up to that new height. The MOJ convened the first National Conference on People's Mediation in 1980. Shortly after, grassroots entities, from Residents' Committees in urban areas to People's Communes (人民公社) in the countryside, to factories, mines, and other work units, (re)instituted people's mediation as a key organizational structure responsible for dispute management. Legislators swiftly enshrined this structure by inscribing it into the PRC's fourth constitution in 1982. Resolving folk disputes then became a constitutional mandate for those who called themselves people's mediators. When the Civil Procedural Law was passed in the same year, followed by the Law of Succession in 1985, legislators once again accentuated the roles of mediators in engendering reconciliation for the aggrieved.[34] In a word, the advent of the reform era overlapped with a spectacular rise of people's mediation—now a prominent fixture on the landscape of conflict resolution.

Figure 3.1 visualizes this prominence by comparing people's mediation to litigation, another mechanism for conflict resolution. Mediators from the early 1980s onward have consistently towered over their counterparts on the bench by processing hundreds of thousands more civil complaints

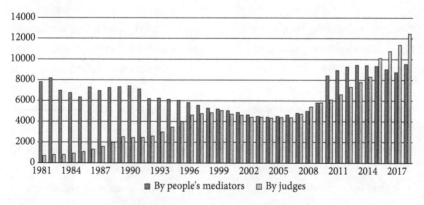

FIGURE 3.1 Folk disputes and first-instance civil suits (in thousands) processed by people's mediators and by judges in China, 1981–2018

SOURCES: *China Law Yearbook* (1987–2013, 2015–2016); *China Statistical Yearbook* (1984–1986, 1999, 2014, 2017–2019); *China Social Statistical Yearbook* (2017–2019); *Historical Statistical Books of the People's Courts, 1949–2016 (The First Volume on Civil Litigation, 1950–2004).*

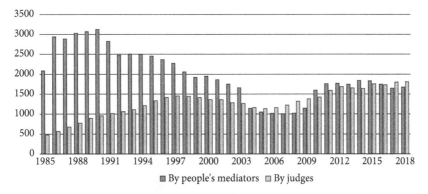

FIGURE 3.2 Marital and family disputes (in thousands) processed by people's mediators and those by judges in China, 1985–2018

SOURCES: *China Law Yearbook* (1987–2018); *China Statistical Yearbook* (2014–2019); *Statistical Communiqué of the People's Courts* (2018).

NOTES:

1. From the mid-1980s onward, people's mediators and judges have used similar categories to classify and document family-related disputes (e.g., divorce, inheritance, child support, eldercare, and others). The discrepancies in this figure thus should not be deemed a mere function of differential record-keeping.
2. This figure includes marital and family disputes that entered the courts of first instance but not the courts of appeal.

each year. This disparity gradually shrunk during the 1990s but did not disappear until 2007. A similar disparity can be found regarding marital and family disputes (see figure 3.2).

Behind these two figures was an emerging reality in socialist China. In 1980, Deng Xiaoping, openly and emphatically, renounced Maoist mass campaigns, asserting that history had proved "launching mass movements frantically...to reform the existing system or to institute a new one has almost never succeeded."[35] The PRC was finally ready to relinquish certain revolutionary practices. At last, violently shaking up millions of women's and men's family lives to create awakened citizenry became a thing of the past. When the Marriage Law was amended in 1980, three decades after its debut, carrying the country from a feudal past into a socialist future was no longer on the lips of legislators. That mission had been accomplished, according to the state. Now the new mission was to pursue the Four Modernizations (四个现代化) by strengthening industry, agriculture, national defense, and science and technology. The ultimate goal was to build a Socialist Material Civilization (社会主义物质文明) in tandem with a Socialist Spiritual Civilization (社会主义精神文明), so the PRC could achieve balanced development by promoting economic growth on the one hand and by instilling within the citizenry a modern socialist morality on the other. These two civilizations, according to the CCP, would ensure that China realizes its developmental ends without losing its soul in the process.[36] To that end, while stressing citizens' rights to the freedom of marriage, legislators underlined their obligations to the state. For one, wives and husbands must comply with family planning policy, which mandated one child per couple. For another, they ought to uphold socialist mores—say, frugality, filial piety, and marital fidelity.[37] Stated otherwise, those disgruntled in marriage no longer had to fear public accusation meetings, show trials, lengthy jail sentences, or other forms of state brutality. Yet they were by no means free from the state's impinging on their daily lives.

People's Judicature (人民司法), a legal journal founded by the SPC in 1957, offers crucial details in this regard. A feature published in 1988 set out to recount a dramatic story. A factory worker with the family name Wu had gone home early, after a sudden blackout at his workplace in Jinan in Shandong Province. The moment Wu stepped into his apartment, he spotted his wife in bed with another man. Enraged, Wu grabbed a kitchen knife and chased the half-naked man, while his wife, still in bed, screamed for help. Two mediators turned up almost immediately. Granny Zhang, as neighbors called her, wasted no time inserting herself between the husband, hungry for blood, and the wife, too scared to utter a word. Staying up all night, Granny Zhang conducted an on-site investigation seeking to get to the bottom of the affair. Once she had calmed the husband down, she admonished the weeping wife for her moral failings. Afterward, Granny Zhang revisited the couple multiple times. Sensing the husband's suppressed rage, she told the young man, "You're thirty-one. The elderly in the family depend on you, and so do the young. The state needs your contributions as well. At your factory, for years, you've been ranked as a model worker. If you [in revenge] end up ruining your reputation, tearing your family apart, how could you answer to all these [individuals and the state]?" Wu, upon hearing this, was so touched that he decided to forgo violence. After monitoring this case for more than three weeks, Granny Zhang was convinced that the couple had reconciled and their marriage would last.[38]

What this highly stylized portrait of Granny Zhang, an exemplary mediator, omits to mention is the source of her authority. What made mediators like Granny Zhang so authoritative in dispute management? To answer that, we must zoom in on those who ran mediation on the ground and untangle their ties to the socialist state. The 1954 regulation, together with subsequent legislation, insisted on staffing people's mediation committees with representatives of the masses.[39] In reality, in urban settings, those in charge of mediation were party cadres at the workplace or party members (retired workers, housewives, and volunteers) embedded in their own neighborhoods; in the countryside, most of mediation work was administered by production team heads, party branch committee members, village security chairs, production brigade heads, and party-branch secretaries—all were state-approved personnel. Few folk disputes could escape the prying eyes of those individuals, for they formed a massive legion. The year 1981 alone saw over 5.75 million mediators installed in work, educational, residential, and governmental organizations nationwide.[40]

More to the point, buttressed by two hitherto well-entrenched institutions of socialism—Leninist party organizations and command economy—mediators operated as the spearhead of the state, extending the PRC's penetration into society, into citizens' domestic lives.[41] Their embeddedness in the workplace, schools, and communities made possible routinized surveillance, monitoring, and interference in mundane disputes over love affairs, divorce, eldercare, child support, and debts. Their presence on the CCP party organizations—along with access to personnel records used to allocate material resources (salaries, housing, and pensions), symbolic rewards (official statuses and honors), and career opportunities among citizens—gave mediators tremendous leverage to induce compliance and obedience in dispute resolution. Moreover, the entrenchment of a command economy meant that, absent a market providing alternatives, ordinary people depended on the state and its local agents for necessities like education, employment, housing, medical care, and retirement pensions. To put it another way, what undergirded people's mediation was the socialist state's organized monopoly over economic and political power. Thanks to this monopoly, mediators were at liberty to deploy an eclectic array of techniques and tactics (see table 3.1 for a summary). They could regularly impose surveillance, monitoring, wanted or unwanted intervention in folk disputes, by brandishing a stick and threatening to strip disputants of vital resources and opportunities, or by dangling a carrot and promising to reward those willing to exhibit deference and subordination in disputation. In practice, mediators invoked state laws and policies, and frequently cited cultural norms such as human relations (人情) and moral right and wrong (道理) in persuasion. In working to keep the aggrieved in line, people's mediation sought to channel human resources into the construction of a socialist civilization.[42]

**

What happened when the socialist state could no longer maintain its monopoly over the allocation of goods, services, and life chances among citizens? Could people's mediation maintain its power or efficacy? The answer seems to be no. As market reform deepened during the 1990s, ordinary women and men increasingly gained access to alternative sources of income, status, and employment opportunities. Their material dependence on the state declined, and so too did their susceptibility to the surveillance and control of Leninist party organizations. These economic and political changes, combined with cultural shifts and greater population mobility, destabilized the bedrock on which people's mediation was founded. Mediators, starting from the early 1990s, steadily lost ground to their counterparts on the bench, with a growing number of civil disputes entering the court system. A similar trend was spotted in regard to marital and family disputes (see figures 3.1 and 3.2). Accordingly, researchers at home and abroad speed to a conclusion: owing to the effects of the PRC's departure from command economy and other social cultural changes, the scope and authority of people's mediation progressively diminished toward the turn of the century.[43]

This conclusion, I fear, is oversimplistic at best and outright erroneous at worst. It overlooks a rather peculiar pattern in the PRC's history:

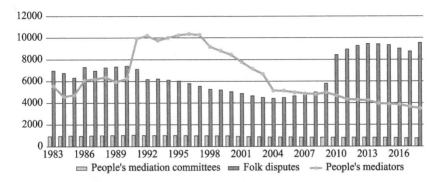

FIGURE 3.3 Number of people's mediation committees, people's mediators, and folk disputes (all in thousands) in China, 1983–2018

SOURCES: *China Law Yearbook* (1987–2016); *China Statistical Yearbook* (1984–1986, 1999, 2017–2019).

following a dramatic surge in the recruitment of people's mediators in 1991, for the next decade or so, China maintained a greater number of mediators than the volume of folk disputes they processed (see figure 3.3). The huge discrepancies between these two measures, it must be noted, cannot be fully explained by ups and downs in the establishment of mediation committees. The number of existing committees has remained relatively stable in the reform era. So, what could account for this sudden and unusual surge in 1991? Did mediators in the subsequent years just sit around, getting so little done that, on average, each handled fewer than one dispute in twelve months? Or did many of those mediators exist only on paper, being part of the PRC's "long and sometimes egregious history of official book cooking," as one researcher put it bluntly?[44] Alternatively, could this surge register a real and significant shift in the state's reaction to folk disputes, as well as a shift in its attempts to permeate society? To answer these questions, we must revisit the end of the 1980s and the beginning of the 1990s, with a sharp focus on 1989.

Meeting with the U.S. president George H. W. Bush on February 26, 1989, Deng Xiaopeng enunciated a new challenge in front of party leadership. China's "overwhelming need is to maintain stability. Without it, everything would be gone, and accomplishments would be ruined," Deng insisted.[45] This unequivocal emphasis on stability reflected party leadership's acute awareness of rising social unrest at home, following the country's transition to a market economy. It also bespoke party elites' wariness over the fate of communism, not least in the Soviet Union and in Central and Eastern Europe. Barely four months went by. Student-led demonstrations—often known as the 1989 Pro-Democracy Student Movement—erupted in Beijing and other parts of the country. Hundreds of thousands of protestors took to the streets to demand fundamental changes in the PRC's ruling. Their call for democracy, free speech, and a free press was promptly met with a bloody crackdown by the government, a moment many have remembered as the Tiananmen Square massacre. To this day, due to official suppression of information, it remains unclear exactly how many protestors were slain, maimed, arrested, jailed, or subsequently pushed into exile.[46] From the viewpoint of the state, the 1989 Student Movement signaled a major crisis in ruling. Scholars, looking back, view that year as a crucial turning point in the PRC's governance. Not long after the crackdown, the PRC began drastically expanding domestic security measures. It did so by amplifying funding and personnel intended to maintain political stability, by incentivizing local authorities to contain social unrest, and by increasing the bureaucratic rank of public security chiefs within the party hierarchy. These developments, in turn, gave rise to a consolidated, sprawling state apparatus, operating with one overarching imperative: stability maintenance (维稳).[47]

In light of the 1989 Tiananmen Square protests, the peculiar pattern we see in figure 3.3 should be examined meticulously against the backdrop of the PRC's reaction to a (perceived or real) crisis in governing. More fundamentally, it should be analyzed as part of the regime's prolonged record of cultivating a repertoire of statecraft to tame society, a process littered with party leadership's elaborate efforts to reclaim and repackage the CCP's revolutionary legacies, to instill new elements into preexisting experience, and, more recently, to wed skills inherited from the Maoist era with those borrowed from liberal democracies. (The so-called socialist rule of law with Chinese characteristics is one striking case in point, bespeaking the PRC's attempts at imbricating differing cultural elements in ruling.) This superb ability to merge the old and the new, inherited and borrowed statecraft, according to political scientist Mary Gallagher, makes the PRC a "genius" in its adaptation to a constantly changing world.[48] For that reason, the post-1989 developments in people's mediation should be viewed as a mix of something old, something new, something borrowed, and something uncertain—to tweak a popular phrase.

Against this backdrop, marital and family disputes would gradually lose their political urgency in the eyes of state actors. Leaving those miserable in marriage to their own devices, to purchase legal services on a market, to mobilize state law piecemeal, and to navigate the court system for individualized recourse would morph into a new, dominant mode of intervention wherein the PRC continuously exerts its influences over citizens' domestic lives. To grasp how these changes came to impinge on Donglin and other women's experiences in disputation, several developments in people's mediation must be flagged.

The first development came days after the Tiananmen Square massacre. On June 17, 1989 , the State Council amended the 1954 regulation on people's mediation. Included in this amendment was a seemingly innocuous clause, demanding that mediators brief Villagers' Committees and Residents' Committees on folk disputes.[49] Informing local authorities of popular grievances among citizens, for the first time, became mediators' regulatory obligations. Within two years, mediators saw their numbers countrywide balloon from six to ten million and stay at that level for years (see figure 3.3). This dramatic expansion was not reflected in the year-by-year volume of folk disputes handled by mediators, in part because manpower had been shifted from dispute settlement to other operations, largely under the radar, away from public scrutiny.

A notice issued by the MOJ, in spring 1991, offers a rare glimpse into the murky operations mediators found themselves undertaking in the aftermath of 1989. Citing Deng Xiaoping's warning to government officials, "Stability shall override all other issues" (稳定压倒一切), the notice stressed the urgency of building a system to "preempt the escalation of folk disputes" (防止民间纠纷激化). To that end, *paicha* (排查), which can be translated as screening and troubleshooting, must be conducted regularly to assess several basic facts: households and individuals susceptible to disputes and conflicts; disputes most likely to explode; and the presence of certain individuals in neighborhoods (juvenile delinquents, ex-convicts, and those recently released from reeducation through forced labor).[50] In taking one step forward, this notice spelled out what kind of information mediators should amass, a development the SPC and the MOJ later characterized as endeavors toward building "a network of intelligence and information on disputes and conflicts" (矛盾纠纷情报信息网络).[51]

By the mid-1990s, the term *folk disputes* had taken on a new connotation. Previously, it had chiefly referred to disputes among citizens. In the wake of 1989, folk disputes as a cultural category had been gradually expanded to include prevailing conflicts between citizens and government agencies. Meanwhile, language like "screening and troubleshooting" and "forestalling the escalation of folk disputes" started infusing official discourse on people's mediation. But what precisely these phrases entailed in practice was less obvious. A series of reports that appeared in the *People's Mediation*, a magazine founded by the MOJ, provide a window onto one episode of local experimentation. In spring 1994, screening and troubleshooting were carried out simultaneously in seventy-three counties, districts, and municipalities in Hubei Province, one report asserted. Within three months, party organs, governments, Offices of Comprehensive Management of Public Security, and Political Legal Committees at multiple levels, along with six checkup work teams dispatched by the Department of Justice in Hubei, coordinated a campaign to tackle prevailing folk disputes. In mobilizing over a million mediators throughout the province, campaign organizers "succeeded in screening 89,720 folk disputes, mediating 83,022, preventing 974 cases of citizen petitioning, preempting 1,703 cases from further escalation, and assisting the police in arresting 578 crime suspects."[52]

In many aspects, these descriptions harkened back to the Maoist-style mass campaigns in the 1950s, albeit in a scaled-down version, a diluted variant political scientist Elizabeth J. Perry terms *managed campaigns*. Mao's invisible hand, Perry contends, is never quite far away from the PRC's governing toolbox.[53] In actuality, a full-blown Maoist political movement did not resurrect in the latter half of the 1990s. The foregoing characterization, which cast *paicha* as a set of concerted, top-down, large-scale campaign efforts, became a rarity in official discourse toward the turn of the century. Deng Xiaoping and other party leaders' abhorrence of certain Maoist legacies, it seems, had kept mass campaigns at arm's length. More to the point, the structural underpinnings that made feasible a certain ruling experience in the Maoist era were no longer in place. With millions of rural residents on the move to join the country's rapidly expanding private sector in metropolises, village cadres saw their grip on community members who used to be tied to farmland weakening. Near-total control over resources and life chances became remote memories for many on the state's payroll.[54] In urban areas, the socialist workplace, which was once known as *danwei* (单位), has likewise changed. As the PRC phased out central planning to embrace a market economy, employers incrementally lost their monopoly over the supply of education, housing, childcare, medical care, and other necessities. They could no longer subject employees to economic dependence or political surveillance.[55] When the twenty-first century finally arrived, people's mediators everywhere faced a dilemma. The economic and political conditions that had previously enabled their work had shifted. Yet, following the 1989 Tiananmen Square protests, party leadership's anxieties over instability had deepened, begetting repeated attempts to remodel people's mediation, to rework its grip on the populace. Women and men mired in their domestic strife and thus in search of state intervention would soon find themselves in a novel reality.

The judicialization of domestic disputes in the new century

Clear-eyed about the dilemma people's mediators faced, the MOJ and the SPC spearheaded a dual-track development during the first decade of the new century. On its face, people's mediation was swiftly remolded into a quasi-judicial institution, following the issuance of four official documents between 2002 and 2004.[56] In enacting these documents, the MOJ and the SPC sought to regularize (规范化), systematize (制度化), and procedural-ize (程序化), a timeworn practice inherited from the Maoist era by turning it into a more lawlike methodology for conflict resolution. In 2010, when the People's Mediation Law was passed, legislators formally affirmed mediators' power to produce legally binding outcomes. This legislative move sanctioned a stance the SPC and the MOJ had taken up earlier, one that equated mediation agreements with valid contracts between disputing parties. As a result of the 2010 legislation, disputants are entitled to approach the courts, demanding judicial confirmation and/or enforcement of their mediation agreements.[57] Today, case files (卷宗) validated by people's mediators bear more than a fleeting resemblance to those signed by judges. These two sets of papers have similar appearance and structure and, more crucially, comparable legal validity in the eyes of the state.[58]

While legislators rendered people's mediation more lawlike, instilling greater formality, regularity, and predictability into this age-old practice, the MOJ went on to pursue another line of development, infusing this practice with more agility, flexibility, and discretionary power. The MOJ did so by further integrating people's mediation into the sprawling state apparatus intended to maintain political stability. And this integration was done not exactly in broad daylight nor by putting state law on the books but rather cloaked in obscurity and outside of the remit of national legislation. When the People's Mediation Law was introduced to the public in 2010 , it made no mention of *paicha*. Legislators dodged the question of how screening and troubleshooting should be conducted as a means of intelligence gathering or as a set of techniques to intercept rising social unrest. Their silence on these matters was no coincidence. Concerted efforts, since the mid-2000s, started surfacing in the officialdom to mask the roles mediators had assumed in stability maintenance. A telling example comes from *China Law Yearbook* (中国法律年鉴).

Under the auspices of the China Law Society (中国法学会)—a mass organization headed by party elites (the current president, Wang Chen, sits on the CCP's Standing Committee of the Central Political Bureau)—*China Law Yearbook* used to publicize both the official categorization of folk disputes and the number of mediated cases within each category. Between 1985 and 2005, a total of ten categories were used to classify grievances that came to the attention of people's mediators: (1) marriage; (2) inheritance; (3) childcare and eldercare; (4) other family disputes; (5) housing and homestead; (6) debts; (7) production and management; (8) neighborly disputes; (9) torts; and (10) others. By checking the tabulation of these categories and the corresponding volume of cases, researchers could attempt an educated guess as to the scope of people's mediation. That option was gone after 2006. Since then, the yearbook has limited data release to five categories only: (1) marital and family disputes; (2) neighborly disputes; (3) housing and homestead; (4) torts; and (5) others. One naturally wonders what happened to the other categories, and what grievances have been removed from the yearbook, and therefore from public awareness, and why? These questions become even more intriguing considering the effects of the 2010 legislation. The passage of the People's Mediation Law, as figure 3.1 shows, has led to instant revitalization of an aged practice, with significantly more cases entering its ambit than in previous decades.

Months after the promulgation of the People's Mediation Law, the MOJ quietly handed a series of tally sheets to millions of mediators across the country. These internal documents offer a rare peek into mediators' responsibilities in stability maintenance. Table 3.2 is a replica of one such tally sheet, which reveals some of the officially designated tasks and functions.[59] Merely reacting to extant folk disputes no longer suffices. Mediators nowadays are expected to enact a much more proactive and expansive approach. Conducting *paicha*, averting disputes in general, and preempting armed fights, organized petitioning, and suicide caused by disputes—these activities must dominate mediators' daily routines, according to the MOJ. As to the question of how *paicha* should be implemented, the SPC and the MOJ—in contrast to legislators who have remained silent on the issue—did not shy away from specificity. Mediators should "further build and improve a network of intelligence and information on disputes and conflicts, upgrade the system for information gathering, reporting, and analysis, and enhance feedback mechanisms." Mediators, furthermore, should "conduct regular *paicha* in villages, residential areas, factories, mines, and other work organizations; conduct frequent, specialized *paicha* for certain professions and industries that involve know-how and technical expertise; and, during important social events, holidays, and sensitive time periods, gather resources and personnel to conduct targeted *paicha*." Together, these activities are meant to "nip disputes and conflicts in the bud," the SPC and the MOJ insisted.[60]

By the time I started investigating people's mediation in Weifeng in late 2010, *paicha*—as a state-sanctioned practice to gather intelligence on citizens and avert disputes in principle—had spawned a litany of grassroots

TABLE 3.2 A tally sheet concerning people's mediation, issued by the MOJ in December 2010

Screening, troubleshooting, and prevention	Prevent organized, armed fights		X	44
			Y	43
	Prevent organized citizen petitioning		X	42
			Y	41
	Prevent folk disputes from turning into criminal cases		X	40
			Y	39
	Prevent folk disputes from turning into suicide		Y	38
	Prevent disputes in general		Y	37
	Screening and troubleshooting		Y	36
Enforcement	Court rulings in favor of mediation agreements		Y	35
	Mediation agreements challenged by lawsuits		Y	34
	Mediation agreements confirmed through court rulings		Y	33
	Medication agreements enforced successfully		Y	32
Mediation circumstances	Format	Written agreements	Y	31
		Oral agreements	Y	30
	Dispute type	Other disputes	Y	29
		Medical disputes	Y	28
		Real estate disputes	Y	27
		Traffic accidents	Y	26
		Environmental protections	Y	25
		Family planning	Y	24
		Land-taking and demolition	Y	23
		Disputes over mountainous or forested land	Y	22
		Disputes over management of village affairs	Y	21
		Labor disputes	Y	20
		Torts and damages	Y	19
		Production and managerial disputes	Y	18
		Contractual disputes	Y	17
		Disputes over housing and homestead	Y	16
		Disputes among neighbors	Y	15
		Marital and family disputes	Y	14
	Source of cases	Conduct mediation upon referral	Y	13
		Conduct mediation upon request	Y	12
		Take an initiative to mediate	Y	11
	Entities responsible	Mediation committees within social organizations	Y	10
		Mediation committees within work organizations	Y	9
		Mediation subcommittees within Residents' Committees	Y	8
		Mediation subcommittees within Villagers' Committees	Y	7
		Total amount of money involved	Z	6
		Difficult and complicated cases	Y	5
		Successfully mediated cases	Y	4
		Number of individuals involved	Y	3
		Total number of cases processed	Y	2
Items			unit	1

SOURCE: the MOJ.

NOTE: This sheet uses three units to compile statistics; the sign of X denotes the number of individuals involved, Y the number of cases or incidents, and Z the amount of money concerned.

experiments and operations. Many of them were meant to tap into the existing organizational infrastructure of people's mediation for the purpose of stability maintenance. To this day, these local practices remain unfettered by the People's Mediation Law. How *paicha* should be enacted as methods of intelligence gathering in a domestic context, how it can be applied to preempt popular contention, and, in this milieu, what rights citizens have and what obligations government officials must shoulder— these issues have remained at the discretion of local state authorities.

In brief, the dual-track development championed by the MOJ and the SPC—and tolerated by legislators—has accomplished something that has long intrigued political scientists, sociologists, and China scholars. How has an authoritarian state like the PRC endured tumultuous changes at home and abroad, while one communist regime after another has faltered around the world and some have disintegrated? One plausible explanation, Mary Gallagher contends, lies in the PRC's capacity to build formal institutions, thus infusing structure, regularity, and norms with its governance, on the one hand, and freeing itself from the strictures of liberal democracy, due process, and accountability to the populace, thereby maintaining agility, flexibility, and discretionary power in ruling, on the other.[61] The post-1989 developments in people's mediation, I argue, testify powerfully to that capability. From the evolution of this once-Maoist practice, I fail to conceive a regime torn between its fixation on political stability and longing for law-based governance. What I discern instead is a regime remarkably dexterous and ingenious at wedding statecraft of varying stripes.

The PRC's remodeling of people's mediation, needless to say, comes with far-reaching implications. As stability maintenance stands high on the agenda of people's mediation in the new millennium, more popular contention has come under its scrutiny. The official classification of folk disputes has expanded from ten to fifteen categories (see table 3.2 for a list of categories the MOJ put in place in 2010). While the scope of people's mediation continues to expand, its attention to citizens' intimate lives has nonetheless shrunk. Indeed, among the forty-four data points listed in table 3.2—that is, forty-four basic facts mediators must check on a

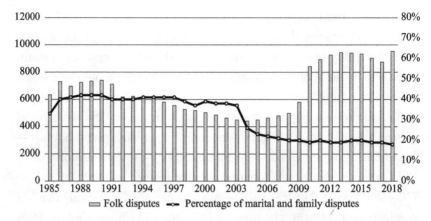

FIGURE 3.4 Folk disputes (in thousands) handled by people's mediators and the percentage of marital and family disputes in China, 1985–2018

SOURCES: *China Law Yearbook* (1987–2016); *China Statistical Yearbook* (2014–2019).

regular basis—marital and family disputes comprise one category and only one point in the tally sheet.

Figure 3.4 presents another piece of evidence in this vein. Between the mid-1980s and 2003, marital and family disputes consistently made up approximately 40 percent of the cases handled by people's mediators. That percentage suffered a dramatic dip in 2004 and has continued to dwindle. By the end of 2018, only 18 percent of mediated cases concerned disputes over marriage or family lives. Even the promulgation of the first national law on people's mediation, in 2010, could not salvage that downward trend.[62]

A question naturally arises. What happened to those marital and family disputes that had dropped out of the ambit of people's mediation? There is no indication that since 2003, Chinese families have had fewer disputes and conflicts than the previous decades. Extant evidence points to the opposite: divorce rates in the new millennium have steadily climbed up among Chinese couples, denoting potentially more, not less, friction in domestic life (chapter 2 provides details on the rise of divorce in Chinese society, see figure 2.1). In view of figures 2.1 and 3.4, one must ask: If a considerable portion of marital and family disputes was no longer attended by people's mediators, where could those disputes go?

A great many marital and family disputes, as the next chapter demonstrates, have entered a burgeoning legal services industry and have been handled by law practitioners in private practice. In other words, the PRC has effectively outsourced part of dispute management to market forces, a theme at the heart of chapter 4. And hundreds of thousands of domestic disputes, including Donglin's case, have landed in courtrooms, a phenomenon chapters 5, 6, and 7 examine by zooming in on divorce law practices inside the People's Courts. Here, a quick comparison serves to drive the message home. In 1985, for every marital or family dispute a judge disposed of, people's mediators went on to tackle four similar cases—a ratio of 1:4. That ratio rose to 1:1 by the end of 2003. Over the next fifteen years, judges nationwide saw their caseload rise from 1.1 million to 1.8 million per year, a 56 percent increase. People's mediators, by contrast, experienced only a 5 percent increase in their handling of domestic disputes in the same period. The sharp contrast between these two measures bespeaks a new reality in the twenty-first century, which I term the *judicialization of domestic disputes*.

This tendency to channel marital and family disputes into the court system seems to echo the PRC's commitment toward legality. Following the CCP's Third Plenary Session of the Eleventh Central Committee in 1978, the PRC set in motion a mission to build a socialist legal system (社会主义法制). Decades of legal reforms have elevated the stature of law in governance. Evidence abounds in regard to the newly gained significance of law in the state's efforts to regulate social and economic life. As for citizens' domestic lives, the PRC has gone quite far to redefine matrimony. When the Marriage Law was amended in 2001, legislators enunciated the nature of matrimony. In a country that used to treat family formation as a key instrument for regime consolidation—a country that took citizens' intimate relationships as a crucial site for political surveillance and social control—the institution of marriage has taken on a new meaning. Today, it embodies a "voluntary contractual relationship grounded in individual emotional satisfaction," a pivotal shift sociologist Deborah S. Davis describes as the "privatization of marriage."[63]

This shift, together with the judicialization of domestic disputes, reaffirms the PRC's reform-era conviction that it must institute a legal system to better governance and safeguard individual freedoms and rights. Driven by this stated commitment, the State Council ushered in an important regulatory change, following the revision of Regulations on Marriage Registration in 2003. This change eliminated the power of village cadres and employers to block divorce (many of whom, like Fan Yongpin, had long overseen people's mediation).[64] Consequently, those aggrieved in marriage could bypass people's mediation by registering their divorce agreements at local governments. Seeking divorce free from state authorities' interference at last became a real, individual choice in China. This new freedom explains that sudden dip in 2004 in figure 3.4. From that point on, people's mediation could no longer stand in the way of women and men actively pursuing divorce.

LEGALITY AND POLITICAL
STABILITY IN A NEW LIGHT

The judicialization of domestic disputes, in its own right, may strike some as a triumphant story of rising individual freedoms in a historically authoritarian context. Some may celebrate the PRC's eventual breakaway from Maoist legacies and its embracing more liberal models of governance. Some may even contend that China, in the new century, has further shifted toward legality. I would have to disagree with that characterization—just as I would oppose the view that treats the recent revival of people's mediation as a sign of the PRC's relapse into the Maoist past and therefore a turn against law.[65]

The PRC's relation to the law, to its Maoist and socialist past, I believe, is more complicated than the recent scholarly works have shown. As mentioned in chapter 1, China scholars have continued to debate whether the reform-era PRC is on a trajectory against or toward legality. Xi Jinping's ascent to the top of party leadership in 2012 has further fueled this debate. Informative and thought-provoking, the debate nevertheless has its limits. This chapter has attempted to move it beyond those bounds in two ways. It maps history differently and furthermore casts legality and political stability in a novel conceptual light in hopes of formulating a more nuanced reading of the interplay of law and politics in an authoritarian state.

Many in the debate, implicitly or explicitly, subscribe to a particular view of the PRC's past and present. One account of the recent legal reforms presents history as essentially a singular, unidirectional progression. The debate, it then follows, centers on the question of whether China is turning toward or away from law.[66] In another account, history acts like a pendulum. Accordingly, the analysis seeks to ascertain how the PRC has swung back and forth between two modalities, one embracing law-based governance and the other stability-oriented ruling.[67] This chapter presents a third account, depicting history as a patchwork of distinct processes; in that sense, it is more like a river, with currents, crosscurrents, and undercurrents. To illustrate this perspective, I show that the Chinese state's gradual retreat from marriage and family life, together with the recent trend to judicialize domestic disputes—one set of historical processes cementing the stature of law in governance—took place in conjunction with the regime's post-1989 enhanced efforts to contain society, to revive age-old institutions to maintain political stability—another set of processes eroding (or at least evading) legality. The concomitance of seemingly contradictory trends is possible because history is rarely singular and because the Chinese state is anything but monolithic.

More crucially, disparate trends can unfold simultaneously, because decades of cultivating a governing tool kit have enabled state actors to mobilize cultural resources in varying configurations to solve different kinds of problems. My use of the term *governing tool kit*, as indicated before, has been informed and inspired by Ann Swidler's theory of culture in action. Unlike many in political science and in sociology who view culture as playing little more than a derivative role in state-making, I draw on Swidler's theory to spotlight the centrality of a regime's tool kit.[68] This tool kit, at its core, is a cultural repertoire, consisting of political ideologies, official discourses, norms, values, and certainly inherited or borrowed ruling methodologies, policy instruments, institutional practices, and arrangements. The mobilization of this tool kit, as Swidler points out, is often piecemeal, unconfined by logical coherence, and geared toward specific scenarios and situations.[69] Also on my mind is Sally Engle Merry's argument that political elites can adopt cultural products, including legal ideals, practices, and institutional arrangements, from one social group (or context) and replay them vis-à-vis a different group (or in another setting). In this manner, those elites engage in what Merry terms *cultural appropriation*, thereby interlacing diverse and sometimes competing and even conflicting cultural influences in ruling.[70]

Taking these theoretical insights to heart, this chapter illustrates how the PRC, an authoritarian regime, has managed to appropriate cultural resources (or what I call *statecraft* at times) from its own past and from liberal democracies. Along this line, I have underscored alacrity, selectivity, and ingenuity behind the PRC's cultural appropriation. More specifically, this chapter details the great lengths to which reform-era decision-makers have gone to upgrade their toolbox for dispute management. They have done so through tireless trial and error, through swiftly responding to crises at critical junctures, and through selectively remodeling the problem-solving skills, strategies, and techniques used by their predecessors. Seen in this light, people's mediation in the twenty-first century is hardly a simple replication of some Maoist prototype. Nor is it a faithful reenactment of certain socialist governing experience. The MOJ and the SPC, in fact, have refashioned this institution by making part of it more lawlike and keeping another part no more susceptible to legal rules and norms than before.

To state the obvious: top decision-makers in the reform era do not simply repeat or recycle history; rather, they reclaim, repackage, and even reinvent prior ruling experience by unlearning certain governing methodologies, by reassembling preexisting institutional practices and arrangements, and by instilling new elements into age-old techniques and tactics for governance. This explains why I would refrain from treating the recent revival of people's mediation as proof of China's relapse into the Maoist past, thus a turn against law. Similarly, while adopting governing experience from liberal democracies—the notion of rule of law as a key example—the PRC has been remarkably conscientious in marking the parameters around such appropriation. In the past two decades, legislators have endowed citizens with greater individual freedoms and legal protections within the realm of intimate relationships.[71] The same, however, cannot be said of citizens' relations to the swelling state apparatus geared toward stability maintenance. Therefore, I hesitate to celebrate the state's retreat from marriage and family life as unbridled progress.

In turning scholarly attention to the so-called governing tool kit, in underlining the PRC's ingenuity and selectivity in cultural appropriation, this chapter casts law and political stability in a new conceptual light. In my analysis, they are not necessarily distinct political ideals, occupying opposite ends of an ideological spectrum. Rather, I view legality and stability maintenance as two sets of statecraft, as differing ruling methodologies, both of which have emerged as part and parcel of the PRC's tool kit. Inside this tool kit, legal components, such as juridical tools, mechanisms, and institutional practices, can exist side by side with nonlegal, extralegal, or even illegal elements. Moreover, state actors' mobilization of one part of the tool kit in one scenario can be more or less insulated from their uses of another part in different scenarios. This multiplicity in a regime's application of a cultural repertoire calls into question certain assessments of the dynamics between law-based governance and stability-oriented ruling. For example, some in China studies have insisted, "any growth in the sociopolitical prestige of legal institutions tends to strengthen their instrumental functionality, while simultaneously weakening the functionality of extralegal forms of administration and dispute resolution."[72] This line of argument, again, betrays a kind of binary thinking pervasive in scholarly accounts of China's legal reforms. Parsimonious as it sounds, this argument scarcely does justice to the PRC's ambidexterity in strengthening legal institutions on the one side, and nonlegal or extralegal ones on the other.

As far as dispute management is concerned, the PRC has not privileged legal over extralegal forms of administration or vice versa in the past two decades. On the contrary, top decision-makers have fortified judicial, quasi-judicial, and extrajudicial tools—by and large at once—in attempts to deploy them to tackle different kinds of social problems. Since 2002, a new classification started permeating official discourse on folk disputes. People's mediators, according to the MOJ and the SPC, should sort popular grievances into two categories: mundane, frequent disputes (常见性、多发性纠纷) and difficult, hot-button disputes (热点、难点纠纷).[73] Marital and family disputes, along with torts, typified the former, whereas widespread discontent with land-taking and demolition, labor relations, and medical malpractice epitomized the latter. In the next decade or so, marital and family disputes and torts had undergone considerable degrees of judicialization, with bigger portions of cases falling into the remit of the judiciary than of people's mediation.[74]

This trend to insert mundane, frequent disputes into judicial space, I must emphasize, has unfolded in tandem with a rather different tendency with regard to difficult, hot-button disputes. Take land disputes as an example of the latter. Recognizing the complexity of land-related grievances and popular demands, the General Office of the CCP Central Committee, the General Office of the State Council, the National People's Congress, the MOJ, and the SPC have issued at least six dozen laws, regulations, and policy directives in the past two decades, many seeking to articulate a multipronged system for conflict resolution.[75] A 2005 SPC document, for instance, enabled the courts to dispose of run-of-the-mill suits over rural land and, meanwhile, turn away some of the most inflammatory issues—judges at lower courts were told to throw out cases disputing compensations for land-taking and demolition, a highly intractable and yet widespread problem in rural China.[76] While circumscribing the judiciary's involvement in land disputes, the PRC proceeded to consolidate quasi-judicial institutions. In 2009, legislators put in place the Law on the Mediation and Arbitration of Rural Land Contract Disputes (农村土地承包经营纠纷调解仲裁法). Catching two pigeons with one bean, this law formally instituted a new mechanism after years of local experimentation: arbitration. In the meantime, it sought to fortify people's mediation, reaffirming its significance as a critical device in state actors' toolbox.

Rather than hanging on one methodology, one mechanism, judicial or extrajudicial, the PRC in recent years has come to a realization that among folk disputes, some are much more complex and potentially subversive than others, and thus must be sorted out and funneled into different state institutions. The practical logic behind this sorting and funneling, at the moment, seems to be this: the more fluid, unpredictable, and menacing popular disputes appear, the more likely they would be tackled by state institutions injected with agility, flexibility, and discretionary power, such as the various government offices in charge of stability maintenance. And the less "troublesome" or "inflammatory" grievances and demands seem, the more likely they would come under the purview of institutions infused with formality, regularity, and predictability, including courts and arbitration commissions. Future research needs to subject this practical logic to systematic, rigorous empirical testing.

All that said, one thing is for sure. The PRC has set in motion processes to build and strengthen a multipronged system of conflict resolution, which somewhat resembles triage. In sorting, shuffling, and reshuffling different kinds of problems among judicial, quasi-judicial, and extrajudicial institutions, the PRC has juxtaposed its legal tools with nonlegal or extralegal devices. In this world, the expansion of legal institutions does not necessarily weaken those nonlegal or extralegal bureaucracies, or vice versa. Legality and extralegality, as two sets of governing methodologies, do not have to be locked in contradictions or conflicts, vying for dominance. However, their coexistence—or, more accurately speaking, the PRC's attempts to imbricate different cultural resources in the texture of its governance—are not unbounded or unproblematic, a theoretical argument I will further develop in chapter 4.

CONCLUSION

Under Xi Jinping's watch, weaving legality into the fabric of governance by layering it with nonlegal and extralegal ruling methodologies has gained further traction. In fact, it has crystalized in an official expression, "diversifying conflict resolution" (多元化纠纷解决). This expression, with its first appearance in the *People's Daily* in the early 2000s, has made deep inroads in official discourse in the following decade. In 2005, Xiamen, a port city on China's southeast coast, became the first municipality to pass local regulations to integrate organizational structures and personnel responsible for reconciliation, mediation, arbitration, litigation, and other official measures for dispute management. In doing so, Xiamen emerged as a front-runner in enacting an official slogan, "Multiplying governmental entities, methods, mechanisms, and levels intended to resolve popular disputes and conflicts" (矛盾纠纷解决主体多元化、方式多元化、环节多元化、层级多元化). In 2014, the CCP's Fourth Plenary Session of the Eighteenth Central Committee formally incorporated the phrase "diversifying conflict resolution" into a key party document. Urging party cadres to simultaneously strengthen "mediation, arbitration, administrative adjudication (行

政裁决), administrative reconsideration (行政复议), and litigation," this document enunciated the importance of "guiding and supporting ordinary people to express their grievances and claims, rationally."[77]

From the early months of 1949—when the CCP deemed mediation a panacea for folk disputes—to 2014, it took the PRC six decades or so to recognize the necessity of tackling popular discontent at multiple fronts by deploying diverse methodologies, techniques, and tactics. The upshot for the aggrieved? Many nowadays must confront byzantine complexity in the state's efforts to employ judicial, quasi-judicial, and extrajudicial institutions to contain different kinds of problems. Figuring out which institution to approach, what institutional logic to follow, and how to align one's own needs and wants with official imperatives in disputation can all be challenging for ordinary people, especially those with limited resources, social connections, or political savvy.

As for the disgruntled in domestic life, the PRC's retreat from marriage and family has profound implications. In the early Maoist era, the state hunted down husbands and wives carrying feudal beliefs and practices. In the socialist era, the state regularly policed the intimate lives of ordinary men and women. Today, wives and husbands, embroiled in conjugal strife, must go to the state themselves—to access official justice. Unlike their predecessors, few can fall back on a political discourse valorizing women's emancipation or socialist citizenship. To name their conjugal grievances, to blame responsible parties, and to stake out claims, women and men in the twenty-first century must navigate a new ideological and discursive terrain. Within that terrain, they are independent rights-holders charged with free will, as far as the state is concerned. Accordingly, it is their individual responsibility—not the government's duty—to locate the right recourse and shoulder expenses associated with legal mobilization and conflict resolution, a theme chapter 4 explores, as it shifts to examine divorcing women's interactions with a market-based legal profession.

CHAPTER 4

The Rise and Fall of Legal Workers

BUSINESS IS BUSINESS

"Without money, who is gonna help you?"

The visitor was weeping, wetting tissue after tissue. Dressed all in black—black leather boots, black stockings, and a black miniskirt—the thirtysomething was obviously into fashion. Yet her purse was frayed, a strap about to fall off at any moment. Her hair was tangled and greasy, and her eyes swollen. A red, wrinkled nose dotted a face that had once been youthful and perhaps radiant. Not anymore. From the moment she had stepped into the Xiqing Legal Workers' Office, she could not hold back tears. Her husband had beaten her again. It was the second time that month that she had knocked on the door to ask for help.

Li Yinxue, a legal worker who had handled divorce suits for years, listened, interjecting intermittently. "Last time you were here, what did I say for a service fee?" That was the first question Li Yinxue asked.

"A hundred yuan. You said a hundred."

"So, you just want me to draft a civil complaint for you?"

"Not exactly." The visitor went on to explain herself. She needed legal representation for her divorce suit.

"Legal representation? Well, that would cost a lot more than a hundred yuan."

"But someone [in the office] told me over the phone that I would pay just a hundred up front?"

Li Yinxue did not dispute that number. Reaching into her purse, she riffled through a stack of invoices. Pulling out a folded piece of paper and flattening it with two thumbs, Li Yinxue turned her discovery over to the visitor. "Look. Here is an invoice, issued by a tribunal. I was there to file a lawsuit. These days, folks have to line up at a bank to pay the litigation fee [charged by the tribunal]. And the litigation fee alone is two hundred sixty yuan." Those intent on taking their spouses to court should prepare for certain significant expenses. That was the unstated but clearly meant message.

For a moment, the visitor forgot about sobbing, perhaps locked away in quiet agony over expenses not yet imaginable. Minutes later, she squeezed out a question: "Well, how much do I have to pay?"

That question, seemingly straightforward, torments many who are discontented in intimate relationships and thus yearn for an out. Sooner or later, they must ask themselves: *Could I afford a divorce, and particularly professional assistance, should legal action become necessary?* To look for answers, some will go all out to search for help. This chapter, by highlighting these individuals' experiences seeking help in the legal services industry, lays bare two theoretical objectives at the heart of the book.

First, it builds on an argument I present in chapter 3. The People's Republic of China (PRC), I have argued, ought to be parsed as a case of an authoritarian regime continually cultivating a cultural repertoire of statecraft. Legality in the form of lawmaking and law-applying has become an integral part of that repertoire, making the regime's governing methodologies more diverse than before. Moreover, the PRC's cultivation of statecraft is often purposive and strategic, but it is not unbounded. In some instances, state actors exhibit notable ingenuity in crafting novel solutions to emerging problems; on other occasions, they demonstrate remarkable efficacy in imbricating the old with the new, inherited ruling experience with borrowed. Ingenuity and efficacy of this kind, however, are far from constant. The PRC's attempts at cultivating and deploying legal techniques, tactics, and personnel, as if they were a set of open-ended devices, waiting to be assembled and reassembled to pursue all goals, do not always deliver. They do not invariably succeed because the Chinese state is often too segmented, too riven, to devise highly consistent or coherent schemes to instrumentalize legality. State fragmentation is thus the key to our understanding of ruling elites' limits in harnessing law and, more broadly speaking, limits in cultural appropriation. In analyzing such limits, I bring into focus the complex interplay of culture and the state—the first theoretical objective of the book.

To concretize these theoretical arguments, this chapter shows that in the reform era the PRC has diversified not only methodologies but also personnel responsible for dispute resolution. This diversification is achieved, partly through revitalizing an army of people's mediators (see chapter 3) and partly through strenuous efforts to transform lawyers and legal workers, two groups of law practitioners who used to be embedded in the state. Arising from this transformation, after decades of reforms, are market-based practitioners along two separate trajectories, one upward and the other downward. Put differently, the PRC, by creating a legal services industry, by incrementally unhooking that industry from the state, has sought to capitalize on the potential of market forces for the purpose of dispute management. And, in that process, it has favored one group (lawyers) over the other (legal workers). The rise and then the fall of legal workers—or, really, the PRC's bitter struggles to refashion this group for new purposes—is a potent testament to ruling elites' limits in mining the utility of law.

These limits, I must emphasize, have enormous repercussions for citizens, especially those hailing from the countryside and/or lacking economic wherewithal. The second goal of the chapter is thus to examine the ways state-driven marketization of legal services has impacted on the disgruntled. To capture such an impact is to unpack a type of professional influences I call *agenda-setting power*. Indeed, sociolegal scholars have long noted the power legal professionals exert as gatekeepers to official justice. Attorneys in the United States, for example, can facilitate ordinary people's access to courts, or block and even derail their attempts to mobilize state law. They can either validate or undercut disputants' interpretations of past events and life experiences. They can shore up clients' expectations for litigation outcomes. So can they dampen or alter such expectations.[1]

This chapter extends this scholarly inquiry by illustrating how law practitioners in rural China assert their professional authority in divorce litigation. They frequently do so by turning away the cash-strapped, oftentimes the most vulnerable in the family and in society. When law practitioners do attend to women's and men's marital grievances, the former tend to reshape the latter's perceptions of discontent and remake or unmake their rights claims. In converting some grievances into disputed issues and others into nonissues, these practitioners become instrumental in presetting decision-making agendas inside courtrooms. This is why I term their influences agenda-setting power. Unpacking the workings of this power in the early moments of legal mobilization, I believe, constitutes the initial step toward reconceiving the notion of disputation resolution—the second theoretical objective of the book.

To sum up, this chapter keeps zooming in and out and in again, to borrow the terminology of cinematography. It opens with a scene of a legal worker tactfully sending away a woman trapped in an abusive relationship, knowing that she could not afford legal services. Zooming out from that scene, the chapter descends in a flashback, recalling the PRC's decades-long development of a legal services industry. By marking the key moments in that development, I show how legal workers rose to prominence in the socialist era and then fell from favor in the new millennium. This historical narrative is followed by an analysis of state fragmentation and limits in cultural appropriation; the goal is to dissect the complex interplay of culture and the state. As the chapter ahead illustrates, culture does not always enable authoritarian rulers; rather, it can constrain and even incapacitate ruling elites' attempts at utilizing law. Toward the end, zooming in again, I provide a close-up view of the lasting consequences of state-driven marketization. In combination, these efforts illuminate the hope and the hopelessness ordinary people experience as they bear the brunt of an authoritarian regime's tussle with legality.

* * *

Back in the Xiqing Legal Workers' Office, Li Yinxue carried on her meeting with the visitor, still in tears. The only legal service provider in a town of approximately forty-eight thousand residents, her office kept its door open to the aggrieved from varying walks of life. But not all were welcome.

"Why don't you pay a thousand yuan for now? We'll sign a service contract shortly after. And I'll take it from there. First things first, I'll draft a civil complaint [for you]." That was Li Yinxue's reply to the visitor's question about service fees. "By the way, do you hold a job somewhere as a laborer?"

In a small town like Xiqing, where locals relied heavily on agriculture, women with cash-paying jobs were more likely than farmhands to pay a professional to get a divorce.

"Not really." The visitor lowered her eyes. "I don't have a job like that."

Silence between their teeth, neither party seemed eager to pick up the conversation. Sitting across from the two women, I wondered how the meeting would unfold.

Just as Li Yinxue was about to resume speaking, someone, a man perhaps in his sixties, stormed into the office.

Before I could scan his face for more details, he shouted, "Pick up your stuff! Go home!" In an instant, he had commandeered the meeting. "You've got no money. Go home."

"No!" the visitor replied immediately, without even looking up at him.

"You have no money. And I've got no money either," said the man.

"You two are related?" Perplexed, Li Yinxue asked, "Y-you're her father?"

"Uh-huh." The man took off his fleece hat, bowing to Li Yinxue, with an embarrassed grimace.

Over the next few minutes, the man wasted little time commanding his daughter what to do and what not to do. "Grab your stuff! Go home!" he yelled again.

"No."

"Without money, who is gonna help you?"

"I don't have any. But I'll earn my own!"

While father and daughter plunged into a shouting match, Li Yinxue tried several times to intercede in their heated exchanges. After much confusion, she finally sorted out the situation.

The young woman, it turned out, was stuck with a physically and emotionally violent husband. A divorce would be out of the question until he received a onetime payment of 200,000 yuan from his wife, an amount unfathomable to countryfolk who banked on good weather for a living. Around the time of this argument, according to the county government, the per capita income for villagers was just 4,937 yuan. Despondent, the woman thought of suing her husband for a divorce. The problem, though, was that she had little knowledge of the court system. And she had no savings or cash income to pay for legal services. In Xiqing and the adjacent areas, legal workers often charged clients anywhere from a few hundred to 2,000 or 3,000 yuan in fees for legal representation in divorce cases. In short, neither the woman nor her natal family could foot the bill for litigation.

Once Li Yinxue fully grasped the situation, she urged the young woman to obey her father. "You should hear your father out," Li Yinxue said.

"I've told you. This is a law firm. They'll charge you for their services!" the man shouted again, as if, with a pitch high enough, his vision of reality would finally register with his daughter. In *that* reality, the disgruntled, however miserable or imperiled, would have no recourse to law unless they had deep pockets.

Li Yinxue made no attempt to correct the man's misconceptions. To begin with, the Xiqing Legal Workers' Office was not a law firm staffed by licensed lawyers in private practice. Rather, it employed a different group of practitioners who had maintained a rather complicated relation with the local state. As for the needy, according to state law, they are entitled to government-funded legal aid. Which is to say, even the poor have a shot—albeit a long shot—at justice.

Instead of injecting a different reality into the conversation, Li Yinxue echoed the father's faulty message and advised the daughter to reconsider divorce. Once it became clear that the two lacked the means to pay for legal services, talk of signing a service contract, or drafting a civil complaint as a necessary step toward divorce litigation, stopped altogether. Shortly after that, Li Yinxue concluded the meeting and showed the visitors the door.[2]

The ups and downs of Township Legal Services

In meeting with a battered woman, Li Yinxue was not entirely unfeeling, I must point out. She heard the woman's grievances, made several attempts to appease her father, and, in the end, offered some useful tips. For example, she stressed the importance of gathering medical records for injuries in case legal action against the husband became an option. That said, Li Yinxue did not take the case. Having recognized her lack of financial means, she instead turned away the aggrieved. What unites this legal worker with many others out there is a market logic that valorizes maximization of profits and minimization of costs. Because of that logic, Li Yinxue, not unlike her male coworkers, must convey a message to the disgruntled: help is on the way if you can afford it. After all, business is business.

Except that a legal workers' office is not exactly a business. The organization, since its foundation in the early 1980s, has been caught in the middle between a fledgling service market, bound to make commodities out of manpower, and a restless state, itching to transform its economy and populace. The organization and its members must consequently chart precarious waters on two fronts, one geared toward delivery of paid services and the other toward provision of public goods. And, in that process, they witnessed the PRC's successive endeavors to cultivate and harness a budding service industry. These endeavors, as the succeeding pages show, are surely intentional in the eyes of state actors. Intentionality, however, does not always translate into consistent, coherent, or integrated policy decisions. Neither does it invariably give rise to the shrewd propaganda, potent symbolism, cogent political ideals, holistic developmental schemes, or well-calibrated models of law enforcement scholars often ascribe to booming authoritarian regimes.[3] To the contrary, the ups and downs experienced by legal workers mirror a state—nearsighted, fractured, full of ambivalence and contradictions. Its attempts to tool and retool legality to suit evolving agendas in ruling are constantly shifting. The consequences? In many instances when wrestling with the law, the PRC has piled the costs on the shoulders of the most vulnerable in society. To grasp these consequences, I argue, is to untangle the nexus between authoritarian legality and social inequality. To that end, we must travel back in time.[4]

At the onset of the 1980s, when the PRC was seeking to rebuild its legal infrastructure in the aftermath of the Cultural Revolution, many took pains to cope with an acute shortage of legal professionals. The year 1982, for instance, recorded some dismal estimates. In a country of over one billion people, lawyers numbered just 11,389. Back then, these practitioners carried an awkward title, lawyer workers (律师工作者), and so did their host organizations, legal advisory offices (法律顾问处), though many of the offices were later renamed law firms (律师事务所). This translated into a ratio of one lawyer for every one hundred thousand individuals in the population. Meanwhile, local governments across the country employed just 27,566 staff to run legal affairs.[5] These employees, dubbed judicial assistants (司法助理员), were usually affiliated with township or district governments or with justice bureaus at the county or municipal level. Their responsibilities abounded and included supervising people's mediation, tackling folk disputes, conducting legal education, and so on. This meant that a handful of government employees, among other duties, had to oversee a massive legion of people's mediators—over five million at that point, and the vast majority of those mediators had little or no legal training. This extraordinary dearth of well-trained legal professionals was echoed in a saying, popular among the plainspoken, "So hard is it to find a lawyer, to obtain notary services, or to launch a lawsuit" (请律师难、办公证难、打官司难).

To satisfy the unmet popular needs for legal know-how and also to prop up grassroots governance, in 1984, the Ministry of Justice (MOJ) began promoting Township Legal Services (乡镇法律服务), a service-oriented organization that first surfaced in Guangdong, Fujian, and Liaoning Provinces.[6] Before long, this organization—with awkward names like *Township Legal Workers' Office* (乡镇法律服务所) and later *Grassroots Legal Workers' Office* (基层法律服务所) (hereinafter legal workers' office)—spread to almost every corner in the land. By the end of the 1990s, the number of the offices in operation had surged to 31,758, employing nearly 100,000 people nationwide (see figures 4.1 and 4.2). At a time when so few lawyers were scattered across so vast a country, the rapid rise of Township Legal Services made a notable difference for the aggrieved. Several distinctions between legal workers and lawyers explain why that was the case.

For most of the 1980s and 1990s, the PRC treated the bulk of lawyers as state legal workers (国家的法律工作者), providing them with public funds and administrative ranks in government-authorized personnel systems (编制).[7] Legal workers, by contrast, never enjoyed that level of state support; from the outset, they were expected to stand on their own feet. The prevailing understanding among officials was that the advent of Township Legal Services, in urban and rural settings alike, was not to

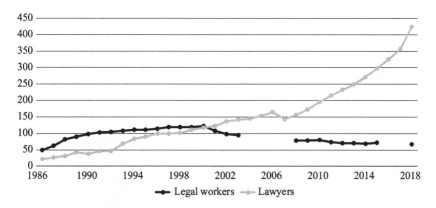

FIGURE 4.1 Number of legal workers and lawyers (in thousands) in China, 1986–2018

SOURCES: *China Law Yearbook* (1988–2016); *China Yearbook of Judicial Administration* (1986–1987, 2002–2004, 2010); *China Social Statistical Yearbook* (2014–2018); *China Statistical Yearbook* (1987–1989, 2019); MOJ 2019; Wang 2008; Zhu 2008.
NOTE: Certain data points were missing for 2004–2007 and 2016–2017.

FIGURE 4.2 Number of legal workers' offices and law firms (in thousands) in China, 1985–2018

SOURCES: *China Law Yearbook* (1988–2016); *China Yearbook of Judicial Administration* (1986–1987, 2002–2004, 2010); *China Social Statistical Yearbook* (2014–2018); *China Statistical Yearbook* (1987–1989, 2019); MOJ 2019; Wang 2008; Zhu 2008.
NOTES:

1. Certain data points were missing for 2004–2007 and 2016–2017.
2. Between 1985 and 1989, *China Statistical Yearbook* used legal advisory offices as a category to document existing organizations employing lawyer workers. From 1990 onward, *China Law Yearbook* switched to a different term, *law firms*. For the sake of brevity, I use only *law firms* in the figure.

burden local governments with budgetary or personnel problems. That was possible only if legal workers, in contrast to lawyers, required neither public funds nor slots in state personnel systems.[8] In 1987, when the MOJ issued the first regulation on Township Legal Services, it formalized this understanding.

Shortly after, legal workers learned that, by decree, they should charge clients for fees—that is, instead of public goods, they would supply the aggrieved with paid services, such as drafting legal documents, representing clients in civil suits, providing consultation to business owners, and so on. Local governments could offer additional funds, but, whenever possible, legal workers were to be responsible for their own economic gains and losses, the MOJ stipulated. While casting this group of law practitioners in the image of self-sustaining business entrepreneurs, the MOJ did not forget to position state agents in the driver's seat. It did so by designating township governments and justice bureaus (at the county, district, or municipal level) as the supervising bodies for legal workers and, more crucially, by making judicial assistants the heads of their offices. The immediate implications were twofold.

For one, following the 1987 regulation, grassroots state actors got the final say about a wide range of issues from the establishment of a legal workers' office in a given locale to the staffing of that office, from licensing to annual auditing. This, in effect, kept legal workers on a tight leash; thereafter, preventing them from challenging state authorities became a walk in the park. Anyone in defiance would soon find it difficult, if not impossible, to retain employment. For another, in picking judicial assistants—nearly always party cadres on local governments' payroll—to run the day-to-day operation of legal workers' offices, the MOJ sought to milk this organization not only for commercial but also for administrative purposes. Legal workers, accordingly, must attend to certain governmental functions, including helping judicial assistants with dispute management, legal education, and other administrative affairs. And when they did so, they were not allowed to charge fees.[9] In brief, legal workers, from the start, have served two masters, the state and the market. And many have done so without the material or symbolic backing the state provided for lawyers in the early years of the reform era.

Several other distinctions set legal workers further apart from their counterparts in law firms, including the size of their host organizations, professional qualifications, and geographic locations. Compared to many law firms in the 1980s and 1990s, legal workers' offices were considerably smaller, nimbler, closer to their clientele, and thus more accessible. They were smaller, for a good many employed only two to four members. They were nimbler in that they could hire anyone with a high school diploma and certain legal knowledge, as a result of the MOJ's lowering the bar for legal practice. Lawyers, by comparison, had to meet notably higher professional requirements to be licensed. Furthermore, whereas law firms chiefly concentrated in urban centers, legal workers often stationed their offices in rural communities, making their services responsive to the needs of villagers and local governments.

To put it briefly, the MOJ at the top, along with local governments at the bottom, rallied behind Township Legal Services early in the reform era. They did so because, at a time marked by a severe shortage of well-trained professionals, legal workers served as functional equivalents of lawyers. And, even better, they performed their duties without demanding the systematic state support lawyers were entitled to. Across the country, legal workers benefited from this burgeoning service industry, which started growing in the mid-1980s and reached its heyday around the turn of the century (see figures 4.1 and 4.2). In those years, Township Legal Services looked—and acted—like a chimera, one part conducting profit-making business with a populace increasingly demanding legal know-how and another part supplying the local state with unpaid (or underfunded) work. This hybrid nature, one might argue, stemmed directly from state actors' intentional efforts to tackle challenges the PRC faced at a particular historical moment. These efforts, however purposive or elaborate, were far from coherent or holistic, I must note.

For example, the MOJ was unable to secure the backing of the National People's Congress, the country's top legislature, which did not recognize legal workers' rights to handle civil suits until 2012, nearly three decades after this group of practitioners burst onto the scene. As for their participation in administrative litigation, legal workers had to wait even longer. Only with the 2014 amending of the Administrative Litigation Law did legislators finally place legal workers on equal footing with lawyers in litigation.[10] This is to say, for decades, the national legislature did not see eye to eye with the MOJ, which in turn thrust legal workers into a gray area. Within that area, judges, lawyers, and litigants could easily cite national procedural laws to dispute the lawfulness of legal workers' job in representing clients in litigation.[11] Many, in consequence, had to fight for their niche in a booming service industry, while fending off suspicion and scrutiny from court insiders. Lawyers, on the other hand, did not fret over the legislature's recognition. Lawmakers, as early as 1954, codified lawyers' role as counsel for litigants. They reconfirmed this role, in 1979, at the outset of the reform era.[12] Speaking of their relations to the state, one might as well compare Chinese lawyers to a family's firstborn and legal workers to the middle child, unattended, uncherished, stuck in fragmentation within the body politic from day one. In the next two decades, these practitioners would be further plunged into vicissitudes and uncertainties. Their fates would be turned upside down at the hands of state actors, who were capricious one moment and indeterminate the next.

* * *

Deng Xiaoping's Southern Tour in early 1992 triggered another wave of policymaking in the PRC. Later that year, the MOJ convened a symposium to discuss the future of Township Legal Services. Soon, participants, including the then vice minister of justice, Zhang Xiufu, and the heads of justice departments and bureaus from dozens of provinces and municipalities, echoed party leadership's renewed commitment to Reform and Opening-Up (改革开放). Reaffirming the connection between market reforms and legal protections, participants raced to the conclusion that legal services at the grassroots level must be further reformed.[13] Behind the conclusion was the belief that the market economy is a rule-of-law economy (市场经济是法治经济), an idea then gaining traction in both political and academic circles.[14]

In 1994, the MOJ rolled out an ambitious, five-year plan, seeking to reshuffle lawyers and legal workers. At the top of the agenda were the initiatives to unhook both groups from the state. For lawyers in state-owned law firms, this meant that they would have to surrender public funds, administrative ranks, and other perks associated with state sector membership. As for legal workers, these initiatives would result in the severance of two entities: justice offices (司法所) and legal workers' offices. In theory, these two entities should operate separately, because the former fell squarely into the category of state bureaucracies, and the latter, as a hybrid, was much harder to box. More accurately, justice offices headed by judicial assistants were supposed to function as liaisons between local governments (at the township or district level) and justice bureaus (at the county or municipal level). Legal workers' offices—also headed by judicial assistants in many places, thanks to the 1987 regulation—were expected to run their profit-making activities independent of justice offices. In practice, the two entities often coalesced due to local governments' budget constraints. Under the circumstances, judicial assistants and legal workers often operated as one team, under two signboards, sharing manpower, budgets, office space, and other resources, a solution tolerated by local governments across the country.[15]

In severing the ties between the two, the MOJ sought to privatize Township Legal Services, along with state-owned law firms. By gradually phasing out state support for law practitioners, policymakers at the top envisaged a legal services industry tailored to the needs of a socialist market economy. Until that point in winter 1994, there had been little indication that the PRC would turn its back on Township Legal Services. All signs had pointed to the opposite direction. In fact, the MOJ showcased a bold vision in that five-year plan: by 1995, it would administer the first, unified qualification examination specifically designed for legal workers; in five years, this group would see their members rise steadily to 135,000 and their host organizations to 38,000.[16]

In reality, however, the MOJ did not hold the first, unified qualification examination for legal workers until 2000. In that year, nearly one hundred thousand practitioners across the country took the examination. The *People's Daily*, in a jubilant tone, celebrated that pivotal moment. The examination would set legal workers on "a path toward scientific, regularized, and institutionalized mechanisms for their admission to legal practice," the paper exclaimed.[17] Accompanying this development was the MOJ's issuance of two measures, in 2000, to streamline its regulations on

Township Legal Services (the organization, by this point, had taken on a new name, Grassroots Legal Services, in many parts of the country).[18]

Around that time, the MOJ joined several state bureaucracies to further privatize both law firms and legal workers' offices, a process officially termed unhooking and restructuring (脱钩改制). Through this process, organizations hosting legal workers would decouple finances, personnel, and routine operations from those of the local state and emerge as "self-running, self-sustaining, self-managing, and self-developing" entities. In legal parlance, these offices would assume the form of partnership (合伙), a structure typically associated with for-profit organizations, the MOJ envisioned.[19] A year later, reports surfaced, estimating that about 59 percent of existing offices nationwide had been unhooked from the state.[20] Notwithstanding various bumps in the road, Township Legal Services, an organization born into a socialist command economy, was on the way to meet the future. To many, it would be a future of legal workers and lawyers growing in tandem into pillars of a booming service market.

That future, alas, never came. On December 11, 2001, China entered the World Trade Organization (WTO). Months later, the minister of justice, Zhang Fusen, publicly declared, "We cannot allow legal workers to turn into substandard lawyers [二律师]. Their offices in metropolitan areas must gradually exit from litigation." This announcement popped up during a speech Zhang gave at the Shanghai Conference, a symposium held by the MOJ in August 2002 to discuss reforms of legal services in large- and midsize cities. To explain his announcement, Zhang quoted national laws. That the country's major procedural laws had yet to recognize legal workers' status as lawful counsel in litigation suddenly became the justification for kicking hundreds of thousands of practitioners out of an area of business that had long been their lifelines. To further support his position, Zhang referenced "countries across the globe," insisting that a good many had their lawyers monopolize legal services. In his words, turning legal workers into "substandard lawyers" would contradict international best practice. Zhang's speech, well publicized, must have turned many heads, sending shivers down the spines of practitioners relying on litigation for their bread and butter.

Later in 2002, justice departments and bureaus nationwide received a set of opinions (意见) from the MOJ. While carefully modulating Zhang Fusen's language (the condescending term *substandard lawyers* was nowhere to be seen in the document), these opinions spelled out the directives the minister of justice put forward at the Shanghai Conference. Legal workers in metropolitan areas must progressively retreat from litigation in the years to come. And they must further "attune themselves to the grass roots, to communities, to the masses" so as to "gear their services to public welfare," "to render their work accessible, at the service of public welfare" (坚持服务的公益性、便民性), and, ultimately, "to prioritize societal benefits" (把服务的社会效益放在第一位), the MOJ demanded.[21]

In media coverage of the Shanghai Conference, the official stance on legal services was even more exact and exacting. The *People's Daily*, Xinhua, and China News Service, for example, went as far as to contend that legal services in urban settings should maintain a nonprofit standing (非营利性)—a position Zhou Yuansheng echoed in an award-winning paper, published in *Justice of China* (中国司法), a magazine under the MOJ's thumb. Zhou, at the time, was the vice director of the Bureau of Lawyers and Notary Publics at the MOJ (司法部律师公证工作指导司).[22] His assertion—"Instead of privileging profit-making activities, legal services must prioritize societal benefits"—reflected the official position. Yet the question remained: In the wake of state-driven marketization, how could legal workers withdraw from litigation—a key source of their income—and remain financially self-sustaining on the one hand, and serve public welfare and prioritize societal benefits on the other? The MOJ did not provide an explanation at the Shanghai Conference or in any follow-up opinions. Nor did it mention anything about those practitioners stationed in rural areas.

One thing is certain, though. The years between 1999 and 2002 marked a dramatic watershed. After two decades of prosperity, Township Legal Services lost momentum at the turn of the century. Within four years, the number of legal workers' offices countrywide was slashed from 35,383 to 26,889 (see figure 4.2). Behind this headlong fall were several key events—for example, unhooking and restructuring, China's entry into the WTO, the Shanghai Conference, and the Sixteenth National Congress of the Chinese Communist Party (CCP), in November 2002, which put forward a catchphrase, "expanding and regularizing legal services" (拓展和规范法律服务), to set the tone for future reforms. Soon after, before the end of 2002, the MOJ had picked two disparate trajectories for the country's law practitioners. Regarding lawyers everywhere, they would see more top-down reforms centering on their practice of law. As for legal workers, their destinies would largely hinge on geography. In major cities, it would be just a matter of time before they quit litigation altogether. On this point, the MOJ insisted that local government officials "unify their understanding, adopt a firm attitude, and take proper measures." Legal workers in the countryside, in the meantime, must consolidate their work.[23] But how? The MOJ did not specify.

Just as many thought that top decision-makers would mull over their next steps, legal workers in both urban and rural areas were sucked into another vortex. The promulgation of the 2003 Administrative License Law prompted the State Council in May 2004 to eliminate certain government agencies' power to issue permits, licenses, and certificates to a range of business owners. The legislative intent was to bring governance further in line with the so-called socialist rule of law. Legal workers soon learned that they would no longer need two permits, one for the establishment of their host organizations and the other for their entry into legal practice. Scarcely had six weeks passed. The State Council reversed part of its earlier decision in June 2004; this time, legal workers were again told that their admission to legal practice would entail a permit issued by provincial or lower-level governments. What about official permission for the establishment of their host organizations? Would such permission be required of legal workers? According to the State Council, the answer would be a resounding no since it had revoked that requirement in May 2004. Yet the answer would become a yes, pursuant to a regulation the MOJ had issued in 2000.[24] It would not be an exaggeration to describe the situation as a clash of titans with regular people smashed in between.

In the section that follows, I draw on the rise and fall of legal workers as a case study to sort out some theoretical takeaways. And I do so with another case study in mind. In the previous chapter, I present the revitalization of people's mediation in the twenty-first century as a "positive" case to illustrate the PRC's alacrity, ingenuity, and efficacy in cultural appropriation. The current chapter, conversely, shifts to offer comparative evidence, attesting to the limits of the PRC's cultural appropriation. To put it another way, the rise and fall of legal workers—a group that prospered in the socialist era and has been trapped in a downward spiral since the turn of the century—constitutes a case leaning more toward the "negative" side. In this way, it brings to our attention a critical question. What has constrained political elites' capacity to remake past ruling experience, to merge the inherited with the borrowed governing methodologies, or to craft novel solutions to emerging problems? The answer, I believe, has a lot to do with state fragmentation.

CULTURE AND THE STATE
State fragmentation and limits in cultural appropriation

From the early 1980s onward, legal workers have time after time found themselves ensnared in state fragmentation—along four distinct dimensions: temporal, spatial, bureaucratic, and ideational. Temporally speaking, elites at the apex of state power have frequently contradicted themselves in decision-making. Policies formed later could wind up contravening or even negating those carried out earlier. One striking case in point concerns the MOJ, the country's top justice agency. After years of preparation, in 2000, the MOJ administered the first, unified qualification examination for legal workers, a moment the *People's Daily* insisted should not pass uncelebrated. Then—bang—it was all over. Since 2001, the agency has discontinued this examination at the national level, although its own regulation unequivocally stipulated this arrangement.[25] Another example involves the State Council, the PRC's central government. In June 2004, it swiftly reversed a decision on legal workers' entry into legal practice, a reversal that separated itself from the previous decision by just six weeks, a mind-blowing policy shift the preceding section discusses. These examples illustrate that the state becomes fractured due to inconsistence in policy formation over time.

Likewise, state fragmentation can emerge following decentralization in policy development across space. Between the mid-1980s and the advent of the new millennium, rural-urban divide scarcely registered as a key parameter in the MOJ's decision-making regarding Township Legal Services. Back then, lawyers everywhere were a rarity. The MOJ thus expected legal workers to fill a void countrywide. The year 2002 marked a tipping point. At the Shanghai Conference, policymakers sought to set legal workers in metropolitan areas apart from those stationed elsewhere. That move soon begat more steps to articulate spatial graduation in policy adjustments.

In 2003, a decision arrived, explicating the MOJ's vision for future reforms. To be exact, in eastern parts of the country, and especially in regions with more developed economies and abundance of lawyers, legal workers would progressively retreat from litigation. In the meantime, their presence in central and western areas, where economic underdevelopment and scarcity of legal professionals persisted, would be preserved and strengthened.[26] This spatially bifurcated approach brought about a significant redistribution of Grassroots Legal Services in the following years. By the end of 2008, 77 percent of legal workers' offices were clustered in rural settings, and only 23 percent or so continued to serve the urban population.[27] Less than a decade into the twenty-first century, legal workers, with a nationwide presence once, now largely concentrated in the countryside. The regulations and policies that governed their practice of law—centralized to a large extent at a time—now became decentralized and disintegrated. Warning against a "one-size-fits-all formula" (一刀切) and "cookie-cutter policy formation" (齐步走), the MOJ refused to set concrete deadlines for legal workers' retreat from litigation anywhere in the country. Nor did it specify how to distinguish regions with "developed economies" and "an abundance of lawyers" from those without such conditions.[28] This reluctance (or inability) to formulate a unitary approach for reforms, coupled with the top legislature's inaction to codify the workings of legal workers, in effect, endowed local governments with full discretion. From the mid-2000s onward, local governments have taken liberties to determine the fate of legal workers, giving rise to a jurisdictional thicket with regulatory practices varying from one province to another, from one municipality to the next. The state, in this view, is spatially divided.

The third dimension of fragmentation stems from a commonality among modern states, which characteristically comprise a multitude of bureaucracies on many fronts and at many levels. Structured horizontally or vertically within the body politic, these bureaucracies constitute—not an autonomous, bounded, unified whole—but rather "a heap of loosely connected parts." And they often contain "ill-defined boundaries between them and other groupings inside and outside the official state borders," political scientist Joel S. Migdal contends. Some of the bureaucracies, inevitably, end up "promoting conflicting sets of rules with one another and with 'official' Law."[29] In this regard, the PRC is hardly an exception. The sheer size of the country, combined with layers of hierarchy within the state apparatus, means that multiple bureaucracies regularly take part in policy formation. Ambivalence, mixed signals, and conflicting cues could dog decision-making processes at any level or front. Moreover, an authoritarian state like the PRC faces a conundrum: ruling elites must strike a delicate balance between mining the utility of law and curbing its subversive potential, a task that further complicates state actors' interactions with various social groups, adding another layer of complexity to state fragmentation, as Rachel E. Stern, another political scientist, points out.[30]

Consistent with the observations of political scientists, my study of Township Legal Services points to a state infested with bureaucratic division and segmentation. This finding is also consistent with the research of sociologist Liu Sida. In three decades, a fragmented state regulatory regime, Liu argues, has produced a highly fragmented market for law practitioners of various stripes.[31] Indeed, rather than acting in consort, the National People's Congress, the State Council, and the MOJ, from time to time, gainsaid one another, emitting confusing and conflicting messages to the public. Consequently, legal workers everywhere have agonized over their fate since the mid-2000s. Many tossed and turned at night, speculating when, where, and under what circumstances their livelihoods would be lost. On this matter, much ink has been spilled by academics and practitioners, and their writings often bear gloomy titles such as "A Look at Legal Workers Stuck in Awkward Conditions," "100,000 'Substandard Lawyers' Facing a Debate on Their Survival," "'Substandard Lawyers' Ready to Step off the Stage?" and so on.[32]

Lastly, state fragmentation can come down in another form, manifesting itself mainly in an ideational sphere, a theoretical insight prior research on authoritarian regimes rarely takes into consideration. While researchers recognize authoritarian states, like the PRC, as far from monolithic, they view fragmentation in terms of either bureaucratic division and segmentation or cracks in power-sharing arrangements between rulers and their elite supporters. Few have explicitly explored how the state may be splintered, rather than unified, in the ideational and, more broadly speaking, cultural realm. Even fewer have unraveled the mechanisms or processes through which culture engenders state fragmentation.[33] Occasionally, researchers do heed the cultural dimensions of authoritarian states. But when they do so, they tend to underscore state actors' ability to conjure up coherent and potent political ideals, theatrics, and signals—Lisa Wedeen's study of rhetoric and symbols in Syria, Nick Cheesman's work on law and order in Myanmar, and Elizabeth J. Perry's article on cultural governance in the PRC are cases in point. What is notably missing in this line of inquiry is a methodical investigation as to how and why autocrats may fail to form consistent, cogent, or integrated ideas in policy development.

On this matter, I turn to a group of institutionalists for insights. Among those institutionalists, some are ardent proponents of organizational institutionalism, and others fall under the rubric of historical institutionalism. Despite that, they are united in one conviction: social actors do not simply have straightforward interests; rather, they have ideas about their interests. What has bolstered this conviction is Max Weber's famous "switchmen" metaphor—that is, while interests serve as the engine of action, providing actors with motivating forces, ideas, acting like the switchmen, frequently determine "the tracks along which action has been pushed by the dynamic of interest."[34] In plain language, interests concern what people want (the ends and the destinations), and ideas inform them of how to get there (the means and the tracks). This Weberian notion of ideas, institutionalists have long maintained, has much to contribute to our understanding of policymaking processes and outcomes.

In this regard, sociologist John L. Campbell's work proves particularly edifying, for it enables us to discern the mechanisms through which culture comes to rupture the state. Classifying ideas along two axes, cognitive/normative and foreground/background, Campbell yields a four-fold typology: (1) programs, (2) paradigms, (3) frames, and (4) public sentiments (see

TABLE 4.1 John L. Campbell's typology of ideas and their effects on policymaking

	Ideational Influences in the Foreground	Ideational Influences in the Background
Cognitive level	**Programs** Cognitive ideas, operating in the foreground of policy formation, by helping decision-makers chart a clear and specific course of action (e.g., ideas that allowed the MOJ to prescribe formal rules and norms to regulate legal workers' practice of law)	**Paradigms** Cognitive ideas, working in the background of policy deliberation, often in the form of taken-for-granted assumptions, categories, and boundaries, thereby limiting the range of options decision-makers can imagine (e.g., the taken-for-granted assumptions behind the MOJ's policymaking, especially the ideas that legal workers must serve as market players as opposed to state employees, and that the state should stand by solely as a regulatory force vis-à-vis the budding legal services market)
Normative level	**Frames** Normative ideas, acting in the foreground of policy formation, by orienting decision-makers' efforts to justify the chosen course of action in relation to the public (e.g., ideas that led the MOJ to discursively and ideologically cast Grassroots Legal Services as nonprofit organizations geared toward promoting public welfare and societal benefits)	**Public sentiments** Normative ideas, operating in the background of policy deliberation, by informing decision-makers of public opinions on fairness, appropriateness, and legitimacy (e.g., ideas that the MOJ invoked to reckon with popular needs and wants concerning legal assistance)

SOURCE: Campbell 2001.

table 4.1).[35] This typology, I believe, carves out an analytical space for researchers to unpack in what ways ideas enable or confine policy formation. Moreover, it provides much-needed leverage to address an understudied issue in China studies and in the literature on authoritarian legality: How come rational and shrewd state actors do not always end with rational or shrewd policy decisions? Indeed, applying Campbell's insights to examine the sedimentation of certain welfare policies in the United States, sociologist Brian Steensland finds that political elites experienced persistent difficulties in shaking up ideas along cognitive, normative, and other dimensions, which in turn undermined the prospect of policy reforms.[36] In my study, I come to discern similar struggles among the PRC's ruling elites.

For example, early in the reform era, decision-makers at the MOJ and many at the grassroots level shared an assumption that unlike lawyers in state-owned law firms, legal workers would stand on their own feet, demanding neither budgetary nor personnel support from the local state, a key feature I underlined earlier in the chapter. That assumption—or, *paradigm*, in Campbell's phrase—sunk in, following the MOJ's regulatory practices in the late 1980s and 1990s (although, in many places, legal workers banked on a grassroots state bureaucracy, justice office, for material and logistic help). The MOJ, at the outset of the new century, went on to institutionalize this assumption by formally severing the ties between legal workers and local governments, a process officially termed *unhooking and restructuring.* In doing so, it sought to further privatize legal services. To the aggrieved, this meant that they had to pay for legal services out of their own pockets, for the state would no longer subsidize such services, either formally or informally. In short, state actors over time have latched onto the cognitive ideas—in the background of policy deliberation—that legal know-how should be traded in a marketplace as paid services as opposed to public goods and that rather than relying on public funding and state support, law practitioners ought to eke out a living as market players.

Yet, in the foreground of policy formation, decision-makers have strived to convey a very different message to the public. The MOJ, since the early 2000s, has made notable efforts to cast Grassroots Legal Services, ideologically and discursively, in the image of public interest organizations. As indicated before, following the Shanghai Conference in 2002, the MOJ instructed legal workers to gear their services to public welfare, to render their work convenient and accessible, and, above all, to prioritize societal benefits. Official media like the *People's Daily* and Xinhua went further, urging Grassroots Legal Services to maintain a non-profit standing, a message echoed by high-ranking officials at the MOJ. In the decades to come, similar attempts persisted in the officialdom. Seen through Campbell's typology, these attempts to dress up legal services—in official ideology and in public discourse—constitute *framing*—that is, deploying normative ideas to justify and legitimize policy choices in relations with ordinary citizens.

It goes without saying that there is a great gap between state actors' background assumptions and foreground frames. The former rests on the ideas of legal workers as market players keeping their businesses afloat by charging clients, thus in no need of public funds or other forms of state support. The latter, on the contrary, are rooted in the notion that these practitioners should pursue the common good rather than seeking profits. So conspicuous is this disjunction that scholars, including Fu Yulin and Fu Hualing, have been writing about this problem since 2004.[37]

To a cynic, such a great gap could be easily explained away by reducing it to an example of the PRC flirting with populism, with party elites merely paying lip service to citizens. Or, perhaps, it is another instance involving "guerrilla policymaking," a Mao-era policy style that has gained a foothold in the reform era. The very style, according to Sebastian Heilmann and Elizabeth J. Perry, prides itself on "a readiness to experiment and learn (even from enemies and foreigners), an agility in grasping unforeseen opportunities, a single-mindedness in pursuing strategic goals, a willingness to ignore ugly side effects, and a ruthlessness in eradicating unfriendly opposition."[38] State actors, in this account, are effortlessly cognizant of their self-interest and uncannily adept at aligning their goals and action, ends and means. Here, regime rationality is not bounded but next to boundless. This characterization of policymaking leaves little room to question state actors' cognition, instrumentality, or creativity in adaptive governance.

Looking beyond China studies, we soon spot a similar problem. In the literature on authoritarian legality, regime behavior is said to result from "rational and shrewd political calculation."[39] Autocrats, it then follows, shore up judicial institutions and strengthen performance of legal professionals—to strategically meet various needs and wants in ruling. Valid and valuable, this inquiry nonetheless seldom heeds what may limit autocrats' ability to exploit legality other than their half-hearted commitment to the rule of law.

Could there be another explanation for the foregoing contradiction between the cognitive-background and normative-foreground aspects of policy formation? I think so. The very contradiction, I argue, attests to the struggles state actors experienced in reimagining and rearranging legal workers' positioning vis-à-vis the state, market, and society—at a critical juncture, the period between 1999 and 2002, when the PRC was undergoing a sequence of key events, including unhooking and restructuring, China's entry into the WTO, the Shanghai Conference, and the CCP's Sixteenth National Congress. What occurred after 2002 is a matter of debate. Some may view the next fifteen years or so as a path-dependent process whereby top decision-makers became locked in indetermination, despite their interest in harnessing Grassroots Legal Services for evolving agendas in ruling. Others may not necessarily view this period through the lens of *path dependence*, a concept institutionalists apply to account for the persistence of institutional arrangements and practices.[40] Irrespective of one's stance on the concept, here is the bottom line.

Between 2003 and 2017, the country's top justice agency did little to lessen the tensions between its background assumptions and foreground frames.[41] Rather, it went on to entrench the disjointedness among what Campbell terms *programs, paradigms, frames,* and *public sentiments.* In fifteen years or so, the MOJ made few attempts to confront the taken-for-granted, almost unquestioned assumption (or *paradigm* in Campbell's words) that legal workers must operate as market players, while the state stands by, solely as a regulatory force, watching over a market economy on the rise. Unable or unwilling to disabuse decision-makers of this sticky idea, the MOJ, in the meantime, could not bring itself to tread the alternative path either. The agency, during those years, continued to stress the necessity of unhooking legal workers from the state in hopes of steering them further toward the market. The goal, as it repeatedly emphasized, was to render these practitioners truly self-sustaining and self-developing in a market economy.

Indeed, if that had been the chosen path, the logical thing to do under the circumstances would have been to formulate policy prescriptions (or *programs*) to level the playing field and to grant legal workers the same kind of market standing Chinese lawyers had long enjoyed. Regrettably, that is not what ensued. Decision-makers at multiple levels, instead, continued to enact various restrictions that had originated in the socialist era. Here is a partial list of restrictions on legal workers' practice of law: up to 2017, these practitioners could not establish new offices without local governments' permission, and private funds were barred from investing in their businesses (lawyers, by contrast, did not need such permission and had obtained the option to use private funds to erect different types of law firms in the early 2000s). In many parts of the country, legal workers still have to turn in management fees (管理费) to justice bureaus or departments, even after paying taxes, practically serving as a cash cow for the local state. While ignoring this burden on legal workers, the MOJ explicitly banned justice bureaus and departments from extracting such fees from lawyers, a decision that came out in 2003.[42] Finally, legal workers, unlike lawyers, are not allowed to handle criminal defense cases and cannot participate in litigation outside the jurisdiction where they were admitted to legal practice.[43] In a word, the socialist past—a past that witnessed the state treating lawyers as the privileged and legal workers as the second class—proves rather hard to dislodge. To say history matters, in this case, is to suggest that the past holds a tenacious grip on the PRC's present-day policy wrangling. And this grip is realized not so much by enabling as by constricting the range of creative adaptation state actors can achieve.

Similarly, between 2003 and 2017, the MOJ continued to exhort legal workers to attune their work to public welfare, to render services convenient and accessible to the masses, and to prioritize societal benefits. Official rhetoric in this vein bespeaks state actors' efforts to evoke normative ideas to grapple with what Campbell calls *public sentiments*. In fifteen years or so, the talk of public welfare and societal benefits did not die down. It rather reached a crescendo in 2014 in a new wave of policy experimentation. This time the MOJ touted its decisions as endeavors toward building a public legal services system (公共法律服务体系). Within this system, legal workers would provide legal aid (法律援助)—essentially unpaid or underpaid services—to "assist the needy and disputants stuck in particular cases." They would also offer "nonprofit legal consultation, advice, and representation in litigation," thereby engaging in a wide range of pro bono work. In addition, they would facilitate local governments to tackle some of the most intractable problems in society, including disputes over land-taking and demolition, labor relations, medical malpractice, environmental problems, food safety, and so on.[44] In a word, legal workers would devote themselves to public services.

Indeed, if that had been the chosen path, the logical thing to do under the circumstances would have been to roll out concrete programs to reorient legal workers toward pursuing the common good. That is not what happened, unfortunately. Not unlike their predecessors at the 2002 Shanghai Conference, decision-makers behind the latest wave of policy experimentation were long on rhetoric but exceedingly short on specific courses of action. How could market-based practitioners commit themselves to public services on the one hand, and remain financially self-sustaining on the other? The MOJ, in 2014, offered a three-sentence answer, which could be summarized as follows: local governments should do more to help those practitioners, perhaps by using public funds to procure their services. That was it. Since then, the highest-level justice agency has stayed tight-lipped as to how to chart a novel path in this direction. This path, known as government procurement of services (政府购买服务), would entail using state revenue to compensate market players for their provision of public goods, including legal assistance. For now, it remains unclear how this path would unfold in the years to come.[45] In short, it proves rather difficult for the PRC to put the socialist past behind, because old ideas remain sticky. And, it is equally, if not more, challenging for decision-makers to instill brand-new ideas into governance and transform them into tangible policy outcomes. Nearly two decades into the twenty-first century, the PRC has yet to fully realign its cognitive and normative ideas surrounding Grassroots Legal Services. Drawing on Campbell's typology of ideas, this chapter illustrates how the state becomes ruptured in the cultural realm.

Unpacking the constitutive roles of culture

To recapitulate, the rise and fall of legal workers in the reform-era as a case study provides a precious window on the PRC's limits in instrumentalizing legality—and, more generally speaking, limits in cultural appropriation. These limits, I argue, in no small measure stem from the reality that the state is often too splintered to devise highly consistent, coherent—let alone holistic or forward-looking—schemes to exploit legality. Overlooking state fragmentation along multiple dimensions could potentially land researchers in two fallacies: either overestimating political elites' capacities to massage law or passing over their promises of legality as little more than linguistic sleight of hand.

Moreover, in highlighting state fragmentation in the ideational sphere, this chapter joins the previous one in a united effort to sharpen a theoretical argument: culture matters, and, to capture the unruliness of authoritarian legality, researchers need to pay greater attention to the constitutive roles of culture in shaping law and politics. To advance this argument, the current chapter, as well as the previous one, uncovers the complex interplay of culture and the state. On the one hand, drawing on Ann Swidler's theory, I have illustrated how culture enables state actors (see chapter 3). By underscoring the enabling effects of culture, I call scholarly attention to state actors' agency, conscious choices, and ingenuity in their cultivation of statecraft. To spotlight these features on the part of state actors is to ensure a thorough breakaway from cultural essentialism, a fallacy that has persisted in China studies.[46] In a constantly shifting world, the PRC's aptitude for cultural appropriation has rendered it exceptionally resourceful and resilient, described in the previous chapter.

The current chapter, on the other hand, shifts to demonstrate how culture constrains state actors. On this front, I join a group of institutionalists who have ruminated on the roles of ideas, broadly construed, in explicating institutional changes and reproduction. Agreeing with John L. Campbell, I maintain that social actors, including those at the pinnacle of state power, do not necessarily have a clear sense of their interests or goals, particularly during periods of great uncertainty. Even when they are indeed clear-eyed about their needs, wants, and self-interest, they still have to coordinate their pursuit of interests with cultural resources at hand, including proper strategies of action, and align their tracks with the final destination in mind, to using Max Weber's "switchmen" metaphor. When they fail to do so, their goals and strategies of action—ends and means—may remain disjointed. This is precisely what happened to the PRC's policy wrangling concerning legal workers, despite ruling elites' enduring interest in using the labor of the group for economic and political purposes. This is to suggest an interest-based, realist account of state actors seeking strategic ends by instrumentalizing legality would not suffice.[47] Neglecting how ideas—such as cognitive schemas, symbolic boundaries, discursive frames, norms, and values—constitute and often confine policy formation, researchers could run two risks. They could either overidealize the state's ability to turn rhetoric into practices or reduce the state to a grab bag of tongue-in-cheek officials, driven by Machiavellian calculations, constantly maneuvering to maximize self-interest.

In view of the constraining effects of culture, we should reckon with both sides of cultural appropriation. The PRC's audacity in imbricating the old with the new, inherited with borrowed governing methodologies, as if these ingredients would magically blend into an organic whole, could cut both ways. It could render the regime adaptable and resilient. But so could it expose state actors to difficulties, challenges, and political fallout they had never expected. After all, cultural resources appropriated from drastically different sources—Confucianism, Maoist legacies, the socialist past, technocracy, and liberal democracy, to name a few—could turn into liabilities as opposed to assets, complicating rather than liberating state actors' options in governance. Besides, these resources could clash with one another, for they often imply competing and even conflicting values, norms, and prescriptions for courses of action.

A final point: when cultural appropriation does not dovetail with proper structural conditions, when the semiotic is utterly divorced from the political or the economic, attempts to cultivate and harness statecraft of varying stripes could fall flat or even backfire. Later in the book, I provide one example along these lines. Recent official rhetoric, seeking to bring back Comrade Ma Xiwu's Way of Judging (马锡五同志的审判方式), a Maoist practice, hardly makes any splash among judges. It falls short of effecting meaningful changes on the ground because official rhetoric has yet to be transfused into organizational structures or practices. In the end, judges talk the talk but rarely walk the walk (see chapter 6 for more details). Examples like this point to the importance of scrutinizing the intricate interplay of culture and structural conditions (or, in the words of William H. Sewell Jr., the interplay of "semiotic structures" and "other structures—economic, political, social, spatial, etc.").[48] To remain mindful of such interplay is, in a way, to preempt cultural determinism, another fallacy still lurking in scholarly works. In summation, cultural appropriation does not serve authoritarian rulers in a neat, straightforward fashion.

UNEQUAL ACCESS TO JUSTICE AND
AGENDA-SETTING POWER

In this section, I shift gears to pursue this chapter's second goal—to untangle the lasting consequences of state-driven marketization of legal services. One consequence, as repeatedly noted, is the downfall of legal workers in the twenty-first century. This downfall did not produce a homogenous effect on Chinese society, I must stress. It has rather impinged more on the have-nots than on the haves, afflicting rural residents more than those residing in urban settings. The fact that certain clusters of the Chinese population make up the core of legal workers' client base is no secret to decision-makers at the top. On this matter, Zhou Yuansheng, the then vice director of the Bureau of Lawyers and Notary Publics, a key division within the MOJ, did not mince his words. In the new millennium, "lawyers have yet to meet the needs of the masses across the country; thus, grassroots services provided by legal workers can help lessen the gap between popular demand and supply." Zhou said so in recognition of a grim reality: by 2004, 206 counties nationwide had yet to employ any lawyers.[49] Wu Ling, a researcher at the Judicial Research Institute of the MOJ (司法部司法研究所), made similar remarks in 2008, acknowledging a persistent lack of lawyers in many parts of the country, a problem particularly severe in rural areas. Wu went on to claim that, for many years to come, "approximately 800 million peasants, together with middle- and low-income urban residents, will count on the services provided by legal workers."[50] In brief, officials were not short on sobering realizations about the persistent shortage of legal professionals in the country. In fact, so vocal were some local officials that they explicitly blamed legal workers' predicaments on flawed policymaking and lawmaking in the 2000s.[51] Such reckoning, however, did not prompt the MOJ to roll back marketization, which piled the cost of legal mobilization on the aggrieved. Nor did it spur top decision-makers to hand out policy prescriptions to reverse the downfall of legal workers. These practitioners, instead, witnessed their membership continue to plummet and their offices shut down nationwide one after another (see figures 4.1 and 4.2).

This is not to suggest that the reform-era PRC has harbored no concerns about the needy, the fragile, or the marginalized in society. As a

matter of fact, the state-driven marketization of legal services—a historical process converting legal know-how into commodities—took place in
tandem with another development, the construction of a state-sponsored
legal aid system (法律援助制度)—a different process transforming expertise into public services. As I have contended in the previous chapter, history is seldom singular, and the Chinese state is anything but monolithic.
These two processes, both state-initiated, could be traced back to 1994.[52]
In the following decade, the MOJ steadily laid the ground for the rise of a
legal aid system throughout the country. By the mid-2000s, the PRC had
promulgated national regulations on legal aid; and what's more, it had
identified several groups as regular beneficiaries: the disabled, the elderly,
minors, women, and the destitute (一般贫困者). Migrant workers (农民
工) made their way onto the list as a new category in 2005, indicating
state authorities' heightened awareness of the group's grievances at the
workplace.[53] In addition, the PRC has gradually expanded its coverage,
with the number of beneficiaries soaring between 1999 and 2018 from
190,545 to approximately 1.52 million (see figure 4.3).

Stated otherwise, the PRC did not simply turn its back on the less
fortunate in society. Rather, the more nuanced argument I am trying to
establish is that the state has barely done enough to protect vulnerable
social groups. The Chinese state, in this case, can hardly be described
as ambidextrous. From the mid-1990s onward, it has kept one hand
strong—the one forcefully pushing for marketization, resulting in the
bulk of the population footing the bill for legal mobilization. Nowadays,
when needing professional help for disputation or litigation, the average
woman and man have few options but to reach into their own pockets.
In the meantime, the PRC's other hand, with much less resolve or vigor,
has rendered legal aid available to only a tiny fraction of the population.
The imbalance between these two hands becomes more discernable once
we compare two measures: the volume of disputation Chinese society has
experienced and the amount of investment the state has made to extend
the availability of government-funded legal aid.

Figure 4.3 makes this comparison plain. Between 1999 and 2018,
judges have seen their caseloads rise by 92 percent. People's mediators
have experienced a similar trend, with a 42 percent increase in the volume

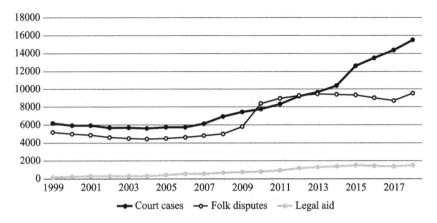

FIGURE 4.3 Number of court cases, folk disputes, and individuals receiving legal aid (all in thousands) in China, 1999–2018

sources: *China Law Yearbook* (2000–2017); *China Social Statistical Yearbook* (2017); *China Statistical Yearbook* (2018–2019); *Statistical Communiqué of the People's Courts* (2017–2018); *Statistics on Chinese Women and Children* (2014–2019).

NOTE:

I use the catchall phrase *court cases* to denote all civil, criminal, and administrative suits that entered either the courts of first-instance or the courts of appeal each year. My data come from two sources: *China Law Yearbook* (2000–2017) and *Statistical Communiqué of the People's Courts* (2018–2019); these two apply somewhat different classifications, though. To make comparison consistent over time, I include only four subcategories in my calculation: the cases handled by the courts of first instance (一审), those by the courts of appeal (二审), retrials (再审), and cases processed through adjudicatory supervision procedure (审判监督程序).

of folk disputes they had to handle. The PRC's investment in legal aid, by comparison, has been limited: the number of beneficiaries grew by only 13 percent in two decades. Here, a caveat must be noted. Figure 4.3 provides a rather conservative estimate of disputation, for it includes only disputes and conflicts that either went into the court system or were brought to the attention of people's mediators. The figure does not factor in popular grievances, rights contention, or civil unrest that transpired outside of courts or people's mediation. The actual gap between popular demand for legal assistance and the supply of government-funded legal aid, in other words, could be much bigger than what the figure indicates.

Another way to look at this problem is to check legal aid budget per capita, a metric widely used to gauge a country's budgetary allocation for the provision of legal assistance as part of public services. Take 2013 as an example. In that year the PRC set aside $0.19 for each citizen; by contrast, the Netherlands spent $34.16, Finland $14.37, Chile $6.60, Spain $3.16, Japan $1.98, South Africa $1.87, Montenegro $0.92, Slovakia $0.42, and Moldova $0.32.[54] Compared to many other countries, the PRC has barely spent enough to ensure citizens' equal access to official justice.

Let me sum up. In the twenty-first century, as Chinese society comes to terms with staggering increases in disputation, litigation, and popular contention,[55] the PRC has soldiered on, forcing its way through marketization of legal services. True, it has done so with an eye to the needy and the vulnerable. In two decades or so, the state has steadily extended legal aid to a variety of social groups and thus shielded certain clusters of the population from the gloomy downsides of a market economy. That said, state endeavors in this vein, compared to the magnitude of disputation in society, are too little, too late. The remainder of this section draws on field research I conducted in Weifeng County in rural Sichuan Province to illustrate the impact of marketization on the aggrieved. As the next few pages show, the decades-long development of a legal services industry has opened the official justice system to some, while shutting the door to many others. Equality before the law remains a myth in rural China.

* * *

In the wake of marketization, the gulf separating the haves from the have-nots, urban residents from those living in remote villages, did not close. Individuals' ability to find and mobilize state law, rather, has been further tied to the depth of their pockets. In a place like Weifeng, legal know-how has turned into a pricey commodity only certain folks can afford. At the same time, government-sponsored legal aid remains hard to come by. Han Donglin, the woman appearing in chapter 3, had to jump through multiple bureaucratic hoops to secure legal aid for her divorce suit. In a decade of research on divorce litigation, I have come across one and only one woman who managed to do so successfully.

Back in early 2010, the time when I conducted field research in Weifeng, this county, home to nearly half a million people, employed just thirteen licensed lawyers and thirty-seven legal workers. The word *wanting* does not even begin to describe the huge disparity between the local demand for legal services and the supply out there. Because of this disparity, lawyers and legal workers took every opportunity to milk the demand-supply gap, as market players typically do. Against this backdrop, I spent nine months straight conducting ethnographic research in two legal workers' offices, one located in a town called Xiqing and the other in Guxiao.

Following legal workers around daily, methodically documenting their routines at the workplace, inside courtrooms, and in rural communities, I came to discern the ways these practitioners acted as business entrepreneurs in every way imaginable. In an article published in *Law & Society Review*, I illustrated how economic incentives profoundly shaped legal workers' case screening and selection. Analyzing a sample of sixty-two face-to-face meetings between legal workers and villagers seeking professional help, this article details how market-informed, economic incentives led to routine decisions to turn away the cash-strapped, however desperate or miserable they might look. What I describe at the beginning of this chapter—Li Yinxue politely turning her back on an embittered wife—was an all-too-common occurrence in the legal services industry.[56]

In another article appearing in *Law & Policy*, I explored how legal workers inserted their professional influences in divorce litigation. Using two research samples—one comprising observations of 60 meetings between legal workers and marital disputants, and the other involving court records for 171 divorce suits—the article shows that gender inequalities did not just result from judges' final rulings inside courtrooms; rather, they had been built into the earlier stages in the course of legal mobilization. Indeed, legal workers played a crucial role in shaping those earlier moments in disputation. And they did so by asserting their influences to reconstruct women's and men's perceptions of conjugal grievances, remake or unmake their rights claims, and channel some but not other disputes into formal court proceedings. In this manner, the legal profession transformed some grievances and claims into contested *issues*— division of marital property and allocation of child custody being the primary examples—and subsequently paved the way for them to enter the formal decision-making arenas inside the court system. Meanwhile, it frequently turned other claims into *nonissues*—women's complaints of domestic violence and marital rape as a striking case in point. As a result, these complaints fell through the cracks long before they could reach the courthouse steps. The legal profession, in that sense, was instrumental in presetting formal decision-making agendas in the official justice system.[57]

Spotlighting the power exerted by the legal profession, in the early moments in legal mobilization, I take the first step toward reconceptualizing the notion of disputation. And I do so by foregrounding interconnected power relations within and outside the official justice system. Accordingly, this section introduces the first type of power relation: agenda-setting power. This power serves to delimit the scope of judicial decision-making later in litigation. It achieves such an effect mainly through excluding certain issues and/or participants from entering formal court proceedings. Ultimately, by routinely evoking this power, the legal profession predetermines the outcomes of divorce litigation, leaving the law's promise of gender equality partially or entirely unfulfilled. Readers can find more details in my 2015 article published in *Law & Policy*.

CONCLUSION

Bridging the two halves of this book, this chapter serves two purposes. Analytically speaking, it concludes the task of articulating the complex interplay of culture and the state—a theoretical objective that has motivated my research over the years. As I have argued before, if the PRC must be a case of some sort, it might as well be studied as an example of an authoritarian regime continually cultivating a cultural repertoire of statecraft. Understanding the intellectual significance of this case, I believe, has crucial implications for political scientists and sociologists.

The PRC as a case contains enormous potential, for it provides fertile ground to fuse two parallel intellectual movements in the social sciences. On the one hand, political scientists and sociologists have tried to rid themselves of the concept of the state, but to no avail.[58] On the other hand, anthropologists and sociologists have attempted to discard the notion of culture, also largely in vain.[59] That we are stuck with these two constructs, however imperfect they may be, has prompted many to explore the alternative path by disaggregating the state or by disassembling culture. Today, to suggest that the state—or culture—is anything but monolithic is almost to repeat a truism. Be that as it may, scholars striving to dissect the former and those busy with deconstructing the latter have yet to build ongoing, fruitful exchanges between themselves. These two intellectual movements, by and large, have remained unconnected.[60] This book, by parsing the ways the PRC has strategically used culture, as well as by scrutinizing the manners with which it has been used by culture, in the context of dispute management and beyond, embarks on a journey in hopes of bridging the two otherwise detached movements, thereby taking a foray into cross-fertilization.

Substantively speaking, the current chapter facilitates the transition from the outside world surrounding the Chinese judiciary to the very inside of the grassroots court system. While chapters 2, 3, and 4 place a heavy emphasis on the early moments preceding marital disputes and divorce litigation, chapters 5, 6, and 7 dive right into the inside of judges' offices, mediation rooms, and courthouse hallways, where formal or informal decision-making transpires. As a whole, this book echoes a key insight sociolegal scholars have long noted: to understand what happens inside the courts, at the end of litigation, a court-centered approach cannot suffice.[61] Connecting the dots between different stages in disputation and illuminating the influences of the legal profession along the way is crucial for researchers who seek to transcend temporal and spatial bounds in their studies of judicial decision-making.

CHAPTER 5

Judging Divorce in the People's Courts

"Judges ought to follow their conscience"

Two weeks after the lull of the Chinese New Year, the Qinchuan People's Tribunal again turned into a bustling office building. Barely nine o'clock in the morning, the halls were already packed with visitors.

Several visitors squatted, bored, and rolled cigarettes by hand. These were villagers from the adjacent areas, waiting around in hopes that they might catch a judge for quick answers to their troubles. Others looked like court regulars, in dark suits, perhaps lawyers or legal workers frequenting the tribunal to handle cases.

At the end of the hallway stood Lan Yu, a forty-six-year-old migrant worker, quietly awaiting her divorce trial. Despite a pending court appearance, she seemed oblivious to her look. Her bare face was covered with wrinkles and sunburn freckles, unruly hair stuck out around her temples, her ponytail sagged down to the shoulder. The cotton-padded jacket Lan Yu wore had faded into a murky gray. Her pants, made of corduroy, a textile popular years ago, were now worn thin. Her leather boots looked like they could fall apart at any moment.

Standing beside Lan Yu were two twentysomethings. They were Lan Yu's children, a son still in college, and a daughter eking out a living as a migrant worker. Later that day, both would testify on behalf of their mother against their father.

Taking Lan Yu's divorce trial as a window, this chapter shines a light on divorce law practices inside the People's Courts. Along this line, I provide a close-up view of the power judges exert, thereby systematically shaping citizens' access to divorce. This power, it turns out, has a long and tortuous history. By connecting the dots between present and past court practices, I specify the mechanisms of power judges have employed to restrain marital dissolution. Three mechanisms stand out: turning divorce petitioners away through case withdrawal, adjudicating against divorce, and stalling marital dissolution by imposing cooling-off periods. Through these mechanisms, the court system has emerged as the vanguard of the People's Republic of China (PRC) in the twenty-first century, keenly defending the state's vision of marriage as a public institution.

Theoretically, the previous chapter and the current one converge at one point: both strive to recast the notion of disputation in terms of interconnected power relations. As the pages ahead show, Chinese judges have combined *formal decision-making power* and *agenda-setting power* to curb divorce. The former, according to Steven Lukes and John Gaventa, is readily recognizable, for it entails power-holders openly and expressly adjudicating on manifest, overt conflicts in society.[1] In divorce litigation, judges routinely evoke this power to determine whose grievances get heard, whose rights claims receive institutional support, and ultimately whose mobilization of state law prevails inside the official justice system.

The workings of formal decision-making power, however, come with certain downsides. Its operation can be time-consuming and costly. It can devour enormous judicial resources in a country with a population increasingly seeking formal remedies for marital grievances and disputes. Besides, in wielding this power, judges expose themselves to internal and external scrutiny. Dissatisfied with their rulings, wives and husbands can take court decisions to appellate courts or to other state bureaucracies, an outcome few on the bench would welcome. Unsurprisingly, over time more judges have resorted to agenda-setting power, which is distinctly different from formal decision-making power.

For one, agenda-setting power enables power-holders to mobilize a set of organizational biases—that is, formal procedures, precedents, and other legal technicalities, as well as informal rules, beliefs, and practices—to delimit the scope of formal decision-making arenas. In so doing, they turn contested issues into nonissues, thereby preempting the aggrieved from political or legal mobilization. Note that these effects are achieved not through power-holders' *substantive decision-making* but rather through *nondecision-making*. By nondecision-making, I refer to not inaction but to a set of practices that suppress and thwart the aggrieved in their pursuit of political or legal redress. In that sense, agenda-setting power operates through a mechanism qualitatively different from that of formal decision-making power.

In divorce litigation, judges have regularly exercised agenda-setting power, as evinced in their frequent attempts to pressure plaintiffs into withdrawing divorce petitions. In this way, judges foreclose those individuals' paths toward courtroom battles without handing out any substantive rulings. Compared to formal decision-making power, the operation of agenda-setting power requires much less time and resources. What's more, nondecision-making can insulate judges from institutional scrutiny. Holding court insiders responsible for their undue influences on plaintiffs' decisions to withdraw suits, in the Chinese context, proves exceedingly difficult. To put it plainly, agenda-setting power frees judges from legal and political accountability.

In sum, by mapping Lukes and Gaventa's theories of power onto the notion of disputation, this chapter advances two interrelated arguments: inside the People's Courts, so much has changed, while so much has not. Unlike their predecessors in the Maoist or the socialist eras, judges nowadays seldom apply highly oppressive or intrusive measures to intervene in citizens' intimate relationships. Instead, they mobilize formal decision-making power and agenda-setting power in the day-to-day practice of law. In terms of methodologies, techniques, and tactics deployed in divorce litigation, much has changed.

On the other hand, while many other state agencies in the reform era have progressively retreated from citizens' domestic lives, the court system has nonetheless entrenched its role in buttressing the institution of marriage. By restricting marital dissolution, judges have continuously upheld the PRC's interest in preserving the public character of marriage. Today, however firmly one might clench the belief that matrimony is a private matter between two individuals, between two families, it is anything but private as far as the Chinese state is concerned. A line of political thinking, which projects a correlative relation between the family and the state, which ties the integrity of matrimony to the cohesion of the nation, has maintained its currency among the PRC's ruling elites at the top and judges at the grassroots level.[2] That the PRC has judicialized marital and family disputes in the new century, a finding presented in the previous chapter, I must stress, should not be interpreted as a sign indicative of the regime's efforts to depoliticize marriage. Rather, over the two past decades, while the state has recalibrated its methodologies for official intervention in citizens' intimate lives, the ideological motivation behind such intervention remains largely intact. In that sense, the personal was—and continues to be—political, likewise the familial.

* * *

Back in that court hallway, I approached Lan Yu. To my surprise, she was rather up-front about her disappointment and disillusion in marriage. At the age of twenty-two Lan Yu left home and moved in with her husband's family. Over the next few years, their relationship soured. Trapped and miserable, she contemplated divorce, but ultimately decided against it. "My kids were still young, in need of care," said Lan Yu. "If I had a divorce, they would grow up in a broken family."

To salvage her marriage, Lan Yu tried everything—praying, pleading, pleasing the in-laws, pressing village cadres to mediate family disputes, and even calling the police to end physical altercations at home. When those attempts failed, she took odd jobs in nearby towns to escape a marriage that became more suffocating by the day. As the kids grew older, occasional work as a menial laborer here and there gradually turned into a lifestyle. Earning a living as a migrant worker was no longer just an escape. It was a necessity to provide enough cash for her children.

"I've lived my life for the kids. And I'll do anything—if necessary, begging on the street—to see my son through college," Lan Yu said. "That's a mother's responsibility."

While Lan Yu worked long and hard hours in a diner in Chengdu, a city about a hundred miles away from home, her husband was having an affair with another woman. He brought her home in broad daylight, humiliating his wife and children. He squandered the family's savings, including the money Lan Yu had put aside for emergencies. He forced the children to weather a harsh winter, after selling grain and poultry to his creditors...He had put his family through a lot over the years.

"I can't live in this muddy pit anymore," Lan Yu told me.

In comparing her marriage to a muddy pit, Lan Yu made up her mind to go through divorce this time. Upon filing a petition for divorce, the mother of two was resolute. She would contest every bit of her property rights to continue supporting her children. Besides, it was Lan Yu—not her husband—who had tirelessly switched back and forth between farmwork in the village and odd jobs in cities while living from hand to mouth. After the 2008 Sichuan earthquake devastated her town, Lan Yu scrambled to take out loans and subsequently renovated their damaged farmhouse. Thanks to her hard work, Lan Yu put a roof back over her family's heads, giving the kids a place they could call home again. In short, every bit of her sense of entitlement to conjugal property was grounded in years of relentless toil, meticulous planning, and painstaking saving.

Speaking of her expectations of Judge Zhao Hongfei, the judge in charge of her divorce suit, Lan Yu did not mince words. "Judges ought to follow their conscience. We country folks would put it that way."[3]

Conscience, it soon turned out, had barely any bearing on the judge's handling of Lan Yu's case.

After several hours, Lan Yu still could not locate her husband, the defendant. Around one o'clock in the afternoon, Judge Zhao could wait no more. The trial would proceed without the defendant, the judge announced.

Lan Yu's counsel, a legal worker in his fifties, read out his client's petition for divorce, in a voice as flat as a stove lid. And thus began the court investigation, the first stage in a civil trial.

"Regarding the farmhouse—" Lan Yu tried to chime in.

"Do you agree with me—or not?" the counsel interrupted Lan Yu.

"Well, you said—"

"What are your claims," Judge Zhao weighed in, "and what do you want?"

"I want. Well. I mean—" Lan Yu stuttered.

"First, do you want a divorce or not?" Before Lan Yu could answer the question, the judge interjected. "Second, what about child support?"

Lan Yu seized the opportunity and explained her son's needs for financial support for college education. But if her husband refused to shoulder this responsibility, as he had for years, Lan Yu would reconsider how to divide the couple's shared property, especially the farmhouse.

Well done, I thought as I listened to Lan Yu's testimony after having received a permission to sit in on the trial.

"Speak up. Clearly." Judge Zhao did not find Lan Yu's answer satisfying. "What precisely are your claims?"

"I want a divorce. And I—"

"Don't bring up other issues now," the counsel cut in again.

"Anyway, I want a divorce."

This time, both the judge and the counsel seemed pleased with the plaintiff's reply.

Moving the court investigation along, Judge Zhao summoned the witnesses Lan Yu brought in, her daughter and son. The two expressed unequivocal support for their mother's petition. They both stressed how their father's temper tantrums, extramarital affairs, and violent behaviors had made it impossible to maintain a normal family life.

Twice, Lan Yu meant to add additional information, while the daughter was testifying. Twice, Judge Zhao censured Lan Yu.

"Stop. Don't you put words into the witness's mouth," said the judge.

"Not really—"

"It's the witness's turn, not yours!" Judge Zhao yelled. "You'll get your turn later."

Lan Yu receded into silence, looking not so much distressed as bewildered.

A few minutes into the trial, the judge announced she would proceed to the next stage, the court debate, and the proceeding would center on the plaintiff's testimony, given the absence of the defendant. At last came the moment for Lan Yu to elaborate on her grievances and rights claims, I gathered. The remainder of the trial, apparently, did not unfold that way.

"The defendant is absent, with no evidence submitted to the court, so cross-examination is out of the question." Judge Zhao turned to Lan Yu. "Plaintiff, state your opinions for the court debate. Now, you can articulate your concerns, thoroughly."

A blank look on her face, Lan Yu had parted her lips, but did not utter a word.

The counsel, sitting next to Lan Yu, leaned forward. "You can talk now."

Relieved, Lan Yu started gathering her thoughts and words, slowly, deliberately. In her eyes, her husband was a "do-nothing," a man with a foul mouth and even fouler temper. His way of living was to "muddle along with no thought of tomorrow." His recent affairs were particularly embarrassing to the family. "The entire town has heard about these," said Lan Yu.

Judge Zhao showed little interest in Lan Yu's marital troubles. Instead, she repeatedly used tag questions in her interactions with the plaintiff. Unlike open-ended questions, which begin with *why, where, when, which, who, what,* or *how,* tag questions comprise certain statements followed by expressions, such as *isn't that true, correct,* or *didn't you.* Like leading questions, tag questions are instrumental for court insiders, especially lawyers and judges, to maintain topic control and to extract desired answers from litigants and witnesses.[4]

Here are some of the leading and tag questions Judge Zhao posed in her exchanges with Lan Yu.

"Right now, all you want is a divorce, right?"

"You no longer want child support. Isn't that true?"

"As for property partition, do you want to deal with that now? Or not?"

"During the court investigation, you mentioned the farmhouse. Do you want to make a claim on the house—or not?"

"You just answer what I ask. OK?"

"You either answer *yes* or you say *no.* Do you have other evidence?"

Lan Yu, all too often, did not respond to the judge's inquiries with a yes/no answer. Time after time, she tried to situate her claims in contingencies. For example, when asked about property division, Lan Yu stressed that her husband should receive a smaller share, if he refused to pay for their son's college tuition, a reasonable consideration from the perspective of a mother and a wife who relied on farming and temporary menial labor for a living.

"There is no such thing as 'if.' I've told you. No 'ifs' inside this court." Judge Zhao cast a quick glance at her watch. "Here, you speak with specificity."

But specificity soon proved to be a tall order. To address the judge's queries about the couple's joint debts, Lan Yu tried to be as specific as possible. She recounted how her family had come to owe thirty thousand yuan in the aftermath of the 2008 Sichuan earthquake. As one of the most devastating disasters in modern Chinese history, that earthquake killed over eighty-seven thousand, left five million homeless, and razed countless buildings in southwest China.[5] Lan Yu's family was among the hundreds of thousands severely affected by the disaster.

Those details did not interest the judge. Minutes into Lan Yu's testimony, Judge Zhao lost her patience. She turned to the court clerk and said, "Just jot down whatever the plaintiff says." After that, she busied herself staring blankly at the floor. Around one thirty in the afternoon, the trial had been completed, the judge declared.[6]

Sitting in the audience seat, I had watched the trial from start to finish. During a court proceeding that lasted about thirty minutes, I caught nearly two dozen interruptions, repeated use of leading and tag questions, and sporadic censure of the plaintiff by the judge. These rhetorical practices effectively reduced the trial into a ritual of formality, the kind judges need to project a façade of procedural integrity. Lan Yu, on the other hand, muddled her way through the trial, only to have her accounts of marital grievances truncated, complaints of spousal abuse omitted, and claims on property and child support dismissed. In the end, her courtroom experience could not have been further from the fair trial the law promised, one that renders justice by "treating facts as the basis" (以事实为依据) and "legal rules as the yardstick of judging" (以法律为准绳).[7]

Turn away petitioners via case withdrawal

Immediately after the trial, Judge Zhao approached Lan Yu's counsel. "The plaintiff brought up issues of debts and property division, but didn't provide evidence. What am I supposed to do?" the judge grumbled, letting out an exaggerated sigh. "So why don't you tell your client to withdraw her case?"

Throughout my field research in Weifeng County, I saw more than a few occasions in which judges urged plaintiffs to withdraw their divorce petitions. Some of those attempts occurred during judges' informal

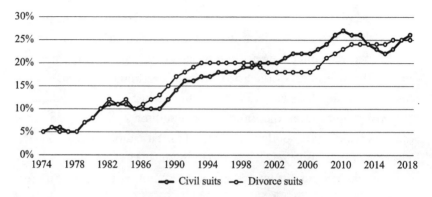

FIGURE 5.1 Percentage of first-instance civil and divorce suits that landed in withdrawal in China, 1974–2018

SOURCES: *China Civil Affairs' Statistical Yearbook* (2018–2019); *China Statistical Yearbook* (2018–2019); *Historical Statistical Books of the People's Courts, 1949–2016 (The First Volume on Civil Litigation, 1950–2004)* and *(The Second Volume on Civil Litigation, 2005–2016).*

meetings with plaintiffs, and others were blended into court-organized mediation sessions. Requests for case withdrawal also surfaced right before or after formal trials. In short, court personnel could raise the issue of withdrawal at almost any stage in litigation.

Indeed, making plaintiffs drop their complaints and rights claims altogether and concluding their cases through a procedure called *withdrawal* (撤诉) have long been an integral part of Chinese judges' toolbox in handling civil litigation. Figure 5.1 illustrates the extent to which this procedure has been entrenched in the People's Courts. From the mid-1970s onward, judges nationwide have increasingly relied on withdrawal to dispose of civil cases in general and divorce suits in particular. The proportion of divorce cases that landed in withdrawal jumped from 5 to 25 percent between 1974 and 2018.

How did the court system arrive at the current levels of withdrawal? To answer the question, we must turn the clock back to 1956, seven years after the Chinese Communist Party (CCP) took over the reins of the country. Back then judges were still waiting for lawmakers to promulgate the procedural rules necessary for civil litigation. Concerned about legal ambiguity, the Supreme People's Court (SPC) in 1956 took up the challenge by compiling a provisional guideline on civil procedures. This guideline advised that if two disputing parties reconciled, or if a plaintiff decided to forgo all complaints, a court could write off that case.[8] But how were judges to classify or document this litigation outcome? The guideline offered no clarification. This ambiguity remained unaddressed for the next two decades.

The year 1974, as the Cultural Revolution was dying down, marked the beginning of the court system's concerted efforts to document case withdrawal in courts at all levels. Five years later, withdrawal as a mechanism to terminate civil suits was included into a provisional SPC regulation on civil procedures.[9] When the first Civil Procedural Law was passed, in 1982, withdrawal was formally recognized as a key mode of case disposition, a tradition honored by subsequent legislators, court administrators, and judges.[10]

For divorce petitioners, the consequences of withdrawal are real and significant. Once a petition is dropped, a plaintiff must wait for at least six months to file the next suit.[11] Meanwhile, challenging a judge's approval for withdrawal on the grounds of coercion, deception, or other improper judicial conduct proves to be a herculean task, if not a simply impossible one. The 1982 Civil Procedural Law provided few remedies for petitioners who deemed their entry into case withdrawal involuntary or erroneous. The law was amended four times over subsequent decades, yet legislators have consistently denied those petitioners the rights to request a retrial at courts of first instance.[12] Similarly, they have persistently refused to grant petitioners the option to seek an appeal to higher courts.[13] Approaching an appellate court for a retrial seems the only redress available under the existing law. The problem with this option, though, is that petitioners must prove errors in the initial court approval for withdrawal.[14] What might constitute such an error? Neither the top legislature nor the SPC has spelled that out. Suffice to say that once a divorce suit passes the stage of withdrawal, there is no turning back.

As far as judges are concerned, however, withdrawal constitutes one of the optimal litigation outcomes. First, it allows judges to conclude a divorce case without handing down any rulings on substantive issues, such as marital dissolution, property partition, or child custody, thereby saving judicial resources and time. Furthermore, court approval for withdrawal is categorically exempt from retrials conducted by courts of first instance and from appeals handled by higher courts. Judges are thus free from worries about internal and external scrutiny. Civil suits concluded by means of adjudication, by contrast, can be subject to retrial and appeal. In other words, whenever judges adjudicate, they risk having their decision-making scrutinized, challenged, or even reversed. Withdrawal, by contrast, enables court insiders to insulate themselves from legal responsibilities resulting from incorrect rulings.

Over the years, the SPC has steadily relaxed disciplinary sanctions against judges for misuse or abuse of withdrawal, thereby making it even harder to hold institutional insiders accountable for misconduct. Back in 1998, judges who forced petitioners into withdrawal by means of duress (胁迫) or cajolement (诱使) could face a number of negative consequences, ranging from a warning to a severe notation in their personnel files.[15] Three years later, the highest court in the land reiterated its stance: "Judges shall not go against litigants' will in applying undue influences to induce case withdrawal or settlements."[16]

A subtle shift occurred around 2009. This time, the SPC reworded the kind of judicial conduct susceptible to disciplinary sanctions. It stipulated, "To advance personal interests (因徇私), judges, who violate litigants' will by pressuring them into withdrawal or settlements, shall be sanctioned."[17] By adding intent— "advancing personal interests"—to the definition of sanctionable conduct inside courtrooms, the SPC narrowed the ambit of its enforcement of ethical rules. In 2010, when the SPC revised the Basic Rules on the Professional Ethics of Judges, a preexisting provision against court personnel's misuse of withdrawal was erased altogether.[18]

The notable change in the SPC's stance on withdrawal, I must point out, took place in tandem with the rise of the notion of harmonious socialist society (社会主义和谐社会), a rhetoric party leadership began promoting after the CCP's Fourth Plenary Session of the Seventeenth Central Committee in 2004. Embodied in that rhetoric was the party leadership's evolving vision of a society in its making. The *People's Daily* spelled out what that society should look like: inside this society, "there would be rapport among people, between individuals and society, and

between humans and nature." What's more, "democracy and legality…
along with stability and order" would be the hallmarks of the so-called
harmonious socialist society.[19]

This official discourse of social harmony made deep inroads into the
court system in short order. Xiao Yang, the then SPC president, extolled
the notion of judicial harmony (司法和谐), a spin-off from the party line,
at the Seventh National Civil Trial Work Conference in 2007. Judicial
work at all levels must be geared toward building a "harmonious legal
order," Xiao declared, thus setting the tone for various policy initiatives
in the decade to follow.[20] Against this backdrop, how effectively judges
could steer citizens away from litigation became a brand-new metric by
which to evaluate the performance of those on the bench. Many would
soon find themselves wrestling with a measure called *rates of withdrawal*
(撤诉率).

About a year after Xiao Yang's speech on judicial harmony, the SPC
stitched together a provisional guideline, ushering in a number of criteria
intended to appraise the fairness, efficiency, and social impact of judging
in lower courts. In 2011, this guideline was formalized as the Case Quality
Assessment System (案件质量评估体系).[21] Under this system, rates of withdrawal became one of the key parameters for the highest court to gauge
judicial decision-making in lower courts. Before long, judges everywhere
found themselves racing to ratchet up their rates of withdrawal. Presidents
of lower courts likewise dove into fierce competitions to improve "case
quality" in hopes of outperforming other jurisdictions.[22]

Not long ago, judges in Weifeng County did not bother to calculate
rates of withdrawal, a term nowhere to be found in the court annals (人
民法院志), spanning from 1941 to 1999. This term was similarly absent
in the annual work reports prepared by the county-level, Basic People's
Court, during the early years of the new millennium. By 2009, the president of the Basic People's Court could not sit still anymore. In the work
report he submitted to the local People's Congress, the president boasted
a "new" achievement: about 58 percent of the civil and economic cases in
his jurisdiction were disposed of through either withdrawal or mediation.
Seen in this light, what Judge Zhao did—rushing through Lan Yu's divorce
trial in an attempt to secure a withdrawal later—is neither idiosyncratic

nor coincidental. Rather, it is a sensible adaptation to organizational demands stemming from a particular institutional environment.

As for Lan Yu, she had no reason to drop her divorce petition. To cover expenses for legal mobilization, she had worked for months as a kitchen helper at a diner in Chengdu. To attend to court proceedings, she took unpaid leave from work several times, commuting back and forth between her workplace in the city and the tribunal in the countryside. To replace a missing marriage certificate, a piece of paper necessary for a divorce petition, she badgered village cadres until they issued a written statement verifying her marital status. To rally her children behind the suit, she dragged herself through heart-wrenching conversations, the kind most mothers dread. All those efforts would have been in vain if Lan Yu simply quit her lawsuit.

When it became clear that Lan Yu would not "cooperate" and that no withdrawal could be secured, Judge Zhao lost no time ruling on the case. Rather than urging Lan Yu to submit proper evidence or retrying her case, the judge turned down her divorce petition, along with all other rights claims.

What happened to Lan Yu begs several important questions. In four decades, withdrawal has quintupled in court disposition of divorce suits. Between 2016 and 2018, it hit a record high, with one in four cases dropping out of the litigation process through withdrawal. Among those cases, how many were withdrawn voluntarily by plaintiffs? How many involved arm-twisting by mendacious, manipulative judges eager to outplay their peers in a fierce competition for "case quality"? Finally, what happened to plaintiffs who refused to withdraw their suits? In practice, the judge who requests withdrawal is usually the one who adjudicates the case at hand. So an "uncooperative" plaintiff like Lan Yu would face the same judge in subsequent court proceedings. In the end, what price would the plaintiff pay for her or his uncooperativeness? We can only conjecture the answers since official statistics offer few clues to these questions.

That said, it is conceivable that judges have been legally, organizationally, and politically incentivized to use—and, very likely, overuse and even abuse—withdrawal in divorce litigation and beyond. Legally speaking, judges concluding divorce suits by means of withdrawal face no risk of having their rulings reversed, for plaintiffs have no rights to challenge such decisions. Organizationally speaking, judges nowadays have little reason to fear disciplinary sanctions against their use of coercion, deception, or manipulation in inducing withdrawal. Finally, those on the bench have, over the past decade, seen up close how the CCP's rhetoric of a harmonious socialist society has translated into a series of penetrating policy initiatives with profound implications for day-to-day judicial activities. A striking case in point is the so-named Case Quality Assessment System, which awards judges for promoting withdrawal and penalizes those who fail to do so. In short, judges have a lot to gain and little to lose in their use of withdrawal in the everyday practice of law.

WHO DESERVES DIVORCE VERSUS WHO GETS DIVORCE

Legal grounds for divorce

Three days after Lan Yu's divorce trial, I visited her in her village. She and I had a candid talk about her courtroom experience. Asked about the judge's decision to turn down her petition, Lan Yu felt at sea. "I explained everything to the judge. So did my kids. But she still insisted that I was not qualified for a divorce," Lan Yu muttered, brow furrowed. "I just don't get it."[23]

Lan Yu's bewilderment at the court decision raises another set of questions. According to the law, whose request for divorce shall be approved? In reality, who obtains divorce inside the People's Courts, and who does not? And why?[24]

Since the founding of the PRC, legislators have continued to refine the answers to the first question. In 1950, when the Marriage Law was promulgated, legislators left out substantive criteria for the adjudication of divorce suits. Instead, the law included only a set of procedural requirements. More specifically, the 1950 Marriage Law stipulated that a divorce could be granted, if both husband and wife wanted it; that in the event of only one party insisting on marital dissolution—also known as an ex parte divorce—mediation must precede any court rulings; and that a divorce could be granted only after mediation failed to bring about reconciliation.[25]

Meanwhile, the country's highest court began experimenting with various substantive criteria in judging divorce. One criterion in particular caught on: the breakdown of mutual affection (感情破裂). The SPC, in dealing with divorce cases concerning soldiers, ethnic minority groups, and foreigners, explicitly encouraged or implicitly sanctioned judges to use mutual feelings between husband and wife (or the lack thereof) as a rule of thumb to determine the fate of a marriage.[26] After a decade of trial and error, judges at the First National Civil Trial Work Conference, in 1963, floated an idea: a formula could be applied in divorce law practices. This formula, known as three examinations and one consideration (三看一参), required judges to examine the foundation of marriage (婚姻基础), to assess a couple's feelings toward each other during marriage (婚后感情), to check the alleged grounds for divorce (离婚原因), and, finally, to factor in the interests of children involved and the potential impact of court rulings on society. In the same year, the SPC formally endorsed the formula by writing it into an official document on civil litigation.[27] From then on, three examinations and one consideration has served as a guiding principle for divorce litigation at times when the letter of the Marriage Law was vague and the legislative spirit behind it volatile. Languages like "foundation of a marriage" and "mutual feelings during marriage" can still be spotted in court decisions to this day, evincing the formula's enduring influence on generations of judges.

Three decades after the passage of the first Marriage Law, the breakdown of mutual affection was inscribed into the law in 1980. In amending the Marriage Law, legislators expressly identified the breakdown of mutual affection in marriage as the sole ground for ex parte divorce. This legislative move reaffirmed the legality of no-fault divorce in China, after a great many couples had obtained divorces inside courtrooms without showing wrongdoings by either party in the marriage.[28] The revised law did not address the question of what circumstances could be viewed as complete collapse of mutual affection, however.

It took the SPC another nine years to clarify the matter. In 1989, it issued a judicial interpretation, marking several circumstances judges could rely on to determine the emotional state of a marriage. These circumstances ranged from a spouse's mental illness to adultery, from vicious habits, such as gambling and drug abuse, to a separation of three or more years due to conjugal discord.[29] This attempt to specify the law on the books signaled a breakthrough: it laid out concrete grounds for divorce and formally introduced the notion of fault (过错) into the PRC's marital regulations. Engaging in adultery or cohabiting with another person, from the SPC's point of view, would render a spouse at fault and thus legally divorceable; in the meantime, the other spouse would become the innocent party in the troubled relationship.[30] By explicitly distinguishing between a spouse at fault (过错方) and another who is not (无过错方), the 1989 judicial interpretation paved the way for subsequent legislators to codify fault-based divorce.

The 2001 amendment of the Marriage Law added more flesh to the bones of the legal rules regarding divorce. Legislators, this time, elaborated the specific grounds for ex parte divorce. Bigamy, cohabitation with another person, domestic violence, spousal abandonment, and vicious habits like gambling and drug use were codified as legitimate justifications for marital dissolution. Moreover, the amended law further specified the notion of fault in the context of divorce by erecting legal rules intended to penalize blameworthy marital conduct—domestic violence, spousal abandonment, and adultery being the primary examples. In this manner, legislators sought to protect the more vulnerable party in the marriage.[31]

After decades of lawmaking and law-applying, a hybrid system has been firmly instituted in Chinese courts. Today, this system recognizes both no-fault divorce and fault-based petition for marital dissolution. The former allows women and men to terminate their marriages on the grounds of the breakdown of mutual affection, and the latter enables them to seek a divorce, as well as financial compensation for specific damages caused by the spouse at fault.[32] Judging by the PRC's black-letter laws, the following groups deserve divorce: women and men whose significant others have agreed upon marital dissolution; individuals capable of proving mutual affection no longer exists in their marriages; and those who have suffered from certain wrongdoings at the hands of a spouse, with corroborating evidence to support their claims of victimization.

Rein in marital dissolution by means of adjudication

While the law on the books establishes formal rules and norms, the question of who gets to divorce inside courtrooms, far too often, hinges on the political calculus of judges. Divorce law practices, from the beginning of the PRC, have been enmeshed with the CCP party leadership's nation-state-building agendas—mobilizing popular support for the nascent regime, firming up grassroots state bureaucracies, creating new socialist citizenry, advancing gender equality, and promoting women's rights, to name but a few examples.[33] Needless to say, all political agendas are not created equal. As the party leadership keeps redefining its top priorities at various historical moments, the court system has grappled with its evolving roles in buttressing authoritarian legality.

Judges, accordingly, have adjusted and readjusted their positions in relation to the institution of marriage. And their approach in divorce law practices has shifted from emboldening women to break free from the feudal family system in the early years of the PRC, to forcefully restricting marital dissolution between the late 1950s and the 1980s, to employing subtle measures to defend the stature of marriage as a bedrock social institution, a trend increasingly salient since the turn of the new century. Figure 5.2 illustrates the trajectory the court system has taken in modifying its approach to divorce litigation over nearly seven decades.

At the core of the figure are two measures: the number of divorce petitions accepted by the courts of first instance nationwide and the percentage of the petitions resulting in court approval for marital dissolution (hereinafter *divorce approval rate*). The first spike in divorce petitions in the history of the PRC appeared in the early 1950s. To rid the populace of the feudal family system, the nascent PRC promulgated the Marriage Law in 1950, vowing to promote the freedom of marriage and divorce, advance gender equality, and protect the rights of women and children (see chapter 3 for a review of the marriage reform of the early 1950s). Scholarship on this period, however, remains divided about the reach and the limitations of the CCP's implementation of the law. Studies conducted by a group of feminist scholars in the 1980s painted a bleak picture. A

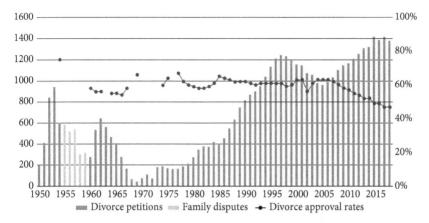

FIGURE 5.2 Number of divorce petitions (in thousands) and divorce approval rates in China, 1950–2018

SOURCES: *China Civil Affairs' Statistical Yearbook* (2018–2019); *China Statistical Yearbook* (2018–2019); *Collection of Archival Records on Judicial Statistics of the People's Courts, 1949–1998 (Civil Litigation); Historical Statistical Books of the People's Courts, 1949–2016 (The First Volume on Civil Litigation, 1950–2004) and (The Second Volume on Civil Litigation, 2005–2016).*

NOTES:

1. Between 1955 and 1959, the SPC did not use *divorce* as a stand-alone category in record-keeping. Rather, divorce was subsumed under a broader category called *family disputes*.

2. To calculate divorce approval rates, I use the number of divorces granted by courts annually as the numerator and the total number of accepted petitions as the denominator.

few years into the campaigns, party leadership retreated from the reform, scaled back its support for women's pursuit of divorce, and eventually left the patriarchal family by and large intact. Empowering women soon gave way to containing the risks of alienating men, especially those in the countryside, where the CCP faced greater resistance to the official ideology of gender equality and tougher challenges for regime consolidation. Once the high tide of Marriage Law campaigns passed in 1953, divorce became increasingly difficult. The marriage reform delayed, and, in effect, failed women's liberation, those feminist scholars concluded.[34]

More recent studies of this period, on the other hand, place a greater emphasis on women's agency in mobilizing the new law and in seeking out official backing for divorce. In reassessing the effectiveness of the 1950 Marriage Law, subsequent scholars contend that women—especially peasants and members of the urban working class—took advantage of the rights enshrined in the law to divorce in considerable numbers, a trend that continued in some regions through the early 1960s.[35]

Thanks to the archival records released by the SPC in 2000, we now have more detailed information about the extent to which the court system was committed to delivering on the promises of the 1950 Marriage Law. Table 5.1 shows some specifics. Soon after the passage of the law, divorce petitions peaked in 1952 and 1953. This upward trend, however,

TABLE 5.1 The court system's handling of first-instance divorce suits in China, 1950–1970

Year	Category	Cases Accepted	Petition Approved	Petition Rejected
1950	divorce	197,060		
1951	divorce	409,500		
1952	divorce	837,900		
1953	divorce	940,369		
1954	divorce	597,993	447,234	164,182
1955	family dispute	579,366	391,309	140,346
1956	family dispute	515,653	288,071	96,042
1957	family dispute	536,841	261,058	112,970
1958	family dispute	305,225	179,385	68,566
1959	family dispute	319,859	173,169	81,031
1960	divorce	275,144	159,098	61,758
1961	divorce	535,710	300,840	100,850
1962	divorce	641,949	360,725	146,433
1963	divorce	560,286		
1964	divorce	462,388	255,347	126,070
1965	divorce	407,407	224,893	121,635
1966	divorce	275,619	149,979	79,584
1967	divorce	165,793	96,712	40,445
1968	divorce	66,305		
1969	divorce	42,736	28,030	9,638
1970	divorce	73,582		

SOURCES: *Collection of Archival Records on Judicial Statistics of the People's Courts, 1949–1998 (Civil Litigation); Historical Statistical Books of the People's Courts, 1949–2016 (The First Volume on Civil Litigation, 1950-2004).*

did not persist, and the number of divorces went down in subsequent years. Starting in 1955, divorce was no longer listed as a stand-alone category in court record-keeping but was subsumed under a broader category called *family disputes* (婚姻家庭纠纷), a practice that was reversed in 1960. Notwithstanding the temporary change in the classification of civil suits, a pattern remains clear: from 1954 onward, the court system accepted far fewer cases related to family disputes and therefore far fewer petitions for divorce. This downward trend lasted through most of the 1960s.

As the country slid into the Cultural Revolution (1966–1976), a decade-long political turmoil ensued. "Smashing the police, the procuratorate, and the judiciary" (砸烂公检法) sprang up as a new slogan for mass frenzied campaigns aimed to rid Chinese society and officialdom of lingering bourgeois influences. Courts everywhere, from the grassroots level all the way to the top, were exposed to ideological, rhetorical, and even physical assaults organized by Red Guards, groups of radicalized and often militarized young people who swore to defend socialism against political enemies at home and abroad.[36] Judges, during this period, frequently resorted to moral criticism, ideological suasion, official pressures, and even coercion to dissuade litigants from seeking marital dissolution.[37] Divorces were rare throughout the 1960s and 1970s, and generally granted on political grounds, such as when individuals sought to distance themselves from spouses accused of being enemies of the revolution.

Deng Xiaoping's rise to the pinnacle of state power in 1977, followed by the CCP's Third Plenary Session of the Eleventh Central Committee the next year, marked the end of Maoist China (1949–1976) and the start of the reform era. Against this backdrop, the Marriage Law was amended in 1980 and expanded popular access to divorce in two distinct ways. The standard, the breakdown of mutual affection, was codified as the legitimate, adequate grounds for divorce. Thereafter, politically motivated divorces, such as those severing ties with a spouse deemed antirevolutionary, ceased to dominate court dockets. Furthermore, procedural requirements for divorce litigation were somewhat relaxed. Whereas the 1950 Marriage Law demanded couples undertake mediation organized by local governments before court rulings over ex parte divorces, the amended law dropped this requirement, thereby guaranteeing citizens the rights to bypass local governments and petition for divorce directly.

The 1980 revision of the Marriage Law, together with other socio-economic and cultural changes in Chinese society, soon translated into a steady growth in popular demand for divorce. Between 1980 and 1999, the number of divorce petitions processed by the courts quadrupled, and divorce approval rates hovered around 60 percent (see figure 5.2). These developments point to the state's step-by-step retreat from citizens' intimate lives. In 2001, when the Marriage Law was revised again, legislators came to redefine matrimony as "a voluntary contractual relationship grounded in individual emotional satisfaction."[38]

At first glance, it seems that, on the cusp of the new century, marriage and divorce were finally on the way to becoming private matters between two individuals, between two families. One might expect that the court system would uphold this new vision endorsed by legislators. Figure 5.3, however, suggests otherwise, attesting to the complex roles of judges in divorce litigation.

Note that, in theory, a first-instance divorce suit can lead to one of the following outcomes: (1) withdrawal; (2) adjudication against divorce (判决不离婚); (3) adjudication for divorce (判决离婚); (4) divorce settlement reached through court-organized mediation (调解离婚); (5) reconciliation between husband and wife (调解不离婚); and (6) other results (e.g., petitions rejected on procedural grounds or transferred to other jurisdictions). In the interest of brevity, I create a category, *petitions approved*, by combining (3) and (4). Doing so allows figure 5.3 to easily capture the proportion of divorce suits that results in court approval for marital dissolution. As for the other category in the figure, *petitions rejected*, it is the equivalent of (2).

Two parallel developments have been unfolding inside the People's Courts during the reform era. On the one hand, courts across the country have opened their doors to more divorce petitions (see figure 5.2). On the other hand, judges have become increasingly restrictive in sanctioning marital dissolution, which is evinced in two measures: from the late 1970s onward, the percentage of rejected petitions has grown steadily,

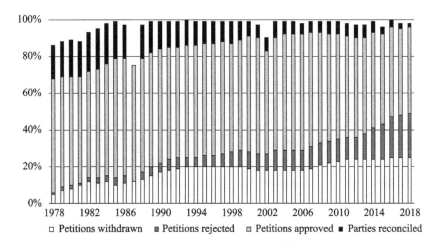

FIGURE 5.3 Outcomes of first-instance divorce suits in China, 1978–2018

SOURCES: *China Civil Affairs' Statistical Yearbook* (2018–2019); *China Statistical Yearbook* (2018–2019); *Historical Statistical Books of the People's Courts, 1949–2016 (The First Volume on Civil Litigation, 1950–2004)* and *(The Second Volume on Civil Litigation, 2005–2016)*.

NOTES:

1. Certain data are missing for 1987.
2. Data for 2002 should be taken with a grain of salt in view of certain inconsistencies between *China Civil Affairs' Statistical Yearbook* and *China Statistical Yearbook*. Such inconsistencies indicate potential errors in the courts' record-keeping. Unfortunately, only the former source contains a detailed breakdown of litigation outcomes; therefore, I have to rely entirely on it to generate this figure.
3. This figure does not include divorce petitions rejected on procedural grounds or those transferred to other jurisdictions. That is why the total for each year does not add up to 100 percent.

whereas the proportion of approved petitions has continued to shrink (see figure 5.3). In 2018, the divorce approval rate dropped to a record low, 47 percent. For the first time in the reform era, divorce approval rates were below 50 percent for four consecutive years.

Together, these two parallel developments speak to the complex roles the court system has assumed in upholding individual rights to divorce on one side and in mounting a public defense for the institution of marriage on the other. While other state bureaucracies have gradually retreated from citizens' intimate relationships in the past two decades, the court system has embarked on a different course. Rather than downscaling public oversight of marital dissolution, it has scaled up its scrutiny of women's and men's domestic lives by consistently holding back divorce in millions of cases. To be precise, about 3.71 million first-instance divorce petitions have been thrown out by judges since the start of the reform era.

The sharp decline of divorce approval rates in recent years, together with the SPC's latest attempts to reform *family trials* (家事审判)—a phrase few had heard of prior to 2016—testifies to a crucial continuity. The court system, from the top to the very bottom, has continued to tie the soundness of individual marriages to the integrity of a modern nation-state, a political vision that has animated much marital lawmaking and policymaking in twentieth-century China. To ensure that this vision would come through, the SPC in the latest reform of family trials solemnly declared, "Resolving family disputes is not just a matter concerning the happiness of individuals and households; indeed, it is tied to the stability and harmony of a society and the advancement of a civilization."[39]

Make no mistake. This is not to suggest that, in curbing marital dissolution, the courts nowadays have relapsed into the tradition of Maoist justice, a style of civil justice that can be traced back to the CCP's marriage reforms in its revolutionary bases in the 1930s and 1940s. Judicial practices associated with the Maoist tradition—such as conducting on-site investigations of marital grievances, mobilizing the masses (relatives, neighbors, coworkers, employers, and community leaders) to settle family disputes, imposing ideological and moral judgments on the disgruntled, and marshaling official pressure to effect reconciliation—are largely absent in present-day divorce law practices.[40] As the following pages illustrate, judges today often apply much subtler, less intrusive measures to limit popular access to divorce than did their predecessors in the Maoist and socialist eras.

DIVORCE LAW PRACTICES ON THE FRONTIERS
Judge Lin's dilemma

Wrestling with divorce suits was a big part of Lin Wenxian's daily routines as a judge. His workplace, also known as the Dingyi People's Tribunal, was among the thousands of People's Tribunals (人民法庭) that form the frontiers of the official justice system. Over a decade or so, the locals brought a great number of divorce cases into Judge Lin's courtroom, too many to remember them all. But Judge Lin specifically recalled a defendant nicknamed "the one-eyed man."

The defendant, a fortysomething husband being sued for divorce, used to make a living as a carpenter. Poor but decent, he was content with his family life, which he shared with a wife, hardworking and kind. A sudden workplace accident plunged the family into unexpected predicaments. After losing part of his vision in the accident, the carpenter became chronically underemployed. The eye injury he had suffered probably caused brain damage as well, prompting erratic behavior at home and in public; neighbors speculated that behind closed doors.

Within a few years, the former carpenter turned into a good-for-nothing—and by some accounts, a petty thief and a nasty bully who frequently took out anger on his wife. With his livelihood being undercut, reputation in tatters, friends estranged, the once happy family man found himself stuck in utter despair. His wife and two kids were the only people he had by his side, the only part of the day-to-day life that he could lean on for a sense of normalcy. But after yet another outburst, yet another beating, the wife finally had enough. Before long, she ran to the tribunal in town and filed a petition for divorce, an act that infuriated her husband. "I'll chop her entire [natal] family into pieces," he ranted.

Upon learning of the defendant's threats of violence, Judge Lin reached out to his village. Perhaps someone could talk sense into the enraged husband. That attempt fell flat in no time. Villagers shunned the one-eyed man as if he carried leprosy. Even the local police in charge of community safety had grown weary of cleaning up the messes that attended his petty offenses. It was abundantly clear to Judge Lin that he was left to his own devices to deal with an agitated, potentially violent defendant.

To mediate the couple's conjugal conflicts, Judge Lin summoned the two parties to his office. The one-eyed man wasted little time turning the mediation into a godsend to extract cash from his wife. His demand was straightforward. With a onetime payment of fifty thousand yuan from his wife—a "breakup compensation," he called it—he would immediately sign divorce paperwork. This amount was almost ten times as much as anyone in the village could earn in a good farming year. The wife, a migrant worker with a menial job in a nearby town, could never afford such a divorce settlement, Judge Lin reckoned. Be that as it may, the judge soldiered on, pleading, reasoning, persuading in hopes of finding a middle ground, a compromise, between the estranged couple.

As the mediation session dragged on, the one-eyed man grew visibly upset. At one point, he just could not hold back his vexation anymore. Suddenly, he grabbed a cell phone from his wife's palm, smashed it in front of the judge, and then went completely silent for a minute or so. Just as everyone in the room waited, hoping he would rejoin the conversation, the one-eyed man pulled out another cell phone and threw it forcefully onto the floor, shouting, "I broke your phone! Now, I'm slamming mine!"

Flabbergasted, Judge Lin called an end to the mediation. "You can't reason with someone like this," said the judge.

On the day the divorce trial was scheduled, the Dingyi People's Tribunal made a special arrangement. The tribunal, which kept no regular security guards of its own, borrowed two bailiffs from the county-level Basic People's Court to maintain order at the trial. The enhanced security measures, apparently, did not stop the one-eyed man from ruining the court proceeding. Minutes into the trial, he jumped up from his seat, dashed across the courtroom, grabbed his wife by her hair, and yanked her head back with full force to keep her from testifying against him before the judge.

The trial, in no time, descended into a hand-to-hand melee. And no one was spared. The defendant was busy with a physical attack against the plaintiff; the court personnel were in shock, with no clue as to how to restore order. It eventually took the two bailiffs, Judge Lin, and a clerk to tackle the one-eyed man, holding him to the ground. Only then could the wife sneak out of the courtroom. Concerned for her safety, Judge Lin ruled against the wife's petition. A court decision that might have led to bloodshed had been avoided, the judge gathered.

Six months passed. The wife came back, again asking the tribunal for a divorce. This time, she was resolute, giving no indication of any potential concession on her part. The one-eyed man was equally unyielding. He would not go anywhere without that breakup compensation, he insisted. When this demand could not be satisfied, he began stalking and harassing the judge. "He followed me everywhere," "he called me repeatedly, even at night," and "he sounded as though he would take my life, if I didn't handle his case 'properly,'" Judge Lin remembered.

Alarmed and frightened, the judge started varying his commute between home and work. He also tweaked his work schedule to make his whereabouts less predictable. That his tribunal was housed in the same building as the township police station—it would take a minute or so to walk from his office to the police chief's—did not give Judge Lin any peace of mind. To find out if the judge was indeed at risk, I talked to other court personnel and police officers stationed in Dingyi. Evidently, Judge Lin was not overreacting. Nor did he overstate the danger posed by an unstable defendant.

The court system in Weifeng had long been underfunded and understaffed. While court financing had notably improved over the preceding decade, the county's six dispatched tribunals continued to struggle with personnel shortages. Most of them were staffed with only one or two judges, together with one court clerk. In the absence of bailiffs, court staff could be easily outnumbered by litigants and their family members. Fending off insults, threats, and potential violence on the part of litigants was an integral part of the job for those sitting on the bench, for as long as they could remember. Meanwhile, police protection remained a luxury for judges. A party cadre, who had served on the Political Legal Committee (政法委员会) of Weifeng for more than two decades, revealed some numbers during an interview: across the county, about 270 police officers were on duty around the time when the one-eyed man was harassing Judge Lin; meanwhile, the county had a population of nearly half a million. To state the obvious: in dealing with angry and potentially violent litigants, judges simply could not count on police protection.

In the end, the one-eyed man had his demand partially satisfied. The Dingyi People's Tribunal ruled in favor of his claim for a breakup compensation, albeit in a smaller amount, five thousand yuan. As for the wife, she got her divorce. To have the one-eyed man agree to this settlement, Judge Lin talked the wife into signing away her rights to marital property. In a closed-door conversation, but not in public, the judge admitted his reservations: there should never be a trade-off between a wife's rights to divorce and her entitlements to marital property. But compromising her property rights in exchange for the husband's concession seemed the only plausible solution. "After all, judges must protect themselves," as one court clerk put it.[41]

Stall divorce by imposing cooling-off periods

Inside China's grassroots court system, Judge Lin is hardly an exception in his daily struggles with divorce cases. Many on the bench have witnessed popular demand for official justice rapidly outpacing what the court system can manage. The imbalance between the supply of and the demand for justice is particularly pronounced in rural areas. In a place like Dingyi, for example, residents have found their domestic lives increasingly volatile year after year, yet their access to the courts has remained curtailed.

This imbalance, on its face, is largely an unfortunate byproduct of the sociodemographic changes of the past four decades in Chinese society. As noted in chapter 2, the bulk of the reform era has seen massive population movements. By the end of 2018, over 288 million rural residents have migrated to cities and towns in search of cash-paying jobs. And approximately 95 million women have left the countryside to toil in the urban workforce. The combination of their newfound geographic mobility, economic independence, and greater awareness of rights as wives, mothers, and property owners has destabilized rural households. When new desires and yearning for respect cannot be satisfied within marriage, women on the move may turn to other forms of intimacy, as indicated earlier in this book. Leaving one's husband for another man and seeking a life with more financial security, emotional satisfaction, and human dignity has become ever-more possible at a time marked by unprecedented internal migration in China.

Rural men, in the meantime, have cultivated various coping strategies in the face of shifting gender roles and relationships in the family. Some are more capable of adapting than others.[42] The one-eyed man is among those less adaptable or optimistic about their future. After all, out of China's population of 1.4 billion, there are approximately 34 million more males than females, a demographic nightmare stemming from a fusion of the state-enforced one-child policy and ingrained cultural preference for sons over daughters.[43] Anxieties over the chance of finding a wife (or a second one after a divorce) are felt palpably in Chinese society, and even more so in the countryside. Dingyi, for example, has seen the shortage of brides further exacerbated by women's prolonged participation in labor out-migration since the early 2000s. Rumor has it that some families got so desperate that they paid off human traffickers to locate daughters-in-law for their unmarried sons. In fact, I ran into a few poor peasant men complaining to judges or government officials about fraudulent sales of women as brides. After making handsome payments, these men soon saw their brides evaporate, along with the bride price. In this context, estranged husbands, caught up in divorce suits, often turn into outraged defendants, taking out their conjugal frustrations on judges.

At a deeper level, the difficulties judges face in divorce litigation point to an entrenched, structural problem. Decades of state-sponsored, top-down court reforms have yet to close the gap between the urban and rural populations' access to official justice. Following the CCP's Third Plenary Session of the Eleventh Central Committee in 1978, which set in motion the plan to build a socialist rule of law, the SPC has championed numerous reform measures.[44] Many have been directed to restore and revitalize the People's Tribunals—a key component of the Basic People's Courts that constitute the lowest rung of the country's four-tiered judiciary.[45] Consolidating this component is of paramount importance, if the administration of justice is to be enhanced at the grassroots level. Symbolically and ideologically, the People's Tribunals embody the CCP's long tradition of sending judges to remote areas where the presence of state law was limited.[46] Today, thousands of these tribunals continue to operate as dispatched offices of the Basic People's Courts, serving communities scattered in agrarian, forested, and mountainous regions and expanding the reach of state law on the frontiers. The political and practical significance of these tribunals cannot be overstated. That said, ongoing court reforms have yet to address some of the most intractable problems.

Figure 5.4 offers a rare glimpse into the SPC's sporadic attempts at improving the working conditions in the People's Tribunals. It shows the number of times the highest court referred to the *People's Tribunals* in annual work reports, spanning from 1980 to 2018. Four peaks stand out, 1988–1989, 1991–1993, 1999–2000, and 2005–2007, each indicating a

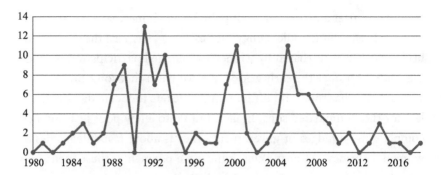

FIGURE 5.4 Number of times the SPC referred to *People's Tribunals* in its annual work reports, 1980–2018

SOURCE: the SPC.

wave of reforms intended to streamline the performance of the existing tribunals. Together, these reforms have brought extraordinary changes in the People's Tribunals.[47]

To begin with, lower courts used to rely on the People's Tribunals to administer justice in both urban and rural jurisdictions. A turning point came in 1999, when the SPC expressly instructed lower courts to dismantle those tribunals in urban settings.[48] Toward the end of 2009, nearly 95 percent of the remaining tribunals stood in rural areas, leaving a tiny proportion to serve urban residents.[49] Top-down court reforms, in other words, have converted the People's Tribunals into a judicial organ specifically addressing the needs of the rural population. Second, a recurring theme of the reforms was to improve court financing and material conditions for judging. A popular saying in the 1980s, "There are no desks for toil, no pots to boil, and sleep only on soil" (办公没有桌, 吃饭没有锅, 睡觉没有窝), illustrates the dire conditions judges had to live with at the grassroots level.[50] Throughout the 1990s, reform agendas were dominated by calls for local governments to lend greater fiscal support to and strengthen the infrastructural capacities of the tribunals, by providing housing, telecommunication, transportation, and office equipment.

As the twentieth century ended, court reforms began striking a distinct chord. *Justice* and *efficiency* burst on the scene as the chief guiding principle for evaluating court performance.[51] Official discourse on court reforms, meanwhile, was sprinkled with catchphrases, such as *regularizing* (规范化), *systematizing* (制度化), and *increasing the scale* (规模化), setting the tone for the consolidation of the People's Tribunals in the new millennium. The year 2005, without exaggeration, should be marked as a critical moment in the history of the PRC. That year, the SPC issued several documents articulating the necessity of safeguarding the material and fiscal well-being of the tribunals.[52] Thanks to those efforts, the central government, between 2006 and 2008, allocated special funds, totaling 2.73 billion yuan, and subsequently funneled them into 5,944 construction projects across the country. The goal was to further shore up the infrastructural capacities of the remaining tribunals, especially those located in the central and western regions.[53] Combined, these reform measures transformed the physical environment in which judges conducted trial work.

When I visited Judge Lin for the first time in summer 2007, he and another judge were using a shaky bungalow as the courthouse. In addition to regular judicial activities, it was their job to fix leaky roofs during the summer rains. Back then, the two had no computers, printers, scanners, or court vehicles. Their daily routines were all squeezed into two rooms, one for trials and the other for meetings with litigants, mediation, and all other tasks. By the time I returned to Dingyi, in January 2010, the old courthouse was gone and a brand-new one had been erected (see figure 5.5). (The building houses both the tribunal and the township police station.) The project tripled the tribunal's square footage, leaving the two judges with too many rooms, some still unoccupied and unfurnished. What's more, it provided major equipment like computers, printers, and an internet connection. Judge Lin no longer rode his motorcycle to turn in court documents to the Basic People's Court located in the county seat. Through the intranet (内部网) established by the county-level court, he could electronically register new cases, conduct scheduling, and submit case records to supervisors without leaving his office. When he had to visit the county seat, he drove a Santana sedan, a standardized vehicle for the courts. His old motorcycle had finally retired.

What has remained largely unchanged, though, is the dearth of talent on the bench. Between 1985 and 2013, the Basic People's Court (including

FIGURE 5.5 The Dingyi People's Tribunal. Photographed by the author in 2010.

all the tribunals) in Weifeng expanded its staff size from 49 to 88, a modest increase dwarfed by a much faster rise in popular demand for justice. The same period saw the number of accepted civil cases triple, jumping from 485 to nearly 1,400. In describing the gap between staff members needed and those available, one judge lamented, "It's like your new crops have yet to be harvested; yet the old ones are already consumed." After decades of state-sponsored court reforms, 4 of the 6 People's Tribunals in Weifeng continued to wrestle with the same old problem: each had only 1 or 2 judges on duty.

This problem, by all accounts, is neither temporary nor local, confined to only a few rural counties. Statistics concerning the People's Tribunals specifically have always been hard to come by, for legislators, the SPC, and lower courts generally treat them as part of the Basic People's Courts as opposed to separate entities. Court record-keeping usually lumps these tribunals with the Basic People's Courts with which they are affiliated. Despite that, determining changes over time is nonetheless possible. In 1992, official estimates put the total number of the People's Tribunals at around 18,000 countrywide, employing nearly 70,000 court staff. This estimate dropped to 10,000 tribunals in 2012, with approximately 37,000 judges and court clerks conducting trial work. It remains unclear how many judges have been dispatched to the tribunals in the years following 2012.[54] These numbers reveal a development that has gone largely unnoticed in the rapidly expanding scholarship on Chinese courts: court personnel–to-tribunal ratio in recent decades decreased from 3.89 to 3.70, a negligible change in numbers, but with crucial implications on the ground. This decrease, I must note, took place at the time when the SPC was turning the People's Tribunals into an institution specifically reserved for the rural population. The end results? Rural residents must bear the brunt of the downsizing of court personnel on the frontiers. The promise the SPC emphatically stressed in 1999—that every People's Tribunal would be equipped with at least three judges, one clerk, and, if possible, bailiffs—has yet to be realized in many rural areas.[55]

Not long after settling the divorce case of the one-eyed man, the Dingyi People's Tribunal reached an unprecedented decision. It became the first tribunal in Weifeng to install a walk-through metal detector, mainly to ensure the safety of the two judges and the clerk (see figure 5.6). Not every tribunal can afford such an arrangement, though. For judges who are dispatched to the remaining tribunals; who regularly encounter angry men resisting state intervention in their marriages; who continue to struggle with personnel shortages; and, in short, for those who just cannot fall back on a metal detector to protect themselves professionally and personally, Judge Lin's approach to divorce litigation—stalling marital dissolution by imposing cooling-off periods on litigants—amounts to a survival strategy.

Prior to 2018, nowhere in the PRC's marital laws or regulations could one locate the term *cooling-off period* (冷静期). Before that point, judges certainly did not apply that terminology to justify their decisions to put

FIGURE 5.6 A walk-through metal detector installed inside the Dingyi People's Tribunal. Photographed by the author in 2010.

a divorce case on hold. Many, however, were savvy enough to capitalize on a particular procedural constraint as a pressure relief valve for highly contested divorce suits. This constraint, which is derived from the Civil Procedural Law, requires plaintiffs to wait for at least six months if they intend to file another divorce suit following a court ruling against marital dissolution.[56] The legislative intent behind this arrangement, one may contend, is to prevent frivolous litigation and preserve judicial resources. Judges who regularly tackle divorce, on the other hand, have come to the realization that they can legally freeze a divorce case, once, twice, three times by invoking this procedural constraint. In turning down a petition and thus forcing a plaintiff into a wait of six months or more, judges can give the defendant time to calm down, release pent-up frustrations, and come to terms with the potentiality of marital dissolution. Moreover, they can preempt the unintended consequences a divorce suit may trigger—suicide, homicide, injuries of disputing parties, attacks on court personnel, and so on. If the plaintiff has her or his mind bent on divorce, the option is always there—just file another petition at the same trial court on one condition: the interval between any two petitions must be at least six months long.

This all sounds good, except that this way of imposing cooling-off periods on divorcing couples remained unregulated and unchecked. For many years, the SPC stood by and made no attempt to bring this court practice under its purview. The year 2018 signaled the highest court's first move toward regulating the application of cooling-off periods in divorce litigation.[57] By then, so entrenched had this practice become that judges everywhere were accustomed to acting as Judge Lin did—that is, routinely (and often indiscriminately) adjudicating against first-time petitioners and then taking follow-up petitions as sine qua non for final judgments on marital dissolution. Filing a second or third petition for divorce, in this view, constitutes corroborating evidence for the claim that mutual affection no longer exists between plaintiff and defendant. Granting a divorce under these circumstances becomes truly justifiable in the eyes of the law.

Using official statistics to gauge the prevalence of this court practice is impossible, because court record-keeping does not distinguish rulings against first-time petitions from those involving second, third, or subsequent petitions. All these judgments are lumped into one category on the books, "adjudication against first-instance divorce suits." Yet, since He Xin, a law professor, first wrote about this practice in 2009, one study after another—conducted in Beijing, Chongqing, Henan, Hunan, Guangdong, Jiangsu, and Zhejiang, together with my own research in Weifeng, part of Sichuan Province—attests to the extent to which Judge Lin's coping strategy has spread widely and become routinized among Chinese judges.[58]

This court practice, of course, generates both benefits and costs, which are distributed unevenly between institutional insiders and outsiders. By dragging divorcing couples through cooling-off periods, judges expect to deescalate conjugal conflicts, release built-up tensions inside courtrooms, and lend greater legitimacy to their decision-making. This "legitimacy," from the SPC's point of view, is reflected in two metrics: rate of first-instance cases in which neither retrial nor appeal is sought (一审服判息诉率) and rate of citizens petitioning against the courts (信访投诉率).[59] As part of the Case Quality Assessment System, these two metrics, along with other criteria intended to evaluate judicial performance, send strong signals to court personnel. In judging, their top priorities are to "settle disputes and end conflicts" (定纷止争), to "conclude cases and put grievances behind" (案结事了), and, last but not least, to prevent discontent over the courts from spilling into other state bureaucracies.[60] These signals compel judges to go all out to appease disgruntled litigants in attempts to stave off legal or extralegal challenges to their judgments. In the context of divorce litigation, they convey a distinct connotation: precautions must be put in place to forestall rural men's violent resistance to official sanction for women's pursuit of divorce and rights contention.[61] Imposing cooling-off periods, in other words, enables judges to finesse their way through judging by placating men without categorically denying women access to divorce, a right that has been repeatedly codified in the history of the PRC.

While judges find their ways out of highly contested divorce cases, women, who make up the bulk of divorce petitioners, come to shoulder the costs. After a court turns down the first petition, a wife must weather the six-month waiting period. What's more, failed petitions can be particularly costly for women who have migrated to cities to work but must return to the countryside to divorce their husbands. Any additional attempts at divorce incur more bills, including litigation fees, service fees (if legal counseling is involved), and travel expenses. As such, many must confront painful decisions in the wake of unfavorable court rulings. Either they stay put, get through the waiting period, lose their income from off-farm employment, and then launch another plea for divorce, or they travel back and forth between their workplaces and the courts as the litigation process drags on—or, worse, they simply give up on divorce altogether.

Aside from financial costs, migrant women must endure legal uncertainty, psychological stress, and emotional turmoil resulting from prolonged courtroom battles. Finally, failed petitions can subject victims of domestic violence to escalated risks and dangers in abusive relationships. Although approximately one in three Chinese families suffers from domestic violence, court-sponsored injunction orders, also known as personal safety protective orders (人身安全保护令), are still a rarity.[62] In 2019, for example, the court system processed over 1.814 million marital and family disputes nationwide; yet only 1,589 cases involved a judge issuing a personal safety protective order to a victim of domestic violence.[63] Obtaining such an order in the countryside is even harder, where even the police often deem beating up one's wife a private matter and thus one to be resolved outside the purview of state law.

CONCLUSION

At the height of their political clout, the People's Tribunals wielded immense power. Established amid the land reform and the Three-Anti and Five-Anti Campaigns (三反、五反运动) between 1951 and 1952, these tribunals formed the vanguard of the PRC's penal machinery against the enemies of the state. Aside from targeting unruly entrepreneurs in the market and corrupt bureaucrats in state agencies, the People's Tribunals were deeply entangled with various mass campaigns, including marriage reform, land reform, and the enforcement of a new election law. Back then, judges stationed in the tribunals had tremendous authority. They could impose heavy fines, confiscate personal belongings, deprive citizens of political rights, send individuals to labor camps, inflict lengthy jail sentences, and even mete out the death penalty.[64]

That revolutionary past is long gone. Also gone with that era is the heavy-handed approaches judges took to intervene in citizens' intimate lives. Today, the freedom of marriage and of divorce is enshrined in black-letter laws and imprinted in the minds of a populace increasingly cognizant of individual rights and freedoms. The PRC's courts, however, cannot afford to leave such freedoms unconstrained. As the historian Nancy Cott has contended, no modern sovereigns can ignore the institution of marriage, because marital practices underlie national belonging and the cohesion of the state.[65] For the same reason, I argue that no modern judiciaries can ignore divorce. And Chinese courts are no exception. This chapter illustrates this point by showing how reform-era judges have restrained marital dissolution among citizens. Three mechanisms have been firmly established to this end: turning away petitioners through withdrawal; adjudicating against divorce; and stalling marital dissolution by imposing cooling-off periods.

These mechanisms suggest that the Chinese judiciary is rather versatile in flexing its muscles over individual choices in domestic lives. To curb divorce, judges have combined formal decision-making power and agenda-setting power. By illustrating how the two operate inside courtrooms, this chapter carries on the theoretical pursuit this book lays out at the beginning. Rather than treating disputation as corollary to individual action (or inaction), sociolegal researchers, I argue, should cast scholarly attention onto institutional practices, especially those configured by prevailing power relations within and surrounding the official justice systems. Doing so will allow us to better capture the complex interplay of law, politics, and inequality. The next chapter continues this line of inquiry by bringing to the fore the dynamics between power and resistance.

CHAPTER 6

Onstage and Offstage

COLLUSION ONSTAGE

"I must have a child"

Nestled along Yuncai Alley, the muddy thoroughfare that connected the outside world to Guxiao, stood the office of three legal workers. Barely a hole in the wall, the office—known as the Guxiao Legal Workers' Office—nonetheless played an important role in local affairs.

Like many other small towns in rural China, Guxiao, population twenty-five thousand or so, had no lawyers. To see a lawyer, villagers had to get on an early bus, endure a bumpy, hours-long ride to the nearest county seat, switch to a cab, a minibus, or more likely a *modi*—a motorcycle carrying passengers for minimal fare—and, if lucky enough, knock on the door of a law firm sometime before sundown.

The out-of-town trip to locate a lawyer could quickly turn into a wild-goose chase. Full-time, licensed lawyers have always been a rarity in Weifeng County, home to nearly half a million residents. As of 2010, just a dozen or so individuals had registered as lawyers across the county, and many preferred to conduct business in urban settings or at least in areas that could be accessed by public transportation.

In an obscure place like Guxiao, the legal workers' office was the most likely option for the locals if they wanted professional opinions about their troubles. Here, few recognized the differences between legal workers and licensed lawyers; the former group has much less formal education, legal training, and professional prestige than the latter (see chapter 4 for more details). Confusing legal workers with lawyers—sometimes even with judges—was hardly an embarrassment to villagers, though. Many would insist that their daily routines had little to do with state law. However, when hit by a streak of bad luck, when embroiled in prolonged, intractable disputes, some would race to the legal workers' office in hopes that the law would take their side.

Wu Manli was one of those actively seeking the help of the legal profession, going so far as to contest their rights inside courtrooms, and only much later realizing that justice is rarely blind. By foregrounding Manli's courtroom experience and by analyzing the institutional conditions that underlie such an experience, this chapter exposes a paradox. Inside the People's Courts, mediation has long maintained its centrality in divorce law practices. Be that as it may, mediation has remained impervious to formal, institutional scrutiny and, paradoxically, permeable to informal, outside influences. Because of this, mediation has served as an arena for those in positions of power to collude in attempts to deny the weaker party in a marriage crucial rights on paper. Consequently, the weaker party—often a wife trying to break away from her husband and in-laws—suffers from a double or even triple whammy: an unsympathetic court system, a co-opted legal profession, and an apathetic conjugal community. Despite all that, women do push back the frontiers of insubordination from time to time. And they do so— not onstage but off, outside of the court system, thereby engaging in what James C. Scott calls the *hidden transcript of resistance.*[1]

Centering power and resistance at once, this chapter advances sociolegal studies along two lines. On the one hand, it builds on and extends research on organizational co-optation of legal professions. "Courts, like many other modern large-scale organizations, possess a monstrous appetite for the cooptation of entire professional groups as well as individuals," Abraham S. Blumberg noted in his study of criminal courts in the United States.[2] Decades of sociolegal research have located ample evidence attesting to the readiness and efficacy of the court system in co-opting attorneys in private practice. This co-optation can occur through several mechanisms, for example, by reshaping attorneys' priorities in case processing, by molding their perceptions of worthy (or unworthy) clients, by bolstering their interdependence with institutional insiders (e.g., police, prosecutors, bondsmen, and so on), and by assimilating them into a homogenizing court culture that often obscures foundational principles, such as due process, fairness, and justice. In the end, rather than faithfully advocating for their clients and upholding crucial rights on the books, attorneys can wind up buttressing the power of the court system.[3] This chapter complements the extant literature by pinpointing the legal and institutional arrangements that have rendered such co-optation possible in the Chinese context.

On the other hand, in writing up this chapter, I intend to expose a blind spot in Blumberg's and many others' research. Sociolegal scholars often fail to entertain the possibility that organizational co-optation of the legal profession may be staged, scripted, and, in some ways, feigned. Such co-optation is, I argue, a function of law practitioners' endeavors to separate their public and hidden performances vis-à-vis power-holders inside the court system. Indeed, the greater the disparity in power differentials between insiders and outsiders to the system, and the more arbitrarily power is exercised, the more the public performance of the legal profession will take on a stereotyped, ritualistic cast. In the words of James C. Scott, "the more menacing the power, the thicker the mask," a mask the disempowered may put on. In piercing that mask, this chapter reveals the face hidden behind. As the pages ahead show, legal workers in rural China, acutely aware of their subordinate standing in courtrooms, often decouple their words and deeds onstage from those offstage. In doing so, they strive to carve out a social space beyond the gaze of the powerful in which they can maintain human dignity and restore a certain degree of professional autonomy. This space, under the right circumstances, can serve as an incubator for the disempowered to launch direct assaults on those in positions of dominance.

* * *

I met Manli for the first time on a chilly spring morning at the Guxiao Legal Workers' Office the day she turned up with 2,300 yuan in her pocket. The money was meant to pay Yan Dejin, a legal worker who had agreed to represent Manli in her divorce suit.

Manli, only twenty-nine, had raised two kids—a son, age thirteen, and a daughter, eleven—with a husband who was more her parents' pick than a love of her own. Open about her husband's quick temper, sporadic outbursts of aggression, and endless failures to provide for his family, Manli did not bother to hide her contempt. Also, she was bitter about her in-laws. "Within this household, I have no say about money. They are in control," said Manli.

Speaking of her kids, her tone noticeably softened. "The boy and the girl are my flesh and blood."

After her daughter turned five, Manli started her journey as a migrant worker in search of cash-paying jobs in adjacent towns and faraway cities, picking cotton in the rural inland in one season, working on a manufacturing assembly line in a coastal area in another. Her footprints could be traced from nearby Chengdu to Xinjiang in the far-off north, from Zhejiang Province in the southeast all the way back to Sichuan in the southwest. Those yearlong trips did not stop Manli from caring for the children she left behind in the countryside. She remained committed to fulfilling her responsibilities as a mother, making regular phone calls, sending home remittance, taking unpaid leave during holidays to visit her family in the village.

As Manli muddled through a life constantly on the move, her marriage fell apart bit by bit. Bickering, fighting, and short-lived truces rotated with the silent treatment. Acerbity and acrimony became the staples of their emotional life. Meanwhile, the quest for a new city life offered Manli a window onto her marriage, through which she came to see the sharp contrasts between the man she had married and the one she desired. Her encounter with a fellow migrant worker, a man Manli described as hardworking, kind, and generous, evolved into a romantic relationship in the space of two years—and eventually led to her decision to end a wretched decade-long marriage.

In asking her husband for a divorce, Manli made one request: custody of either of the two children. "I have no preference," she told him. "I will take it, whether you give me the boy or the girl."

But her husband, Sun Hongfu, had no intention of negotiating with Manli. His reaction to her request was ice-cold. She could walk away from their marriage, but child custody was out of the question. Soon Manli's in-laws cut off her contact with the children. Unable to meet the kids in person or talk to them over the phone, Manli grew more and more desperate.

Upon learning of Manli's situation, a friend put her in touch with the legal workers' office in town. Despairing, Manli decided to give it a try. The office swiftly charged her 2,300 yuan, not a small amount for someone like Manli, whose monthly wages as a migrant worker had stagnated around 1,000 yuan for a couple of years.

Recognizing the steep price tag for legal services, Manli was hopeful. After all, Dejin, the legal worker who agreed to handle her case, promised customer satisfaction with his services. "The world out there may be crooked. But some do stand by their moral scruples," said Manli. That was how she justified her decision to hire a law practitioner.[4]

For almost four months, Manli waited and waited but did not hear anything from her counsel. In midsummer, word finally came from Dejin: the Guxiao People's Tribunal was ready to hear her divorce case.

Inside the legal workers' office, I met Manli again on the day of the court proceeding. Wearing a bright-colored T-shirt, cropped jeans, and running shoes, she looked brisk and confident. Manli's mother, a quiet peasant woman with a severely humped back, had come with her.

On the way to the tribunal, located one block away from the office, I asked Manli if she had changed her mind about child custody.

"No."

Would it make any difference whether she got custody of her son or her daughter?

"No."

Would she ask for custody of both children? When this question came up, Manli did not respond right away. Silence descended on our conversation. Minutes later, Manli muttered, "That's unlikely." Her husband would not let go of both children, she explained.

When we arrived at the tribunal, there was no sign of Sun Hongfu. Dejin, Manli's counsel, was already there, chatting and laughing with court personnel, seemingly in a good mood. The moment Dejin saw Manli, he motioned her to meet for a private chat.

"Why don't you let Sun Hongfu have the kids?" Dejin whispered in an empty hallway.

"No way. I must have a child," said Manli, point-blank.

At that moment, the judge in charge of the case, Qian Shuting, a baby-faced woman in her late twenties with impeccable makeup and polished nails, walked up and interrupted the conversation between Dejin and his client.

Judge Qian ran over some details about the day's court proceeding with Dejin. She then asked if his client, Manli, had accepted the "arrangement."

Dejin shook his head.

"Carry on," Judge Qian said and walked away.

What "arrangement"? Hearing the exchange between the judge and Dejin, I was intrigued, but did not ask any questions in the moment.

Once the judge was gone, Dejin resumed his conversation with Manli. "You're working as a migrant worker. That's not good for the children."

"Not good for the children? No, I don't see any problems." Manli frowned. "I have the ability [to care for my kids]. Otherwise, I wouldn't ask for custody."

Dejin lost his tongue for a moment. Then he walked away and disappeared at the end of the hallway.

To convince a bystander like me, Manli once again stressed how much the kids meant to her. "[Marital] property isn't that important to me. I have two hands, capable of earning my own livelihood. I just want custody," Manli insisted.

When Dejin showed up a few minutes later, he did not wait long to bring up the issue of child custody. His talking points remained unchanged, but he tried a different tack this time. Judge Qian would help Manli reach a speedy divorce settlement with her husband if she agreed to give up custody altogether. Refusing this arrangement, Dejin pointed out, could result in the court's outright rejection of her divorce petition, which would leave Manli no choice but to wait for another six months to file a second petition.

"Six months later, I'll come back, demanding custody all over again." Manli, unpersuaded, uttered her reply word by word.

After several more futile attempts, Dejin made no headway in his attempt to "reason" with his client.

Then Judge Qian weighed in by summoning Manli, her mother, and Dejin into a conference room behind closed doors. She got to the point right away. "Why bother with custody? You're a young woman. You're still young," Judge Qian said.

"I want custody. And I'm not that young. Almost thirty," Manli replied.

"Almost thirty? You want custody, but you are bound to get remarried," Judge Qian continued.

Dejin chimed in. Once remarried, Manli would shoulder the burden of raising one child from her previous relationship and potentially a new one from her current marriage, Dejin reminded his client.

"I'm not afraid of 'burden.' To care for my kids, I won't consider remarriage," said Manli.

Unwilling to take no for an answer, Dejin shifted his tactics. For the next few minutes, he went on and on about the technical difficulties of enforcing court rulings in child custody cases, portraying a bleak prospect for Manli's contest over her rights as a mother.

Judge Qian sat stone-faced as she watched the exchanges between Dejin and Manli. At one point, she cut in with a sharp question. "You're determined to get a divorce, aren't you?"

Shortly after Manli confirmed that, the judge went on, "I'll level with you. If you really want a divorce, you'd better comply. If you do that—leaving the kids to him—you'll lose no time getting a divorce. Otherwise, you'll have to wait for the next round of court hearings. Six months later, there is still no guarantee that I'll grant you a divorce." Judge Qian paused for a moment, followed by a loaded question. "Now, do you want a divorce—or a kid?"

"I want a divorce. And I also want a kid." Manli's reply was remarkably terse, straight to the point. In the face of mounting pressure from the judge and her counsel, Manli stood her ground.

Around noon, Sun Hongfu, Manli's estranged husband, showed up at the tribunal, together with his father, a relative, and a lawyer named Liu Baoshan.

The moment Liu Baoshan—or "Lawyer Liu," a term court regulars used to address him—strolled into the judge's office, he grabbed an armchair, seated himself, reclined, with one leg touching the floor and the other dangling over the armrest. No hello, no self-introduction, no greetings to the judge or anyone else in the room. Soon, he started complaining about the summer heat, a sentiment immediately echoed by a court clerk. "Only fatties like you and I truly understand the hassles of summertime," the clerk joked.

Judge Qian also treated Lawyer Liu in a different manner. She paid hardly any attention to the discomfort of the other visitors who were all standing—and sweating. Yet the moment she saw Lawyer Liu wiping sweat off his face with his palm, she dug through piles of documents lying around the desk, found a pack of facial tissues, and handed him one. Nobody else received such consideration from the judge.

While Lawyer Liu was making himself as comfortable as possible in his chair, drinking tea from his travel mug, enjoying the cool air produced by the only table fan in the room, everyone else waited. After some stretching, some chitchatting with the judge, and quite a bit of tea drinking, Lawyer Liu finally announced that he was ready for the proceeding. In that case, the mediation would begin, Judge Qian confirmed.

From that moment on, a strange coalition—among Dejin, Lawyer Liu, and Judge Qian—began taking shape. Representing the plaintiff, the defendant, and the court system, respectively, the three teamed up, each taking a turn to echo another, with their attention exclusively directed at Manli. Their comments were all geared toward one goal: to make Manli drop her claim on child custody.

Dejin opened the mediation session, resuming his role as a thankless messenger by asking Manli if she would reconsider Judge Qian's earlier "suggestion."

Before Manli could reply, Lawyer Liu cut in. "You can always visit your kids [at Sun Hongfu's place]. You can buy them gifts. You can give them money. Or not. The point is that the living conditions at his place, compared to yours, are better."

"Who says he has better conditions?" Manli replied, barely registering any annoyance at the lawyer's comments. "I can take care of my kids."

Upon hearing Manli's rebuttal, Judge Qian could not sit back anymore. "But the kids have been staying with the husband. What can you do about it?"

"Exactly! The kids have been living with the guy," Dejin repeated after the judge. "Suppose the court grants you custody, but the guy refuses to hand over the kid. There is nothing you can do about it."

"Even if the court gives you custody, you think the enforcement [of such a ruling] would be effortless." Lawyer Liu took another sip of his tea. "The court is in no position to enforce its rulings on child custody by force."

"We are not going to forcibly enforce court rulings on child custody. So, don't hold your breath." Judge Qian made no secret whose side she was on.

The remainder of the mediation session unfolded just like this. Dejin, Lawyer Liu, and Judge Qian each repeated and reinforced one another's arguments about the legal and the practical difficulties of Manli's quest for custody.

Blindsided, strong-armed, and cornered though Manli was, she tried hard to stay the course, repeatedly emphasizing that she must have one child. Her resistance crumbled, however, as fatigue and isolation kicked in. Her voice gradually lost vitality. Her face no longer featured that lively look. She seemed so exhausted, her upper body bent forward, shoulders slumped, head slouched, as if the pressure of the mediation had turned her into a hunchback.

An hour after noon, Manli signed divorce paperwork, agreeing to let her husband raise both their son and daughter.[5]

Dealmaking in the shadow of power

Manli's courtroom experience left me aghast. For days, I mulled over why Manli's counsel, the husband's lawyer, and the judge had behaved that way during the mediation. To find out what had happened, I reached out to Liu Baoshan, her husband's lawyer. I also sat down with Dejin, Manli's counsel. The two, in turn, helped me put Manli's custody battle in perspective. It turned out that Sun Hongfu, the defendant, had gained the upper hand early in the litigation process. He did so by mobilizing his kinship ties to secure the help of Liu Baoshan, who was not just experienced and armed with legal know-how but well-connected and in possession of the right kind of "political know-who."[6] As a longtime partner at a law firm founded by Judge Qian's father, Lawyer Liu was reasonably smug about his influence in the local court system. Here, nobody needed to study the fine points of the law to know who would prevail inside the courtroom, Lawyer Liu told me.[7]

Manli, on the other hand, had no such connections. Her family did not know any powerful figures, much less a prominent lawyer friendly with the judge who would be hearing her case. In seeking legal assistance, Manli had to rely on a total stranger, Dejin, a mid-career legal worker, who had neither the status nor the local court connections of her husband's lawyer. What had further tipped the scales against Manli was Dejin's quiet realization that he could never afford to cross a judge like Qian Shuting. Growing up with a father who founded the first law firm in Weifeng and an uncle who headed the county-level Basic People's Court, Judge Qian was a rising star in the eyes of fellow judges. At the age of twenty-eight, she had already served for several years as the president of the Guxiao People's Tribunal, a position that was meant to serve as a springboard to high office. Judge Qian, sooner or later, would surpass her uncle, making her way to the top of the local party leadership, Dejin divulged.[8] Such insider knowledge led him to pick a side with little hesitation. Despite recognizing that Judge Qian should have recused herself from Manli's case, given her connections with the defendant's lawyer, Dejin nevertheless played along. No word was uttered to oppose the judge's presiding over the case. No attempt was made to defend Manli's rights to an unbiased court hearing.

In 2018, when I returned to Weifeng to conduct a follow-up study of divorce litigation, I learned that Judge Qian had left the court system. A year after she mediated Manli's divorce case, she was promoted to the vice director of the Weifeng Justice Bureau, a county-level government agency in charge of local legal affairs. Around 2015, she received another promotion, allowing her to move up the state bureaucratic ladder once again. This time she became the vice procurator-general of the Weifeng People's Procuratorate. Dejin's speculations about Judge Qian's bright future had become reality. Unfortunately, I was unable to locate Manli. Nearly seven years had passed since the day I watched her mediation session. When was the last time Manli saw her kids? I could only imagine.

A PARADOX UNDERNEATH DIVORCE SETTLEMENTS
The imperviousness of mediation

It is tempting to label Manli's courtroom experience as an exceptional case of rule-breaking on the part of one judge and two law practitioners, thereby setting it apart from the hundreds of thousands of divorce suits settled inside the People's Courts every year. True, it is not every day that a defendant brings in a mighty lawyer who maintains strong ties with state agencies. Not every judge is untouchable, coming from a political family with multiple relatives and friends holding public office. What happened to Manli, however, is neither random nor unique. It is rather symptomatic of entrenched systemic problems with divorce law practices in Chinese courts. To unpack these problems, we must examine the role of mediation in judges' efforts to dispose of civil cases.

From the outset of the People's Republic of China (PRC), legislators have privileged mediation over adjudication in divorce suits. The 1950 Marriage Law unequivocally made court-organized mediation a procedural must for contested divorces. "Divorce shall be granted, if both husband and wife desire it," the law declared, but "in the event of contested divorces, mediation must be attempted; only after mediation fails to yield a reconciliation between the parties can the court grant a divorce."[9] The Supreme People's Court (SPC) took it one step further in 1956. While compiling the first procedural guideline for civil litigation, the SPC expanded the application of mediation to all divorce cases, regardless of whether or not marital dissolution was contested.[10] In the aftermath of the Cultural Revolution (1966–1976), which shook the country to the core, the SPC sought to restore the civil justice system. It did so in part by strengthening procedural rules for civil litigation. Mediation was again marked as a mandatory procedure for divorce suits.[11] Later legislators followed suit as they amended the Marriage Law in 1980 and then in 2001. Their message to the courts across the country was loud, clear, and consistent: when dealing with divorce, judges must carry out mediation.[12]

The PRC's strong emphasis on mediation is by no means confined to the letter of the law. Judges, from the mid-1950s onward, persistently favored mediation over adjudication in civil litigation in general and in divorce suits in particular. Figures 6.1 and 6.2 illustrate the initial patterns. The mid-1980s witnessed the centrality of mediation waning in day-to-day court practices, setting in motion a downward trend that was further reinforced by the 1991 revision of the Civil Procedural Law. Whereas previous legislators underscored the importance of conciliation in dispute resolution, the amended law no longer emphasized court-induced

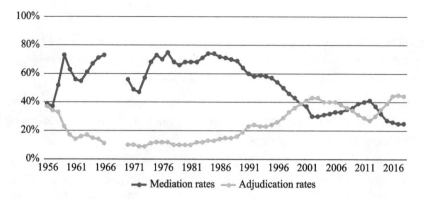

FIGURE 6.1 Mediation and adjudication rates in first-instance civil suits in China, 1956–2018

SOURCES: *China Law Yearbook* (2003–2019); *Historical Statistical Books of the People's Courts, 1949–2016 (The First Volume on Civil Litigation, 1950–2004).*
NOTE: Certain data are missing for 1967, 1968, and 1969.

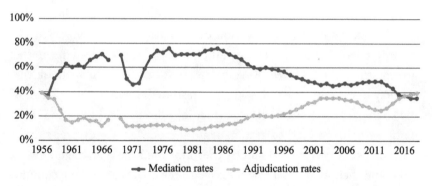

FIGURE 6.2 Mediation and adjudication rates in first-instance divorce suits in China, 1956–2018

SOURCES: *China Statistical Yearbook* (2018–2019); *Historical Statistical Books of the People's Courts, 1949–2016 (The First Volume on Civil Litigation, 1950–2004) and (The Second Volume on Civil Litigation, 2005–2016).*
NOTE: Data are missing for 1968.

settlements in case disposition.[13] The popularity of mediation thus dwindled through the last decade of the twentieth century.

A watershed moment came in 2004. Mediation stepped back into the spotlight as a result of the SPC's initiatives to renew the tradition of concluding civil disputes outside of formal trials.[14] A slogan soon permeated

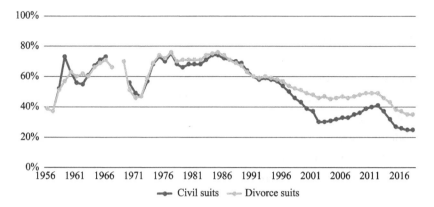

FIGURE 6.3 Mediation rates in first-instance civil and divorce suits in China, 1956–2018

SOURCES: *China Law Yearbook* (2003–2019); *China Statistical Yearbook* (2018–2019); *Historical Statistical Books of the People's Courts, 1949–2016 (The First Volume on Civil Litigation, 1950–2004)* and *(The Second Volume on Civil Litigation, 2005–2016)*.
NOTE: Certain data are missing for 1967, 1968, and 1969.

official discourse: "Whenever possible, mediation shall be attempted; when it is time for adjudication, formal rulings should be handed out; combine mediation and adjudication so as to conclude cases and put grievances behind" (能调则调, 当判则盼, 调判结合, 案结事了). Party leadership's promotion of a harmonious socialist society (社会主义和谐社会), a trend I discussed in the previous chapter, coalesced with this reemphasis on mediation. In later years, courts countrywide received another directive from the SPC. This time, judges were told to "prioritize mediation, and supplement it with adjudication" (调解优先, 调判结合). Funneling popular disputes and conflicts into mediation, in other words, became a new fad under the leadership of Wang Shengjun, who served as the president of the SPC from 2008 to 2013.[15] This renewed emphasis on mediation lasted until Zhou Qiang took over the reins of the SPC in 2013. After that, courts at all levels backpedaled, leading to another downturn in mediation rates.

Amid the foregoing fluctuations—some triggered by legislative changes and others by policy shifts—judges have developed greater dependence on mediation in divorce law practices than in other areas of civil litigation. Figure 6.3 illustrates this pattern by showing two measures: the percentage of mediated civil cases and that of mediated divorce suits. In short, mediation has consistently eclipsed adjudication in divorce suits for most of the PRC's history, albeit with ups and downs in popularity.

Notwithstanding its centrality in nearly six decades of divorce law practices, mediation has remained impervious to formal scrutiny, but permeable to informal, outside influences. This paradox must be unpacked, if we intend to uncover the inner workings of mediation, as a dominant mode of case disposition. Doing so entails a methodical examination of the nuts and bolts of mediation. More specifically, it entails a meticulous investigation of when, where, and how mediation is conducted, who can participate, and who is most likely to have the final word.

For decades, judges have exercised full discretion in determining the time, place, and circumstances in which mediation can be administered. In terms of timing, they can engage in mediation at almost any point in the process of litigation, so long as formal rulings are still pending.[16] During my field research in Weifeng, I watched judges attempting mediation on various occasions. Some tried to do so soon after plaintiffs filed divorce petitions, and others sought to reach settlements during pretrial conferences. Often, judges treated trials as the optimal occasions not necessarily to adjudicate but to gather wife and husband in the same room in hopes of finding a middle ground for settlements. Efforts to induce agreements on marital dissolution and related issues usually preceded and immediately followed trials, as if they were prologue and epilogue of the same play. So seamless was the transition from one act to the other that the demarcation between mediation and adjudication frequently became obscured beyond recognition.

Transitioning back and forth between mediation and adjudication is logistically possible, in no small part due to a longtime tradition in the People's Courts—that is, divorce cases are typically tried by a single judge as opposed to a collegial panel of three or more judges. Moreover, the judge in charge of mediation is often the one who will go on to adjudicate the case in hand if that is necessary.[17] Assuming two roles at once, judges are mediators and also adjudicators. These institutionalized arrangements give those on the bench tremendous bargaining power in relation to litigants. Threatening "uncooperative" litigants with unfavorable rulings—the tactic Judge Qian applied in Manli's case—has long been readily available in judges' toolboxes to conclude divorce cases.

As for the locale for mediation, judges have always been at liberty to pick and choose. In Weifeng, many preferred to hold settlement meetings in their offices, conference rooms, or mediation rooms. These places share one commonality: they are unmonitored and underregulated spaces with no surveillance cameras and few formal rules governing judges' words or deeds in interactions with litigants. Unlike trials, which necessitate transcribing verbal exchanges between judges and other participants, mediation sessions involve no such documentation. No paper trail is to be left behind, exposing the mediation process to internal or external scrutiny. There is no recourse for litigants, counsel, court supervisors, or appellate courts wishing to review the process leading to divorce settlements after the process is concluded. Put more plainly, when it comes to judicial conduct in mediation, judges can easily stay above the fray.

Once divorce suits are settled, challenging judges' approval of mediation outcomes is a formidable—if not impossible—task. Since 1956, the SPC has explicitly denied litigants the right to challenge mediation outcomes through appeal. Legislators have repeatedly countenanced the SPC's stance on this matter, first through the promulgation of the Civil Procedural Law in 1982 and then through four amendments to that law in the decades to come.[18] When the law was revised in 2012, legislators blocked another important route. Previously, in principle, litigants could demand that trial or appellate courts conduct retrials for mediated divorce cases. That option disappeared after 2012.[19] The end result, following decades of lawmaking in the PRC, is that litigants are left with no legal redress for mediated cases and that judges rarely fret over their approval of divorce settlements.

Just as black-letter laws insulate judges from the negative repercussions of mediation, the court system, as an institution, has been similarly unwilling to hold its insiders accountable for unprofessional, unethical conduct. In fairness, I must point out that at every step along the way—from the SPC's early attempt at specifying procedural rules necessary for civil litigation, in 1956, to its latest provisions on mediation—the highest court has time and again stressed, "Mediation is a voluntary process and must be carried out in accordance with the law."[20] Voluntariness (自愿) and lawfulness (合法), in other words, have been consecrated in lawmaking and policymaking with regard to mediation. Decades of repeated emphases on these two principles, however, have yet to translate into concrete, enforceable disciplinary rules against institutional insiders. To rein in judicial misconduct, four versions of the Judges' Law, together with over a dozen SPC provisions, have been put in place since the early 1990s.[21] The vast majority of them remain silent on judges' misuse or abuse of mediation.

In 2001, the SPC broke its own silence. "Judges shall not go against litigants' will or apply undue means to induce case withdrawal or settlements," the highest court stipulated in a document intended to lay out ethical rules for judging. Meanwhile, the SPC was careful enough to expressly demarcate the scope of sanctionable misconduct in mediation. Merely breaching the principle of voluntariness or lawfulness would not suffice. Rather, only when judges have done so to "advance their personal interests" (因徇私) could they be subject to disciplinary sanctions.[22] In emphasizing the intent behind judicial misconduct, the SPC did not widen, but rather narrowed the reach of its enforcement of ethical rules. In 2010, when the foregoing document was revised, the highest court went even further: it simply got rid of the article against judges' use of undue means to induce settlements, signaling another retreat from previous efforts to curb misuse of mediation (see chapter 5 for a more detailed account of the context in which such regulatory changes took place).[23]

The leakiness of mediation

Taken together, the foregoing legal and institutional arrangements have turned mediation into a black box, making it exceedingly hard to hold judges responsible for their abuse of power in divorce settlements. Using the metaphor of a black box to characterize mediation inside the People's Courts must, however, come with a caveat. Mediation, though impervious to formal scrutiny, has long been permeable to informal, outside influences. The latter characteristic can be described as the "leakiness of the judicial field in China"—to borrow the phrase used by Ng Kwai Hang and He Xin, two scholars who have spent decades studying Chinese courts. Among other findings, Ng and He stress that Chinese judges are socially embedded, with their decision-making susceptible to the social ties they have formed within and outside the judiciary. When these ties are "rock solid," rather than superficial or indirect, they can sway judges in their case processing and rulings.[24]

My field research in Weifeng led to findings highly consistent with Ng's and He's argument. More specifically, I found that the more powerful (or resourceful) party in marriage—oftentimes the husband—could mobilize his social ties to recruit allies within or outside the court system and, subsequently, channel such allies' influences into the mediation process, thus further enhancing his own bargaining power in divorce settlements. Consequently, the wife—the weaker party in the marriage—would suffer more from preexisting power differentials and/or inequalities in marriage, family, and communal life. To understand how the mediation process opens itself to external social influences, we must once again travel backward in history.

On October 9, 1944, a woodcut created by the renowned revolutionary artist Gu Yuan appeared in the *Liberation Daily*, the official newspaper of the Chinese Communist Party (CCP) in its revolutionary bases. Featured at center stage of the artwork was Ma Xiwu, a judge mediating a marital dispute in an open court surrounded by litigants, family members, and fellow villagers (see figure 6.4). Famous for his practice of taking court personnel to villages, conducting on-site investigations, and mobilizing multiple parties to tackle disputes, Judge Ma was the CCP's handpicked choice to incarnate its treasured tradition in governance. This tradition, known as the mass line (群众路线), required court personnel to follow a formula: relying on the masses (依靠群众), investigating and conducting research (调查研究), and mainly using mediation to address popular discontent (调解为主). To widely disseminate the formula among the courts in the revolutionary bases, party cadres turned Gu Yuan's artwork into an iconic image, dubbed Judge Ma's style of justice "Comrade Ma Xiwu's Way of Judging" (马锡五同志的审判方式), and subsequently popularized both the image and the phrase in official discourse.[25]

As the CCP rose to power in 1949, it strove to pass its revolutionary legacies on to younger generations of judges. "Applying the mass line" (实行群众路线) was formally written into the PRC's 1975 constitution and into the SPC's 1979 guideline for civil litigation. From 1982 onward, the Civil Procedural Law has time and again affirmed judges' authority to invite "relevant organizations and individuals" (有关单位和个人) to participate in mediation and to assist the courts to resolve disputes and conflicts.[26] Starting in 2006 and 2007, as mediation emerged as a key vehicle for the party leadership to build a harmonious socialist society, courts across the country were told to "bring societal forces" (引入社会力量) into settlements.[27] The SPC pushed the envelope further in 2012, by encouraging judges to select specially invited mediators (特邀调解员) from a wide range of choices, including "deputies to the National People's Congress, members of the National Committee of the Chinese People's Political Consultative Conference, people's jurors, specialists, lawyers, arbitrators, and retired law practitioners."[28] By 2017, over sixty thousand individuals had been chosen to conduct specially invited mediation (特邀调解) alongside judges, according to an estimate provided by Zhou Qiang, the president of the SPC.[29] In brief, the court system over the past decades has made myriad efforts to insert non-litigants into mediation, subjecting this mode of case disposition to outside influences, formal or informal.

FIGURE 6.4 "Comrade Ma Xiwu mediating a marital dispute" by Gu Yuan. Photographed by the author in the Sichuan Art Gallery in 2016. Fair use.

FIGURE 6.5 A trial room at the Qinchuan People's Tribunal. Photographed by the author in 2010.

Those influences can be spotted in the physical layout of mediation rooms inside the grassroots court system. In Weifeng, adjudication was typically held in trial rooms, which divided space into distinct areas for court personnel, litigants, counsel, and audience (see figure 6.5). Mediation rooms, on the contrary, featured no such spatial separation. Instead, participants could sit anywhere around one big table. The nameplates on the table read the varying roles of participants: mediators, specially appointed mediators, disputing party A (被调解[甲方]), disputing party B (被调解 [乙方]), and litigants' relatives and friends (亲友) (see figures 6.6 and 6.7).

There is more to this mediation room than meets the eye. Courthouses, like many other physical spaces, can conceal or distort truths—just as they can expose truths, sociologist Thomas F. Gieryn warns.[30] My observations of court-organized mediation reveal complex realities on the ground. During my stay in Weifeng, I rarely spotted judges reaching out to local communities or government agencies, requesting assistance for

FIGURE 6.6 A mediation room at the Xiqing People's Tribunal. Photographed by the author in 2010.

FIGURE 6.7 Nameplates on the desk inside the mediation room. Photographed by the author in 2010.

dispute resolution, or recruiting laymen to mediate divorce suits.[31] The severe shortage of court personnel, coupled with a heavy caseload—a problem I detailed in chapter 5 —makes it unrealistic for judges to regularly go down to villages to dispense justice among the masses. Comrade Ma Xiwu's Way of Judging, for the most part, remains a symbol of the Maoist past, lurking in official discourse, while making little splash among those currently on the bench. Judges nowadays know all too well where political rhetoric ends and judicial realities begin. The burden of relying on the masses to resolve disputes, consequently, piles on the shoulders of the two parties in litigation. Whoever can retain influential, outside allies—someone like Liu Baoshan or local political elites, such as village cadres and government officials—will more likely gain the upper hand in divorce settlements. Put differently, power dynamics inside the courtroom hinges, to a large extent, on the two litigants' abilities to mobilize the outside world, especially their kinship ties in local communities and governments. Through this mobilization, gender differences in society at large find ways to infiltrate disputation and litigation.

Women in Weifeng generally face greater difficulties than men in mobilizing family and communal support for divorce for two specific reasons. For one, like Manli, many follow the tradition of patrilocal residence. Once married, they relocate from their natal families to conjugal families, from natal villages to those where their husbands and in-laws live. In conforming to a deep-seated tradition, married women become and often stay as outsiders in their conjugal communities, even after years or decades of residence. This outsider status, in turn, makes it hard for these women to invoke kinship ties to obtain communal support in dispute resolution. Getting a village cadre, a relative, or a neighbor to testify in the courtroom on contested issues, such as domestic violence, extramarital affairs, and spousal abandonment, is a herculean task for many on the verge of divorce. What's more, women's participation in labor migration has further tilted the playing field. As they spend years or even decades toiling in the urban workforce in places far from home, their connections with conjugal (and natal) communities have been diluted, their outsider status being further reinforced.

Unsurprisingly, Manli opted out of approaching village cadres for help. "If they [cadres] took my side, wouldn't they offend the Suns?'" (Sun was the family name of Manli's husband.) That was Manli's reply, when I asked her whether she had contacted community leaders for her custody battle. She was sober about her disadvantages in legal mobilization, recognizing a grim reality that her husband was part of a village where a significant proportion of residents shared the same family name, Sun, and was bonded by overlapping kinship ties. Few in her community would rally behind her suit.

Other women echoed Manli's point. Ma Mingyan, a native of Yunnan Province, was acutely aware of her outsider status in Weifeng, a county in southern Sichuan Province. Upon divorce, Mingyan did not talk to anyone in her village. To explain her decision to keep the matter to herself, Mingyan walked me through the intricate ties that linked her conjugal family to the key decision-makers sitting on the Villagers' Committee, the main governing body at the grassroots level. Even Lan Yu, a fortysomething who had lived in her conjugal village for over two decades, had little faith in local political elites. "Party cadres at the grassroots level...when they are in a good mood, they may step in and help you with your problems. When they are not, well, they won't lift a finger," she said. "They don't care if it's an ox beating up a horse or a horse beating up an ox." With this colloquial expression, Lan Yu vividly depicted local officials' indifference to women's marital grievances and disputes.[32] In fact, only two among the thirty-two divorcing women I interviewed spoke positively of village cadres' roles in dispute resolution. In both cases, the women deviated from the tradition of patrilocal residence. Rather than relocating to the conjugal family, they had continued to reside in their natal villages throughout their marriages.

Divorcing men, by contrast, held rather different views of political elites in their communities. In interviews, few voiced disappointment or resentment toward village cadres. Staying close to their natal villages proved critical for their legal mobilization at the time of marital dissolution. A sample of 198 divorce cases, processed by the Guxiao Legal Workers' Office between 2003 and 2011, sheds additional light on this matter. Whereas nearly 42 percent of the male petitioners in the sample successfully gathered affidavits from village cadres, allowing them to show official backing for their pursuit of divorce, only 17 percent of their female counterparts managed to do so (chapter 7 provides a systematic analysis of the cases in the sample). To sum up, the two gender groups are hardly on par with each other with regard to their abilities to convert social connections into effective legal mobilization. Relying on the masses to resolve disputes—the party line the CCP has enshrined through decades of lawmaking and policymaking—has drastically different implications for female and male litigants.

Table 6.1 recapitulates the legal and institutional arrangements that have enabled the court system and the legal profession to collude in their attempts to deny women crucial rights on the books. This collusion is desirable, because the grassroots court system and the market-based legal profession have vested interest in reining in women's legal mobilization. By suppressing their rights claims upon divorce, both judges and paid counsel benefit from reducing time investment in case processing. For judges, tossing wives' custodial and property claims out of divorce settlements allows them to simplify and expedite court proceedings, thereby decreasing docket size and boosting "efficiency" on paper. Similarly, in keeping wives from seeking child custody and marital property, law practitioners can maintain a quick turnaround, minimize resource investment in each divorce case, and, in turn, maximize fee revenues in the long run. Dejin, Manli's counsel, was going to keep the 2,300 yuan she paid him up front, whether he won the case or not. He would not get paid any more if she won her custody battle.[33]

Moreover, by holding back women's rights contention, both judges and law practitioners try to avoid confronting the entrenched male ascendancy in rural households and in communities. In the past decade, preserving the so-called harmonious socialist society has trumped the needs of protecting citizens' lawful rights in many domains, including marriage and family life—a trend scholars at home and abroad have repeatedly noted. Within this context, undercutting women's rights rarely registers as a political problem for policymakers at the commanding heights or for those on the front line of dispute management.[34] In the end, divorcing women often find themselves in uphill battles, simultaneously wrestling with a callous

TABLE 6.1 The paradox behind divorce settlements in rural China

	Imperviousness	Leakiness
Legal/ institutional arrangements	• Mediation process is undocumented, unmonitored, and underregulated. • Mediation outcomes are not subject to appeal or retrial. • Few ethical rules have been put in place to hold judges accountable for misconduct in mediation.	• The party line, relying on the masses to resolve popular disputes, has made deep inroads in lawmaking and policymaking. • Judges can invite relevant organizations and individuals to participate in mediation. • Courts can select laymen to conduct specially invited mediation alongside judges. • Litigants can recruit and bring their own allies into mediation.
Implications	• Litigants have few formal remedies for mediated divorce cases. • Holding judges responsible for their abuse of power in mediation is nearly impossible.	• Power dynamics within the courtroom becomes a function of the two disputing parties' abilities to mobilize the outside world. • Because rural women face greater difficulties than men in seeking communal support for divorce, they are often forced into uphill battles inside courtrooms.

court system, a co-opted legal profession, and a conjugal community apathetic to their marital grievances and disputes, these battles all too often resulting in stark gender inequality in litigation outcomes, a theme the next chapter details.

The legal profession's tendency to be co-opted by court (and community) insiders has long drawn scholarly attention. Criminal defense attorneys in the United States, for example, are said to operate like double agents. While marketing their legal expertise to clients, they often end up serving the organizational needs of the court system (for example, concluding cases through plea bargaining as opposed to a combative, trial-by-jury process).[35] In civil litigation, attorneys can be co-opted as well. Rather than zealously advocating for their clients, they usually take a conciliatory approach in disputation in hopes of satisfying clients on the one hand and preserving their social ties in local communities on the other.[36] The co-optation of the legal profession by the court system is, however, rarely absolute, leaving law practitioners no space for disobedience or defiance.

As the remainder of this chapter shows, when legal workers are onstage, in the presence of court insiders, they routinely display deference, cooperativeness, and allegiance to the official justice system. Wearing a mask, following a script, and enacting a public performance is a necessity for legal workers to sustain their practice of law. But once we peer behind that mask, go beyond the scripted play onstage, and search for backstage or offstage activities, we may spot a world of insubordination, resistance, and subversion that has been hidden from the gaze of the powerful.

RESISTANCE AND SUBVERSION OFFSTAGE
Manli's choice

Outside was a sunny midsummer afternoon. White jasmine was blooming. Sweet corn was growing enthusiastically, everywhere, as if it could not wait to be picked. After a brief lunch break, villagers were ready for another round of tea plucking on the hills that meandered through Guxiao.

Inside was a dim passage, reeking of sterilant, the kind of smell most often found in a medical clinic. This clinic was housed in a brick building, about a five-minute walk from the Guxiao People's Tribunal, a perfect shelter for those whose hopes for justice were dashed and who thus yearned for a secluded corner to compose themselves in. Wrapped in the pungent smell, Manli and I sat in silence in the waiting area for visitors from nearby villages. It was a quiet afternoon with few patients around. That quiet was precisely what Manli needed after signing away her parental rights to her husband.

As silence deepened, I felt compelled to say something, anything, knowing nothing could console a mother who just lost her fight for custody. "You didn't anticipate this result, did you?"

"No. I thought I would surely get one kid. After all, I can provide better conditions [for child-rearing]," Manli said.

"Better conditions? You mean you can take the kid to Chengdu?"
Manli nodded.

Before filing a divorce petition, Manli had set up a small business in Chengdu, a city with much better schools. Like many other migrant workers of rural origin, Manli was eager to put down roots in a place where she could find quality education for her children.

"But how come he sided with Sun Hongfu?" Manli suddenly changed the topic.

Not sure which person Manli was referring to, I asked her who said what.

"He said I'd better drop custody." Manli's face twisted, eyebrows nearly clashing. "Why didn't he defend me?"

Of course, the unidentified "he" was Yan Dejin, Manli's counsel.

"I paid him twenty-three hundred yuan. That's twenty-three hundred going down the toilet," said Manli, with a shiver in her voice. "But you know what? I would pay thirty-three hundred, if only I could get a kid."

To muster two or three thousand yuan for another custody battle, Manli would have to toil in cotton fields or on an assembly line for two or three months. As a migrant worker, she was making a meager salary, largely living hand to mouth. But setting aside expenses, would Manli maintain her faith in the court system or the legal profession after what she had just gone through in divorce settlements? With that question in mind, I asked Manli about her view of her courtroom experience.

"It's not fair. And it's not reasonable."

What would count as a fair and reasonable court ruling, then?

"Each parent gets one child."

Would she still believe in the impartiality of the court system?

"There is no such thing as 'impartiality.' Not in this world. You'll get justice if you're rich. If not, no justice for you," said Manli. She then commented on the legal profession. "They'll root for you if you have more money. Or they'll side with him if he has deeper pockets."

At the beginning of her divorce suit, Manli held a bright outlook on individuals practicing law in suits and those in black robes, maintaining that some would "stand by their moral scruples" despite a crooked world out there. That outlook was gone, her faith in the law shattered, her confidence in the legal profession wiped out. What now? When the official justice system failed, would women like Manli take matters into their own hands? I had had this question turning over in my head ever since I saw that offstage exchange between Dejin and Manli.

Earlier that day, in the middle of the court-organized mediation, Dejin divulged something to his client. After Judge Qian made her first attempt

at dissuading Manli from seeking child custody, which fell flat immediately, she arranged a recess. The moment the judge walked out of the
conference room, Dejin leaned over and whispered to Manli, "There is
another way to go about this."

That other way, according to Dejin, was to pretend to concede in the
mediation. Once the husband signed the divorce paperwork, Manli would
be at liberty to help herself regarding custody.

"You're gonna wait outside the school," Dejin lowered his voice,
quickly casting a wary glance at the room's entrance. "The moment the
kid comes out, you're gonna grab the little one. Run! Teachers won't have
time to intervene."

"What if it didn't work out?"

"It'll definitely work out," Dejin insisted. "But you must hold your
tongue and remain tight-lipped before and after."

"Wouldn't the Suns' family guard the school?"

"Who could possibly guard the school, day in, day out?" Dejin
cleared his throat. "You have to remember the law. The law says the
courts can't physically enforce their rulings on child custody." Dejin
paused for a moment. "Now, you have to wait. Wait until the school
semester starts."

For a while, Manli was mute, her head lowered, gaze fixed on the
floor, one hand on her lap and the other slowly rubbing a knee. She then
mumbled like someone who was sleep-talking, "The kids will go back to
school in September. September 2."

Dejin went on, barely paying any attention to Manli's pondering.
"You're the [kids'] guardian. There's nothing Sun Hongfu can do to you.
We got another case, also involving two kids, one boy and one girl. Both
the guy and his wife wanted the kids. The court ruled in favor of the
guy. But the wife would not comply. Eventually, she seized the kids and
disappeared. They still can't find her to this day."

Dejin kept peddling the idea that Manli might well snatch a kid from
the husband after the divorce settlement. But Manli was ambivalent...

While my mind began wandering the conference room, floating around
that offstage talk, a voice brought me back into the smelly, dim passage.

"Could I appeal?" Manli asked. I could feel her gaze on my face.

I had to tell Manli what I knew about the law. Mediation outcomes were not subject to appeal. The only plausible legal solution to her predicament was to sue her ex-husband to demand a formal change in the allocation of child custody. In that case, going back to the court would be inevitable. Alternatively, a mother in Manli's shoes could resort to self-help. God might help those who help themselves, as Dejin pointed out. Manli, in other words, had to decide which route she would take, the legal or the extralegal one.

"I must get a kid," Manli declared forcefully, in almost the same tone she had four months earlier, when we first met.

But how? Would Manli hire another counsel for another courtroom battle over custody?

"That's impossible," Manli replied instantly. "These lawyers—you get one for your side, he gets one for his side. Under the table, they all eat from the same plate. It's a corrupt world out there."

What about snatching a kid from the Suns' family?

"Why would I file a lawsuit, if I decided to steal?"

Just as I thought Manli had vetoed Dejin's scheme, she went on with a narrative a mother determined to get her child back would entertain.

"I could arrange a vehicle. The school will close around three or four o'clock. A friend of mine has a car. And I'll pay for gas. Afterward, the car can take us to Chengdu..." Manli was lost in her imagination.[37]

Sitting in the dim light of the passage, Manli and I carried on the conversation. Neither of us had a clue where it was heading. She clearly needed more time to mull over her options in the wake of the derailed courtroom battle, I told myself at the end of the day.

In the months that followed, I heard from Manli a few times. She was busy with her business in Chengdu. She found a new rental home. She learned how to use a computer, email, and QQ, an instant messaging software. She was saving as much cash as she could. She would open her own grocery store once she had enough savings. Her relationship with her boyfriend stabilized. They were now living together...Meanwhile, her ambivalence about child custody—either going back to the court to duke it out, in front of a judge, or executing the scheme Dejin suggested, outside the purview of the law—grew stronger day by day.

Weeks before New Year's Day, I found Manli in a stinky, poorly lit internet café on the outskirts of Chengdu, a place far enough away that it might allow for a new start for the divorced. Running the internet café with her boyfriend, Manli was trying to put the divorce suit behind her. When asked about her plan for child custody, Manli replied, "Forget it. It's better this way. I don't want to get entangled with the Suns anymore."[38]

Public versus hidden performance

To a cynic, Manli's decision to forgo child custody might amount to another example of women's quiescence in the face of glaring injustice stemming from disputation and litigation. Similarly, a cynic might readily dismiss the offstage talk—the one in which Dejin tried to nudge Manli into child abduction—as yet another manifestation of the legal profession's insincerity toward its clientele. After all, sociolegal scholars have long noted the court system's tendency to co-opt the legal profession, eviscerating its professional commitments and undercutting its duties to clients.[39] It is little wonder that those in the legal profession sing one tune in the presence of judges and another when they are left alone with their clients. At this point, one might ask: Isn't that the Janus-faced nature of the legal profession? What more can we read into that fleeting moment when Dejin peddled the idea of Manli taking matters into her own hands?

That moment is, I believe, pivotal, for it spotlights the falling of the curtain that separates the legal profession's public and hidden performances vis-à-vis those on the bench. Judges are far too often exposed to the former while being blocked from viewing the latter. Spending at least six hours in two legal workers' offices, five days a week, for nine months—following Dejin and his coworkers around, and accompanying them to various court proceedings, dinner meetings, and holiday gatherings—enabled me, in contrast to judges, to discern the dramatic discrepancies between the legal profession's onstage performance and offstage conduct.

Onstage, legal workers routinely play out acts of deference in face-to-face interactions with judges and other court personnel—bowing their heads, lowering their voices, feigning smiles, and using official titles, such as *judge* (法官), *provision head* (庭长), and *president* (院长), to address court insiders. To convey the outward impression of homage, legal workers habitually engage in rituals to reconfirm their subordinate positions in the court system. A telling example is *jingyan* (敬烟)—that is, offering cigarettes as a gesture of humility.

In Weifeng, most legal workers were male, and so were the judges in the People's Tribunals. In power-laden encounters between these two male groups, sharing cigarettes became a highly ritualistic practice. The sharing was, of course, never meant to be a two-way exchange. During my stay in Weifeng, I never saw a judge offer a cigarette to a legal worker. Invariably, it was the other way around. Simply handing a cigarette to a judge would not suffice. A veteran in the legal profession would extend the ritual by bending over slightly, maintaining eye contact, and monitoring the judge's facial expression and body language—to determine whether he needed to light the cigarette right away. If the cigarette went directly to the judge's mouth, the legal worker would immediately pull out a lighter, create a flame, and gently bring it to the tip of the cigarette. Depending on the judge's rank, seniority, and formal or informal influences among peers and, additionally, depending on how desperate a legal worker felt about the case he was representing, he might have to decide what to do with the rest of the cigarettes in his pocket. Dejin, for example, always kept extra unopened packs in his briefcase, knowing that he might need more than a single cigarette to break the ice.

The legal profession's systemic subordination to the court system, a well-documented reality,[40] means that trading a slap for a slap, an insult for an insult, is out of the question, although legal workers frequently find their egos bruised and dignity crushed at the hands of court insiders. Indeed, enduring judges' slights, condescension, sarcasm, rudeness, angry outbursts, and routine extortion, while concealing one's embarrassment, bitterness, resentment, and moral indignation, is an integral part of legal workers' experiences inside courtrooms. The ability to manage one's emotions and particularly to choke back one's negative feelings about authorities—efforts sociologists call *emotional labor*—is crucial for legal workers' survival in the official justice system.[41]

Small wonder then that Li Yinxue, a female legal worker in her mid-forties, never lost her cool inside the courthouse, not even in front of a foul-mouthed judge who occasionally addressed her as "stupid woman" (瓜婆娘) and "silly broad" (傻婆娘). Her reaction was to keep her chin up, as if nothing could get under her skin. When a judge scorned Dejin for his penmanship and then his writing, including his diction, Dejin listened soundlessly, holding a steady grin on his face. Smiling away indignity within these four walls seems to be a Hobson's choice for law practitioners who anticipate returning to the same court to wrestle with the same judge day after day, year after year. Even Wang Xin, the head of the Guxiao Legal Workers' Office, one of the most established practitioners in Weifeng, could not escape servility. When a judge demanded a bribe, Wang Xin readily complied by passing point-by-point instructions to his client, a female plaintiff on her third attempt to divorce a mentally disabled husband. His essential point was that she ought to pay the judge's dinner, as well as other expenses related to her suit. And she had to do so quietly and discreetly.[42]

Succumbing to material exploitation, conducting emotional labor, and staging everyday rituals of homage are all crucial elements of the legal profession's public performance, orchestrated for a particular audience: those in black robes. Symbolic and ritualistic as this performance may be, it achieves rather practical ends. The plain truth is that the court system needs the legal profession to keep its clients in line, thereby making judging more manageable. The choreography of a credible performance of cooperation thus entails genuine—or feigned—efforts on the part of the legal profession to "manage" its clients, especially their expectations for litigation outcomes. And that is precisely what Dejin tried to deliver in front of Judge Qian: to make his client, Manli, forgo child custody, so the judge could satisfy Lawyer Liu and close the case expeditiously. By holding divorcing women's rights contention in check, the legal profession seeks to visualize its allegiance to the court system and reaffirm its place in a power structure in which judges sit atop the hierarchy, counsel in the middle, and female clients at the bottom.

This allegiance, played out for the judges' benefit, is not the whole story. Out of judges' earshot, outside the courthouse, law practitioners often maintain another set of speeches, memories, and practices that dispute, negate, and defy the dominance of court insiders. These speeches, memories, and practices constitute the hidden transcript of resistance the disempowered may engage in. Gossip, rumors, slander, character assassination, curses, backbiting, and double-dealing are the mundane weapons those in subordinate positions can take up to push back the boundaries of insubordination.

Indeed, rather than deference, contempt was one of the core emotions legal workers generally felt toward court insiders. And they were not afraid to air their true feelings behind closed doors. For example, when a judge asked Li Yinxue to make her client withdraw a divorce petition, she did not oppose the request on the spot. But upon returning to her office, located in the same neighborhood as the Xiqing People's Tribunal, Li Yinxue could not keep her discontent bottled up anymore. "Why on earth would I do that?" she asked, attempting a sneer. "Yang Meihua [the client] has filed the suit and paid the litigation fee, already." By raising a derisive rhetorical question, Li Yinxue vocalized her resentment toward the judge, toward a court system that sought to meet bureaucratic needs, like ratcheting up the rate of withdrawal, at the expense of citizens' access to justice. In the end, Li Yinxue did not bother to talk to her client about withdrawal.[43]

Dejin, likewise, found his way to unload his bitterness as a court regular. Meeting with coworkers, friends, and acquaintances at the mahjong tables, Dejin, a man with a facility for words, regularly ventured into lively narration of his latest encounters with court insiders. In his stories, each judge carried distinct features, hence a befitting nickname. One judge, an army veteran in his late fifties, was called a "white-eyed wolf" (白眼狼), owing to his insatiable appetite for bribes and perpetual lack of respect for legal workers. Another judge was named a "smiley tiger" (笑面虎) for his combination of seemingly friendly mannerisms and secretly wicked demeanor toward litigants. While portraying those judges as corrupt and abusive, Dejin did not forget to recast himself in his narratives. Constantly pitting his wits against those in black robes, outsmarting his opponents on the other side of the aisle, bringing local party cadres to heel, exploiting loopholes in the law...graphic details as such abounded in Dejin's recollections of his decade-long legal practice.[44]

Dejin is certainly not the only legal worker famous (or infamous) for his bluffing, bragging, and blustering. Talking big is hardly uncommon among law practitioners in Weifeng and elsewhere. Whether their stories of courtroom adventures are truths, half-truths, or outright untruths is beside the point. The crux of the matter is that, in this type of narration, law practitioners are anything but powerless, and court insiders are scarcely as omnipotent as they wish to appear. Featuring a multitude of rhetorical tactics—hyperbole, caricature, metaphor, mockery, travesty, farce, and so on—this narration powerfully attests to the legal profession's capability to dispute and negate court insiders' dominance in formal decision-making arenas.

A skeptic might now argue against taking such mundane forms of insubordination too seriously. Li Yinxue's reluctance to play along with the judge is, the skeptic might argue, at best ephemeral and at worst inconsequential. Dejin's indulgence in his tales of (more or less imagined) formidable pushback from underdogs inside courtrooms, in this view, merely renders otherwise insufferable situations tolerable. Elevating subordinate groups' trivial, opportunistic, and self-interested attempts at chipping away at domination may end up romanticizing powerlessness, the skeptic might insist.[45]

This skepticism is myopic, I believe, for it overlooks the potentiality of commonplace insubordination. Li Yinxue is not an outlier when it comes to resistance to the court system's fixation on case withdrawal. Nationwide, approximately 20 percent of first-instance divorce suits ended in withdrawal between 2003 and 2011 (see figure 5.1 in chapter 5). A sample of 198 divorce cases, retrieved from the Guxiao Legal Workers' Office, however, suggests that, during that period, the cases handled by legal workers featured much lower rates of withdrawal: only 10 percent of female petitioners, along with 16 percent of male petitioners, eventually withdrew their divorce suits (chapter 7 provides a closer look at this sample). A comparison of the national statistics and the office's records points to two possibilities. One, petitioners who go as far as to hire legal professionals to pursue divorce are more resistant to case withdrawal than the general population. Or two, there has been plenty of pushback from legal workers who recognize that the procedure of withdrawal diminishes their clients' prospect of marital dissolution.

My observations of practitioner-client interactions in two legal workers' offices confirm the second possibility. As chapter 5 illustrates, judges routinely turn down first-time divorce petitions; in consequence, plaintiffs must endure at least two separate petitions to legally dissolve their marriages. In ignoring judges' call for withdrawal, legal workers like Li Yinxue try to keep their clients on the right track. Carrying clients through the first petition and swiftly proceeding to the second one is a strategic move, for many legal workers are cognizant of an unspoken rule: a second-time divorce petition generally stands a better chance of advancing a client's quest for divorce. Repeated refusal to comply with judges' demands for withdrawal, in other words, is neither ephemeral nor inconsequential. It rather amounts to profession-wide resistance to an overbearing court system that has been mired in its own bureaucratic needs and wants. However limited, this resistance matters, for it helps divorcing women and men—the vast majority of whom have no prior experience in wrestling with the judiciary—navigate the system and avoid bureaucratic traps.

Dejin's narration of corrupt court insiders, I must point out, takes everyday resistance one step further. Every time he recounted his courtroom experiences, he exposed the hypocrisy, irregularity, and systemic abuses among those in positions of power. Circulating accounts of this kind among his peers serves an important purpose. It allows law practitioners to share experiences of indignity at the hands of legal authorities, to verbalize otherwise pent-up frustrations and indignation against power-holders, and to validate individual opinions about the official justice system, all of which contribute to an us-versus-them outlook, thereby counteracting the atomizing conditions of subordination. Shared experiences, sentiments, and identities, in turn, provide the grounds for the emergence of a dissident subculture.

Dejin's attempt to push Manli into parental kidnapping thus must be viewed against the backdrop of this subculture among legal workers. The very subculture does not just dispute or negate the dominance of court insiders in formal decision-making arenas. Rather, it seeks to subvert prevailing power structures in the courts and in rural communities. By exposing judges' limits in enforcing rulings on child custody, by revealing the police's inability to curb parental abduction as well as local communities' failures to catch "deviant" mothers on the run, Dejin informed—and emboldened—rural women who would otherwise possess little insider knowledge of the cracks in the extant power structures. Indeed, Dejin's talk of self-help did turn into a real and effective disputing strategy in some cases.

Deng Pingping, a widow who was suing her in-laws over an inheritance dispute, did precisely as Dejin had suggested—waiting outside of her son's school, snatching the five-year-old the moment he stepped out, and concealing their whereabouts ever since. By seizing physical control of her son, Pingping quickly turned her suit on its head. Unable to secure the police's or the local community's intervention in parental abduction, Pingping's in-laws had no choice but to approach her to renegotiate the terms of inheritance. They did so in hopes of regaining the custody of the boy, the sole heir of their deceased son. To track the progression of this dispute, I interviewed Pingping seven times at various points in her struggles to actualize her spousal, property, and custodial rights. From those interviews, I learned a great deal about Dejin's influence on her decision to hide her son from her in-laws, a move that amounted to a serious assault on male dominance in rural communities.[46]

Like Dejin, many legal workers in Weifeng were clear-eyed about the Achilles' heel of the grassroots court system—the limited ability to enforce its own rulings. In theory, if after divorce a parent ignores a court ruling and refuses to cede child custody, the other parent can ask the court to take forceful measures (强制措施). A judge, according to the Civil Procedural Law, can then impose a fine or period of detention on the noncomplying parent.[47] In practice, the law is often toothless, because divorcing (or divorced) women are highly mobile. Their extended participation in labor migration has equipped many of them with geographic mobility, financial resources, and certain social networks in the cities where they have lived and worked. Those resources and networks can come in handy, should the women decide to run away from court judgments disfavoring them as mothers, property owners, and/or victims of domestic violence.

Using labor migration as a means to shirk legal responsibilities and consequences arising from divorce litigation—a strategy I have seen time and again in my field research—would not be possible without the legal profession's goading, coaching, and urging. In that sense, legal workers in rural China serve as cultural ambassadors. In disseminating a dissident subculture, they sow the seeds of disobedience and defiance in divorcing women. Moreover, they guide the women to spot the openings, lapses, and cracks in the official justice system. Finally, they teach women on the verge of divorce important skills, tactics, and lessons for self-help, so the latter can affront patriarchy in the underbelly of the law.

CONCLUSION

In his seminal 1967 study of criminal defense attorneys in the United States, Abraham S. Blumberg shed light on the legal profession's tendency to be co-opted by the court system. In the decades since, sociolegal scholars have time after time generated similar findings, bespeaking the courts' ability to reorient attorneys toward the needs, goals, and interests of the official justice system.

In recent years, studies of the Chinese legal profession have noted a similar tendency among lawyers in private practice. Criminal defense lawyers, for instance, must confront a duality in the everyday practice of law. On the one hand, they often seek justice by trying to hold state power, including the power of the judiciary, in check. Many, on the other hand, rely on their ties to state actors to mount a good defense for clients. Heavy reliance on ties with police, procuracy, and courts, however, can cut both ways, offering lawyers protections and convenience in case processing, but also thrusting them more deeply into systemic subordination to state power. As some assume the role of pragmatic brokers, using their ties with state authorities to pursue economic gains, they wind up throwing higher political and professional ideals out the window.[48]

This chapter builds on extant research on organizational co-optation of legal professionals. It complements this literature by teasing out the legal and institutional arrangements that render such co-optation possible. Divorce settlements in rural China, I argue, offer a unique window into the inquiry of how certain arrangements inside courtrooms have occasioned collusion between judges and law practitioners. This collusion would not be feasible without certain power relations. Judges' attempts at prodding divorcing women into settlements would be merely empty threats, were they not equipped with formal decision-making power. Likewise, pushing clients into unfair settlements would not be possible, were legal workers deprived of their power to funnel some but not other contested issues into formal court proceedings.

Decision-making power and agenda-setting power, in other words, enable the court system and the legal profession to coordinate their attempts to deny women crucial rights on paper. This enabling effect is particularly insidious, for it evades formal, institutional scrutiny. Bringing down judges on the grounds of duress, cajolement, or other unethical and unprofessional conduct is highly unlikely in the People's Courts. The former judge Qian Shuting, who mediated Manli's divorce case, is living proof of the institutionalized impunity Chinese judges have long enjoyed.

While building on the extant literature, this chapter also exposes certain limitations in scholarly inquiries. Blumberg and many other researchers, I argue, fall short of exploring the limits of the court system's ability to co-opt the legal profession. Consequently, they fail to consider an alternative explanation: organizational co-optation of the legal profession may be staged, scripted, and feigned. This problem is particularly salient in recent studies of Chinese legal professionals.

Over two decades or so, researchers have placed Chinese lawyers in a number of groupings: politically embedded lawyers; state-adjacent lawyers; *weiquan* lawyers (*weiquan* literally means rights defense in Chinese); activist lawyers; human rights lawyers; moderate lawyers; radicalized lawyers; progressive elites; pragmatic brokers; notable activists; grassroots activists; routine practitioners, and so on. Corresponding to each grouping, researchers claim, is one set of distinct self-identities, practices, and specific positioning in relation to the state or society. Starting with definitional fiat, researchers then proceed to spell out how each group stands out, owing to its style of legal practice.[49] So far, there has been some critical reflection on this approach, which strives to catalog law practitioners by applying increasingly refined labels and classifications.[50] The fundamental assumption behind this approach, nevertheless, has remained unquestioned. Here, the unstated assumption is that practitioners carry their identities around, along with their distinctive style of legal practice and positioning to state or societal actors, as if identities, practices, and social relationships could stay static across space and over time. The legal workers in this chapter, however, prove otherwise.

These practitioners defy easy categorization in that they often buttress power in one setting and then go on to dispute, negate, and even subvert the same power relation in another context—all of which could take place in the course of a single lawsuit. By separating the legal profession's public and hidden performances, I hope to shine a light on the variation, complexity, and dynamics in practitioners' interactions with clients, community members, and court insiders. In those interactions, which identity practitioners assume (e.g., counsel or business entrepreneurs; court regulars or rural community members; or someone's kith and kin), how they position themselves in relation to power-holders and the disempowered, and what strategies of action they take often hinge on situational contexts and other contingencies. This is to say, the same group of practitioners can contribute to social reproduction of power and inequality in one time and space, and so can they resist and undermine power and inequality in another context. For that reason, placing practitioners in static categories, however refined they might be, runs the risk of pigeonholing and stereotyping those in the legal profession.

CHAPTER 7

Issues and Nonissues

ANOTHER DAY, ANOTHER DIVORCE

"I might as well burn myself to death"

The man was having an affair. Looking no further, Wang Guiping knew her marriage was in peril. He Jun, her husband of two decades, had moved in with the other woman. He had brought her to a few family gatherings. Their kin had heard an earful about her—her looks, her work, her vices big and small. Their mutual friends had sat around mahjong tables with her on holidays. Their neighbors had spotted her coming and going at a thousand-square-foot apartment, a property the He family had recently purchased in the bustling county seat. Their eighteen-year-old son had met with his father's girlfriend. What Guiping considered as *theirs*, now was on the verge of becoming *hers*.

Like millions of other rural women toiling in China's booming urban economies, Guiping had managed to scrape by, her world divided between a family life in a western inland village and a cash-paying factory job in an eastern coastal city thousands of miles away. Her routines during those twelve years of migration alternated between tilling farmland and attending to the young and old at home, in one season, and churning out products on assembly lines, earning meager wages, and succumbing to homesickness, in another. Her marriage to He Jun, the man she had hoped to grow old with, would survive separation across time and space, Guiping told herself. "We were two lovebirds back then," she remembered.

That past seemed even more remote now. Despite that, Guiping still resisted the idea of taking the easy way out. "Divorce is no light matter," she insisted. "Besides, the man may turn around, eventually, if I give him one more consideration, one more opportunity."

For months, Guiping fought to keep that dream alive. The smallest gestures from her husband, a phone call or a greeting as commonplace as "Have you eaten?" fed her hopes. Perhaps their life would go on to remain *theirs*, after all.

A violent assault burst her bubble one midsummer evening. Having started a brawl, He Jun pinned his wife to the ground. He pushed her face against the cement. He twisted her arm from behind. Holding her in that position, he cursed her in every way imaginable. And he threatened to kill her on that spot. Repeatedly. There and then, it hit Guiping: her marriage was beyond salvable.

On a blisteringly hot day later that summer, I ran into Guiping at the Xiqing People's Tribunal. She was there to hear a judge's ruling on her divorce petition without even the faintest inkling of what was to come. Hours later, she would find herself betrayed not only by her husband but also by the court system and her own counsel. That realization would plunge her more deeply into despair, so deeply that reducing herself to ashes would seem the only way out.

Placing Wang Guiping alongside Li Zhiqing, Han Donglin, Lan Yu, Wu Manli, and the young woman of chapter 3, whose name I failed to learn, this chapter joins the previous ones in a concerted effort to reconceive the notion of dispute resolution. To do so, as indicated before, is to study dispute resolution in terms of interconnected power relations. Conceptually and empirically, this entails an untiring analysis of how the People's Republic of China (PRC) has over time exerted three types of influence in shaping the terrain of conflict management: *agenda-setting power, decision-making power,* and *consciousness-formation power.* Where chapters 4, 5, and 6 explore the nexus between the first two types, the current chapter focuses on the second and the third. Taking Guiping's courtroom experience as a window, this chapter peers into judges' exercise of decision-making power in litigation. By invoking this power, those on the bench expressly determine who—husband or wife—prevails inside courtrooms in conflicts over child custody, property division, and other issues. Meanwhile, judges also routinely apply agenda-setting power with which they seek to thwart and suppress rights claims brought by some but not other litigants. In doing so, they push highly contested matters, such as domestic violence, out of formal deliberation. In the end, litigation often neglects the most vulnerable in marriage, especially victims of spousal abuse and abandonment, leaving them utterly alone in their suffering.

Whether judges exert decision-making or agenda-setting power, their deliberation centers on a set of manifest conflicts over identifiable, specific grievances and interests—infidelity, domestic violence, property division, and allocation of child custody are the most typical examples. Oftentimes, so nakedly do they wield their authority inside courtrooms that it is virtually impossible to overlook the effects of judicial conduct on women's rights contention. When power asserts itself this way—unapologetic, unveiled, over well-delineated issues—it lends itself to resistance, insubordination, and certainly to scholarly scrutiny. Indeed, a close inspection of litigation outcomes reveals stark gender disparities. Most of the women in this book walked away from their divorce suits with little or no marital property, child support, or any remedies for wrongdoings, including domestic violence and desertion. Their male counterparts, by contrast, managed to retain child custody and conjugal property; those responsible for adultery, spousal abuse, or marital rape invariably escaped penalty. Suffice to say that, within the walls of the courthouse, the links between state power and gender inequality are scarcely invisible.

Consciousness-formation power, on the other hand, operates in much less conspicuous ways, and its impact on women's legal mobilization tends to elude the most watchful eyes. To unveil the workings of this power, the latter half of the chapter brings to light a stark contrast: upon divorce, women like Guiping make herculean efforts to actualize their spousal, custodial, and/or property rights; many, however, remain silent about their lawful entitlement to landholding. In other words, some matters are disputed vehemently, while others remain nonissues, unquestioned and unchallenged in legal mobilization by citizens. Why?

The answer, I argue, lies in the perverting potential of state power and particularly its capacity to induce compliance, quiescence, and a profound sense of powerlessness among citizens. To flesh out this argument, I show that the PRC, through decades of lawmaking and policymaking, has entrenched a reform-era land regime, which is by and large compatible with a patriarchal-patrilineal-patrilocal family structure that has reigned supreme in rural China for centuries. This land regime, one may contend, is premised on state-endorsed male dominance both at home and in society at large. Contesting rights to landholding, in this context, is not just legally or politically unactionable; it is all but unspeakable and unthinkable to many women. Better put, state power has configured women's discourse and practices, and so has it shaped their consciousness, as well as their ideas of grievances, interests, and possibilities of contestation in situations of latent conflicts. The most insidious exercise of power over the disempowered, it turns out, is the kind that can keep interests from being recognized, grievances from being voiced, and disputes from arising in the first place.

* * *

When the estranged couple turned up at the tribunal on that sizzling morning in mid-July, Guiping and her husband could not have looked more average. Also unremarkable was their path to divorce, one so typical as to be banal. They married young, they sweated blood to make a living, they grew older and apart, while hitting every rung on the climb to a middle-class life. They then decided to part ways. Now, they became another case number in front of Chen Heping, a veteran judge in his late fifties.

The couple's son had recently turned eighteen, old enough to stand on his own feet, so child custody was not in question. The only remaining issue, according to the judge, was to determine who should get what at the time of divorce. For that purpose, Judge Chen summoned Guiping, the plaintiff, to his office, while keeping the defendant and his counsel in a separate room.

"How about this?" The judge cast a look at his desk, case files piling on top of one another, printouts scattered all over, mail unopened. "Regarding property division—"

"I-I've been thinking," said Guiping. "I mean. Aren't I entitled to the farmhouse—"

Judge Chen frowned and interrupted Guiping. "I've discussed that with He Jun. The farmhouse, renovated years ago, is not worth mentioning."

Guiping and her family, for nearly a decade, had lived in a brick farmhouse an hour east of the county seat. Having obtained a loan of twenty thousand yuan in 2001, Guiping worked out a plan to rebuild the property. To do so within budget, she took a two-month break from her factory job, speedily turning herself into a bricklayer, carpenter, pipe fitter, plumber. Construction is said to be a man's job, but Guiping did it with no less vim or vigor. To her mind, the farmhouse was obviously worth mentioning.

"As for the recently purchased apartment," Judge Chen carried on his speech, "it was obtained during your marriage, but its ownership has been settled. If you insist on property partition, let's talk about how to divide the debts [resulting from the purchase]."

Guiping harbored a different view. Both her and He Jun's natal families had chipped in financially to make it possible for the couple to afford a property whose value was expected to rise in the years to come. While the deed listed their son as the sole owner, Guiping and her siblings' monetary contributions should be recognized by law, she told me later.

Judge Chen apparently did not believe so. "The apartment, when you bought it, the ownership went to your son. Now, neither you nor your husband can make claims on that property." Dropping that announcement, the judge returned to his attempts to tidy his desk.

Standing in a corner of the office, I was unsure where to look— Guiping's sun-damaged face, her mud-covered sandals, or the judge's hands, hurling around folders, pencils, notepads, dotting the dreadful silence in the room with intermittent noise.

Suddenly, Judge Chen looked up and turned to Guiping. "Come on. Do you want a divorce or not? If yes, you'd better act fast. Act decisively. That way, you'll get a divorce in thirty seconds."

"I must get a divorce," said Guiping.

"Then why are you being so insistent on property division? Why not just stay married and keep everything [in your marriage]?" The judge tossed something into the trash can without a second look. "In my view, this case is super simple."

That "simplicity," it turned out, hinged on Guiping's "decisiveness," which is to say, her willingness to forgo marital property in its entirety.

"You expect to hold on to every piece of property. How is that possible?" the judge grumbled. "You two still owe relatives thirty thousand yuan after purchasing the apartment. Why not let the guy take care of the debts? So you can walk away."

"That's it?" asked Guiping.

"That's it!" Judge Chen, annoyed, repeated. "Otherwise, you two might as well just stay married."

"But he has forced me into a corner."

"So?"

"No, I can't stay married."

Judge Chen took the opportunity to circle back to his earlier point. Guiping stood no chance of obtaining any shares of the recently purchased apartment, he insisted. The only way to free Guiping from her marriage with "no strings attached" was to preserve her son's ownership of the apartment and make He Jun pay off the debts.

At the time the couple was thirty thousand yuan in debt. Guiping was liable for half of it, according to the Marriage Law. The same law also entitled her to half of the couple's shared property, including the farmhouse, investments in the apartment, agricultural machinery, home furniture, and other items whose combined value far exceeded fifteen thousand yuan. It made no sense, mathematically or legally, for the wife to forsake her property rights altogether, just to relieve herself of the debts. Unsurprisingly, Guiping stood there, red-faced and wordless.

Her silence inflamed the judge. With a career spanning from the army to the bench, from operating military gear to wielding the gavel, Judge Chen was not known for his geniality. Among court regulars, gossip ran rampant, graphically detailing the judge's distinct ways to "deliver justice." When Guiping made another attempt to emphasize her property claims, Judge Chen yelled, "Stop hustling!" From the top of his lungs came another shout. "It's hard enough mediating divorce cases!"

"I must get a divorce. Because—"

"In that case," Judge Chen cut Guiping off again, "I'll prepare the paperwork. Arrange for the guy to cover the debts. End of story!"

"But..."

Both visibly upset, the judge and the plaintiff unleashed a torrent of arguments and counterarguments, yelling and pleading, for the next ten minutes or so. At one point, Guiping asked in a high-pitched tone, "What about the grain storage?"

"Grain storage? How much could that be worth these days? Why don't you grab some bowls and chopsticks [upon divorce]?" the judge replied.

"It's over five hundred kilos of grain. I planted it. I harvested it," said Guiping, ignoring the judge's mockery.

At another point, when asked to withdraw her petition and "forget about divorce," Guiping implored, again, "Without a divorce, I'd be stuck in a living hell." Tears in her eyes, she could barely piece together her next sentence. "The man...My heart. Shattered already."

"All right. Let's just settle the case, then." Judge Chen lowered his voice upon seeing her tears. Looking out his window as if he were curious about the whereabouts of a cool breeze, he mumbled, "This summer is unbearable. Why waste time here, going back and forth? I'll talk to the guy again. Tell him to clear the debts." The judge directed his next command to Guiping: "As for you, let go of the property."

"Fine. I'll do that," Guiping gave in.

Satisfied, Judge Chen cast another glance at his desk while making one more flight into derision: "Marital property, huh? Why don't you grab some chickens?"[1]

***

Shortly after Guiping signed divorce papers under the judge's watchful eyes, I approached her. She readily accepted my request for an interview. Outside the tribunal, the two of us found a quiet street corner, strewn with trash, including a wooden bench to sit on. There, Guiping and I dove into a conversation about her marriage and divorce, the past and the present in her family life.

Halfway through the conversation, Guiping jumped off the bench, suddenly panicked. It had just occurred to her that she had left behind her keys to the couple's apartment, where she kept all her personal possessions, cash, clothing, and other everyday necessities. Retrieving those items would be impossible if He Jun made it home first. That horrifying realization that she had lost all her belongings accumulated in a two-decade-long relationship abruptly set in. Guiping bolted, leaving me with a despairing look on her face and her parting words: "What am I gonna do? I might as well burn myself to death."[2]

I never heard from Guiping again. Over the next few months, many times I returned to that tribunal, and many times I revisited the legal worker involved in Guiping's case, hoping to locate her. Nobody brought up her name again. The dispute had been settled, case closed, justice served.

Guiping's courtroom experience, in many respects, strikes me as woefully familiar. To reach speedy settlements and clear court dockets, Judge Chen is probably no more cavalier than his colleagues who appear in the previous chapters. His attempts to stifle rights contention by a wife who, compared to the husband, is often the more vulnerable party in litigation stem from the same playbook judges routinely use in courtroom interactions. Inside this playbook is a long list of judicial techniques and tactics black-letter laws hardly ever speak of: deceit, derision, humiliation, intimidation, manipulation, thinly veiled or naked threats, deliberate misinterpretation of legal rules and norms, to name a few. Those engaging in such conduct rarely fret over consequences, whether legal or political, owing to the PRC's enduring efforts to imbricate certain revolutionary legacies, especially mediation, with other reform measures in the People's Courts (see chapter 5 for an analysis of the continued centrality of mediation in present-day divorce law practices and its implications for women's rights contention).

Guiping's counsel, a legal worker named Li Yinxue, is no more incompetent than most of her coworkers. During the aforementioned mediation, Li Yinxue stood beside Guiping, but did not stand up for her. Nobody informed Guiping of her lawful entitlement to the couple's joint property, after being married for more than two decades. Nobody cited her rights to damages—that is, the kind of compensations victims of adultery and domestic violence are entitled to under the Marriage Law.[3] Nobody defended her access to adequate legal counseling. The simple truth is that Guiping did not receive quality legal services. Nor did the other women in this book. After paying handsome legal fees out of their own pockets, few received competent or sufficient legal representation in disputation or in litigation (chapters 3 and 5 provide in-depth analyses of the legal profession's failures to protect the rights and interests of female clients).

Guiping's husband, morally flawed and, in theory, legally liable, suffered no consequences in the courtroom. Not only did he retain the couple's joint property but also waltzed his way through the proceeding. Nobody checked whether his conduct—abandoning and assaulting his wife and cohabiting with another woman—constituted spousal abandonment, domestic violence, or bigamy, all of which are codified offenses.[4] This husband, I must point out, is no more fortunate than many other men out there. As the pages ahead show, the courts seldom hold husbands responsible for adultery, desertion, extreme cruelty, or neglect, although lawmakers have repeatedly condemned these behaviors.

Guiping's conjugal community, with time, was inundated with rumors and gossip about her husband's infidelity. Some in her village had even witnessed his violent assault on Guiping, a detail I learned from my conversation with her. Yet nobody showed up at the tribunal to testify on her behalf. Nobody other than the legal worker accompanied her to her court proceeding, and nobody was there to offer emotional or moral support. Her husband, on the other hand, turned up in the company of two relatives. Guiping's aloneness inside the courtroom is far from unique. Women on the verge of divorce often face social isolation, because community members tend to treat married-in wives as outsiders and their husbands and in-laws as insiders. This outsider-insider divide, a reality chapter 5 lays bare, makes it hard for women to marshal communal support for their rights contention. By comparison, men upon divorce are much more effective in mobilizing their natal villages to back up their legal action. Guiping's courtroom experience, in other words, mirrors the realities of the wider world outside the tribunal. In China's sprawling countryside, women's isolation and fragility within the court system is all but a corollary to their isolation and fragility at home and in community.

Stark gender disparities in litigation outcomes

Over the years, I have seen many women—of rural origin, at various stages of life, with varying experiences in labor migration—entering divorce litigation and expecting fairness and equity down the road. The majority, however, only come to have their notions of justice, fairness, and equity being gutted in the end. Guiping's divorce, in that sense, is just another garden-variety case in the People's Courts. Indeed, a systematic analysis of litigation outcomes shows in detail how poorly women have fared compared to men in the grassroots court system.

During my stay in Weifeng County, I reviewed all the records of divorce cases processed by the Guxiao Legal Workers' Office between 2003 and 2011. This effort led to a meticulous examination of over three thousand pages of legal documents, including divorce petitions filed by plaintiffs, witness testimonies, other forms of evidence, court judgments, mediation agreements, and, in some instances, counter-petitions prepared by defendants. After clearing incomplete records, I formed a sample of 198 divorce cases, of which 167 were wife-initiated, and 31 were husband-initiated (see table 7.1 for more details). This overwhelmingly gendered pattern in the initiation of divorce is by and large consistent with the national statistics. As indicated before, throughout the history of the PRC, the vast majority of divorce petitions have been filed by wives, not husbands. The latest estimate, conducted by the Supreme People's Court (SPC) in 2018, suggests that approximately 70 percent of divorce suits nationwide were lodged by women rather than men.[5]

Using this sample, I analyzed how litigation outcomes varied by several factors: gender; the initiation of divorce (wife-initiated versus husband-initiated); modes of case disposition (mediation versus adjudication); and, finally, contested issues (e.g., child custody, property division, and domestic violence). To sort out litigation outcomes along those lines, I created four codes: (1) husband prevails; (2) wife prevails; (3) split; and (4) no decision. For example, if a judge granted sole custody to a father, I marked that outcome as *husband prevails*. If sole custody went to a mother, I labeled that as *wife prevails*. If a judge assigned joint custody to father and mother, that ruling was coded as a *split*.

Regarding property division, if a court granted all marital property to a husband, I recorded that as *husband prevails*; conversely, if a ruling allowed a wife to obtain all conjugal property, that result was coded as *wife prevails*. As for *split*, in this context, it refers to a situation in which a judge divided property between the two disputing parties. Finally, if a

TABLE 7.1 A sample of divorce suits in Guxiao and nearby townships, 2003–2011

	Wife-Initiated Divorce	Husband-Initiated Divorce
Litigants' characteristics	Means or Percentage	
Plaintiff's age	35	37
Defendant's age	38	34
Years of marriage	12	11
Children's characteristics		
Number of children	1	0.87
Average age of the oldest child	12	12
Oldest child male	49%	79%
First-time petition or not		
First petition	90%	100%
Second petition	10%	0
Counsel or village cadres involved		
Plaintiff represented by counsel	96%	87%
Defendant represented by counsel	34%	29%
Affidavits provided by village cadres	17%	42%
Case disposition		
Parties reconciled	0	0
Petition withdrawn	10%	16%
Petition rejected	12%	7%
Divorce approved via adjudication	29%	32%
Divorce approved via mediation	49%	45%
Total cases	167	31

SOURCE: the Guxiao Legal Workers' Office.

judge was mute on property partition, I used *no decision* to indicate that situation. Together, these analytical strategies enabled me to numerically specify variations in litigation outcomes in a way that was at once systematic and parsimonious.

Tables 7.2 and 7.3 show how allocation of child custody, a highly contested issue in divorce litigation, varied by gender and other factors.

TABLE 7.2 Allocation of child custody in the husband-initiated suits ($n_1=16$)

	Mediated Cases	Adjudicated Cases
Husband prevails	75%	100%
Wife prevails	25%	0
Split	0	0
No decision	0	0
Total	12	4

NOTE: Among the 31 husband-initiated suits, 25 resulted in a judge dissolving the marriage in question, of which only 16 involved children under the age of 18.

TABLE 7.3 Allocation of child custody in the wife-initiated suits ($n_2=110$)

	Mediated Cases	Adjudicated Cases
Husband prevails	74%	47%
Wife prevails	26%	53%
Split	0	0
No decision	0	0
TOTAL	72	38

NOTE: Among the 167 wife-initiated suits, 129 resulted in a judge terminating the marriage in question, of which 110 involved children under the age of 18.

Overall, women rarely came out ahead in custodial disputes. Men, by contrast, stood a much better chance of holding on to their custodial rights upon divorce. For example, among the husband-initiated divorces, 75 percent of the cases resulted in a judge assigning sole custody to fathers via mediation; as for the adjudicated cases, judges invariably ruled in favor of fathers (see table 7.2). In the wife-initiated suits, fathers maintained a similar advantage; in 74 percent of the mediated cases, judges backed fathers' requests for custody. In one and only one scenario did mothers fare at all better than fathers. When judges could not reach settlements in the wife-initiated suits and had to adjudicate on custody, they favored mothers more than fathers by a small margin: 53 percent of those rulings supported women's custodial claims, and 47 percent upheld men's (see table 7.3).

At first glance, gender disparities seemed less stark in court rulings on property division. On this subject, judges' most typical reaction was inaction. Among the 198 suits, 129 resulted in a judge dissolving the marriage in question, of which 110 cases involved conjugal property jointly owned by wife and husband. Yet 84 out of the 110 cases—that is, 76 percent—featured no court decision on property partition. Put plainly, judges more often than not left the issue out of their rulings altogether. This happened again and again, not because women did not contest their property rights but because judicial silence on this matter derived from two prevailing pitfalls in the official justice system. For one, as indicated in chapter 3, the legal profession frequently failed to convert women's property claims into written requests, and subsequently failed to channel such requests into formal court proceedings. For women seeking to actualize their rights upon divorce, the consequences were dire: their demands for marital property had fallen through the cracks early on in the process of litigation.

The other pitfall, as Guiping's courtroom experience illustrates, has a lot to do with judges' elaborate efforts to block women's acts of contestation. In this way, those on the bench sought to simplify and expedite case disposition. Moreover, judges often traded women's property rights in exchange for men's cooperation in conflict resolution. Eventually, Guiping and many other women emerged from litigation with a piece of court paperwork utterly silent about their rights as property owners in marriage.[6] Silence of this kind can be hugely consequential. Absent formal court rulings, divorcées must either give up conjugal property altogether or negotiate privately with their ex-husbands in hopes of accessing housing and other possessions—a situation unlikely to yield satisfying results, given those women's isolation and vulnerability in their former conjugal communities. Finally, when judges did rule on property partition, they rarely sided with wives. Only 7 percent of the husband-initiated suits, together with 2 percent of the wife-initiated divorces, produced an outcome in which the wife prevailed (see tables 7.4 and 7.5).

In divorce litigation, another frequently contested matter is domestic violence. Out of the 198 suits, 97 contained myriad accounts depicting a wife's physical, mental, or emotional suffering at the hands of her

TABLE 7.4 Property division in the husband-initiated suits (n_3=25)

	Mediated Cases	Adjudicated Cases
Husband prevails	7%	0
Wife prevails	7%	0
Split	20%	0
No decision	66%	100%
Total	15	10

NOTE: Among the 31 husband-initiated suits, 25 resulted in a judge dissolving the marriage in question—that is, 25 cases entailed property division.

TABLE 7.5 Property division in the wife-initiated divorce suits (n_4=110)

	Mediated Cases	Adjudicated Cases
Husband prevails	42%	7%
Wife prevails	2%	0
Split	18%	5%
No decision	38%	88%
Total	66	44

NOTE: Among the 167 wife-initiated suits, 129 resulted in a judge terminating the marriage in question, of which 110 entailed property division (and the other 19 cases did not involve joint property, thus there was no need for partition).

husband—that is, nearly half of these cases attributed conjugal discontent, partially or entirely, to violence against women. Reading between the lines, I found it impossible to go over case records without a growing feeling of revulsion. Women's complaints of spousal abuse were everywhere, albeit in abbreviated form. They were scattered in interview notes (询问笔录), a log legal workers kept to record their initial encounters with prospective clients. Those complaints were also embedded in conference minutes (会议记录), which documented legal workers' meetings with disputants outside courtrooms. Moreover, women's accusations of domestic violence made their ways into divorce petitions, alternatively known as civil complaints (民事诉状), a document detailing petitioners' marital grievances and rights claims. Finally, evidence prepared by the women themselves or by their counsel attested to the prevalence and the severity of abuses in intimate relationships. Such evidence included medical records, photos of injuries, witness testimonies, and occasionally formal statements issued by village cadres and local government officials, all of which were meant to substantiate wives' accounts of their victimization in marriage.

In addition to case records, I myself witnessed at least eight women testify to their experiences as victims of domestic violence during court-organized mediation or formal trials. Their narrations of spousal abuse all fell on deaf ears. Judges and court clerks ignored them like they had turned a blind eye to the pages upon pages of civil complaints mentioned above. No judges or court clerks followed up on these complaints. No questions were raised during mediation sessions or trials. No investigations were conducted within or without courtrooms. The overall pattern was remarkably consistent: not a single case in the sample generated a court decision that expressly identified a husband as a perpetrator and thus the party responsible for domestic violence; not a single case demanded a violent, abusive spouse pay damages to his victim, although the Marriage Law decrees otherwise. Everywhere I looked in my data collection, I could not find any indication of judicial attempts to address violence against women.[7]

A skeptic might now raise questions about the quantity or quality of evidence the women submitted to the courts. After all, in divorce litigation, the burden of proof lies on the complainant. If she fails to back her plaints with solid evidence, it is no surprise that she would face an unfavorable court decision. Evidence in this context scarcely matters, though. A divorce suit filed by a woman named Feng Min in 2003 sheds some light on the relevance—or really irrelevance—of evidence. To back up her claims of victimization, Feng Min, along with two legal workers, amassed an enormous body of proof: hospital records, village clinic records, and eyewitnesses' testimonies signed by seventeen individuals, including neighbors and village cadres. Additionally, the Villagers' Committee (村民委员会), the Office of Mediation (调解办公室), the Justice Office (司法所), and the police station—part of the grassroots state apparatus in charge of conflict resolution—issued formal statements to corroborate Feng Min's accounts as a victim. Copious evidence, however, did not persuade the court into ruling in favor of the wife. A judge mediated and eventually settled the case, dissolving the couple's marriage, allowing Feng Min to raise their daughter and her husband to enjoy sole custody of their son. Nowhere in the court-approved settlements could I spot even a modicum of judicial redress for domestic violence; this once highly contested issue was completely obliterated from judicial decision-making. Another eleven cases in the sample also contained considerable evidence indicative of a wife's suffering from spousal abuse. None of those cases prompted a judge to break the silence on violence against women. Put bluntly, the quality or quantity of evidence made no difference. Nor did the modes of case disposition. Whether judges disposed of cases via mediation or adjudication, they were unalterably stuck in their silence. These findings are consistent with the most recent studies of divorce litigation in China. In their research on this subject, He Xin and Kwai Hang Ng have repeatedly reported that in divorce suits, Chinese judges often undermine the rights of battered women, despite clear evidence of their prolonged suffering at home, despite lawmakers and other state actors' frequent vows to protect women from domestic violence.[8]

Year after year, the PRC has enshrined gender equality, inscribing it into countless laws, regulations, and policy directives. In 2001, when the Marriage Law was amended, legislators again reiterated some of the PRC's foundational principles: for example, the marriage system shall be based on "equality between men and women," "the lawful rights of women...shall be protected," and "maltreatment or desertion of any family members shall be prohibited." Moreover, the revised law, for the first time in the history of the PRC, stipulated civil penalties for blameworthy conjugal conduct, including bigamy, domestic violence, and spousal desertion, thereby entitling victims to seek damages upon divorce.[9] During the decade that followed, a number of national laws were upgraded to protect wives and other family members from domestic violence. In 2008, the SPC handed down concrete guidelines to lower courts so that judges could properly handle cases involving violence against women.[10] Seven years later, legislators promulgated the first anti-domestic violence law. In short, the PRC has no shortage of formal norms and rules intended to safeguard women's rights in marriage.

Judicial realities, on the other hand, are a world apart from legal prescriptions. In exercising decision-making power, judges regularly favor husbands over wives, assigning child custody to the former at the expense of the latter's lawful interests. In doing so, they align state power with the deep-seated patrilineal tradition in rural China. Moreover, judges routinely block women from mobilizing state law to challenge male dominance in property possession; in a similar vein, they time and again suppress women's painstaking attempts to confront male control over women's bodies and minds. Judicial inaction, in this context, constitutes a distinctive type of deliberation, or *nondecision* as some call it.[11] By regularly falling back on nondecision-making, judges in effect silence the aggrieved, deny them judicial redress, and push their rightful demands for state intervention out of formal decision-making arenas. In the end, rather than serving as the weapons of the weak, the courts operate at the service of the dominant gender group in Chinese society.

THE CONTESTED AND THE UNCONTESTED
A blind spot in rights contention

For years, Guiping's lament, "I might as well burn myself to death," has weighed on me. Was that lament a sign of resistance or resignation by a woman whose quest for justice was left in tatters? Had I been able to conduct a more in-depth interview with Guiping, I might address that question with certainty. Unfortunately, I could not locate her in the wake of that court proceeding. One thing is clear, though. Like many other women in this book, Guiping was cognizant of her rights as a wife and property owner, albeit with limited knowledge of the letter of the law. That cognizance had brought her to a courtroom battle over marital dissolution and property division. It had also spurred her to vehemently protest the judge's blatant disregard for her lawful rights and interests in marriage. Because of that cognizance, she was overcome with moral indignation upon realizing that the official justice system had abandoned her, just like her husband had. Guiping and many other women like her who seek to mobilize state law to actualize their rights, I must emphasize, are neither "cultural dopes" nor "structural dopes"—their actions in disputation are by no means predetermined by a patriarchal culture or social structures in Chinese society.[12]

Nevertheless, women's legal mobilization is bounded. On their way to divorce, while actively seeking spousal, custodial, and/or property rights, women all too often remain silent on their rights to landholding, although one national law after another has pledged to safeguard their lawful interests in land use in the countryside. The Marriage Law, in particular, insists that wives' rights in land use must be protected by law at the time of divorce.[13] Moreover, several mechanisms, including litigation, arbitration, and people's mediation, have been established to ensure that the aggrieved, be they women or men, can formally and openly contend for their land rights. Women, however, rarely take divorce litigation as a means to retain arable land and related income. Throughout my 2010–2011 field research in Weifeng, everywhere I looked, I found scant evidence indicative of women's attempts to secure landholding upon or after marital dissolution. Several findings attested to this blind spot in women's rights contention.

The first finding stemmed from the aforementioned sample of 198 divorce suits. Basically, contention over landholding was completely missing from court records. Nowhere in the divorce petitions could I find any traces of wives making claims on farmland, homesteads (宅基地), or other types of land. Nowhere in court rulings—either civil judgments (民事判决书) or civil mediation agreements (民事调解书)—could I spot any attempts by judges to partition couples' rights to land use at the end of their marriages. The absence of claim-making by wives, together with the nonexistence of decision-making on the part of judges, could have serious implications. Without a court ruling that formally designates a divorcée as a landholder, her ex-husband would very likely exercise de facto control over land and related resources. Following divorce, she would have to negotiate with him privately to regain access to farmland, a discussion unlikely to yield satisfying results, given their recent face-off in court.

Why did these women refrain from claiming rights to landholding, if they had gone so far as to take their husbands to court? Perhaps some did contest the matter, but somehow their claim-making slipped through the cracks, leaving few traces in court records. This speculation prompted me to extend my inquiries from written records to on-site observations. During my field research in Weifeng, I conducted observations in five People's

Tribunals, in Guxiao, Xiqing, and three nearby townships. By observing formal trials, mediation sessions, and informal face-to-face interactions between litigants and court personnel, I explored whether women were contentious about their land rights. These observations, over time, gave rise to the second finding: inside courtrooms, women—be they plaintiffs or defendants in divorce litigation—hardly ever demanded continued land use in their conjugal villages. In twenty months of field research, I never encountered a wife pursuing judicial remedies for her postdivorce access to land. Landholding, in other words, remained a nonissue in virtually all court proceedings, both formal and informal. Female litigants, their counsel, court clerks, and judges were all silent on this matter.

That women did not openly dispute land possession in front of court personnel should not be the end of my investigation, I reckoned. After all, sociolegal scholars have long insisted that researchers move beyond a court-centered approach by examining the earlier stages of disputation. Among other rewards, doing so allows researchers to problematize the role of the legal profession in shaping the paths disputants take and the specific goals they pursue in the course of conflict resolution.[14] With this scholarly advice in mind, I spent nine months in two legal workers' offices, one in Guxiao and the other in Xiqing, documenting and analyzing face-to-face interactions between women in pursuit of legal assistance and law practitioners in rural communities. My attempts at expanding inquiries from court proceedings to earlier moments in legal mobilization proved rewarding.

Inside these two offices, time after time, I witnessed women of different generations, varying educational backgrounds, and diverse work experiences making strenuous efforts to find and use state law. A good many came in with thought-out questions. Some asked explicitly how divorce litigation could free them from wrecked marriages, or how legal action could help them secure child custody or retain conjugal property upon divorce. Others raised questions of whether or how the court system could rein in a violent husband or obnoxious in-laws. What's more, women often went all out to win over potentially sympathetic counsel. To that end, they took pains to amass financial resources, to mobilize kinship ties to bond with legal workers, and to make both moral arguments and emotional pleas to underscore their need for expert support. In brief, the women I met during the field research were anything but hapless victims of patriarchy.

Fully recognizing women's agency, I must nonetheless stress the third finding: in neither office did I ever come across a wife requesting assistance for courtroom battles over land possession, use, or management. Conscious and vocal about their rights in marriage, few women attempted to cling to landholding upon divorce. In meeting with (prospective) counsel, few expressed their interest in farmland, and even fewer posed questions as to how to contest land rights inside or outside courtrooms. The initial finding described earlier—namely, that claim-making by wives was absent in court records—should thus not be attributed to the inaction of the legal profession. Put simply, it is not that the legal profession overlooked or deliberately blocked women's endeavors to seek land-related entitlements; rather, women themselves scarcely ever brought up this issue in their meetings with counsel.

What if divorcing women opted out of legal action due to concerns about its confrontational nature and instead preferred nonconfrontational solutions? What if some wound up holding closed-door negotiations with village cadres and government officials under the impression that local political elites might back their land use in the wake of divorce? Keeping these what-if questions in mind, I visited a number of grassroots bureaucracies in Weifeng, including seven Villagers' Committees at the village level; the Justice Office, the Office of Justice and Mediation (司法调解办), the Office of Letters and Visits and the Masses (信访与群众办公室), the Office of Comprehensive Management of Public Security (综治办), and the Center for Integrated Mediation for Disputes and Conflicts (矛盾纠纷大调解中心)—all at the township level; and, finally, four county-level agencies, the Women's Federation (妇女联合会), the Housing Management Office (房屋管理所), the Legal Aid Center (法律援助中心), and the Political Legal Committee (政法委员会). From these official entities, I learned a lot about how local state actors approached conflict management in general and how they went about stability maintenance (维稳) in particular.

At the Xiqing Justice Office, I gathered hundreds of pages of internal memorandums prepared by local officials between 2006 and 2010. These official records detailed mundane, frequent disputes among villagers, such as grievances over eldercare and debts. They also documented difficult, hot-button disputes, including popular contention over land-taking and demolition, environmental pollution, and incidents that triggered organized mass petitioning (群体性上访), suicide, homicide, and other serious criminal offenses. In combination, these official documents offered a rare glimpse of the prevailing grievances and rights contention the local state had closely monitored. Again, nowhere in those documents could I locate any signs of women wrestling with political elites to secure landholding upon or after divorce. After conducting eighteen in-depth interviews with local officials and village cadres, after combing through hundreds of pages of internal memorandums, I had to grapple with the fourth finding: outside the court system, scarcely any women launched political action to retain postdivorce access to farmland.

Finally, I triangulated the aforementioned archival, observational, and interview data with the information retrieved directly from divorcing women. To this end, I conducted sixty in-depth interviews with thirty-two women who were either considering marital dissolution or were already in the midst of divorce litigation. During the interviews, the vast majority made no mention of landholding when asked about their expectations for litigation outcomes. Many instead insisted that, once divorced, they would continue eking out a living as migrant workers in cities. Seen from this viewpoint, seeking postdivorce access to farmland seemed pointless.

This finding was unsurprising. As indicated in chapter 1, labor migration, over the past four decades, has empowered millions of rural women everywhere in the country, enabling many to forge new identities, gain economic independence, and re-envision and readjust their intimate lives. Participation in the urban labor force has also emboldened rural women to find out their rights at home and in the workplace, thus enhancing their willingness and ability to resist rights infringements in various social domains. Labor migration alone, however, is unlikely to provide rural women with long-term job security. Nor does it offer the same kind of social welfare urban residents have long enjoyed. Arable land, in the long run, will remain a crucial safety net for China's millions of migrant workers.[15] Women's quiescence on landholding at the time of divorce would very likely subject them to economic dependence or even destitution in the future. Acquiescence and inaction, one might argue, is hardly in those women's best interest.

To sum it up, everywhere I checked, there was nary a sign of women's contestation of landholding. Inside courtrooms, few wives took divorce litigation to materialize their lawful interests as land users. Outside the court system, few engaged in open or hidden resistance, overt or covert contestation, to push back against male dominance in land possession. Why didn't women contest their land rights, if they had already gone so far as to approach the legal profession for expert help and had petitioned the courts for judicial remedies for their marital grievances? What could account for this blind spot in their contentious acts? More fundamentally, in legal mobilization by citizens, why do some matters become fiercely disputed, and others stand unquestioned and uncontested? To address these questions, I believe that we must untangle the power structures behind the PRC's reform-era land regime.

Power and powerlessness in land possession

Between the late 1970s and the early 1980s, a time when the PRC sought to leave behind the Maoist era and usher in the Reform and Opening-Up (改革开放), a series of land policies were put in place. These policies, which later came to be known as the Household Responsibility System (家庭联产承包责任制) (HRS), enabled individual households to break away from People's Communes (人民公社), a key feature of the Maoist era, and to contract plots of arable land from collectives in the countryside. Approximately 95 percent of rural households—that is, over 175 million families—had formed contractual agreements with their collectives by the end of 1983.[16] Shortly afterward, they gained the rights to possess, use, and profit from collectively owned land and became obliged to pay taxes, fees, and in-kind quotas set by rural collectives and local governments. The promulgation of the Land Administration Law and the General Principles of the Civil Law, in 1986, codified these rights and obligations.[17] Subsequent lawmaking and policymaking has repeatedly affirmed the standing of the HRS as a bedrock institution in rural China.

The institutionalization of the HRS, on its face, has little to do with gender. In practice, gender—in the form of ingrained social norms, customary practices, and cultural categories—has profoundly structured the HRS, plunging women in certain regions, age cohorts, and/or of marital status into land dispossession.[18] Several mechanisms have contributed to women's and men's unequal access to land, despite the PRC's repeated promises to the contrary. First, from the onset of the HRS, rural collectives in certain parts of the country have treated their male and female members differently, even though farmland was supposedly distributed on a per capita basis. Many granted unmarried adult women smaller portions of land than their male counterparts, reasoning that the former group could marry outsiders and leave for conjugal families elsewhere and that the latter would stay put and bring wives into their natal families. Young men, therefore, deserved to receive bigger portions of land than young women. Following the same logic, villages in many regions allocated more land to boys than to girls. Some went so far as to deny young women allotted land altogether.[19] Although state laws and policies make no reference to patrilocality—a social norm dictating married couples reside with or near husbands' parents—it has left indelible imprints on land distribution under the HRS.

Next, state policies and laws seeking to consolidate land tenure have further tipped the scales against women in certain age cohorts. Around 1987, a policy that could be translated as "no increase in land allocation when households expand, and no decrease otherwise" (增人不增地, 减人不减地), first surfaced in Guizhou Province. Within a few years, the central government disseminated the policy to the rest of the country to curtail rural collectives' discretion in land readjustment on the basis of demographic changes in families, such as the birth of children, the demise of family members, and a daughter either leaving or arriving to marry. This policy was intent on boosting landholders' confidence in the stability of the HRS, thereby ensuring their long-term investment in agricultural production.[20] In 1998, when the Land Administration Law was amended, legislators went a step further by codifying the central government's extension of land tenure from fifteen years (or ten years in some areas) to three decades. This extension—or "no change for thirty years," as some call it—enabled rural households to secure their land-holding for extended periods.[21] Moreover, the amended law restricted rural collectives from changing the terms for land contracting; without the consent of the majority of their members, rural collectives could not alter landholding unilaterally.[22]

By severing land distribution from demographic changes in households and by limiting the circumstances for land reallocation, these laws and policies aimed to fortify the HRS. Well-intentioned, they were nonetheless weighted more heavily against female than male family members. After land tenure was extended to three decades or longer (nationwide this extension was completed between 1994 and 1998), rural collectives became increasingly unwilling or unable to adjust land contracting to accommodate the advent of newborns.[23] Consequently, individuals who were born after the late 1990s remained de jure landless in the course of their childhoods, with no land allotted in their names for extended periods. If they intended to become landholders, one of the few options was to inherit their parents' or grandparents' land use rights.

Both women and men, according to state law, are eligible for such inheritance. Legislators, in fact, have insisted that women should enjoy equal rights with men of inheriting family property.[24] In reality, patrilineality has retained wide currency in the countryside, leading many to prioritize their sons over daughters in succession. Robbed of the opportunity to inherit land under contract from their birth families, those daughters may face de jure landlessness for years to come. But even when daughters do inherit land use rights from their parents or grandparents, many can still face de facto land dispossession later in life. In honor of the tradition of patrilocal postmarital residence, women usually leave their natal families to reside with their husbands and in-laws when they get married. This relocation makes it difficult, if not impossible, for married women to effectively exercise rights over land contracted to their birth families. Meanwhile, in most cases, demanding village cadres assign additional land to their conjugal families would prove futile. Rural collectives have their hands tied, following the enactment of the 1998 Land Administration Law. Few are willing or able to modify land distribution to accommodate newly arrived brides, barring extraordinary circumstances.[25]

Moreover, changes in women's marital status can further reinforce their structural disadvantages in land use. Since the consolidation of the policy called "no change for thirty years" in the late 1990s, divorcées everywhere in the countryside have faced a dilemma. Once they sever their ties to conjugal families, effectively exercising rights over land would be difficult, even if they remain landholders on paper. Their continued use of arable land would be subject to the whims and mercy of their ex-husbands and former in-laws, on the one hand. Returning to their natal communities to demand a readjustment in land allocation is an equally unpromising prospect, on the other hand. As mentioned before, rural collectives have seen their discretion in land reallocation limited by the implementation of the 1998 Land Administration Law. As a result, divorced women would have few options other than calling on their parents for help; for many, cobbling together a living in the urban labor force would seem the only realistic solution to landlessness. Despite the PRC's one vow after another to uphold women's land rights and the Marriage Law's promise to protect such rights irrespective of changes in women's marital status, the reality on the ground tells a very different story. Over the last three decades, study after study has demonstrated the connections between marital dissolution and women's experiences of land dispossession.[26]

Caught up in a patchwork of ostensibly gender-neutral policies, seemingly progressive state laws, and deep-seated social norms in favor of patrilocality and patrilineality, women in the countryside frequently experience de jure or de facto landlessness. Both government agencies and scholars, over the years, have documented long-term, widespread land dispossession among rural women. For example, the All-China Women's Federation, along with the National Bureau of Statistics, has carried out systemic inquiries. In 2001, they launched the Second Survey on Chinese Women's Social Status, followed by a third in 2010 and a fourth in 2019. This national survey has provided some of the most compelling evidence to date on women's and men's unequal access to land. It estimated that, around the turn of the century, about 9.2 percent of rural women had no land. That estimate jumped to 21 percent of rural women by 2010; around that time, 11 percent of rural men were landless.[27]

Beneath the gap between rights promised and rights delivered is, I must stress, a set of entrenched power structures. To begin with, lawmakers exert legislative prerogative to define citizens' lawful rights in land use. Rural collectives exercise administrative authority in land allocation and contracting. Heads of households—usually senior males—maintain practical control over the distribution of land-related resources and opportunities among family members. Lastly, judges, arbitrators, and local government officials routinely assert their influences in families and in communities by determining who prevails in land disputes. Everywhere I look within these interconnected networks of power relations, the deck has been stacked against women.

Four decades after the HRS was put into place, the Marriage Law has yet to recognize land rights as part of conjugal property, thus suitable for partition at the time of divorce. This lacuna in the law—intentional or otherwise—makes it impossible for wives to cite national legislation to justify their claims on landholding at the end of marriage. The SPC, the highest court in the land, has similarly skirted this issue, though its leaders have time and again expressed concerns about women's land rights.[28] Yet, rather than issuing proper guidelines to lower courts to spell out divorcing women's entitlement to landholding, the SPC has repeatedly passed the buck to legislators, insisting on lawmaking as *the* solution to the prevailing violations of women's land rights. Owing to the SPC's inaction, judges in lower courts are under no obligation to divide couples' land rights in divorce litigation. With gender equality on their lips, lawmakers and justices at the pinnacle of state power have yet to set in motion a top-down, concerted process to address widespread infringements of women's rights to land possession, use, and management. Nor have they made systemic efforts to hold rural collectives accountable for undercutting the equality of women and men in land use.

Indeed, under the HRS, rural collectives—also known as rural collective economic organizations (农村集体经济组织)—have remained at liberty to determine who can or cannot enjoy their membership, an issue at the heart of the distribution of land and related benefits. In four decades, lawmakers and the SPC have consistently refrained from imposing a standard definition for the membership of rural collectives. Their silence on this matter means that women who relocate upon marriage, divorce, or widowhood would have no choice but to live with uncertainty about their standing as members of particular rural collectives. A given collective could either recognize a married-in, divorced, or widowed woman, thereby including her in the distribution of economic gains derived from land-related transactions. Or it could deny her such benefits on the grounds of her lack of membership. Put more plainly, women's claims on landholding and related interests are often at the mercy of their residing communities.[29] The entrenchment of the "no change for thirty years" policy from the late 1990s onward has further freed rural collectives from legal and moral obligations to mitigate landlessness among women. In short, rather than uprooting the patriarchal-patrilocal-patrilineal family structure in rural China, the institutionalization of the HRS has reproduced and reinforced that very structure.

Taken together, the sedimentation of the foregoing power structures has given rise to a social context in which contending for certain rights is not only legally and politically unactionable but also, in many instances, nearly unimaginable and unutterable for the disempowered. Consequently, women on the brink of divorce, as much as they strive to actualize their spousal, custodial, and/or property rights, often remain quiescent with regard to their lawful entitlement to landholding. Of the thirty-two women I interviewed, only three stood out as exceptions. Instead of acquiescence and inaction, the three sought to quietly evade entrenched power relations at home and in communities. None of those three openly disputed land use in their divorce suits; afterward, none of them approached their ex-husbands or village cadres in an attempt to regain access to farmland. Beneath this strategic façade of obedience, however, were deliberate and elaborate efforts to continuously profit from land use. One woman persuaded her ex-husband into keeping their separation as a secret, so that she could continue farming the land under the names of her former in-laws. The other two women, both forward-looking, anticipated their conjugal villages transferring collectively owned land to real estate developers in the future. That foresight prompted them to use divorce papers to change their household registration status, or *hukou* (户口). Previously, their *hukou* had been bundled with that of the husband's household. Shortly after divorce, they had the local police separate their residence from the ex-husband's. An independent residence, these two women divulged, might help them benefit from future land transfer without their having to worry about their ex-husbands' opposition or obstruction.

By contrast, most of the women I interviewed did not utter a word about landholding. Anger or angst over prospective land dispossession was noticeably missing in our conversations. Which is to say, the women in this book bear little likeness to the storytellers studied by sociologists Patricia Ewick and Susan Silbey. By narrating mundane oppositions to authorities, the disempowered can expose otherwise taken-for-granted social structures, and, in turn, temporally and spatially extend individual acts of resistance, Ewick and Silbey observe.[30] Few of the women I talked to had engaged in such acts to reckon with their structural disadvantages in land use.

Nor did the women in my study display much affinity with *everyday resisters*. According to James C. Scott, although tight-lipped about injustice and inequality in the presence of power elites, everyday resisters quietly push back the frontiers of insubordination. And they often do so beyond the gaze of the powerful by strategically deploying "weapons of the weak," such as foot dragging, dissimulation, false compliance, pilfering, feigned ignorance, and sabotage. Domination, as Scott discovered in peasant societies in Southeast Asia, is hardly ever unalterable, and hegemonic power does not invariably achieve an absolute ideological grip on subordinate groups. Group members' compliance and quiescence is, in fact, usually a strategic façade put on in front of those in positions of power. Offstage, in secluded settings, the disempowered often find ways to defy, undercut, and even subvert the prevailing power relations.[31] In my study, however, only flimsy evidence could be located to indicate such resistant practices among divorcing women vis-à-vis power elites in charge of landholding; the three divorcées mentioned above serve as the exception rather than the rule in this regard.

Moreover, the women in this book barely resemble *rightful resisters* in rural China. In their study of popular contention in China's vast countryside, political scientists Kevin J. O'Brien and Li Lianjiang find that, in the face of stark iniquity, villagers often cultivate an elaborate repertoire of resistant acts. Many turn political or economic domination to their advantage in order to curb the exercise of power. For example, when local government officials abused their authority and neglected the letter of the law, villagers were quick to intervene. They did so by innovatively employing the rhetoric, values, and commitments promoted by the central government, by locating and exploiting the divisions among local power-holders, and by mobilizing support from the wider public. Hegemonic power, in this view, does not necessarily reap obedience or deference. Nor does it invariably diminish social conflicts by means of ideological indoctrination, mystification, or naturalization of the status quo. Rather, the structure of domination can breed popular contention, in part because it contains cracks and openings the disempowered can exploit, and in part because it offers rich soil for the aggrieved to reinterpret and retool the discursive, symbolic, and ideological instruments at the service of power elites. Rightful resisters, under this microscope, can be remarkably adept at appropriating "the master's tool to challenge the master." Regrettably, this is not what I found in my field research.

Rather, the data I gathered in Weifeng during the 2010–2011 field research provided evidence highly consistent with Steven Lukes's and John Gaventa's theories of power and powerlessness. According to these two, when an unequal distribution of power is so egregious and entrenched, domination could seem almost immutable. With time, subordinate groups would come to view their powerlessness as natural and inevitable, and insubordination as inconceivable and unactionable. Stated otherwise, the sedimentation of interlocked power structures can preempt manifest conflicts—in no small part through shaping group members' conceptions of their interests, along with their perceptions of alternative lines of action. This is precisely what I found at my research sites in rural Sichuan.

Under the HRS, gender has been routinely instrumentalized to implement and justify unequal distribution of land between women and men. The power structures that have enabled such practices have been so ingrained and highly integrated—from top legislature to the highest court in the land, from local governments to rural collectives, to individual households—that structural openings for rightful resistance to male dominance in landholding are barely visible.[32] Indeed, a sense of powerlessness was palpably felt among divorcées and their family members. When I asked a peasant man in an interview why his daughter did not contest her land rights upon divorce, this man, who had served as a village cadre for more than two decades, sighed. Quoting the "no change for thirty years" policy, he insisted that any rights contention by a divorcée would be a "nonstarter."[33]

Rural women's participation in labor migration, ironically, has further complicated the problem. While enhancing their ability to find and use state law, off-farm employment, especially the kind requiring longtime absence in one's conjugal community, often dilutes women's ties to community members, thrusting them more deeply into social isolation. Embroiled in sequestered struggles over marital discontent, women seeking divorce are in effect atomized, unable to have their resentment toward power-holders validated by similarly situated individuals. For that reason, those women form a social class in itself, but far from a class for itself, with scarcely any group consciousness of its own making.[34] In the end, the PRC's reform-era land regime, combined with the atomizing effects of labor migration, has achieved a nearly hegemonic grip on women's legal mobilization, foreclosing the possibility of thinking, speaking, and acting in their best interests on one particular front: landholding.[35]

CONCLUSION

Rather than laying the axe to the root of inequality and injustice, the grassroots court system often reinforces and reproduces social ills in the Chinese family and in society. Starting out with high hopes, women pursuing legal action soon come to the realization that few on the bench or in the legal profession treat seriously their lawful rights and entitlements, although the PRC, in seven decades, has made numerous promises to advance gender equality in almost every social domain. Divorce litigation, in the end, proves liberating in a rather minimal sense: it enables women to flee unhappy relationships, but has done so by callously curtailing their spousal, custodial, property, and land rights. Instead of banishing the distinctions, old as time, of breadwinner and homemaker, of master and dependents, legal mobilization reaffirms men's dominance in the home and in the community, while keeping women in a subordinate position.

This is happening day in and day out, in no small part because state actors, within and without the official justice system, have aligned their power with the entrenched gender norms and practices in society. Over time, this alignment has crystalized in mutually reinforcing power relations that crisscross the family, community, and state bureaucracies on multiple fronts and levels. Neither rural women's participation in labor migration nor decades of top-down court reforms have fundamentally shifted the arc of the political universe. Throughout the reform era, judges have continuously exercised decision-making and agenda-setting power, so that they can dismiss women's rights claims as wives, mothers, and property owners. Outside courtrooms, lawmakers and policymakers at the commanding heights, together with government officials and village cadres down in the trenches, have instituted one barrier after another, making it exceedingly difficult for women to realize their rights to landholding. Male household heads, in the meantime, have continued to rein in domestic matters, such as lineage, inheritance, property arrangements, and land use.

When power relations remain ingrained and interlocked, they constrain not merely the discourse or the behaviors of the disempowered, they limit what individuals can imagine as alternative courses of action. In that sense, power effects consciousness. In illuminating the workings of consciousness-formation power, I join Steven Lukes and John Gaventa in their defending of the *third dimension of power*—the one that shapes individual minds and group consciousness.[36] In doing so, this chapter completes the task of mapping Lukes's and Gaventa's first, second, and third dimensions of power onto the terrain of disputation. And it fulfils the promise I have made at the beginning: this book sets out to revamp the notion of dispute resolution by moving power to center stage. This reconceptualization, I hope, will give birth to more sophisticated understandings of the potential as well as the grave pitfalls of legality in a continuously evolving authoritarian state.

Epilogue

IN THE SUMMER OF 2018, I found my way back to Weifeng County in southern Sichuan Province, the place where I have conducted multiple rounds of field research since 2006. Over the course of a decade or so, I have visited Weifeng so many times that it has come to feel almost like my second home. Yet every time I returned, I found my research site undergoing a sea change on a scale and at a pace far beyond what I could grasp immediately. Gentrification, a word constantly on the lips of my students back in New York City, had been unfolding in Weifeng at breakneck speed.

During an extended stretch of field research between 2010 and 2011, I had stayed at an elementary school in the middle of the bustling downtown area in the county seat. By the time I came back to Weifeng in summer 2018, the school had been razed to make way for new urban developments. Shopping malls, high-rise apartments, and restaurants had edged out the area's longtime residents. Displacement as such had occurred across the county, which was home to nearly half a million residents; about 70 percent of the local population, as of 2018, were still officially classified as part of the agricultural as opposed to nonagricultural population. Villagers who had once ensconced themselves in farmhouses scattered across the vast countryside were now concentrated in apartment complexes on the outskirts of the county seat. Having lost their farmland to real estate developers and local governments, they became urban *hukou* holders living off pensions provided by the state. Urbanization, that unstoppable juggernaut, has remade the urban and rural geography of Weifeng—and perhaps everywhere else in the country. Meanwhile, the legal services industry, courts, and citizens' rights contention have likewise continued to evolve.

These days, legal workers like Li Yinxue no longer toss and turn at night, fearing for their livelihoods. As noted in chapter 4, the Ministry of Justice (MOJ) struggled for nearly two decades to remake a group of law practitioners who had burst onto the scene in the early years of the reform era. Following the 2002 Shanghai Conference, the country's top justice agency sought to incrementally shut legal workers out of litigation, particularly those based in metropolitan areas. Sooner or later, this policy prescription would have stripped Li Yinxue and her peers of their main source of income, pushing the group further to the periphery of the legal services market. For the next fifteen years or so, legal workers nationwide waited with bated breath, perseverating on the gloomy prospect that it could be just a matter of time that their livelihoods vanished. Decision-makers at the MOJ, meanwhile, hesitated, unable to embrace or jettison the country's socialist past, which cast Grassroots Legal Services partially as a profit-making business and partially as a state-funded entity in charge of certain administrative functions. Failing to reconceive legal workers' positioning in relation to the state, market, and society, the MOJ just left the group in limbo.

In 2017, a breakthrough at last. That year, the MOJ amended two key regulations on Grassroots Legal Services, taking crucial steps to shake itself out of indecision. For the first time, the top justice agency explic-itly recognized that a legal workers' office could assume the form of a general partnership (普通合伙), thereby opening the door for private funds to invest in Grassroots Legal Services, a notable departure from the agency's prior restrictions on these offices.[1] Meanwhile, a legal workers' office, according to the amended regulation, can now also operate as a public institution (事业单位) and is thus eligible for state budgetary and personnel support.[2] The latter change, as far as I can tell, marks a radical breakaway from the MOJ's longstanding position that legal workers had to be unhooked from the state so that they could act in the capacity of truly self-managing and self-sustaining market players.

Together, these regulatory changes suggest that the MOJ, once again, has reclaimed and repackaged the country's socialist legacies, by preserv-ing something old and by adding something new. On the one hand, the agency has finally come to level the playing field by granting legal workers the kind of market standing their rivals—lawyers—have enjoyed since the early 2000s. From 2017 onward, legal workers, like lawyers, have been able to funnel private funds into their practice of law. They can also establish new offices without local governments' permission. What's more, unlike their predecessors, legal workers nowadays are under no obligation to facilitate the work of local justice bureaus and departments after the revised regulations stripped the provisions imposing administrative functions on Grassroots Legal Services. In other words, the MOJ has strengthened legal workers' positioning in the market economy, making it easier for them to compete with lawyers and other rivals.

On the other hand, decision-makers at the MOJ have finally abandoned the attempts to unhook legal workers from the state, an initiative the agency began in 1994. *Unhooking and restructuring* (脱钩改制), the slogan that defined the state's marketization of legal services on the cusp of the new millennium, has faded into the background. Over two decades, decision-makers have slowly grappled with the complex reality that the country needs not just lawyers but also legal workers. The latter group has assumed—and will continue to assume—a crucial role in meeting popular needs for legal assistance, and its survival is particularly critical for low-income residents in both urban and rural settings. Therefore, it is of great importance for the state to lend material and logistical support to Grassroots Legal Services. Thanks to the regulatory changes introduced in 2017, legal workers now can apply for a legal person certificate of public institution (事业单位法人证书) and thus become eligible for public funding. After a relentless, decades-long push for marketization, the People's Republic of China (PRC) has finally begun reversing some of its earlier reform agendas.

In October 2020, the MOJ and the Ministry of Finance teamed up, further articulating a policy termed *government procurement of services* (政府购买服务). This policy allows local governments to use their revenues to compensate market players for their provision of public goods, including legal assistance.[3] At the moment, it is too early to tell whether or how this policy development, combined with the aforementioned regulatory changes, will affect ordinary people's access to justice. One thing is for sure, though. To keep the official justice system accessible, to make litigation truly affordable for the aggrieved, the PRC's decision-makers must learn the lesson that the decades of top-down, state-driven marketization have stripped the most vulnerable and the neediest of access to justice.

* * *

Courts across the country have continued to evolve in recent years as well. They have to in part because the Chinese family has continued to change. By the end of 2018, the crude divorce rate—that is, the number of divorces per 1,000 people—has climbed steadily from 0.2 in 1978 to 3.2 four decades later. In that same year, the United States saw a rate of 2.9 divorces per 1,000 individuals.[4] Chinese marriage, as an institution, seems more fragile than ever before. Against this backdrop, the Supreme People's Court (SPC) ushered in a pilot program intent on streamlining court practices involving family trials (家事审判). To place this initiative into perspective, the highest court emphasized that resolving family disputes was not just a matter concerning the happiness of individuals and households; instead, "it is tied to the stability and harmony of a society and the advancement of a civilization."[5] Since then, *family trials*, a phrase hitherto nonexistent in the court lexicon, has begun permeating the discourse of the highest court.

Judging by the extant evidence, the most recent court reforms stand out in several respects. First, they are emphatically and specifically geared toward reforming court performance concerning marriage and the family. To this end, the SPC has dabbled in neologism and, more crucially, upgraded its classification of judicial statistics. For almost seven decades, judges at all levels were accustomed to lumping all domestic disputes into one, somewhat fuzzy category—marital and family disputes (婚姻家庭纠纷). Under this umbrella term were several subcategories: (1) divorce (离婚), (2) child support (抚养), (3) eldercare (赡养), and (4) inheritance (继承). Today, judges sitting on the SPC, along with those in lower courts, must sort official statistics into nine subcategories: (1) divorce, (2) upbringing (抚养), (3) eldercare (赡养), (4) maintenance (扶养), (5) adoption relations (收养关系), (6) guardianship (监护权), (7) visitation (探望), (8) inheritance (继承), and (9) other matters.[6] The court system, in other words, has adopted a more elaborate scheme of classification to track the volume as well as the specific kinds of domestic friction entering the official justice system.

The latest round of court reforms, I must stress, also features a striking level of coordination among state bureaucracies. A year after the SPC showcased the foregoing pilot program in 2016, the highest court teamed up with fourteen agencies in concerted efforts to institute an interministerial joint conference system (联席会议制度). Within this system, the SPC, under the leadership of the Central Political-Legal Affairs Commission of the Chinese Communist Party (CCP) (中央政法委), is expected to convene leaders from the following agencies annually: the Office of the Comprehensive Administration of Public Security Commission under the CCP's Central Committee (CAPSC) (中央综治办); the Supreme People's Procuratorate; the Ministry of Education; the Ministry of Public Security; the Ministry of Civil Affairs; the Ministry of Justice; the National Health and Family Planning Commission (国家卫生计生委); the State Administration of Press, Publication, Radio, Film, and Television (新闻出版广电总局); the National Working Committee for Women and Children under the State Council (国务院妇儿工委办公室); the All-China Federation of Trade Unions (全国总工会); the Central Committee of the Communist Youth League (共青团中央); the All-China Women's Federation; the Working Commission for the Care of Children (中国关工委); and the National Council on the Aging (全国老龄办). The goal of this joint conference system, it is said, is to explore new frontiers in the reform of family trials, to diversify nonjudicial mechanisms intended for conflict management, and to monitor and screen marital and family disputes in society at large.[7] I have not seen *this* level of coordination within the state apparatus since the nascent PRC launched its family revolution in the early 1950s.

Finally, recent reforms have rendered divorce harder—not easier—for the average woman and man. Before the end of 2018, the SPC mapped out a comprehensive, detailed plan consisting of forty-nine itemized reform measures, all of which were intent on deepening the reform of family trials. Here, I focus on one of these measures: the 2018 plan formalized an entrenched, and yet hitherto informal, practice among judges. As indicated in chapter 5, judges in lower courts have long sought to stall marital dissolution by routinely turning down first-time petitions for divorce. Consequently, wives and husbands, embroiled in conjugal discord, must wait for at least six months before they can make another attempt at marital dissolution inside a courtroom. Though long established and widespread, this practice was not backed up by any substantive legal rules; instead, judges mainly relied on a procedural constraint established by the Civil Procedural Law to impose informal cooling-off periods on litigants. In 2018, the SPC formally and expressly named—and thus legalized—the practice of inserting a cooling-off period no more than three months into divorce litigation on one condition: both plaintiff and defendant must agree on this arrangement.[8] Here is the upshot: judges nowadays can openly and justifiably put divorce suits on hold. Whether litigants genuinely consent to this arrangement or not, however, is open to question. After all, the SPC did not specify what procedures judges should use to obtain such consent. Nor did it spell out the consequences for those on the bench who fail to seek litigants' consent.

The term *cooling-off period for divorce* (离婚冷静期) made its way from court lexicon into public discourse after the National People's Congress promulgated the new Civil Code (民法典) in May 2020. Article 1077 of the new Civil Code soon caught the attention of the general public, which can be translated as follows: where either party is unwilling to divorce, he or she may withdraw a divorce registration application within thirty days after such an application is received by the marriage registration authority; within thirty days after the expiration of the period, both parties shall personally visit the marriage registration authority to apply for the issuance of a divorce certificate, and failing to do so will cause the divorce registration application to be treated as withdrawn. As many academics have noted, this article practically means that, after a couple submits a divorce application to the marriage registration authority, they must wait for thirty days, thus a cooling-off period, before the wife and the husband have their relationship formally terminated. Note that this requirement is intended for *all* couples seeking to dissolve their marriages by registering their divorce agreements at local governments.[9] Starting on January 1, 2021, the day the new Civil Code came into effect, all divorcing couples—whether they approach the court system or local governments—must face the so-called cooling-off period.

To sum up, the newly introduced cooling-off period, together with the SPC's other reform measures, attests powerfully to the PRC's enduring interest in buttressing the institution of marriage. Two decades into the twenty-first century, this institution has taken on new significance as decision-makers at the pinnacle of state power continuously grapple with the practical and the ideological import of marriage. Their efforts to elevate the political significance of this institution must once again, I argue, be analyzed against specific historical and social backdrop. In recent years, divorce rates have risen while marriage rates have fallen, as have birth rates among Chinese couples. In fact, birth rates have dropped to their lowest level in the seven decades since the formation of the PRC in 1949.[10] Additionally, the Chinese population is aging at a pace that unnerves many within and without the officialdom. Several estimates speak to the magnitude of the demographic challenges the PRC's ruling elites face. In 2010, there were 111 million Chinese age sixty-five and older—approximately 8.2 percent of the total population. By 2050, the proportion of the population age sixty-five or older will jump to 26.9 percent—that is, over 400 million individuals.[11]

Considering those sociodemographic changes, future research needs to consider several important questions. In the decades to come, how will top decision-makers adjust and readjust the relation between the state and the institution of marriage? What roles will this institution assume in the PRC's ever-evolving governing tool kit? Will it remain a key vehicle ruling elites deploy to advance their demographic, political, or ideological agendas? If so, how will state law facilitate or constrain such deployment? How will such deployment affect individual freedoms and rights in intimate relationships and beyond? Inside courtrooms, how will those on the bench calibrate and recalibrate divorce law practices to dovetail litigation with the PRC's larger agendas in ruling? How will ordinary women and men wrestle with the potential—and the pitfalls—of authoritarian legality? All these questions warrant scholarly attention.

* * *

In conducting a follow-up study of divorce litigation in Weifeng in summer 2018, I noticed some important changes on the ground. These days, land seems to be on everyone's mind. During the first decade of the new century, the central government abolished the agricultural tax and increased subsidies for agricultural products, making farming more profitable than it was in the 1990s. Villagers in Guxiao and Xiqing, the two townships that have been my research sites since 2006, are now more enthusiastic about farming. Moreover, two trends—land conversion and land transfer—have accelerated here and elsewhere in the country, prompting many to think long and hard about their interest in landholding.

Land conversion, as part of state-driven urbanization plans, has spurred local governments to facilitate and, oftentimes, to force the transfer of land ownership from rural collectives to the state.[12] In recent years, turning arable land into construction land, absorbing rural-born individuals into the urban population, boosting domestic consumption, and especially using land sales for revenue have become increasingly appealing in the eyes of state actors who have their minds bent on development and modernization.[13] In the process, more than 88 million rural residents have lost their rights to village land. According to one estimate, by 2026, approximately 250 million rural residents will reside in cities, rapidly expanding China's middle class.[14]

Land transfer, by contrast, allows rural households to pass their land use rights to fellow villagers, agribusinesses, and other commercial entities without effecting any changes in land ownership. Since 2013, the central government's reform agenda has focused on deepening rural land reform, instituting new mechanisms for land transfer, and scaling up agricultural production.[15] A new, official initiative called the separation of three rights (三权分置) emerged against this backdrop, which aimed to further refine rural land rights by dividing them into three distinct categories: (1) the right to own land (所有权), (2) the right to contract land (承包权), and (3) the right to manage land (经营权). Previously, under the Household Responsibility System (HRS), the right to ownership went to rural collectives, and the other two rights were bundled together, under the names of household members. The latest round of land reform, championed by the CCP Central Committee and the State Council, has sought to separate the second category from the third, so that rural households can keep the right to contract land, and transfer management rights to agribusinesses or other third parties. The ultimate goal, according to top decision-makers, is to use the market as a mechanism to pool land resources, to funnel industrial capital into agricultural production, and to streamline China's rural economy.[16] The separation of these three rights, within just a few years, has accelerated a nationwide shift in land management. Between 2010 and 2017, the amount of contracted land that has changed hands through transfer (转包、转让), leasing (出租), exchanges (互换), and shareholding (入股) has doubled.[17] By 2017, more than 70 million rural households had participated in land transfer, shifting over 512 million *mu* (nearly 85 million acres) of contracted land from the original contract holders to others. A year later, it was estimated that approximately 37 percent of the farmland under the HRS has been transferred in one way or another.[18]

Caught up in these two developments, families in Guxiao and Xiqing must consider seriously their immediate and long-term interest in landholding. In recent years, the county government's attempts to erect new factories on collectively owned land, together with the central government's encroachment on farmland to build multiple dams along the Min River, have forced villagers to contend with a harsh new reality: sooner or later, many of them will experience temporary or permanent land dispossession. Within this context, contesting land rights, upon or after divorce, is no longer as unthinkable or unutterable as before. The signs of rights contention are now visible in court records. One case in point is a divorce suit that I learned about during the most recent trip to my research sites. In a township next to Xiqing, a woman with the surname Zhong sued her husband for divorce in June 2016. A key part of her divorce petition was to stake her claim on the 122,500 yuan her conjugal family had received as compensation in the wake of land expropriation. What I could not find during my 2010–2011 field research can now be easily spotted in divorce case records. Using divorce litigation as a key site to contest one's rights to benefit from land use will, I imagine, become ever more plausible amid the rapid rise of land conversion and transfer.

Outside the court system, a new terrain for rights contention is emerging. Previously, women seeking divorce were largely isolated from one another. Absent contact with individuals in similar circumstances, divorcing (or divorced) women were in effect atomized, unable to have their anger, frustration, and bitterness validated by similarly disempowered individuals. As more rural collectives muddle through land expropriation and/or transfer, land possession, use, and management will all be subject to renegotiation, contention, and potentially disputation. Put another way, China's latest rural land reform will inevitably introduce uncertainty and unpredictability in the HRS, with new cracks and fissures appearing in the power structures once fully ingrained and integrated. Recent reform measures can make women more aware of others who face a similar prospect of land dispossession. This awareness, in turn, can help reduce these women's atomization—a crucial condition for subordinate groups to accept and normalize their powerlessness. In the near future, we may see more women asserting their land rights, upon or after divorce, by forging a new alliance with individuals bearing similar interest in landholding, by treading new paths for rights contention (e.g., using arbitration as a novel forum for dispute resolution), and perhaps by dipping their toes into collective resistance, as seen in other parts of the countryside.[19]

Notes

INTRODUCTION

1. Interview with WJH on May 10, 2010; interview with DL on July 19, 2010. Throughout the book, I use the following notations to indicate my data sources. All interviews are marked by the initials of respondents and the days I conducted the conversations. And all participant observations are labeled according to the locations and dates.

2. National Bureau of Statistics of China. 2019. "2018 Monitoring Report of Migrant Workers" (2018年农民工监测调查报告).

3. China Justice Big Data Service 2018.

4. This definition of culture stems from Sewell (2005), 152–174, who surveys and critiques some of the most influential conceptions of culture in the social sciences over the twentieth century. Based on this review, Sewell defines his own vision: culture "should be understood as a dialectic of system and practice, as a dimension of social life autonomous from other dimensions both in its logic and in its spatial configuration, and as possessing a real but thin coherence that is continually put at risk in practice and therefore subject to transformation." In this book, I follow Sewell by employing a similar notion of culture, albeit in more straightforward language.

5. Swidler 2001, 19. Also see Swidler (1986) for her elaboration of a theory of culture in action.

6. In addition to Ann Swidler's theory of culture in action, anthropologist Sally Engle Merry's 1998 article, "Law, Culture, and Cultural Appropriation," provides another important inspiration for my study of law and politics in the PRC. While Merry draws on the notion of *cultural appropriation* to depict how dominant social groups take cultural resources, practices, and meanings from subordinate groups (or vice versa), I apply that same concept to characterize authoritarian rulers' creative use of cultural materials retrieved from different origins. Despite this difference, my application is consistent with Merry's and Swidler's emphasis on the human agency, conscious choices, flexibility, and ingenuity underlying social actors' use of culture. This emphasis, I must insist, does not automatically lead to a utilitarian view of culture (or legality). Nowhere in my analysis do I suggest that authoritarian rulers regularly resort to cost-benefit analysis in their deployment of cultural resources. Nor do I imply that these rulers cultivate and employ cultural materials, including law and courts, to advance a set of transcendent, preconceived, and agreed-upon "functions" or "purposes." In chapter 1, I detail why I find it problematic to employ a utilitarian or a functionalist approach to unpack legality in nondemocratic contexts.

7. See Albiston, Edelman, and Milligan (2014) for a critique of the individualistic, behavioristic tendency in the studies of conflict resolution.

8. Throughout the book, I use pseudonyms for the places such as Weifeng, Chuanyu, Guxiao, Xiqing, Qinchuan, Dingyi, and other townships in southern Sichuan Province. Also, all the individual names are pseudonyms.

9. That I interviewed more divorcing women than men reflects two realities: one, for most of the twentieth century, Chinese women have outnumbered men in the initiation of divorce, a gendered pattern well-documented in both English and Chinese literature. For discussions of this gendered pattern, see Stacey (1975), 77; Johnson (1983), 117–118; Platte (1988), 441–442; Ocko (1991), 351–352; Bailey (1993), 60; Bernhardt (1994), 195; Palmer (1995), 123; Xu and Ye (2002), 34; Xu (2007), 199; and China Justice Big Data Service (2018). Two, as a female researcher, I experienced persistent difficulties in obtaining divorcing men's consent to interview. This limitation, while regrettable, had limited impact on my study, which set out to explore women's experiences in legal mobilization and in litigation.

10. In 2000, the SPC published a series of books, entitled *Collection of Archival Records on Judicial Statistics of the People's Courts, 1949–1998)* (全国法院历史资料汇编, 1949–1998), allowing researchers to plumb the PRC's earliest efforts to methodically register judicial activities. The SPC, in 2018, released another book series under the title, *Historical Statistical Books of the People's Courts, 1949–2016)* (人民法院司法统计历史典籍,1949–2016). Combined, these two book series constitute some of the PRC's most systematic endeavors to compile and publicize judicial statistics.

11. Geertz 1973, 3–30; Scott 1990, 1–16, 17–23; Burawoy 1998.

12. Feagin, Orum, and Sjoberg 1991; Ragin and Becker 1992. See also Gieryn (1983, 2018) as good examples of using comparative case studies to advance theoretical arguments.

13. For a discussion of the literary techniques employed by journalists, especially those pioneering the New Journalism, see Wolfe (1996), 15–36. I learned the fourth technique from Frederick Kaufman, a professor of journalism at the City University of New York, whose teaching has made possible my experimentation with feature writing.

14. Sontag 2001, 15. For a penetrating analysis of the prevailing dichotomies in literary and film critique, such as style versus content, manners versus matter, form versus theme, mask versus face, and so on, see Sontag's 1965 essay, "On Style."

15. Quoting William Blake's poem, Clifford Geertz lamented anthropologists' tendency to move from "ethnographic miniatures" to "wall-sized culturescapes of the nation." In this way, Geertz raised methodological questions about how ethnographers could link the microscopic and the macroscopic. For more details, see Geertz (1973), 20–23.

16. Schindler and Schäfer (2021) provide the latest review of inadequate reflections on the practice of writing among ethnographers.

17. Swidler 1986, 2001.

18. Scott 1990.

19. Gaventa 1980, vii.

CHAPTER ONE

1. See Shapiro (2008) for a review of the expansion of studies of courts in authoritarian regimes.

2. Moustafa 2007, 2014; Ginsburg and Moustafa 2008; Solomon 2015; Gallagher 2017; Whiting 2017; Curley, Dressel, and McCarthy 2018; Zhang and Ginsburg 2018. Also see Cheesman (2015), 9–11, and Hurst (2018), 16–19, for summaries of the most recent studies of judicial institutions in nondemocratic settings.

3. Mahoney (2000) identifies four theoretical models scholars employ to explain institutional genesis, evolution, and changes. Among researchers studying authoritarian legality, the functionalist and the utilitarian models have gained wide currency; the other

two models, power- and legitimacy-based, have yet to receive the same level of attention or acceptance.

4. Moustafa 2014, 283.

5. Mahoney 2000, 519. See also Hall and Taylor (1996) for a similar critique of the functionalist view in institutional analysis. For one thing, once created, institutions can generate unintended consequences or effects. Thus, in explaining the origin of an institution largely in terms of the effects that follow from its creation, scholars can incidentally take the unintended for the intended purposes actors attached to the genesis of a given institution. For another, a functionalist view hardly offers a satisfactory explanation for the inefficiencies an institution brings. Which is to say, a functional explanation would fall flat in a scenario in which an institution persists, although it is barely functional, achieving little means-ends efficiency. Finally, see Thelen (1999) for a resounding rejection of the functionalist view, contending that institutions stem from concrete, often conflictual historical processes rather than from transcendent, preconceived "functions" or "functional purposes."

6. For a poignant critique of positivist epistemology, which leads sociologists to bracket off time and space from their causal inference in hopes of locating decontextualized "causal laws" across all instances of a given kind of empirical phenomena, see Steinmetz (2004). See also Sewell (2005), 1–21, for a broader critique of social scientists' fixation on "lawful regularities" of the world they study—a kind of regularities that are achieved only by bracketing social temporalities out of scientific consciousness.

7. Thelen 2003, 215. Also see Pierson (2000), 14, for a similar argument. Rather than assuming a connection between the intentions of the actors responsible for the genesis of a given institution and the institutional effects that ensue, Pierson argues that we should go back and look, empirically verifying the nexus between actors' intentions and institutional effects. After all, a nexus of this kind is primarily an empirical matter.

8. Gallagher 2017, 31.

9. Pierre Bourdieu (1987) critiques the instrumentalist view of legality, but for a different reason. Those subscribing to this view, according to Bourdieu, often treat law as direct reflections of economic or political dominance, while overlooking the symbolic structures of what he terms the *juridical field*. As far as I can tell, his critique is a characteristically culturalist one. I will come back to this point later, when I critique the extant literature for its inattention to culture.

10. For a discussion of how rational choice theorists conceive the notion of *bounded rationality*, see Campbell (2004), 15–17,

11. Migdal 2001, 15–22. Also see Lieberthal (1992) on the notion of *fragmented authoritarianism*. Finally, Stern (2013) presents a study of political ambivalence in policymaking and lawmaking in the PRC. This ambivalence, as Stern points out, in no small measure derives from the reality that the Chinese state is anything but a monolith.

12. Mahoney 2000; see also Hall and Taylor (1996), Thelen (1999), and Campbell (2004), 1–30, for comparisons of the explanatory logics at the heart of rational choice institutionalism, organizational institutionalism (also known as *sociological institutionalism* among political scientists), and historical institutionalism.

13. For more details on the New Institutionalism in organizational sociology, see Powell and DiMaggio (1991). For a discussion of the differences between the *logic of instrumentality* and the *logic of appropriateness*, see March and Olsen (1989, chapter 2), and also see Campbell (2004), 17–23. Drawing on the works of John Meyer, Brian Rowan,

and other pioneers in the New Institutionalism, Campbell contends that organizations like nation-states, business firms, and schools adopt formal structures and practices—not necessarily to increase efficiency or to reduce costs relative to benefits, as rational choice theories indicate—but rather to adapt to an institutional environment that defines what is appropriate and what is legitimate. By highlighting organizations' responsiveness and sensitivity to the normative and the cognitive dimensions of the fields they occupy, Campbell underscores how the explanatory logic of appropriateness sets the New Institutionalism apart from rational choice theories and structural functionalism.

14. Outside organizational sociology, a group of sociologists and political scientists, who call themselves *historical institutionalists*, have made similar efforts by placing culture center stage in their studies of the genesis, evolution, and changes of modern institutions. See Hall and Taylor (1996), Thelen (1999), and Campbell (2004), 23–27, for in-depth discussions of historical institutionalism.

15. Suchman and Edelman 1996.

16. Ng and He 2017.

17. Sewell 2005, 159. Of course, there are always exceptions to every rule. Occasionally, researchers do place culture—especially legal consciousness, discourses, and ideas—front and center in their studies of law, courts, and/or politics in nondemocratic contexts. Gallagher (2006), He (2013b), Wang (2013), Cheesman (2015), Liu (2018), and Wang and Truong (2021) are cases in point. But even among these studies, few attribute causal priority to culture in the analysis of the genesis, evolution, and reproduction of institutions; even fewer go as far as to specify cultural causal mechanisms in shaping policy development or institutional changes.

18. Swidler 1986, 2001.

19. Merry 1998.

20. The 2015 Anti-Domestic Violence Law, Articles 23–32.

21. Institutionalists of various stripes generally view path dependence, bricolage, translation, and diffusion as the key mechanisms through which institutional changes take place. See Campbell (2004), 1–30, 62–89, for discussions of the specific mechanisms rational choice, organizational, and historical institutionalists favor in order to explain institutional changes. In this book, I frame diffusion, translation, bricolage, and path dependence in terms of *active strategies* as opposed to *mechanisms*. Behind this decision is a recognition: institutionalists from time to time struggle to locate human agency in the processes of institutional evolution and changes. Consequently, according to Campbell (2004), some portray such changes as "mindless and excessively mechanical transfer of [institutional] principles and practices" from one context to another. See Hirsch (1997) and Campbell (2004), 20–22, for their critique of the limitations of organizational institutionalism. Ann Swidler's theory of culture in action, I believe, provides the much-needed remedy for this problem, thanks to her sensitivity to social actors' agency and creativity in their use of cultural resources. Considering her argument that culture can shape actors by providing them with specific strategies of action, I come to view diffusion, translation, bricolage, and path dependence as willful actions ruling elites adopt to craft somewhat novel solutions to challenges and difficulties in governance.

22. See Lee and Zhang (2013) and Gallagher (2017), 46–51, for reviews of the debates in which sociologists and political scientists have grappled with the phenomenon of durable authoritarianism in the post–Cold War era.

23. Minzner 2011, 938.

24. Zhang and Ginsburg 2018.

25. Liebman 2014; Yang 2017, 25. For reviews of the recent debates on Chinese legal reforms, see Minzner (2011), Peerenboom (2014), Chen (2016), Zhang and Ginsburg (2018), and Zhang (2021).

26. For discussions of cultural logics, see Swidler (2001), 187–204, and Valentino (2021). For sociological studies of binary codes in popular discourse and in policy development in the United States, see Alexander and Smith (1993) and Steensland (2006).

27. Cheesman 2015; Curley, Björn, and McCarthy 2018; Clarke 2020.

28. In actuality, it was Chen Yun, another CCP party elite, who repeatedly used the colloquial expression "crossing the river by groping the stepping-stones" to characterize the PRC's emergent, experimental, and pragmatic approach to market reforms in the post-Mao era. See Yu (2017) for the origin of this expression in the CCP's official discourse. That said, Deng Xiaoping endorsed Chen Yun's use of the expression and elevated it to the extent that party cadres later came to view the so-called theory of groping as an embodiment of Deng's political philosophy. For a detailed account of the relationship between Chen Yun and Deng Xiaoping, see Vogel (2011), 717–721. Also see Ouyang (2014) as an example of how Chinese academics and CCP party cadres have sought to indoctrinate Deng Xiaoping's political thoughts.

29. Vogel 2011.

30. Swidler 2001, 191–194.

31. Bourdieu 1990, 80–97.

32. Mitchell 1991; for a discussion of Mitchell's notion of a cultural "state effect," see Steinmetz (1999), 8.

33. See Steinmetz (1999) for a refined review of the lack of concern for culture, as well as some of the false leads in the studies of state formation in sociology and in political science. For similar reviews, see Migdal (2001), 236–241; Steensland (2006); and Xu and Gorski (2018).

34. Social scientists used to treat culture as a singular, bounded, coherent, stable, and integrated system of meanings, symbols, and practices. That era is long gone. See Ortner (1984), Merry (1998), and Sewell (2005), 152–174, for reviews of how anthropologists, sociologists, and other analysts revised their views of culture in the second half of the twentieth century.

35. Campbell 2004, 90–123.

36. Campbell 2001. Also see Steensland (2006) for an illuminating and meticulous study of how cultural categories, such as the deserving versus the undeserving poor, have profoundly shaped the ideological foundation of the American welfare state. Using the rise and fall of guaranteed annual income proposals in the United States in the 1960s and 1970s as a "negative" case, Steensland shows that when political elites failed to uproot entrenched cultural categories in public discourse, in collective schemas, and in social programs, their attempts to shake up welfare policies hardly generated any enduring effects. Steensland's study suggests that top decision-makers in liberal democracy can face mounting challenges as they strive to undo certain cultural influences in policy development. The same, I argue, can be said about ruling elites in authoritarian regimes like the PRC. I believe so because, whether in liberal or illiberal states, culture can impinge on politics through multiple mechanisms—say, by configuring expert deliberation and public discourse, by exerting schematic influences on state or societal actors' cognition and perceptions, and

most fundamentally, by institutionalizing social programs that often serve to reinforce and reproduce preexisting cultural establishments.

37. Moustafa 2007, 15.

38. Within sociology, many are accustomed to the dichotomy between culture and social structures. This dichotomization, as Sewell (2005) contends, is problematic, because culture—just like social structures—assumes certain structural properties and can be analyzed through structuralist perspectives. Thus, it is ill-conceived to attach *structures* to one part of the dichotomy but not the other. While I recognize Sewell's critique, here I use this conventional dichotomy to get across my argument about the inherent risks involved in the PRC's cultural appropriation.

39. Cultural analysts nowadays generally recognize that culture and social structures may or may not be isomorphic with each other and that perfect cultural coherence is almost nonexistent in any societies. For discussions of the dynamics between culture and social structures, see Geertz (1973), 142–169; Merry (1998); Sewell (2005), 164–168; and Xu and Gorski (2018), 518.

40. Powell and DiMaggio 1991; Campbell 2004.

41. Many sociolegal studies have examined individual choices in conflict resolution. Here, I cite only some of the most well-known works: Black 1976; Merry 1979; Miller and Sarat 1980–81; Felstiner, Abel, and Sarat 1980–81; Mather and Yngvesson 1980–81; Zemans 1982; Engel 1984. See Wagner-Pacifici and Hall (2012) and Albiston, Edelman, and Milligan (2014) for reviews of the studies that focus on individual behaviors in disputation.

42. Edelman 2005, 2016; Edelman et al. 2011.

43. For more details about legal ambiguity around EEO law, see Edelman (2016), 42–44.

44. See Edelman et al. (2011), 906, for a discussion of the case *McDonnell Douglas Corporation v. Green* (1973).

45. Edelman et al. 2011.

46. Edelman et al. 2011, 902; Edelman 2016, 171.

47. Dobbin 2018, 542.

48. See DiMaggio and Powell (1991), 11-15, for an account of why the New Institutionalism, unlike the old version of institutional analysis in organizational sociology, deliberately downplayed conflicts of interests within and between organizations. This decision, unfortunately, led to unintended consequences. See Thelen (1999), 384 and 387, for a critique of the New Institutionalism in organizational sociology. While emphasizing the significance of shared cultural scripts, organizational institutionalists often obscure political struggles among competing scripts, thereby conceiving of institutional changes largely resulting from the displacement of one script by another. Also see Hirsch (1997) and Campbell (2001) for similar critiques of organizational institutionalists' inattention to political conflicts and power struggles in institution building and policymaking.

49. Gaventa 1980; Lukes 2005.

50. See Lukes (2005), 16–19, and Gaventa (1980), 5–8, 13–14, for their discussions of the first dimension of power.

51. Regarding the "two faces of power," see Bachrach and Baratz (1962). Also see Lukes (2005), 20–25, and Gaventa (1980), 8–11, 14–15, for their discussions of the second dimension of power.

52. For discussions of the third dimension of power, see Lukes (2005), 25–29, and Gaventa (1980), 11–13, 15–25.

CHAPTER TWO

1. Qi 2018.

2. In 1978, the court system processed a total of 186,232 divorce suits nationwide; that number rose to 1,377,073 in 2018. For more details about the system's handling of divorce suits in 1978, see *Collection of Archival Records on Judicial Statistics of the People's Courts, 1949–1998 (Civil Litigation)*, 44; also see *China Statistical Yearbook*, 2019, 779, for data concerning the year 2018.

3. National Bureau of Statistics 2019.

4. Interviews with LZQ on January 18 and on February 1, 2010.

5. United Nations 2018b.

6. Woetzel et al. 2009, 13; United Nations 2018a.

7. The State Council, 1955, the Directive Concerning the Establishment of a Regular *Hukou* Registration System (国务院关于建立经常户口登记制度的指示). For a review of the *hukou* system in the PRC, see Cheng and Selden (1994) and Chan and Li (1999).

8. Cheng and Selden 1994, 644.

9. The Standing Committee of the National People's Congress, 1958, Regulations on Household Registration System of the People's Republic of China (中华人民共和国户口登记条例), Article 1.

10. For a discussion on the PRC's policy changes regarding *hukou* and population movements, see Zhang (2001), 24–28.

11. The State Council, 1984, Notification on the Issue of Allowing Peasants to Enter Cities and Towns and to Obtain Residence (国务院关于农民进入集镇落户问题的通知); and the Ministry of Public Security, 1985, Notification on the Issuance of Provisional Regulations on the Management of the Population Living Temporarily in Cities and Towns (公安部印发《公安部关于城镇暂住人口管理的暂行规定》的通知).

12. Meng and Zhang 2001, 486; National Bureau of Statistics 2019.

13. National Bureau of Statistics 2010, 2012, 2014, 2015, 2016, 2017, 2018, and 2019.

14. Threewitt 2017.

15. Interviews with LZQ on November 20 and on December 17, 2010.

16. Interview with Dr. Xiao Suowei on November 29, 2018.

17. For a review of scholarly works on the discourse of *suzhi* in contemporary China, see Jacka (2009).

18. Observation conducted inside the Xiqing People's Tribunal on January 19, 2010.

19. Interview with LZQ on December 17, 2010.

20. See Davis (2014a) for a discussion of the regulatory change introduced in 2003.

21. Among scholars who applied utilitarian perspectives to unpack the nexus between female employment and marital instability, the most famous example is the work of economist Gary S. Becker (1981). Within sociology, researchers have debated whether and how the increase in the employment of women resulted in the rise of divorce in Western countries during the second half of the twentieth century. Three theories have dominated this debate: role specialization theory, economic opportunity theory, and institutional theory. I have reviewed this debate elsewhere, see Li (2015a).

22. This literature is too large to be cited in its entirety. Here I can provide a partial list: Lee 1998; Fan 1999; Zhang 2001; Gaetano and Jacka 2004; Jacka 2005; Ngai 2005; Fu 2008; Yan 2008; Chang 2009; Gaetano 2015.

23. Ma and Cheng 2005; Feng 2006; Shu 2007; Jin, Ren, and Yue 2008; Zheng 2008; Sudhinaraset et al. 2012; He and Cao 2014; Choi 2016; Choi and Peng 2016; Xiao 2018; Sun 2019.

24. Citing Max Weber, Clifford Geertz pioneered interpretive anthropology. For his discussion on the centrality of meanings in cultural analysis, see Geertz (1973), 3–30.

25. At the time of interviewing, six women were considering marital dissolution, and twenty-six had initiated or completed divorce litigation. In some cases, I managed to interview a respondent several times. This is how I ended with a total of sixty interviews with thirty-two women.

26. Interviews with DHQ on December 21, 2010, and on January 11, 2011; interviews with WL on March 1 and on December 11, 2010.

27. Interviews with YYQ on April 8, 2010, and on March 19, 2011.

28. Interviews with SXL and DYX, respectively, on November 22, 2010.

29. Wang and Zuo 1999; Meng and Zhang 2001; Wu 2004; Wang, Zuo, and Ruan 2002; Cox 2007; Démurger et al. 2009; Wang and Fan 2012.

CHAPTER THREE

1. Interview with ZXY on November 23, 2010.

2. The two phrases *folk disputes* (民间纠纷) and *civil disputes* (民事纠纷) overlap somewhat in denotation. There is, however, a crucial distinction in state actors' use of these two phrases in official discourse: the former has been consistently associated with the cases processed by people's mediators, and the latter with those handled by judges.

3. For a thoughtful review of the dispute pyramid model, see Albiston, Edelman, and Milligan (2014).

4. Edelman 2005, 2016; Edelman et al. 2011.

5. Tilly 1985.

6. Yang 2017, 35.

7. Minzner 2011; Liebman 2014; Peerenboom 2014; Yang 2017. For reviews of the recent debate on China's legal reforms, see Chen (2016), Zhang and Ginsburg (2018), and Zhang (2021).

8. Interviews with ZXY on November 23 and 25 and on December 25, 2010.

9. The 1987 Organic Law of the Villagers' Committees [for Trial Implementation], Article 2; the 1998, 2010, and 2018 Organic Law of Villagers' Committees, Article 2.

10. Interview with CFP on December 20, 2010.

11. See "The Key to Folk Disputes Is Mediation, a Decision Made by the North China People's Government" (民间纠纷重在调解，华北人民政府颁发决定), published in the *People's Daily* on March 17, 1949.

12. To parse the use of *folk disputes* and related expressions in official discourse, policymaking, and lawmaking, I analyzed a sample of texts that comprised seventy national laws, regulations, and policy decisions, hundreds of entries retrieved from *China Law Yearbook, China Statistical Yearbook, China Social Statistical Yearbook, The People's Republic of China Yearbook, Historical Statistical Books of the People's Courts, 1949–2016 (The First Volume on Civil Litigation, 1950–2004)*, and 759 news articles published by the *People's Daily* between 1946 and 2019.

13. Cott 2000, 6.

14. The 1950 Marriage Law, Article 1.

15. For an analysis of how the derogatory signifier *feudal* (封建) came to be associated with cultural backwardness and political disunity in the early twentieth century in China, see Friedman (2006), 67–103.

16. Between 1950 and 1953, the courts of first instance countrywide processed a total of 2,967,993 marital and family disputes, among which 2,384,829 were divorce petitions.

In other words, divorce made up appropriately 80 percent of the domestic strife handled by the court system during this period. For details, see *Historical Statistical Books of the People's Courts, 1949–2016 (The First Volume on Civil Litigation, 1950–2004)*, 6–16.

17. Diamant 2000; Friedman 2006; Hershatter 2011.

18. Bennett 1976, 18.

19. Perry 2011.

20. Strauss 2006.

21. Johnson 1983.

22. Stacey 1983; Friedman 2006; Hershatter 2011; Cong 2016; Altehenger 2018.

23. Diamant 2000, 88–91.

24. The 1950 Marriage Law did encounter overt and covert resistance and even violent pushback from the average man and their parents. Women in search of divorce were, not infrequently, met with obstruction, revenge, and even murder. For more details as to how different social groups reacted to the law during the 1951 and then the 1953 campaigns, see Johnson (1983), Diamant (2000), and Wang and Mu (2020).

25. See "Improve the Work of People's Mediation, Strengthen the Unity of the People, and Promote Production and Construction" (做好人民调解工作, 加强人民团结推动生产建设), published in the *People's Daily* on March 23, 1954.

26. The Administration Council, 1954, Interim Rules on People's Mediation Committees (人民调解委员会暂行组织通则), Articles 2 and 5.

27. The Ministry of Justice, 1954, Two Replies Regarding the Interim Rules on People's Mediation Committees (司法部关于《人民调解委员会暂行组织通则》的两个问题的复函).

28. *China Yearbook of Judicial Administration* 1995, 33.

29. *China Law Yearbook* 1987, 782.

30. See "Report on the Work of the Supreme People's Court" (关于最高人民法院工作的报告), published in the *People's Daily* on July 3, 1957.

31. The Anti-Rightist campaign in 1957 and 1958, which sought to purge rightist bourgeois within the Party, led to further twists and turns. People's mediation committees, in some areas, were converted into adjustment committees (调处委员会). The latter, it seems, put a greater emphasis than the former on ideological control, political discipline, and administrative coercion in dispute settlement. Scholars are generally circumspect about the differences between people's mediation committees and adjustment committees, owing to the scarcity of reliable archival records. See Han (1981) as an exception, though. When the SPC, in 2000, publicized some of the PRC's earliest record-keeping, one crucial detail surfaced. Party leadership's endorsement of people's mediation (and its variants) did translate into widespread grassroots practices. The years of 1959 and 1960 saw adjustment committees effortlessly eclipse the court system. Mediators nationwide processed a total of 4,766,618 folk disputes in two years (the bulk involved civil cases, and only a small portion concerned minor criminal matters); judges, meanwhile, disposed of 692,577 civil suits, a tiny fraction of those handled by mediators outside courtrooms. For more details, see *Collection of Archival Records on Judicial Statistics of the People's Courts, 1949–1998 (Civil Litigation)*, 25 and 27.

32. See "The SPC President, Xie Juezai, Reporting on the Work of the Supreme People's Court" (谢觉哉院长作最高人民法院工作报告), published in the *People's Daily* on January 1, 1965.

33. Clarke 1991; Lubman 1997, 1999; Huang 2010; Read 2012.

34. The 1982 Constitution, Article 111; the 1982 Civil Procedural Law [for Trial Implementation], Article 14; the 1985 Law of Succession, Article 15.

35. See Deng Xiaoping's speech, "The Reform of the Party and the State's Leadership System" (党和国家领导制度的改革), at the Enlarged Meeting of the Political Bureau of the CCP Central Committee on August 18, 1980.

36. See Dynon (2008) for a study of the origin, persistence, and evolution of the CCP's reform-era narratives surrounding various types of civilization (文明).

37. Several official documents shed light on the PRC's motivations behind the 1980 revision of the Marriage Law: Notice of the State Council on Carefully Enforcing the New Marriage Law (国务院关于认真贯彻执行新婚姻法的通知), issued in 1980; Notice of the Supreme People's Court, the Ministry of Justice, the Ministry of Civil Affairs, the All-China Federation of Trade Unions, the Communist Youth League Central Committee, and the All-China Women's Federation on Further Disseminating the Marriage Law (最高人民法院、司法部、民政部、总工会、共青团中央、全国妇联关于深入宣传婚姻法的通知), issued in 1981; and, Notice of the State Council on Further Publicizing and Enforcing the Marriage Law (国务院关于进一步宣传贯彻婚姻法的通知), released in 1981. Also see Palmer (1995), Woo (2003), and Davis (2014a) for scholarly discussions of the 1980 Marriage Law.

38. Zhang 1988.

39. The 1954 Interim Rules on People's Mediation Committees, Article 5; the 1982 Constitution, Article 111; the 1982 Civil Procedural Law [for Trial Implementation], Article 14.

40. *China Yearbook of the New Era of Reform and Opening Up*, 1981, 619.

41. For an illuminating study of the two pillar institutions of socialism, Leninist party organizations and command economy, see Walder (1986).

42. See Han (1981), Clarke (1991), Wall and Blum (1991), and Lubman (1999) for detailed studies of people's mediation in the early years of the reform era.

43. Lubman 1999; Halegua 2005; Di and Wu 2009; He 2013; Zhang 2013; Liu 2016.

44. Read 2012, 221.

45. Memorandum of Conversation between George H. W. Bush and Chairman Deng Xiaoping in Beijing, February 26, 1989, History and Public Policy Program Digital Archive, Memcons and Telcons, George Bush Presidential Library and Museum.

46. It is unclear how many protesters were killed or jailed by the Chinese government during or after the 1989 Pro-Democracy Student Movement. The estimate varied from a few hundred to thousands. See Kristof (1989); Lusher 2017; *BBC*, December 23, 2017.

47. Wang and Minzner 2015.

48. Gallagher 2017, 36–51.

49. The State Council, 1989, Regulations on the Organization of the People's Mediation Committees (人民调解委员会组织条例), Article 5.

50. The MOJ, 1991, Notice on Further Preventing the Escalation of Folk Disputes (司法部关于进一步加强防止民间纠纷激化工作的通知).

51. The SPC and the MOJ, 2007, Opinions on Further Strengthening the Work of People's Mediation under the New Circumstances (最高人民法院、司法部关于进一步加强新形势下人民调解工作的意见).

52. Two articles, "Transforming the Old Mindset and Serving the Overall Interests: A Summary of the Work of People's Mediation in Hubei Province (1)" (转变观念，服务大局—河北省人民调解工作纪实[一]), and "A Million Members of Xiang Army Launching the First Battle of *Paicha*" (百万湘军打响排查治理第一战役), were published in the *People's Mediation* in 1995. They exemplified how *paicha*, at one point in the wake of the 1989

Pro-Democracy Student Movement, was enacted as a series of concerted, top-down, large-scale campaign efforts.

53. Perry 2011.

54. Yan 1995.

55. Walder 1995.

56. See Opinions of the Supreme People's Court and the Ministry of Justice on Further Strengthening the Work of People's Mediation under the New Circumstances (最高人民法院、司法部关于进一步加强新时期人民调解工作的意见); Some Provisions of the Supreme People's Court on Trying Civil Cases Involving Agreements Reached Through People's Mediation (最高人民法院关于审理涉及人民调解协议的民事案件的若干规定); Some Provisions Concerning the Work of People's Mediation (人民调解工作若干规定). All three documents were issued in 2002. And see also Opinions of the Supreme People's Court and the Ministry of Justice on Further Consolidating the Work of People's Mediation for the Purpose of Maintaining Social Stability (最高人民法院、司法部关于加强人民调解工作切实维护社会稳定的意见), released in 2004.

57. The 2010 People's Mediation Law, Articles 31, 32, and 33. See also Some Provisions of the Supreme People's Court on Trying Civil Cases Involving Agreements Reached Through People's Mediation, Article 1, and Some Provisions Concerning the Work of People's Mediation, Article 5.

58. I would like to thank Fu Hualing for generously sharing his collection of mediation case files with me.

59. See Notice of the Ministry of Justice on Printing and Distributing Case Files and Statistical Reports Regarding People's Mediation (司法部关于印发人民调解文书格式和统计报表的通知) for more details on the paperwork the MOJ handed down in 2010.

60. The SPC and the MOJ, 2011, Opinions on Carefully Enforcing the People's Mediation Law of the People's Republic of China and Strengthening and Innovating Social Management (最高人民法院、司法部关于认真贯彻实施《中华人民共和国人民调解法》加强和创新社会管理的意见).

61. Gallagher 2017, 46–51.

62. Note that in 2016, the SPC and other state bureaucracies initiated another round of reform, seeking to improve their handling of marital and family disputes. This round of reform called for greater professionalism and specialization in handling family trials (家事审判), on the one hand, and renewed an emphasis on deploying people's mediation to settle domestic disputes, on the other. In the epilogue, I will discuss in the PRC's latest approaches to marital and family disputes and the broad implications.

63. Davis 2014a. See also Alford and Shen (2004) for a review of the 2001 revision of the Marriage Law.

64. The State Council, 2003, Regulations on Marriage Registration (婚姻登记条例), Article 11. Also see the 1994 Managing Rules on Marriage Registration (婚姻登记管理条例), Article 9. A comparison of these two articles reveals a significant regulatory change. In 2003, in revising the 1994 rules, the State Council revoked a requirement that upon divorce husband and wife must present to local government a statement prepared either by their employers or Residents' Committee (in urban settings) or Villagers' Committee (in rural settings) to verify the state of their marriage. Prior to 2003, when a couple failed to provide such a statement, they could not register their divorce at the local government. The 2003 regulatory change, in other words, practically eliminated the power of employers and village cadres to block citizens' pursuit of divorce.

65. Minzner 2011.

66. Minzner 2011; Peerenboom 2014; Chen 2016; Zhang and Ginsburg 2018.

67. Liebman 2014; Yang 2017.

68. For discussions of widespread indifference to culture in the studies of modern states, see Steinmetz (1999), Migdal (2001), 236–241, Steensland (2006), and Xu and Gorski (2018).

69. Swidler 1986, 2001.

70. Merry 1998.

71. See Alford and Shen (2004), Palmer (2007), Davis (2014b), and Li and Friedman (2015) for discussions of how marital regulations in the twenty-first century have endowed citizens with more individual freedoms and rights. That said, even within intimate relationships, legislators have been rather selective in terms of the kinds of rights granted to wife and husband. For example, after four decades of implementing the Household Responsibility System (家庭联产承包责任制), the Marriage Law has yet to recognize rural couples' access to farmland as part of their conjugal property, thus suitable for partition at the time of divorce. Chapter 7 analyzes the PRC's lawmaking in this regard, as well as its impact on women's legal mobilization and rights contention upon divorce.

72. Zhang and Ginsburg 2018, 7.

73. This classification first appeared in a 2002 document, Opinions of the Supreme People's Court and the Ministry of Justice on Further Strengthening the Work of People's Mediation under the New Circumstances. See also Opinions of the Supreme People's Court and the Ministry of Justice on Further Consolidating the Work of People's Mediation for the Purpose of Maintaining Social Stability.

74. A few estimates reveal the extent to which torts, as one type of folk disputes, have been judicialized in the reform era. In 1984, for every tort case that landed in a courtroom, six similar cases came to the attention of people's mediation—a ratio of 1:6. That ratio, by the end of 2018, had jumped to 1:0.6, a ninefold increase in three decades, bespeaking the judiciary's enhanced role in dealing with torts. This comparison is based on data points retrieved from *China Law Yearbook* (1987–2016), *China Statistical Yearbook* (1985–1986, 2014, 2019), *China Social Statistical Yearbook* (2017–2018), and *Collection of Archival Records on Judicial Statistics of the People's Courts, 1949–1998 (Civil Litigation).*

75. To analyze the PRC's attempts to resolve land-related disputes, I analyzed a sample of ninety-two national laws, regulations, and policy decisions, issued between 1950 and 2018.

76. The SPC, 2005, Interpretations of the Issues Concerning the Application of Law in Disputes over Rural Land Contracting (最高人民法院关于审理涉及农村土地承包纠纷案件适用法律问题的解释), Article 1.

77. The CCP Central Committee, 2014, Decisions on Major Issues Concerning the Comprehensive Promotion of the Rule of Law in Governance (中共中央关于全面推进依法治国若干重大问题的决定).

CHAPTER FOUR

1. Hosticka 1979; Mather and Yngvesson 1980–81; Sarat and Felstiner 1995; Kritzer 1997, 1998; Mather, McEwen, and Maiman 2001.

2. Observation conducted in the Xiqing Legal Workers' Office on December 8, 2010.

3. Scott 1998; Wedeen 2015; Cheesman 2015; Gallagher 2017; Perry 2017; Curley, Björn, and McCarthy 2018.

4. To trace how the PRC developed various legal professions in the reform era, I analyzed a sample of texts that consisted of 111 national laws, departmental

regulations, and policy directives, hundreds of entries retrieved from *China Law Yearbook*, *China Statistical Yearbook*, *China Social Statistical Yearbook*, *The People's Republic of China Yearbook*, and *China Yearbook of Judicial Administration*, and *Justice of China*, and 233 news articles published by the *People's Daily* between 1985 and 2020.

5. All the estimates come from *China Statistical Yearbook* (1984), 11. For a detailed account of the PRC's efforts to build and name various entities providing legal services in the Maoist and then in the socialist era, see Liu (2001).

6. The two phrases, *Township Legal Services* and *Grassroots Legal Services*, are largely equivalents, both referring to legal workers' host organizations. That said, the former was widely used in the 1980s and 1990s; after 2000, the latter gained currency in official discourse, policymaking, and lawmaking. In the remainder of the chapter, I use the former in writing of the last two decades of the twentieth century and switch to the latter for the years in the new millennium.

7. The 1980 Interim Regulations of the People's Republic of China on Lawyers (中华人民共和国律师暂行条例), Article 1. For in-depth studies of Chinese lawyers' ties with the state, see Liu (2001), Michelson (2007), Liu (2011), Liu and Halliday (2011), and Stern and Liu (2020).

8. For a discussion of the motivations behind the official promotion of Township Legal Services in the 1980s, see *China Law Yearbook* (1988), 693–697.

9. Three regulations specified legal workers' obligations to fulfil certain administrative functions: the 1987 Interim Provisions of the Ministry of Justice Concerning Township Legal Workers' Offices (司法部关于乡镇法律服务所暂行规定); the 1991 Working Rules on the Operation of Township Legal Services (乡镇法律服务业务工作细则); and the 1997 Notice of the State Planning Commission and the Ministry of Justice on the Issuance of the Administrative Measures for the Service Charges of Township Legal Services (国家计委、司法部关于印发《乡镇法律服务收费管理办法》的通知).

10. When Civil Procedural Law was amended in 2012, lawmakers codified for the first time the role of legal workers as lawful counsel in litigation; see Article 58. See also the 2014 Administration Litigation Law, Article 31, for a similar stipulation.

11. In Weifeng and many other places, judges and especially those stationed in rural areas tolerated legal workers' practice of law inside courtrooms, even though the country's major procedural laws did not recognize the legality of this group's involvement in litigation until 2012 and then 2014. Judges did so in no small part because they were cognizant of the scarcity of lawyers in their jurisdictions.

12. The 1954 Organic Law of the People's Courts of the People's Republic of China (中华人民共和国法院组织法), Article 7, and the 1979 Organic Law of the People's Courts of the People's Republic of China (中华人民共和国法院组织法), Article 8.

13. *China Law Yearbook* 1993, 141–142.

14. Peerenboom 2002, 55.

15. For studies of the relations between legal workers' offices and justice offices, see Fu (2004, 2011), Fu (2004, 2015), You (2005), and Liu (2011).

16. The MOJ, 1994, Notice on the Issuance of a Five-Year Plan for the Development of the Administration of Justice (司法部关于印发《中国司法行政工作五年发展纲要》的通知).

17. Wang 2000.

18. The MOJ, 2000, Measures for the Administration of Grassroots Legal Workers' Offices (基层法律服务所管理办法), and Measures for the Management of Grassroots Legal Workers (基层法律工作者管理办法).

19. The MOJ, 2002, Notice on the Issuance of the Opinions Toward Unhooking and Restructuring of Grassroots Legal Workers' Offices (司法部关于印发《基层法律服务机构脱钩改制实施意见》的通知).

20. *China Law Yearbook* 2001, 229.

21. The MOJ, 2002, Opinions on Strengthening Legal Services in Communities in Large- and Mid-Sized Cities (司法部关于加强大中城市社区法律服务工作的意见).

22. For media coverage of the 2002 Shanghai Conference, see Li (2002), Ye (2002), and Wu (2002). For Zhou Yuansheng's article, see "Reflection on Further Regulating the Order of the Legal Services Market" (关于进一步规范法律服务市场秩序的思考), published in the *Justice of China* in 2004.

23. At the National Forum for the Heads of Justice Departments and Bureaus, held between December 26 and 28, 2002, the MOJ set two different paths for legal workers stationed in large- and mid-sized cities and those in the countryside. For a discussion of this forum, see the article, "Further Expanding and Regulating the Delivery of Legal Services (进一步扩展和规范法律服务工作)," published in *Chinese Lawyers* in 2003.

24. The State Council, 2004, "Decisions on Abolishing and Adjusting Items Requiring Administrative Permissions (the Third Batch)" (国务院关于第三批取消和调整行政审批项目的决定). In June 2004, the State Council reversed its prior decision on legal workers' entry into legal practice. For more details, see "Decisions on Preserving Certain Items Requiring Administrative Permissions" (国务院对确需保留的行政审批项目设定行政许可的决定). In 2012, the State Council, once again, adjusted the kind of official permits legal workers would need to be licensed. This time the authority to issue permits to legal workers was delegated from the provincial governments (or their delegates at a lower level) to those at the municipal level. See "Decisions on Abolishing and Adjusting Items Requiring Administrative Permissions (the Sixth Batch)" (国务院关于第六批取消和调整行政审批项目的决定). As for the MOJ's 2000 stipulation on the requirements for the establishment of a legal worker's office in a given locale, see Measures for the Administration of Grassroots Legal Workers' Offices, Article 11.

25. The MOJ, 2000, Measures for the Management of Grassroots Legal Workers, Article 7.

26. *China Law Yearbook* 2004, 199.

27. Wang 2008, 35.

28. For more details on the MOJ's stipulations on legal workers' gradual retreat from litigation, see "Opinions on Strengthening the Legal Services in Communities in Large- and Mid-Sized Cities," released in 2002.

29. Migdal 2001, 22.

30. Stern 2013, 3–7, 97–122. See also Lieberthal (1992) for a discussion of fragmented authoritarianism and its impact on policymaking in the post-Mao China.

31. Liu 2017.

32. Li 2004; Chen 2008; Zhang 2008.

33. Political scientists and sociologists have long noted that the Chinese state is far from a monolith. Lieberthal (1992) and Stern (2013), for example, explore how the Chinese state is structurally and bureaucratically fragmented and its implications for policy formation. Similarly, Liu (2017) analyzes how a fragmented state regulatory regime, in the past three decades, has led to a fragmented legal services market. In this analysis, Liu mainly stresses the bureaucratic divisions in the state and the structural segmentation in the market. The foregoing works, I must note, pay little attention to the question of how culture may split

the state—ideologically, discursively, cognitively, or symbolically—thereby presenting unique challenges and difficulties in state actors' policy reforms.

34. Weber 1946, 280. For discussions of how Max Weber has inspired generations of scholars to explore the social effects of ideas, see Swidler (1986, 2001), Campbell (2001, 2004), and Schmidt (2008).

35. Campbell 2001.

36. Steensland 2006.

37. Fu 2004, 2011; Fu 2004, 2015.

38. Heilmann and Perry 2011, 22.

39. Moustafa 2007, 15.

40. Thelen (1999) and Mahoney (2000) provide in-depth discussions of the concept of path dependence. See Capoccia and Kelemen (2007) for more details on the notion of critical juncture.

41. The year 2017 must be marked as another tipping point. The MOJ, in that year, amended two key regulations on Grassroots Legal Services, signaling significant policy shifts. I discuss these developments in the epilogue.

42. The Ministry of Justice and the Ministry of Finance, 1990, Notice on the Issuance of Measures for the Financial Management of Township Legal Workers' Offices (司法部、财政部关于印发《乡镇法律服务所财务管理办法》的通知), Articles 10 and 13. As for the MOJ's decision to revoke management fees for law firms and lawyers, see Opinions on Expanding and Regulating the Legal Services Provided by Lawyers (司法部关于拓展和规范律师法律服务的意见), issued in 2003.

43. The MOJ, as early as in 1991, restricted legal workers' practice to the jurisdictions in which they were admitted to law. See Working Rules on the Operation of Township Legal Services, Article 24. It reiterated this restriction later, in 2002, 2015, and 2017, respectively.

44. The MOJ, 2014, Opinions on Further Advancing the Construction of a Public Legal Services System.

45. A detailed note must be included to explain how the PRC's stance on government procurement of legal services has evolved in the past decade. When the MOJ suggested, in 2014, that local governments use public funds to purchase legal services from practitioners in private practice, there were few national laws or regulations specifying how this could be done on the ground. In October 2020, the Ministry of Justice and the Ministry of Finance teamed up, taking the first step to articulate policy prescriptions in the new direction. For details, see Opinions of the Ministry of Justice and the Ministry of Finance on Establishing and Improving the Mechanisms for Government Procurement of Legal Services (司法部、财政部关于建立健全政府购买法律服务机制的意见). This move reconfirms top decision-makers' stance that legal workers should maintain their standing as market players and that local governments could use revenues to compensate this group for provision of public services. In the epilogue, I discuss the latest developments in this regard.

46. For a critique of the scholarly tendency to essentialize and stereotype Chinese culture, see a discussion of rights consciousness versus rule consciousness in Gallagher (2017), 55–62. See also Sewell (2005), 152–174, for a broader critique of cultural essentialism. In his critique, Sewell revisits the identity crisis among anthropologists in the 1980s and 1990s, a crisis stemming from scholars' reflections on past practices of essentializing, exoticizing, and othering the cultures of peoples whose ways of life were deemed different from white middle-class Euro-Americans.

47. For a penetrating critique of interest-based theories of organizations, politics, political economy, international relations, and economics, see Campbell (2004), 90–92. See also Wedeen (2015) for a similar argument that politics is not just about material interests or the groups articulating them; rather, culture, in the form of rhetoric, symbols, and ideologies, is central rather than epiphenomenal to politics.

48. Sewell 2005, 167.

49. Zhou 2004, 50.

50. Wu 2008, 68.

51. A report issued by the Department of Justice in Shanxi Province is a case in point. Government officials who prepared the report were rather blunt about the predicaments legal workers had experienced in the new century. According to the report, policymaking had been flawed at both the national and the local level. See "Survey Report on Strengthening the Legal Services in Rural Shanxi Province" (陕西省农村法律服务工作调研报告), published in the *Justice of China*, in 2009, for more details.

52. In 1994, the MOJ, on the one hand, announced the decision to build a publicly funded legal aid system; see *China Law Yearbook* (1998), 181. On the other hand, that same year, it released a five-year plan, envisioning future reforms to unhook lawyers and legal workers from the state, thereby setting in motion a trend to privatize legal services. See Notice of the Ministry of Justice on the Issuance of a Five-Year Plan for the Development of the Administration of Justice.

53. See the 2003 Regulations on Legal Aid (法律援助条例), Article 10, for social groups eligible for state-sponsored legal aid. From 2005 onward, *China Law Yearbook* started listing migrant workers as a distinct category entitled to such aid.

54. United Nations Office on Drugs and Crime 2016, 93.

55. Many have studied popular grievances and right mobilization in China in the twenty-first century. Here, I can provide only a partial list of scholarly works: Perry and Selden 2000; Diamant, Lubman, and O'Brien 2005; Gallagher 2006, 2017; Michelson 2006; Read and Michelson 2008; He, Wang, and Su 2013; Lee and Zhang 2013; Chuang 2014; Fu 2014; Pils 2016; Lu, Zheng, and Wang 2017; Chan 2019.

56. Li 2016.

57. Li 2015b.

58. See Skocpol (1985) and Mitchell (1991) for reviews of political scientists' attempts to get rid of the concept of the state.

59. Merry (1998) and Sewell (2005), 152–174, offer reviews of anthropologists and sociologists' efforts to replace culture with other conceptual constructs.

60. See Aretxaga (2003) for a review of the recent attempts to analyze modern states from cultural perspectives. Note that the works in this review are primarily conducted by anthropologists, not sociologists or political scientists.

61. Felstiner, Abel, and Sarat 1980–81; Mather and Yngvesson 1980–81; Mather 1990.

CHAPTER FIVE

1. Gaventa 1980; Lukes 2005.

2. Viewing marriage and the family as the cornerstones of a nation-state, a line of political thinking, can be traced back to Confucianism. During the New Culture (1915–1923) and May Fourth (1919) movements, young urban intellectuals recast this view by rendering marriage and family reforms as China's inescapable path toward modernity. Both the Nationalist government and the Chinese Communist Party (CCP) inherited this political

thinking and subsequently translated it into a series of marital regulations. For discussions of the nexus among family formation, nation-state building, and modernity, see Diamant (2000), Li and Friedman (2015), and Cong (2016).

3. Interview with QYL on February 24, 2011.

4. Conley and O'Barr 1998, 15–38.

5. Information Office of the State Council 2008.

6. Observation conducted at the Qinchuan People's Tribunal on February 24, 2011.

7. The 1982 Civil Procedural Law [for Trial Implementation], Article 5; the 1991, 2007, 2012, 2017 Civil Procedural Law, Article 7.

8. The SPC, 1956, Summary of Civil Procedures for the People's Courts at All Levels (各级人民法院民事案件审判程序总结).

9. The SPC, 1979, Provisions of the People's Courts on the Procedural Rules of Civil Litigation [for Trial Implementation] (人民法院审判民事案件程序制度的规定[试行]).

10. The 1982 Civil Procedural Law [for Trial Implementation], Articles 112 and 114.

11. In principle, a petitioner can bypass the six-month procedural constraint, if she or he can prove that new circumstances and/or grounds for divorce have emerged since the withdrawal. See Opinions of the Supreme People's Court on Several Issues Regarding the Enforcement of the Civil Procedural Law of the People's Republic of China (最高人民法院关于适用《中华人民共和国民事诉讼法》若干问题的意见), Article 144, issued in 1992. See also Interpretation of the Supreme People's Court on the Application of the Civil Procedural Law of the People's Republic of China (最高人民法院关于适用《中华人民共和国民事诉讼法》的解释), Article 214, released in 2015; Interpretation of the Supreme People's Court on the Application of the Civil Procedural Law (the 2020 Revision) (最高人民法院关于适用《中华人民共和国民事诉讼法》的解释[2020修正]), Article 214, released in 2020.

12. The following provisions have foreclosed the path for plaintiffs to demand retrials at the courts of first instance, where civil cases are disposed of through withdrawal: the 1982 Civil Procedural Law [for Trial Implementation], Article 84; the 1991, 2007, and 2012 Civil Procedural Law, Article 111; and the 2017 Civil Procedural Law, Article 124.

13. The following provisions have repeatedly denied plaintiffs the right to appeal to higher courts to challenge trial courts' approval for case withdrawal: the 1982 Civil Procedural Law [for Trial Implementation], Article 122; the 1991 and 2007 Civil Procedural Law, Article 140; and the 2012 and 2017 Civil Procedural Law, Article 154.

14. The 1991 and 2007 Civil Procedural Law, Article 178; the 2012 and 2017 Civil Procedural Law, Article 199.

15. The SPC, 1998, Notice on the Issuance of Disciplinary Measures for Court Trials [for Trial Implementation] (最高人民法院关于印发《人民法院审判纪律处分办法[试行]》的通知), Article 37.

16. The SPC, 2001, Notice on the Issuance of the Basic Rules on the Professional Ethnics of Judges of the People's Republic of China (最高人民法院关于印发《中华人民共和国法官职业道德基本准则》的通知), Article 5.

17. The SPC, 2009, Notice on the Issuance of Disciplinary Rules for the People's Court Personnel (最高人民法院关于印发《人民法院工作人员处分条例》的通知), Article 44.

18. The SPC, 2010, Notice on Reissuing the Basic Rules on the Professional Ethnics of Judges of the People's Republic of China (最高人民法院关于重新印发《中华人民共和国法官职业道德基本准则》的通知).

19. Liu 2012.

20. Li 2013.

21. See Notice of the Supreme People's Court on the Issuance of Interim Guiding Opinions Regarding the Implementation of the Case Quality Assessment System (最高人民法院印发《最高人民法院关于开展案件质量评估工作的指导意见［试行］》的通知), issued in 2008; and Guiding Opinions on Launching the Case Quality Assessment System (关于开展案件质量评估工作的指导意见), released in 2011.

22. Kinkel and Hurst 2015.

23. Interview with QYL on February 27, 2011.

24. To track how divorce laws have evolved in the PRC on paper and in practice, I examined a sample of texts, including ninety-four national laws, judicial interpretations, and policy documents, and hundreds of entries retrieved from *China Civil Affairs' Statistical Yearbook*, *China Law Yearbook*, *China Statistical Yearbook*, *Collection of Archival Records on Judicial Statistics of the People's Courts, 1949–1998 (Civil Litigation)*, and *Historical Statistical Books of the People's Courts, 1949–2016 (The First Volume on Civil Litigation, 1950–2004)* and *(The Second Volume on Civil Litigation, 2005–2016)*.

25. The 1950 Marriage Law, Article 17.

26. A few documents reveal the SPC's early attempts to apply the breakdown of mutual affection as a principle for judging in divorce litigation: Reply of the Supreme People's Court Regarding Article 19 of the Marriage Law (最高人民法院对婚姻法第十九条的解释意见之答复), issued in 1951; Reply of the Supreme People's Court Concerning the Divorce of Yan Peikuan and Tokudome Nobuko (最高人民法院关于颜佩宽与德留信子离婚问题的批复), issued in 1954; and, Reply of the Supreme People's Court Regarding Divorces among Ethnic Minority Groups (最高人民法院关于兄弟民族离婚纠纷问题的批复), released in 1955.

27. The SPC, 1963, Opinions on Several Issues Regarding the Enforcement of Policies Related to Civil Disputes (最高人民法院关于贯彻执行民事政策几个问题的意见).

28. The 1980 Marriage Law, Article 25.

29. The SPC, 1989, Several Specific Opinions on How in Divorce Cases the People's Courts Determine Whether Mutual Affection Breaks Down between Husband and Wife (最高人民法院印发《关于人民法院审理离婚案件如何认定夫妻感情确已破裂的若干具体意见》).

30. The SPC, 1989, Several Specific Opinions on How in Divorce Cases the People's Courts Determine Whether Mutual Affection Breaks Down between Husband and Wife, Article 8.

31. The 2001 Marriage Law, Articles 32 and 46.

32. For detailed discussions of marital regulations in the PRC, see Bailey (1993), Palmer (1995, 2007), Diamant (2000), Woo (2003), Huang (2005), and Davis (2014b), and Li and Friedman (2015).

33. Stacey 1983; Johnson 1983; Diamant 2000; Friedman 2006; Hershatter 2011; Li and Friedman 2015; Cong 2016; Altehenger 2018; Wang and Mu 2020.

34. Andors 1983; Johnson 1983; Stacey 1983; Wolf 1985; see also Friedman (2006).

35. Judd 1998; Diamant 2000; Cong 2016.

36. He 2007, 18–33.

37. For studies of divorce law practices under the influences of the Maoist justice, see Bailey (1993), Diamant (2000), Huang (2005), Cong (2016), and Wang and Mu (2020).

38. Davis 2014a.

39. The SPC, 2016, Notice on Implementing a Pilot Program in Reforming the Methods and Working Mechanisms of Family Trials in Certain Courts (最高人民法院关于在部分法院开展家事审判方式和工作机制改革试点工作的通知).

40. For studies of divorce law practices in the 1930s and 1940s, see Bailey (1993), Cong (2016); for a comparison of the Maoist style and present-day divorce law practices, see Huang (2005) and He (2009).

41. Interviews with ZM on February 28 and with YJQ on March 16, 2011.

42. Choi and Peng 2016.

43. Denyer and Gowen 2018.

44. Lubman 1997; Peerenboom 2002, 2014; Cabestan 2005; Clarke 2007; Grimheden 2006; Liebman 2007, 2014; Minzner 2015; Chen 2016; Huang 2016; Zhang 2016; Zhang and Ginsburg 2018.

45. The Chinese court system comprises four tiers: the Supreme People's Court at the top, the High People's Courts at the provincial level, the Intermediate People's Courts at the municipal level, and the Basic People's Courts at the bottom. In terms of organizational composition, the People's Tribunals form a component of the Basic People's Courts. And their rulings are deemed the equivalent of formal judgments made by the Basic People's Courts.

46. Su 2000.

47. To trace the SPC's efforts to improve the performance of the People's Tribunals, I analyzed a sample of official texts, including eighty-seven national laws and policy initiatives, seventy-two entries retrieved from the *China Law Yearbook*, and the annual work reports prepared by the highest court between 1980 and 2018.

48. The SPC, 1999, Notice on the Issuance of the Five-Year Reform Outline for the People's Courts (最高人民法院关于印发《人民法院五年改革纲要》的通知). This document laid out three priorities for the reform of the grassroots court system: to equip the People's Tribunals with at least three judges, one clerk, and, if possible, bailiffs; to abolish tribunals that did not meet the basic conditions for judging and those incapable of exercising judicial power independently or fairly; and to dismantle existing tribunals stationed in urban areas.

49. The SPC, 2009, Notice on Further Advancing the Work of the People's Tribunals in 2009 (最高人民法院关于进一步做好2009年人民法庭工作通知).

50. This popular saying was retrieved from an official document; see Notice of the Supreme People's Court on Circulating No. 69 File Issued by the General Office of the State Council in 1988 (最高人民法院关于转发"国办发［1988］69号"文件的通知), released in 1988.

51. Grimheden 2006.

52. In 2005, the SPC issued four documents to lay out its plans to shore up the existing People's Tribunals: Notice on the Issuance of the Second Five-Year Reform Outline for the People's Courts (最高人民法院关于印发《人民法院第二个五年改革纲要》的通知); Notice on the Issuance of Planning for the Material Construction of the People's Courts during the National Eleventh Five-Year Plan (最高人民法院关于印发《国家"十一五"规划期间人民法院物质建设规划》的通知); Notice of the General Office of the Supreme People's Court on Several Issues Regarding the Strengthening of Specialized Construction of the People's Tribunals (最高人民法院办公厅关于加强人民法庭专项建设若干问题的通知); and Notice on Decisions to Consolidate the Work of the People's Tribunals (最高人民法院印发《关于加强人民法庭工作的决定》的通知).

53. Hu and Chen 2011, 85.

54. *China Law Yearbook* 1993, 86; *China Law Yearbook* 2013, 153. See also Clarke (2003), 179–180, for an account of the changes in the number of People's Tribunals nationwide since the early 1990s.

55. The SPC, 1999, Notice on the Issuance of the Five-Year Reform Outline for the People's Courts, Item 27.

56. The 1982 Civil Procedural Law [for Trial Implementation], Article 84; the 1991 and 2007 Civil Procedural Law, Article 111; the 2012 and 2017 Civil Procedural Law, Article 124. Note that once a divorce petition is withdrawn, a plaintiff will be subject to the same six-month constraint. More specifically, the plaintiff must wait for at least six months to file another petition for divorce, until she or he can prove that new circumstances or grounds have emerged in this divorce case. For more details, see note 11 in this chapter.

57. In 2018, the SPC for the first time specified the circumstances in which judges could formally impose a cooling-off period in divorce litigation. One, the waiting period shall not last for more than three months; and two, both parties in a divorce suit must agree on this arrangement. For more details, see Opinions of the Supreme People's Court on Further Deepening the Reform of the Methods and Working Mechanisms of Family Trials [for Trial Implementation] (最高人民法院关于进一步深化家事审判方式和工作机制改革的意见[试行]), Item 40.

58. See He (2009) for a study of how judges had routinely turned down first-time divorce petitions. For similar studies, see Ma (2005), Liu (2012), Chen and He (2014), Jiang and Zhu (2014), Luo (2016), Luo (2017), and Zhang (2018).

59. Kinkel and Hurst 2015, 942.

60. The SPC in its annual work reports used two expressions: *dingfen zhizheng* (定分止争) and *dingfen zhizheng* (定纷止争). Between 2005 and 2007, it used the former term, which could be traced back to the seventh century BC and means ascertaining ownership first and then putting an end to disputes. In 2010, the SPC tweaked the traditional expression and started using the latter term, whose meaning was changed to simply settling disputes and ending conflicts. For a discussion of the differences between these two phrases, see Wang (2014).

61. Concerns about divorce litigants' personal safety, apparently, are not limited to the rural population. In fact, the SPC, in 2017, issued a notice, exhorting lower courts to further the reform of family trials. For more details, see Notice of the Supreme People's Court on Trying Cases Regarding Marriage and Family Disputes in Accordance with the Law and Effectively Safeguarding the Parties' Lawful Rights, Interests, and Personal Safety (最高人民法院关于依法妥善审理婚姻家庭案件切实保障当事人合法权益和人身安全的通知).

62. About one in three Chinese families suffers from domestic violence. This estimate comes from an official document. See Guidelines for Hearing Marital Cases Involving Domestic Violence (涉及家庭暴力婚姻案件审理指南), issued in 2008 by the China Institute of Applied Jurisprudence (中国应用法学研究所), a research organ affiliated with the SPC.

63. The 2020 SPC annual work report.

64. Fan 2013.

65. Cott 2000.

CHAPTER SIX

1. Scott 1990.

2. Blumberg 1967, 39.

3. Eisenstein, Flemming, and Nardulli 1988; Uphoff 1992; Van Cleve 2016.

4. Interview with WY on March 1, 2010.

5. Observation conducted at the Guxiao People's Tribunal on July 9, 2010.

6. Michelson 2007.

7. Interview with LYX on July 11, 2010.

8. Interview with YDJ on July 13, 2010.

9. The 1950 Marriage Law, Article 17.

10. The SPC, 1956, Summary of Civil Procedures for the People's Courts at All Levels (各级人民法院民事案件审判程序总结).

11. The SPC, 1979, Provisions of the People's Courts on the Procedural Rules of Civil Litigation [for Trial Implementation] (人民法院审判民事案件程序制度的规定[试行]).

12. The 1980 Marriage Law, Article 25, and the 2001 Marriage Law, Article 32.

13. In 1991, when the Civil Procedural Law was revised, legislators removed Article 6, which stressed the role of mediation in civil litigation. A new provision, Article 9, was added to the amended law with an emphasis on a general principle: mediation must be carried out voluntarily and lawfully. For detailed reviews of the shifting roles of mediation in Chinese courts in the reform era, see Huang (2006), Ma (2008), Fu and Cullen (2011), and Li, Kocken, and Van Rooij (2018).

14. The SPC, 2004, Provisions on Several Issues Concerning Civil Mediation in the People's Courts (最高人民法院关于人民法院民事调解工作若干问题的规定). Also see the 2007 Notice of the Supreme People's Court on the Issuance of Several Opinions on Further Enhancing the Positive Roles of Judicial Mediation in the Construction of a Harmonious Socialist Society (最高人民法院印发《最高人民法院关于进一步发挥诉讼调解在构建社会主义和谐社会中积极作用的若干意见》的通知). Finally, see the 2010 Notice of the Supreme People's Court on the Issuance of Several Opinions on Further Implementing the Work Principle of "Giving Priority to Mediation and Combining Mediation with Adjudication" (最高人民法院印发《关于进一步贯彻"调解优先、调判结合"工作原则的若干意见》的通知).

15. For discussions of the surge of mediation in Chinese courts between 2004 and 2013, see Kinkel and Hurst (2015) and Li, Kocken, and Van Rooji (2018).

16. Regulations on the timing of mediation are scattered in multiple versions of the Civil Procedural Law and various SPC provisions. Key examples include the 1982 Civil Procedural Law [for Trial Implementation], Article 111; the 1991 and 2007 Civil Procedural Law, Article 128; the 2003 Several Provisions of the Supreme People's Court on the Application of Summary Procedures in Civil Trials (最高人民法院关于适用简易程序审理民事案件的若干规定), Article 14; the 2004 Provisions on Several Issues Concerning Civil Mediation in the People's Courts, Article 1; the 2012 and 2017 Civil Procedural Law, Articles 122 and 142; the 2015 Interpretation of the Supreme People's Court on the Application of the Civil Procedural Law of the People's Republic of China (最高人民法院关于适用《中华人民共和国民事诉讼法》的解释), Article 225; the 2018 Opinions of the Supreme People's Court on Further Deepening the Reform of the Methods and Working Mechanisms of Family Trials [for Trial Implementation] (最高人民法院关于进一步深化家事审判方式和工作机制改革的意见[试行]), Item 10. A close reading of these legal rules and regulations suggests that, over time, legislators and the SPC have gradually moved mediation to the earlier stages in the litigation process. The most recent SPC documents indicate that mediation can be attempted as early as the suit-filing stage.

17. For a thorough review of the combination of mediatory and adjudicatory justice under a single court system in the history of the PRC, see Huang (2006). In 2016, the SPC brought up the idea of assigning different judges to conduct mediation and adjudication as two distinct modes of case disposition. See Item 30 in Opinions of the Supreme People's Court on the People's Courts Deepening the Reform Intended to Diversify the Mechanisms for Conflict Resolution (最高人民法院关于人民法院进一步深化多元化纠纷调解机制改革的意见), issued in 2016. To what extent and in what ways this reform initiative has altered power dynamics in mediation still awaits empirical investigation.

18. The SPC, 1956, Summary of Civil Procedures for the People's Courts at All Levels, Section 5. Also see Provisions of the People's Courts on the Procedural Rules of Civil Litigation [for Trial Implementation], Section 7, issued in 1979; the 1982 Civil Procedural Law [for Trial Implementation], Article 144; the 1991 and 2007 Civil Procedural Law, Article 147; and the 2012 and 2017 Civil Procedural Law, Article 164. Together, these legal rules have instituted and entrenched a tradition in the People's Court: in principle, court decisions that lead to judgements (判决书) or rulings (裁定书) are appealable; by contrast, court approval of mediation outcomes are not appealable, for it involves a different kind of decision-making, as well as documentation known as civil mediation agreements (民事调解书).

19. The 1991 Civil Procedural Law allowed litigants, including those in divorce litigation, to dispute mediation outcomes through retrials conducted by trial or appellate courts (see Article 180). When the law was revised in 2007, legislators put one restriction in place: once a marriage is dissolved via adjudication, litigants can no longer request retrials at that trial or any appellate court (see Article 183 in the revised law). In 2012, legislators imposed another restriction: divorce litigants whose marriages have been terminated by means of either adjudication or mediation can no longer demand such retrials (see Article 202 in the 2012 Civil Procedural Law). These two legislative changes, in effect, closed the path for litigants to use retrial as a mechanism to challenge judges' approval of divorce settlements.

20. In lawmaking and policymaking, legislators and the SPC have consistently underscored the principles of voluntariness and lawfulness in mediation. Examples include the 1982 Civil Procedural Law [for Trial Implementation], Article 100; the 1991 Civil Procedural Law, Article 88. Also see the 1992 Notice of the Supreme People's Court on Releasing the Opinions on Some Issues Concerning the Application of the Civil Procedural Law of the People' Republic of China (最高人民人民印发《关于适用<中华人民共和国民事诉讼法>的意见》的通知), Item 92; the 2004 SPC Provisions on Several Issues Concerning Civil Mediation in the People's Courts, Article 12; the SPC Provisions on Several Issues Concerning Civil Mediation in the People's Courts (the 2008 Revision) (最高人民法院关于人民法院民事调解工作若干问题的规定[2008修正]), Article 12; the 2007, 2012, and 2017 Civil Procedural Law, Article 9. And finally, the 2010 Notice of the Supreme People's Court on the Issuance of Several Opinions on Further Implementing the Work Principle of "Giving Priority to Mediation and Combining Mediation with Adjudication," Item 16.

21. Wang and Liu 2016.

22. The SPC, 2009, Notice on the Issuance of Disciplinary Rules for the People's Court Personnel (最高人民法院关于印发《人民法院工作人员处分条例》的通知), Article 44.

23. The SPC, 2010, Notice on Reissuing the Basic Rules on the Professional Ethnics of Judges of the People's Republic of China (最高人民法院关于重新印发《中华人民共和国法官职业道德基本准则》的通知).

24. For a thorough examination of how *guanxi* (关系) comes to shape judicial decision-making in Chinese courts, see Ng and He (2017), 142–166.

25. See Cong (2016), 175–208, for a detailed account of how the CCP elevated Ma Xiwu's style of judging to political symbolism. See also Lubman (1999), 40–70, and Huang (2005) for in-depth discussions of the links between the Maoist justice and mediation.

26. The 1982 Civil Procedural Law [for Trial Implementation], Article 99; the 1991 and 2007 Civil Procedural Law, Article 87; and, the 2012 and 2017 Civil Procedural Law, Article 95.

27. The SPC, 2007, Several Opinions on Further Enhancing the Positive Roles of Judicial Mediation in the Construction of a Harmonious Socialist Society, Item 11.

28. The SPC, 2012, Notice on the Issuance of a Comprehensive Plan to Expand the Pilot Reform Geared Toward Coordinating Litigation and Non-Litigation in Conflict Resolution (最高人民法院印发《关于扩大诉讼与非诉讼相衔接的矛盾纠纷解决机制改革试点总体方案》的通知), Item 4.

29. The SPC, 2017, Report on Deepening Judicial Reforms Comprehensively (最高人民法院关于人民法院全面深化司法改革情况的报告).

30. Gieryn 2018, 100–121.

31. There was one exception, though. If a divorce suit could potentially result in a malicious, violent incident (恶性暴力事件), such as suicide, homicide, and attacks on litigants or court personnel, judges would be more likely to contact local communities and/or government agencies to seek assistance for conflict management. In 2017, the SPC raised concerns about those malicious incidents in marriage and family disputes. See Notice of the Supreme People's Court on Trying Cases Regarding Marriage and Family Disputes in Accordance with the Law and Effectively Safeguarding the Parties' Lawful Rights, Interests, and Personal Safety (最高人民法院关于依法妥善审理婚姻家庭案件切实保障当事人合法权益和人身安全的通知). See also He (2017).

32. Interviews with WY on July 9, 2010; with ZY on January 4, 2011; with QYL on February 27, 2011.

33. In an article published in *Law & Policy*, I examined how fee structures could impact on the legal profession's divorce law practices. See Li (2015b) for more details.

34. He and Ng 2013a; He 2017, 2020; Ng and He 2017.

35. Blumberg 1967; Eisenstein, Flemming, and Nardulli 1988; Uphoff 1992.

36. Landon 1985, 1988.

37. Interview with WY on July 9, 2010.

38. Interview with WY on December 11, 2010.

39. Blumberg 1967; Landon 1985, 1988; Uphoff 1992; Van Cleve 2016.

40. Michelson 2007; Liu and Halliday 2011.

41. For the concept of emotional labor, see Hochschild (1979); see also Pierce (1995) for a study of how the legal profession engaged in emotional labor daily.

42. Observation conducted in a People's Tribunal in Chuanyu County on January 6, 2010; and observation carried out in the Xiqing People's Tribunal on April 13, 2010.

43. Observation conducted in the Xiqing Legal Workers' Office on May 13, 2010.

44. Throughout my stay in Weifeng, I had numerous conversations with Yan Dejin, a legal worker and a key informant, who helped me grasp the various aspects of the hidden performance conducted by the legal profession in rural China.

45. For a summary of objections to the study of commonplace resistance, see Ewick and Silbey (1998), 184–189.

46. Inside the Guxiao Legal Workers' Office, I met Deng Pingping for the first time on January 19, 2010, the day she turned up to seek out legal assistance for her dispute over inheritance. On March 8, 2011, I held my last interview with her in a small town outside Chengdu, where she and her son were hiding from her in-laws. Tracking her case in the course of thirteen months allowed me to conduct seven interviews to examine the impact of several social forces—including her natal family's support, fellow migrant workers' informal knowledge of state law, and the legal profession's influences—on the process and outcomes of her legal mobilization.

47. The 1982 Civil Procedural Law [for Trial Implementation], Article 166; the 1991 and 2007 Civil Procedural Law, Articles 102 and 216; and, the 2012 and 2017 Civil Procedural Law, Articles 111 and 236. Note that, legally speaking, it is unclear if parental abduction is a criminal act in China or not. On the one hand, it is a widespread practice. Some even estimate that, in 2019 alone, approximately eighty thousand children in China were snatched by their parents during custodial battles. See Yeung (2021) for a report on the prevalence of the problem. On the other hand, few laws or regulations have stipulated against parental kidnapping. When the Law on the Protection of Minors was amended in 2020, legislators added a clause: parents "must not use methods such as stealing or hiding children to fight for custody rights" (see Article 24). This is one of the few national laws that explicitly bars parental abduction. For the moment, it is too early to tell whether this legislative change will lead to the criminalization of parental kidnapping in practice.

48. Liu and Halliday 2011.

49. Michelson 2007; Fu and Cullen 2011; Liu 2011; Liu and Halliday 2011; Givens 2013; Liu and Stern 2021.

50. See Stern and Liu (2020) for their call for future work on "varieties of legal professionalism."

CHAPTER SEVEN

1. Observation conducted at the Xiqing People's Tribunal on July 14, 2010.

2. Interview with YJG on July 14, 2010.

3. The 2001 Marriage Law, Articles 17 and 46.

4. The 2001 Marriage Law, Articles 32 and 45; the 2009 Criminal Law, Articles 258 and 260.

5. China Justice Big Data Service 2018.

6. Judges typically issue one of the two court documents in divorce suits: civil judgments (民事判决书), if a case is disposed of via adjudication; or civil mediation agreements (民事调解书), if a lawsuit is settled via mediation.

7. In the sample of 198 divorce suits, I also looked for signs of domestic violence against men but could not find any complaints raised by husbands.

8. He and Ng 2013a, 2013b; Wang 2013; He 2017, 2021; Michelson 2019.

9. The 2001 Marriage Law, Articles 2, 3, 13, 45, and 46.

10. The 2005 Law on the Protection of Women's Rights and Interests, Articles 38 and 46; the 2006 Law on the Protection of Minors, Article 10; the 2008 Law on the Protection of Disabled Persons, Article 9. Additionally, the SPC made similar efforts to underscore the importance of shoring up judicial redress for domestic violence. In 2001, it issued a judicial interpretation to spell out the PRC's first official definition of domestic violence. See Interpretation No. I of the Supreme People's Court on Several Issues Regarding the Application of the Marriage Law of the People's Republic of China (最高人民法院关于适用《中华人民共和国婚姻法》若干问题的解释[1]), Article 1. Seven years later, the China Institute of Applied Jurisprudence (中国应用法学研究所), a research organ affiliated with the SPC, handed down a set of guidelines to lower courts, seeking to regularize court practices in cases involving domestic violence. See Guidelines for Hearing Marital Cases Involving Domestic Violence (涉及家庭暴力婚姻案件审理指南).

11. See Gaventa (1980), 14, 95, 189–190, and 201, for his discussions of the notion of *nondecision*.

12. For a lucid discussion of cultural determinism, structural determinism, and human agency, see Giddens (1979), 48–59.

13. The 2001 Marriage Law, Article 39.

14. Felstiner, Abel, and Sarat 1980–81; Mather and Yngvesson 1980–81; Mather 1990.

15. Chuang 2014.

16. *China Economic Systems Reform Yearbook* 2000–2001, 168.

17. The 1986 Land Administration Law, Article 12; the 1986 General Principles of the Civil Law, Article 28.

18. A large number of studies have examined gender inequality in land possession, use, and management in rural China. Below I provide only a partial list of these studies: Zhu 2000; Sargeson 2006, 2008, 2012; Li and Bruce 2005; Hare, Li, and Englander 2007; Judd 2007; Liaw 2008; Zhang et al. 2008; Sargeson and Song 2010; Song and Dong 2017; Chan 2019; Li 2020.

19. Sargeson 2012; Kong and Unger 2013.

20. Liu and Shi 2016.

21. When the Rural Land Contracting Law came out in 2002, it endowed landholders with greater security in land tenure: for farmland, the duration of land contracting was extended to thirty years; for grassland, thirty to fifty years; and for forestland, thirty to seventy years; see Article 20.

22. The 1998 Land Administration Law, Article 14.

23. This is not to suggest that periodic readjustments of land allocation disappeared altogether in the wake of the enactment of the 1998 Land Administration Law. For discussions of land reallocations in the late 1990s and the early 2000s, see Kong and Unger (2013) and Wang, Riedinger, and Jin (2015).

24. The 1992 Law on the Protection of Women's Rights and Interests (LPWRI), Article 31; 2005 and 2018 LPWRI, Article 34; see also 2002 and 2009 Rural Land Contracting Law (RLCL), Articles 31 and 50; and the 2018 RLCL, Articles 32 and 54.

25. Hare, Li, and Englander 2007; Judd 2007; Liaw 2008; Song and Dong 2017.

26. Li and Bruce 2005; Hare, Li, and Englander 2007; Liaw 2008; Zhang et al. 2008; Sargeson 2012; Wu 2016.

27. The All-China Women's Federation and the National Bureau of Statistics held the first round of the Survey on Chinese Women's Social Status in 1991. But it is unclear whether that survey looked specifically at gender disparities in land use and management. At the time of this writing, the results of the 2019 survey have yet to be released. After they become publicly available, we may find out whether the gender gap in land use has expanded or contracted over the past decade. For more details, see All-China Women's Federation (2012), 5.

28. In 2005, after a great deal of research, the Judicial Committee of the SPC (最高人民法院审判委员会) concluded that the crux of the problem—widespread land dispossession in the countryside—laid in legal ambiguity surrounding the definition of *rural collective membership*; therefore, the committee reasoned that the proper solution must come from the Standing Committee of the NPC, the national legislature. As of late 2018, the head of the First Civil Division of the SPC again emphasized lawmaking as *the* solution to the vagueness of the term *rural collective membership*, insisting that the NPC pass laws to better protect women's land rights. See Li (2020) for a detailed discussion of how top legislators and the SPC have failed to curtail landlessness among rural women.

29. In promulgating the Rural Land Contracting Law first in 2002, and in revising the law in 2009 and again in 2018, legislators have consistently evaded the task of defining

rural collective membership. Their silence on this matter has left millions of rural women with little certainty about their standing as members of a particular community. This uncertainty, in turn, may thrust their claims on land rights into legal limbo. See Chan (2019) for a detailed discussion in this regard.

30. Ewick and Silbey 2003.

31. Scott 1985, 1990; see also Wedeen (2015) for an illuminating study of the entanglement of domination and everyday forms of resistance in an authoritarian context.

32. For a discussion of the structural and cognitive conditions that render rightful resistance possible, see O'Brien and Li (2006), 25–49.

33. Interview with YDR on June 21, 2018.

34. For a discussion of "class in self" versus "a class for itself," see Bourdieu (1987) and (1991), 229–251.

35. In the summer of 2018, I conducted another round of field research in Weifeng. This time, I found some noticeable changes in women's attempts at retaining landholding upon divorce. In the epilogue, I provide a discussion of these recent changes.

36. For a thought-provoking debate between James C. Scott and Steven Lukes, in which the former questions the notions of *hegemony* and *false consciousness* and the latter casts doubts on the concept of the *hidden transcripts* of resistance, see Scott (1990), 70–107, and Lukes (2005), 124–134.

EPILOGUE

1. Until 2017, legal workers could not establish new offices without local governments' permission, and private funds were barred from investing in their businesses. For more details on these restrictions, see Measures for the Administration of Grassroots Legal Workers' Offices (基层法律服务所管理办法), Article 11, issued by the MOJ in 2000.

2. The MOJ, 2017, Measures for the Administration of Grassroots Legal Workers' Offices (2017 Revision) (基层法律服务所管理办法[2017修订]), Article 7; see also Yang (2018).

3. For more details, see Opinions of the Ministry of Justice and the Ministry of Finance on Establishing and Improving the Mechanisms for Government Procurement of Legal Services (司法部、财政部关于建立健全政府购买法律服务机制的意见), issued in 2020.

4. *China Civil Affairs' Statistical Yearbook* 2019, Table B-37; Centers for Disease Control and Prevention 2020.

5. The SPC, 2016, Notice on Implementing a Pilot Program in Reforming the Methods and Working Mechanisms of Family Trials in Certain Courts (最高人民法院关于在部分法院开展家事审判方式和工作机制改革试点工作的通知).

6. *China Statistical Yearbook* 2019, 779. Note that there are subtle differences among the three subcategories: disputes over upbringing (抚养), eldercare (赡养), and maintenance (扶养). The first category involves disputes between parents and young children in need of care; the second focuses on discord between aging parents and their adult children responsible for eldercare; and the third deals with rights and obligations among other family members.

7. For more details regarding the establishment of a joint conference system, see two documents that came into effect in 2017: Opinions of the All-China Women's Federation, the CAPSC, and the SPC on the Prevention and Resolution of Marital and Family Disputes (全国妇联、中央综治办、最高人民法院等关于做好婚姻家庭纠纷预防化解工作的意见); and Opinions of the SPC, the CAPSC, and the Supreme People's Procuratorate on the Establishment of a Joint Conference System in Reforming the Methods and Working

Mechanisms of Family Trials (最高人民法院、中央综治办、最高人民检察院等关于建立家事审判方式和工作机制改革联席会议制度的意见).

8. The SPC, 2018, Opinions on Further Deepening the Reform of the Methods and Working Mechanisms of Family Trials [for Trial Implementation] (最高人民法院关于进一步深化家事审判方式和工作机制改革的意见[试行]), Item 40.

9. Jiang 2020; Weng 2020.

10. *China Civil Affairs' Statistical Yearbook* 2019, Table B-36; Campbell 2019; BBC, January 17, 2020.

11. Fang et al. 2015.

12. Pils 2016.

13. Gallagher 2017, 6–14.

14. Chuang 2020, 3–4.

15. For more details on the latest round of rural land reform, see Several Opinions on Comprehensively Deepening Rural Reforms and Accelerating Agricultural Modernization (关于全面深化农村改革加快推进农业现代化的若干意见), issued by the Central Committee of the Chinese Communist Party and the State Council in 2014.

16. Liu 2022.

17. By 2010, approximately 200 million *mu* of land had been transferred (Gao 2015). For the most recent statistics in this regard, see Ministry of Agriculture and Rural Affairs, Reply to Suggestion No. 8778 at the Second Session of the Thirteenth National People's Congress (对十三届全国人大二次会议第8778号建议的答复), issued on September 25, 2019.

18. *China Reform Yearbook* 2018, 303.

19. For studies of land-taking and collective resistance in places like Wukan, Guangdong Province, see Fu (2014) and Lu, Zheng, and Wang (2017).

References

ENGLISH LANGUAGE

Albiston, Catherine R., Lauren B. Edelman, and Joy Milligan. 2014. "The Dispute Tree and the Legal Forest." *Annual Review of Law and Social Science* 10: 105–131.

Alexander, Jeffrey C., and Philip Smith. 1993. "The Discourse of American Civil Society: A New Proposal for Cultural Studies." *Theory and Society* 22(2): 151–207.

Alford, William, and Yuanyuan Shen. 2004. "Have You Eaten? Have You Divorced? Debating the Meaning of Freedom in Marriage in China." In *Realms of Freedom in Modern China*, edited by William C. Kirby, 234–263. Stanford: Stanford University Press.

Altehenger, Jennifer. 2018. *Legal Lessons: Popularizing Laws in the People's Republic of China, 1949–1989*. Cambridge & London: Harvard University Press.

Andors, Phyllis. 1983. *The Unfinished Liberation of Chinese Women, 1949–1980*. Bloomington: Indiana University Press.

Aretxaga, Begoña. 2003. "Maddening States." *Annual Review of Anthropology* 32(1): 393–410.

Bachrach, Peter, and Morton S. Baratz. 1962. "Two Faces of Power." *American Political Science Review* 56(4): 947–952.

Bailey, Martha J. 1993. "Mediation of Divorce in China." *Canadian Journal of Law & Society* 8(1): 45–72.

BBC. 2017. "Tiananmen Square Protest Death Toll 'Was 10,000.'" Accessed January 31, 2020. https://www.bbc.com/news/world-asia-china-42465516

———. 2020. "Chinese Birth Rate Falls to Lowest in Seven Decades." Accessed March 23, 2021. https://www.bbc.com/news/world-asia-china-51145251

Becker, Gary S. 1981. *A Treatise on the Family*. Cambridge: Harvard University Press.

Bennett, Gordon. 1976. *Yundong: Mass Campaigns in Chinese Communist Leadership*. Berkeley: Center for Chinese Studies, University of California.

Bernhardt, Kathryn. 1994. "Women and the Law: Divorce in the Republican Period." In *Civil Law in Qing and Republican China*, edited by Kathryn Bernhardt and Philip C. C. Huang, 187–214. Stanford: Stanford University Press.

Black, Donald. 1976. *The Behavior of Law*. San Diego, New York, Boston, London, Sydney, Tokyo, and Toronto: Academic Press.

Blumberg, Abraham S. 1967. "The Practice of Law as Confidence Game: Organizational Cooptation of a Profession." *Law & Society Review* 1(2): 15–40.

Bourdieu, Pierre. 1987. "The Force of Law: Toward a Sociology of the Juridical Field." *Hastings Law Journal* 38 (5): 814–853.

———. 1987. "What Makes a Social Class? On the Theoretical and Practical Existence of Groups." *Berkeley Journal of Sociology* 32: 1–17.

———. 1990. *The Logic of Practice*. Stanford: Stanford University Press.

———. 1991. *Language and Symbolic Power*. Cambridge: Harvard University Press.

Burawoy, Michael. 1998. "The Extended Case Method." *Sociological Theory* 16(1): 4–33.

Cabestan, Jean-Pierre. 2005. "The Political and Practical Obstacles to the Reform of the Judiciary and the Establishment of a Rule of Law in China." *Journal of Chinese Political Science* 10(1): 43–64.

Charlie, Campbell. 2019. "China's Aging Population Is a Major Threat to Its Future." *Time*, February 7, 2019. Accessed December 27, 2021. https://time.com/5523805/china-aging-population-working-age/

Campbell, John L. 2001. "Institutional Analysis and the Role of Ideas in Political Economy." In *The Rise of Neoliberalism and Institutional Analysis*, edited by John L. Campbell and Ove K. Pedersen, 159–189. Princeton and Oxford: Princeton University Press.

———. 2004. *Institutional Change and Globalization*. Princeton: Princeton University Press.

Capoccia, Giovanni, and R. Daniel Kelemen. 2007. "The Study of Critical Junctures: Theory, Narrative, and Counterfactuals in Historical Institutionalism." *World Politics* 59(3): 341–369.

Centers for Disease Control and Prevention. 2020. "Marriage and Divorce." Accessed March 23, 2021. https://www.cdc.gov/nchs/fastats/marriage-divorce.htm

Chan, Kam Wing, and Li Zhang. 1999. "The Hukou System and Rural-Urban Migration in China: Processes and Changes." *China Quarterly* 160: 818–855.

Chan, Peter C. H. 2019. "Do the 'Haves' Come Out Ahead in Chinese Grassroots Courts?—Rural Land Disputes Between Married-Out Women and Village Collectives." *Hastings Law Journal* 71(1): 5–78.

Chang, Leslie T. 2009. *Factory Girls: From Village to City in a Changing China*. New York: Spiegel & Grau.

Cheesman, Nick. 2015. *Opposing the Rule of Law: How Myanmar's Courts Make Law and Order*. Cambridge: Cambridge University Press.

———. 2018. "Rule-of-Law Ethnography." *Annual Review of Law and Social Science* 14: 167–184.

Chen, Albert H. Y. 2016. "China's Long March Towards Rule of Law or China's Turn Against Law?" *Chinese Journal of Comparative Law* 4(1): 1–35.

Cheng, Tiejun, and Mark Selden. 1994. "The Origins and Social Consequences of China's Hukou System." *China Quarterly* 139: 644–668.

Choi, Susanne Y. P. 2016. "Gendered Pragmatism and Subaltern Masculinity in China: Peasant Men's Responses to Their Wives' Labor Migration." *American Behavioral Scientist* 60(5–6): 565–582.

Choi, Susanne Yuk-Ping, and Yinni Peng. 2016. *Masculine Compromise: Migration, Family, and Gender in China*. Berkeley: University of California Press.

Chuang, Julia. 2014. "China's Rural Land Politics: Bureaucratic Absorption and the Muting of Rightful Resistance." *China Quarterly* 219: 649–669.

———. 2020. *Beneath the China Boom: Labor, Citizenship, and the Making of a Rural Land Market*. Oakland: University of California Press.

Clarke, Donald C. 1991. "Dispute Resolution in China." *Journal of Chinese Law* 5: 245–296.

———. 2003. "Empirical Research into the Chinese Judicial System." In *Beyond Common Knowledge: Empirical Approaches to the Rule of Law*, edited by Erik G. Jensen and Thomas C. Heller, 164–192. Stanford: Stanford University Press.

———. 2007. "Introduction: The Chinese Legal System Since 1995: Steady Development and Striking Continuities." *China Quarterly* 191: 555–566.

———. 2020. "Order and Law in China." GW Law Faculty Publications & Other Works. Accessed March 6, 2021. https://scholarship.law.gwu.edu/faculty_publications/1506/

Cong, Xiaoping. 2016. *Marriage, Law and Gender in Revolutionary China, 1940–1960*. New York: Cambridge University Press.

Conley, John M., and William M. O'Barr. 1998. *Just Words: Law, Language, and Power*. Chicago and London: University of Chicago Press.

Cott, Nancy. 2000. *Public Vows: A History of Marriage and the Nation*. Cambridge and London: Harvard University Press.

Cox, Lawrence. 2007. "Freedom of Religion in China: Religious, Economic and Social Disenfranchisement for China's Internal Migrant Workers." *Asian-Pacific Law & Policy Journal* 8(2): 370–430.

Curley, Melissa, Björn Dressel, and Stephen McCarthy. 2018. "Competing Visions of the Rule of Law in Southeast Asia: Power, Rhetoric and Governance." *Asian Studies Review* 42(2): 192–209.

Davis, Deborah S. 2014a. "Privatization of Marriage in Post-Socialist China." *Modern China* 40(6): 551–577.

———. 2014b. "On the Limits of Personal Autonomy: PRC Law and the Institution of Marriage." In *Wives, Husbands, and Lovers: Marriage and Sexuality in Hong Kong, Taiwan, and Urban China*, edited by Deborah S. Davis and Sara L. Friedman, 41–61. Stanford: Stanford University Press.

Démurger, Sylvie, Marc Gurgand, Shi Li, and Ximing Yue. 2009. "Migrants as Second-Class Workers in Urban China? A Decomposition Analysis." *Journal of Comparative Economics* 37(4): 610–628.

Deng, Xiaoping, and George Bush. 1989. "Memorandum of Conversation between George H. W. Bush and Chairman Deng Xiaoping in Beijing." Accessed February 15, 2020. https://digitalarchive.wilsoncenter.org/document/116507

Denyer, Simon, and Annie Gowen. 2018. "Too Many Men." *Washington Post*, April 18, 2018. Accessed January 19, 2019. https://www.washingtonpost.com/graphics/2018/world/too-many-men/?utm_term=.06049a00dbcb

Di, Xiaohua, and Yuning Wu. 2009. "The Developing Trend of the People's Mediation in China." *Sociological Focus* 42(3): 228–245.

Diamant, Neil. 2000. *Revolutionizing the Family: Politics, Love, and Divorce in Urban and Rural China, 1949–1968*. Berkeley, Los Angeles, and London: University of California Press.

Diamant, Neil Jeffrey, Stanley B. Lubman, and Kevin J. O'Brien, eds. 2005. *Engaging the Law in China: State, Society, and Possibilities for Justice*. Stanford: Stanford University Press.

Dobbin, Frank. 2018. "The Sorry State of Civil Rights." *Contemporary Sociology: A Journal of Reviews* 47(5): 541–543.

Dynon, Nicholas. 2008. "'Four Civilizations' and the Evolution of Post-Mao Chinese Socialist Ideology." *China Journal* 60: 83-109.

Edelman, Lauren B. 2005. "Law at Work: The Endogenous Construction of Civil Rights." In *Handbook of Employment Discrimination Research: Rights and Realities*, edited by Laura Beth Nielsen and Robert L. Nelson, 337-352. The Netherlands: Springer.

———. 2016. *Working Law: Courts, Corporations, and Symbolic Civil Rights*. Chicago: University of Chicago Press.

Edelman, Lauren B., Linda H. Krieger, Scott R. Eliason, Catherine R. Albiston, and Virginia Mellema. 2011. "When Organizations Rule: Judicial Deference to Institutionalized Employment Structures." *American Journal of Sociology* 117(3): 888–954.

Eisenstein, James, Roy B. Flemming, and Peter F. Nardulli. 1988. *The Contours of Justice: Communities and Their Courts.* Boston: Little, Brown.

Engel, David M. 1984. "The Oven Bird's Song: Insiders, Outsiders, and Personal Injuries in an American Community." *Law & Society Review* 18(4): 551–582.

Ewick, Patricia, and Susan S. Silbey. 1998. *The Common Place of Law: Stories from Everyday Life.* Chicago and London: University of Chicago Press.

———. 2003. "Narrating Social Structure: Stories of Resistance to Legal Authority." *American Journal of Sociology* 108(6): 1328–1372.

Fan, C. Cindy. 1999. "Migration in a Socialist Transitional Economy: Heterogeneity, Socioeconomic and Spatial Characteristics of Migrants in China and Guangdong Province." *International Migration Review* 33(4): 954–987.

Fang, Evandro Fei, Morten Scheibye-Knudsen, Heiko J. Jahn, Juan Li, Li Ling, Hongwei Guo, Xinqiang Zhu, Victor Preedy, Huiming Lu, Vilhelm A. Bohr, Wai Yee Chan, Yuanli Liu, and Tzi Bun Ng. 2015. "A Research Agenda for Aging in China in the 21st Century." *Ageing Research Reviews* 24: 197–205.

Feagin, Joe R., Anthony M. Orum, and Gideon Sjoberg, eds. 1991. *A Case for the Case Study.* Chapel Hill and London: University of North Carolina Press.

Felstiner, William L. F., Richard L. Abel, and Austin Sarat. 1980–81. "The Emergence and Transformation of Disputes: Naming, Blaming, Claiming...." *Law & Society Review* 15(3–4): 631–654.

Friedman, Sara L. 2006. *Intimate Politics: Marriage, the Market, and State Power in Southeastern China.* Cambridge: Harvard University Asia Center.

Fu, Diana. 2008. "A Cage of Voices: Producing and Doing *Dagongmei* in Contemporary China." *Modern China* 35(5): 527–561.

Fu, Hualing. 2014. "What Does Wukan Offer? Land-Taking, Law, and Dispute Resolution." In *Resolving Land Disputes in East Asia: Exploring the Limit of Law,* edited by Fu Hualing and John Gillespie, 173–193. Cambridge: Cambridge University Press.

———. 2015. "Away from Grass-Roots? The Irony of the Chinese Rural Legal Service." *Diogenes* 60(3–4): 116–132.

Fu, Hualing, and Richard Cullen. 2011. "From Mediatory to Adjudicatory Justice: The Limits of Civil Justice Reform in China." In *Chinese Justice: Civil Dispute Revolution in China,* edited by Margaret Y. K. Woo and Mary E. Gallagher, 25–57. New York: Cambridge University Press.

Fu, Yulin. 2011. "Dispute Resolution and China's Grassroots Legal Services." In *Chinese Justice: Civil Dispute Resolution in Contemporary China,* edited by Margaret Y. K. Woo and Mary E. Gallagher, 314–339. New York: Cambridge University Press.

Gaetano, Arianne M. 2015. *Out to Work: Migration, Gender, and the Changing Lives of Rural Women in Contemporary China.* Honolulu: University of Hawai'i Press.

Gaetano, Arianne M., and Tamara Jacka, eds. 2004. *On the Move: Women and Rural-to-Urban Migration in Contemporary China.* New York: Columbia University Press.

Gallagher, Mary E. 2006. "Mobilizing the Law in China: 'Informed Disenchantment' and the Development of Legal Consciousness." *Law & Society Review* 40(4): 783–816.

———. 2017. *Authoritarian Legality in China: Law, Workers, and the State.* New York: Cambridge University Press.

Gaventa, John. 1980. *Power and Powerlessness: Quiescence and Rebellion in an Appalachian Valley.* Urbana and Chicago: University of Illinois Press.

Geertz, Clifford. 1973. *The Interpretation of Cultures.* New York: Basic Books.

Giddens, Anthony. 1979. *Central Problems in Social Theory: Action, Structure and Contradiction in Social Analysis*. Berkeley and Los Angeles: University of California Press.

Gieryn, Thomas F. 1983. "Boundary-Work and the Demarcation of Science from Non-Science: Strains and Interests in Professional Ideologies of Scientists." *American Sociological Review* 48(6): 781–795.

———. 2018. *Truth-Spots: How Places Make People Believe*. Chicago and London: University of Chicago Press.

Ginsburg, Tom, and Tamir Moustafa, eds. 2008. *Rule by Law: The Politics of Courts in Authoritarian Regimes*. New York: Cambridge University Press.

Givens, John Wagner. 2013. "Sleeping with Dragons; Politically Embedded Lawyers Suing the Chinese State." *Wisconsin International Law Journal* 31(3): 734–774.

Grimheden, Jonas. 2006. "The Reform Path of the Chinese Judiciary: Progress or Stand-Still?" *Fordham International Law Journal* 30 (4): 1000–1013.

Halegua, Aaron. 2005. "Reforming the People's Mediation System in Urban China." *Hong Kong Law Journal* 35: 715–750.

Hall, Peter A., and Rosemary C. R. Taylor. 1996. "Political Science and the Three New Institutionalisms." *Political Studies* 44(5): 936–957.

Hare, Denise, Li Yang, and Daniel Englander. 2007. "Land Management in Rural China and Its Gender Implications." *Feminist Economics* 13(3–4): 35–61.

He, Xin. 2009. "Routinization of Divorce Law Practice in China: Institutional Constraints' Influence on Judicial Behavior." *International Journal of Law, Policy and Family* 23(1): 83–109.

———. 2017. "'No Malicious Incidents': The Concern for Stability in China's Divorce Law Practice." *Social & Legal Studies* 26(4): 467–489.

———. 2021. *Divorce in China: Institutional Constraints and Gendered Outcomes*. New York: New York University Press.

He, Xin, and Kwai Hang Ng. 2013a. "In the Name of Harmony: The Erasure of Domestic Violence in China's Judicial Mediation." *International Journal of Law, Policy and the Family* 27(1): 97–115.

———. 2013b. "Pragmatic Discourse and Gender Inequality in China." *Law & Society Review* 47(2): 279–310.

He, Xin, Lungang Wang, and Yang Su. 2013. "Above the Roof, Beneath the Law: Perceived Justice Behind Disruptive Tactics of Migrant Wage Claimants in China." *Law & Society Review* 47(4): 703–738.

Heilmann, Sebastian, and Elizabeth J. Perry. 2011. "Embracing Uncertainty: Guerrilla Policy Style and Adaptive Governance in China." In *Mao's Invisible Hand: The Political Foundations of Adaptive Governance in China*, edited by Sebastian Heilmann and Elizabeth J. Perry, 1–29. Cambridge (Massachusetts) and London: Harvard University Asia Center.

Hershatter, Gail. 2011. *The Gender of Memory: Rural Women and China's Collective Past*. Berkeley, Los Angeles, and London: University of California Press.

Hirsch, Paul M. 1997. "Review Essay: Sociology Without Social Structure: Neoinstitutional Theory Meets Brave New World." *American Journal of Sociology* 102(6): 1702–1723.

Hochschild, Arlie Russell. 1979. "Emotion Work, Feeling Rules, and Social Structure." *American Journal of Sociology* 85(3): 551–575.

Hosticka, Carl J. 1979. "We Don't Care about What Happened, We Only Care about What Is Going to Happen: Lawyer-Client Negotiations of Reality." *Social Problems* 26(5): 599–610.

Huang, Philip C. C. 2005. "Divorce Law Practices and the Origins, Myths, and Realities of Judicial 'Mediation' in China." *Modern China* 31(2): 151–203.

——. 2006. "Court Mediation in China, Past and Present." *Modern China* 32(3): 275–314.

——. 2010. *Chinese Civil Justice, Past and Present*. Lanham: Rowman & Littlefield.

——. 2016. "The Past and Present of the Chinese Civil and Criminal Justice Systems: The Sinitic Legal Tradition from a Global Perspective." *Modern China* 42(3): 227–272.

Hurst, William. 2018. *Ruling Before the Law: The Politics of Legal Regimes in China and Indonesia*. Cambridge, New York, Port Melbourne, and New Delhi: Cambridge University Press.

Jacka, Tamara. 2005. *Rural Women in Urban China: Gender, Migration, and Social Change*. London and New York: M. E. Sharpe.

——. 2009. "Cultivating Citizens: *Suzhi* (Quality) Discourse in the PRC." *Positions: Asia Critique* 17(3): 523–535.

Johnson, Kay Ann. 1983. *Women, the Family, and Peasant Revolution in China*. Chicago and London: University of Chicago Press.

Judd, Ellen R. 1998. "Reconsidering China's Marriage Law Campaign: Toward a De-orientalized Feminist Perspective." *Asian Journal of Women's Studies* 4(2): 8–26.

——. 2007. "No Change for Thirty Years: The Renewed Question of Women's Land Rights in Rural China." *Development and Change* 38(4): 689–710.

Kinkel, Jonathan J., and William J. Hurst. 2015. "The Judicial Cadre Evaluation System in China: From Quantification to Intra-State Legibility." *China Quarterly* 224: 933–954.

Kong, Sherry Tao, and Jonathan Unger. 2013. "Egalitarian Redistributions of Agricultural Land in China through Community Consensus: Findings from Two Surveys." *China Journal* 69: 1–19.

Kristof, Nicholas D. 1989. "Crackdown in Beijing; Troops Attack and Crush Beijing Protest; Thousands Fight Back, Scores Are Killed." *New York Times*, June 4, 1989. Accessed August 11, 2020. https://www.nytimes.com/1989/06/04/world/crackdown-beijing-troops-attack-crush-beijing-protest-thousands-fight-back.html

Kritzer, Herbert M. 1997. "Contingency Fee Lawyers as Gatekeepers in the Civil Justice System." *Judicature* 81(1): 22–29.

——. 1998. "Contingent-Fee Lawyers and Their Clients: Settlement Expectations, Settlement Realities, and Issues of Control in the Lawyer-Client Relationship." *Law & Social Inquiry* 23(4): 795–821.

Landon, Donald D. 1985. "Clients, Colleagues, and Community: The Shaping of Zealous Advocacy in Country Law Practice." *American Bar Foundation Research Journal* 10(1): 81–111.

——. 1988. "LaSalle Street and Main Street: The Role of Context in Structuring Law Practice." *Law & Society Review* 22(2): 213–236.

Lee, Ching Kwan. 1998. *Gender and the South China Miracle: Two Worlds of Factory Women*. Berkeley, Los Angeles, and London: University of California Press.

Lee, Ching Kwan, and Yonghong Zhang. 2013. "The Power of Instability: Unraveling the Microfoundations of Bargained Authoritarianism in China." *American Journal of Sociology* 118(6): 1475–1508.

Li, Ke. 2015a. "Divorce, Help-Seeking, and Gender Inequality in Rural China." PhD dissertation, Indiana University, Bloomington.

——. 2015b. "'What He Did Was Lawful': Divorce Litigation and Gender Inequality in China." *Law & Policy* 37(3): 153–179.

———. 2016. "Relational Embeddedness and Socially Motivated Case Screening in the Practice of Law in Rural China." *Law & Society Review* 50(4): 920–952.

———. 2020. "Land Dispossession and Women's Rights Contention in Rural China." *China Law and Society Review* 5 (1): 33–65.

Li, Ke, and Sara L. Friedman. 2015. "Wedding Marriage to the Nation-State in Modern China: Legal Consequences for Divorce, Property, and Women's Rights." In *Domestic Tensions, National Anxieties: Global Perspectives on Marriage, Crisis and Nation*, edited by Kristin Celello and Hanan Kholoussy, 147–169. New York: Oxford University Press.

Li, Li. 2013. "Judicial Strategies in Chinese Group Action Cases: A Realistic Reaction to Judicialization." *Hong Kong Law Journal* 43(1): 317–347.

Li, Yedan, Joris Kocken, and Benjamin Van Rooij. 2018. "Understanding China's Court Mediation Surge: Insights from a Local Court." *Law & Social Inquiry* 43(1): 58–81.

Li, Zongmin, and John Bruce. 2005. "Gender, Landlessness and Equity in Rural China." In *Developmental Dilemmas: Land Reform and Institutional Change in China*, edited by Peter Ho, 308–337. London and New York: Routledge.

Liaw, H. Ray. 2008. "Women's Land Rights in Rural China: Transforming Existing Laws into a Source of Property Rights." *Pacific Rim Law & Policy Journal* 17(1): 237–264.

Lieberthal, Kenneth G. 1992. "Introduction: The 'Fragmented Authoritarianism' Model and Its Limitations." In *Bureaucracy, Politics, and Decision Making in Post-Mao China*, edited by Kenneth G. Lieberthal and David M. Lampton, 1–30. Berkeley, Los Angeles, and Oxford: University of California Press.

Liebman, Benjamin L. 2007. "China's Courts: Restricted Reform." *China Quarterly* 191: 620–638.

———. 2014. "Legal Reform: China's Law-Stability Paradox." *Daedalus* 143(2): 96–109.

Liu, Charles Chao. 2001. "China's Lawyer System: Dawning Upon the World Through a Tortuous Process." *Whittier Law Review* 23: 1037–1098.

Liu, Lawrence J., and Rachel E. Stern. 2021. "State-Adjacent Professionals: How Chinese Lawyers Participate in Political Life." *China Quarterly* 247: 793–813.

Liu, Qian. 2018. "Legal Consciousness of the Leftover Woman: Law and Qing in Chinese Family Relations." *Asian Journal of Law and Society* 5(1): 7–27.

Liu, Sida. 2011. "Lawyers, State Officials and Significant Others: Symbiotic Exchange in the Chinese Legal Services Market." *China Quarterly* 206: 276–293.

Liu, Sida, and Terence C. Halliday. 2011. "Political Liberalism and Political Embeddedness: Understanding Politics in the Work of Chinese Criminal Defense Lawyers." *Law & Society Review* 45(4): 831–866.

Liu, Tiantian. 2022. "'Enclosure with Chinese Characteristics': A Polanyian Approach to the Origins and Limits of Land Commodification in China." *Journal of Peasant Studies*: 1–29. Accessed February 10, 2022. https://doi.org/10.1080/03066150.2021.1979967.

Lu, Yao, Wenjuan Zheng, and Wei Wang. 2017. "Migration and Popular Resistance in Rural China: Wukan and Beyond." *China Quarterly* 229: 1–22.

Lubman, Stanley B. 1997. "Dispute Resolution in China After Deng Xiaoping: Mao and Mediation Revisited." *Columbia Journal of Asian Law* 11(2): 229–391.

———. 1999. *Bird in a Cage: Legal Reform in China After Mao*. Stanford: Stanford University Press.

Lukes, Steven. 2005. *Power: A Radical View*. New York: Palgrave Macmillan.

Lusher, Adam. 2017. "At Least 10,000 People Died in Tiananmen Square Massacre, Secret British Cable from the Time Alleged." *Independent*, December 23, 2017. Accessed

August 11, 2020. https://www.independent.co.uk/news/world/asia/tiananmen-square -massacre-death-toll-secret-cable-british-ambassador-1989-alan-donald-a8126461.html

Ma, Eric, and Lau Ling Helen Cheng. 2005. "'Naked' Bodies: Experimenting with Intimate Relations among Migrant Workers in South China." *International Journal of Cultural Studies* 8(3): 307–328.

Mahoney, James. 2000. "Path Dependence in Historical Sociology." *Theory and Society* 29(4): 507–548.

March, James G., and Johan P. Olsen. 1989. *Rediscovering Institutions: The Organizational Basis of Politics.* New York: Free Press.

Mather, Lynn. 1990. "Dispute Processing and a Longitudinal Approach to Trial Courts." *Law & Society Review* 24(2): 357–370.

Mather, Lynn, Craig A. McEwen, and Richard J. Maiman. 2001. *Divorce Lawyers at Work: Varieties of Professionalism in Practice.* New York: Oxford University Press.

Mather, Lynn, and Barbara Yngvesson. 1980–81. "Language, Audience, and the Transformation of Disputes." *Law & Society Review* 15(3–4): 775–822.

Meng, Xin, and Junsen Zhang. 2001. "The Two-Tier Labor Market in Urban China: Occupational Segregation and Wage Differentials Between Urban Residents and Rural Migrants in Shanghai." *Journal of Comparative Economics* 29(3): 485–504.

Merry, Sally Engle. 1979. "Going to Court: Strategies of Dispute Management in an American Urban Neighborhood." *Law & Society Review* 13(4): 891–925.

———. 1990. *Getting Justice and Getting Even: Legal Consciousness among Working-Class Americans.* Chicago and London: University of Chicago Press.

———. 1998. "Law, Culture, and Cultural Appropriation." *Yale Journal of Law & the Humanities* 10(2): 575–603.

Michelson, Ethan. 2006. "The Practice of Law as an Obstacle to Justice: Chinese Lawyers at Work." *Law & Society Review* 40(1): 1–38.

———. 2007. "Lawyers, Political Embeddedness, and Institutional Continuity in China's Transition from Socialism." *American Journal of Sociology* 113(2): 352–414.

———. 2019. "Decoupling: Marital Violence and the Struggle to Divorce in China." *American Journal of Sociology* 125(2): 325–381.

Migdal, Joel S. 2001. *State in Society: Studying How States and Societies Transform and Constitute One Another.* Cambridge: Cambridge University Press.

Miller, Richard E., and Austin Sarat. 1980–81. "Grievances, Claims, and Disputes: Assessing the Adversary Culture." *Law & Society Review* 15(3–4): 525–566.

Minzner, Carl F. 2011. "China's Turn Against Law." *American Journal of Comparative Law* 59(4): 935–984.

———. 2015. "Legal Reform in the Xi Jinping Era." *Asia Policy* 20: 4–9.

Mitchell, Timothy. 1991. "The Limits of the State: Beyond Statist Approaches and Their Critics." *American Political Science Review* 85(1): 77–96.

Moustafa, Tamir. 2007. *The Struggle for Constitutional Power: Law, Politics, and Economic Development in Egypt.* New York: Cambridge University Press.

———. 2014. "Law and Courts in Authoritarian Regimes." *Annual Review of Law and Social Science* 10: 281–299.

Ng, Kwai Hang, and Xin He. 2017. *Embedded Courts: Judicial Decision-Making in China.* Cambridge, New York, Port Melbourne, New Delhi, and Singapore: Cambridge University Press.

Ngai, Pun. 2005. *Made in China: Women Factory Workers in a Global Workplace*. Durham and London: Duke University Press.

O'Brien, Kevin J., and Lianjiang Li. 2006. *Rightful Resistance in Rural China*. New York: Cambridge University Press.

Ocko, Jonathan. 1991. "Women, Property, and Law in the People's Republic of China." In *Marriage and Inequality in Chinese Society*, edited by Rubie S. Watson and Patricia Buckley Ebrey, 313–346. Berkeley, Los Angeles, and Oxford: University of California Press.

Ortner, Sherry B. 1984. "Theory in Anthropology Since the Sixties." *Comparative Studies in Society and History* 26(1): 126–166.

Palmer, Michael. 1995. "The Re-Emergence of Family Law in Post-Mao China: Marriage, Divorce and Reproduction." *China Quarterly* 141: 110–134.

———. 2007. "Transforming Family Law in Post-Deng China: Marriage, Divorce and Reproduction." *China Quarterly* 191: 675–695.

Peerenboom, Randall. 2002. *China's Long March Toward Rule of Law*. Cambridge: Cambridge University Press.

———. 2014. "The Battle Over Legal Reforms in China: Has There Been a Turn Against Law?" *Chinese Journal of Comparative Law* 2(2): 188–212.

Perry, Elizabeth J. 2011. "From Mass Campaigns to Managed Campaigns: 'Constructing a New Socialist Countryside.'" In *Mao's Invisible Hand: The Political Foundations of Adaptive Governance in China*, edited by Sebastian Heilmann and Elizabeth J. Perry, 31–61. Cambridge (Massachusetts) and London: Harvard University Asia Center.

———. 2017. "Cultural Governance in Contemporary China: 'Re-Orienting' Party Propaganda." In *To Govern China: Evolving Practices of Power*, edited by Vivienne Shue and Patricia M. Thornton, 29–55. Cambridge: Cambridge University Press.

Perry, Elizabeth J., and Mark Selden, eds. 2000. *Chinese Society: Change, Conflict and Resistance*. London and New York: Routledge.

Pierce, Jennifer L. 1995. *Gender Trials: Emotional Lives in Contemporary Law Firms*. Berkeley, Los Angeles, and London: University of California Press.

Pierson, Paul. 2000. "Increasing Returns, Path Dependence, and the Study of Politics." *American Political Science Review* 94(2):251–267.

Pils, Eva. 2016. "Resisting Dignity Takings in China." *Law & Social Inquiry* 41(4): 888–916.

Platte, Erika. 1988. "Divorce Trends and Patterns in China: Past and Present." *Pacific Affairs* 61(3): 428–445.

Powell, Walter W., and Paul J. DiMaggio, eds. 1991. *The New Institutionalism in Organizational Analysis*. Chicago and London: University of Chicago Press.

Ragin, Charles C., and Howard S. Becker, eds. 1992. *What Is a Case?: Exploring the Foundations of Social Inquiry*. Cambridge: Cambridge University Press.

Read, Benjamin L. 2012. *Roots of the State: Neighborhood Organization and Social Networks in Beijing and Taipei*. Stanford: Stanford University Press.

Read, Benjamin L., and Ethan Michelson. 2008. "Mediating the Mediation Debate: Conflict Resolution and the Local State in China." *Journal of Conflict Resolution* 52(5): 737–764.

Sarat, Austin, and William L. F. Felstiner. 1995. *Divorce Lawyers and Their Clients: Power and Meaning in the Legal Process*. Oxford and New York: Oxford University Press.

Sargeson, Sally. 2006. "Introduction: Women and Policy and Institutional Change in Rural China." *Journal of Contemporary China* 15(49): 575–583.

———. 2008. "Women's Property, Women's Agency in China's 'New Enclosure Movement': Evidence from Zhejiang." *Development and Change* 39(4): 641–665.

————. 2012. "Why Women Own Less, and Why It Matters More in Rural China's Urban Transformation." *China Perspectives* (4): 35–42.

Sargeson, Sally, and Yu Song. 2010. "Land Expropriation and the Gender Politics of Citizenship in the Urban Frontier." *China Journal* 64: 19–45.

Schindler, Larissa, and Hilmar Schäfer. 2021. "Practices of Writing in Ethnographic Work" *Journal of Contemporary Ethnography* 50(1): 11–32.

Schmidt, Vivien A. 2008. "Discursive Institutionalism: The Explanatory Power of Ideas and Discourse." *Annual Review of Political Science* 11: 303–326.

Scott, James C. 1985. *Weapons of the Weak: Everyday Forms of Peasant Resistance.* New Haven and London: Yale University Press.

————. 1990. *Domination and the Arts of Resistance: Hidden Transcripts.* New Haven and London: Yale University Press.

————. 1998. *Seeing Like a State: How Certain Schemes to Improve the Human Condition Have Failed.* New Haven and London: Yale University Press.

Sewell Jr., William H. 2005. *Logics of History: Social Theory and Social Transformation.* Chicago and London: University of Chicago Press.

Shapiro, Martin. 2008. "Courts in Authoritarian Regimes." In *Rule by Law: The Politics of Courts in Authoritarian Regimes,* edited by Tom Ginsburg and Tamir Moustafa, 326–332. New York: Cambridge University Press.

Shirk, Susan L. 2018. "China in Xi's 'New Era': The Return to Personalistic Rule." *Journal of Democracy* 29(2): 22–36.

Skocpol, Theda. 1985. "Bringing the State Back In: Strategies of Analysis in Current Research." In *Bringing the State Back In,* edited by Peter B. Evans, Dietrich Rueschemeyer, and Theda Skocpol, 3–37. Cambridge, New York, Melbourne, and Madrid: Cambridge University Press.

Solomon, Peter H. 2015. "Law and Courts in Authoritarian States." *International Encyclopedia of the Social & Behavioral Sciences* 2: 427–434.

Song, Yueping, and Xiao-Yuan Dong. 2017. "Domestic Violence and Women's Land Rights in Rural China: Findings from a National Survey in 2010." *Journal of Development Studies* 53(9): 1471–1485.

Sontag, Susan. 2001. *Against Interpretation and Other Essays.* New York: Picador.

Stacey, Judith. 1975. "When Patriarchy Kowtows: The Significance of the Chinese Family Revolution for Feminist Theory." *Feminist Studies* 2(2): 64–112.

————. 1983. *Patriarchy and Socialist Revolution in China.* Berkeley, Los Angeles, and London: University of California Press.

Steensland, Brian. 2006. "Cultural Categories and the American Welfare State: The Case of Guaranteed Income Policy." *American Journal of Sociology* 111(5): 1273–1326.

Steinmetz, George. 1999. "Introduction: Culture and the State." In *State/Culture: State-Formation After the Cultural Turn,* edited by George Steinmetz, 1–49. Ithaca and London: Cornell University Press.

————. 2004. "Odious Comparisons: Incommensurability, the Case Study, and 'Small N's' in Sociology." *Sociological Theory* 22(3): 371–400.

Stern, Rachel E. 2013. *Environmental Litigation in China: A Study in Political Ambivalence.* New York: Cambridge University Press.

Stern, Rachel E., and Lawrence J. Liu. 2020. "The Good Lawyer: State-Led Professional Socialization in Contemporary China." *Law & Social Inquiry* 45(1): 226–248.

Strauss, Julia C. 2006. "Morality, Coercion and State Building by Campaign in the Early PRC: Regime Consolidation and After, 1949–1956." *China Quarterly* 188: 891–912.

Suchman, Mark C., and Lauren B. Edelman. 1996. "Legal Rational Myths: The New Institutionalism and the Law and Society Tradition." *Law & Social Inquiry* 21(4): 903–941.

Sudhinaraset, May, Kristin Mmari, Vivan Go, and Robert W. Blum. 2012. "Sexual Attitudes, Behaviors and Acculturation Among Young Migrants in Shanghai." *Culture, Health & Sexuality* 14(9): 1081–1094.

Sun, Wanning. 2019. "Rural Migrants and Their Marital Problems: Discourses of Governing and Knowledge Production in China." *Critical Policy Studies* 13(1): 43–60.

Swidler, Ann. 1986. "Culture in Action: Symbols and Strategies." *American Sociological Review* 51(2): 273–286.

———. 2001. *Talk of Love: How Culture Matters.* Chicago and London: University of Chicago Press.

Thelen, Kathleen. 1999. "Historical Institutionalism in Comparative Politics." *Annual Review of Political Science* 2(1): 369–404.

———. 2003. "How Institutions Evolve: Insights from Comparative Historical Analysis." In *Comparative Historical Analysis in the Social Sciences*, edited by James Mahoney and Dietrich Rueschemeyer, 208–240. Cambridge, New York, Port Melbourne, Madrid, and Cape Town: Cambridge University Press.

Threewitt, Cherise. 2017. "Which Cars Were Made in China and Sold in the U.S. in 2017?" *U.S. News & World Report*, July 26, 2017. Accessed January 6, 2021. https:// cars.usnews.com/cars-trucks/cars-made-in-china-2017

Tilly, Charles. 1985. "War-Making and State-Making as Organized Crime." In *Bringing the State Back In*, edited by Peter B. Evans, Dietrich Rueschemeyer, and Theda Skocpol, 169–191. Cambridge, New York, Melbourne, and Madrid: Cambridge University Press.

United Nations. 2018a. "Around 2.5 Billion More People Will Be Living in Cities by 2050, Projects New UN Report." Accessed December 31, 2020. https://www.un.org/develop ment/desa/en/news/population/2018-world-urbanization-prospects.html

———. 2018b. "The World's Cities in 2018." Accessed December 31, 2020. https://www .un.org/en/events/citiesday/assets/pdf/the_worlds_cities_in_2018_data_booklet.pdf

United Nations Office on Drugs and Crime. 2016. "Global Study on Legal Aid: Global Report." Accessed July 15, 2021. https://www.unodc.org/documents/justice-and-prison-reform/LegalAid/Global_Study_on_Legal_Aid_-_FINAL.pdf

Uphoff, Rodney J. 1992. "The Criminal Defense Lawyer: Zealous Advocate, Double Agent, or Beleaguered Dealer?" *Criminal Law Bulletin* 28(5): 419–456.

Valentino, Lauren. 2021. "Cultural Logics: Toward Theory and Measurement." *Poetics: Journal of Empirical Research on Culture, the Media and the Arts* 88. Accessed October 2021. https://www.sciencedirect.com/science/article/abs/pii/S0304422X21 000589

Van Cleve, Nicole Gonzalez. 2016. *Crook County: Racism and Injustice in America's Largest Criminal Court.* Stanford: Stanford University Press.

Vogel, Ezra F. 2011. *Deng Xiaoping and the Transformation of China.* Cambridge and London: Belknap Press of Harvard University Press.

Wagner-Pacifici, Robin, and Meredith Hall. 2012. "Resolution of Social Conflict." *Annual Review of Sociology* 38: 181–199.

Walder, Andrew G. 1986. *Communist Neo-Traditionalism: Work and Authority in Chinese Industry.* Berkeley, Los Angeles, and London: University of California Press.

————. 1995. "The Quiet Revolution from Within: Economic Reform as a Source of Political Decline." In *The Waning of the Communist State: Economic Origins of Political Decline in China and Hungary*, edited by Andrew G. Walder, 1–25. Berkeley, Los Angeles, and Oxford: University of California Press.

Wall Jr., James A., and Michael Blum. 1991. "Community Mediation in the People's Republic of China." *Journal of Conflict Resolution* 35(1): 3–20.

Wang, Feng, and Xuejin Zuo. 1999. "Inside China's Cities: Institutional Barriers and Opportunities for Urban Migrants." *The American Economic Review* 89(2): 276–280.

Wang, Feng, Xuejin Zuo, and Danching Ruan. 2002. "Rural Migrants in Shanghai: Living under the Shadow of Socialism." *International Migration Review* 36(2): 520–545.

Wang, Hui, Jeffrey Riedinger, and Songqing Jin. 2015. "Land Documents, Tenure Security and Land Rental Development: Panel Evidence from China." *China Economic Review* 36: 220–235.

Wang, Jian. 2013. "To Divorce or Not to Divorce: A Critical Discourse Analysis of Court-Ordered Divorce Mediation in China." *International Journal of Law, Policy and Family* 27(1): 74–96.

Wang, Juan, and Hongqin Mu. 2020. "'It's Not Just About the Divorce': Law, Politics, and Mediation in Communist China." *Journal of Comparative Law* 15(2): 160–178.

Wang, Juan, and Nhu Truong. 2021. "Law for What? Ideas and Social Control in China and Vietnam." *Problems of Post-Communism* 68(3): 202–215.

Wang, Wenfei Winnie, and C. Cindy Fan. 2012. "Migrant Workers' Integration in Urban China: Experiences in Employment, Social Adaptation, and Self-Identity." *Eurasian Geography and Economics* 53(6): 731–749.

Wang, Yuhua, and Carl F. Minzner. 2015. "The Rise of the Chinese Security State." *China Quarterly* 222: 339–359.

Weber, Max. 1946. "The Social Psychology of the World Religions." In *From Max Weber, Essays in Sociology*, edited by H. H. Gerth and C. Wright Mills, 267–301. New York: Oxford University Press.

Wedeen, Lisa. 2015. *Ambiguities of Domination: Politics, Rhetoric, and Symbols in Contemporary Syria*. Chicago and London: University of Chicago Press.

Whiting, Susan H. 2017. "Authoritarian 'Rule of Law' and Regime Legitimacy." *Comparative Political Studies* 50(14): 1907–1940.

Woetzel, Jonathan, Lenny Mendonca, Janamitra Devan, Stefano Negri, Yangmei Hu, Luke Jordan, Xiujun Li, Alexander Maasry, Geoff Tsen, and Flora Yu. 2009. "Preparing for China's Urban Billion." Accessed December 1, 2018. https://www.mckinsey.com/~/media/McKinsey/Featured%20Insights/Urbanization/Preparing%20for%20urban%20billion%20in%20China/MGI_Preparing_for_Chinas_Urban_Billion_full_report.pdf

Wolf, Margery. 1985. *Revolution Postponed: Women in Contemporary China*. Stanford: Stanford University Press.

Wolfe, Tom. 1996. *The New Journalism*. London: Picador.

Woo, Margaret Y. K. 2003. "Shaping Citizenship: Chinese Family Law and Women." *Yale Journal of Law and Feminism* 15(3): 99–134.

Wu, Weiping. 2004. "Sources of Migrant Housing Disadvantage in Urban China." *Environment and Planning A* 36(7): 1285–1304.

Wu, Yi. 2016. *Negotiating Rural Land Ownership in Southwest China: State, Village, Family*. Honolulu: University of Hawai'i Press.

Xu, Xiaohong, and Philip Gorski. 2018. "The Cultural of the Political: Toward a Cultural Sociology of State Formation." In *Routledge Handbook of Cultural Sociology*, edited by Laura Grindstaff, Ming-Cheng M. Lo, and John R. Hall, 515–524. London and New York: Routledge.

Yan, Hairong. 2008. *New Masters, New Servants: Migration, Development, and Women Workers in China*. Durham and London: Duke University Press.

Yan, Yunxiang. 1995. "Everyday Power Relations: Changes in a North China Village." In *The Waning of the Communist State: Economic Origins of Political Decline in China and Hungary*, edited by Andrew G. Walder, 215–242. Berkeley, Los Angeles, and Oxford: University of California Press.

Yang, Dali L. 2017. "China's Troubled Quest for Order: Leadership, Organization and the Contradictions of the Stability Maintenance Regime." *Journal of Contemporary China* 26(103): 35–53.

Yeung, Jessie. 2021. "In China, 80,000 Children Were 'Snatched' in 2019 by Parents Fighting for Custody, Report Says." *CNN*, May 22, 2021. Accessed August 23, 2021. https://www.cnn.com/2021/05/22/china/china-divorce-child-custody-abduction-intl-hnk-dst/index.html

Zemans, Frances Kahn. 1982. "Framework for Analysis of Legal Mobilization: A Decision-Making Model." *American Bar Foundation Research Journal* 7(4): 989–1071.

Zhang, Hongwei. 2013. "Revisiting People's Mediation in China: Practice, Performance and Challenges." *Restorative Justice* 1(2): 244–267.

Zhang, Li. 2001. *Strangers in the City: Reconfigurations of Space, Power, and Social Networks within China's Floating Population*. Stanford: Stanford University Press.

Zhang, Linxiu, Chengfang Liu, Haomiao Liu, and Lerong Yu. 2008. "Women's Land Rights in Rural China: Current Situation and Likely Trends." In *Gender and Natural Resource Management: Livelihoods, Mobility and Interventions*, edited by Bernadette P. Resurreccion and Rebecca Elmhirst, 87–108. London: Earthscan.

Zhang, Qianfan. 2016. "Judicial Reform in China: An Overview." In *China's Socialist Rule of Law Reforms Under Xi Jinping*, edited by John Garrick and Yan Chang Bennett, 17–29. London and New York: Routledge.

———. 2021. "The Communist Party Leadership and Rule of Law: A Tale of Two Reforms." *Journal of Contemporary China* 30(130) 578–595.

Zhang, Taisu, and Ginsburg, Tom, "Legality in Contemporary Chinese Politics." Accessed March 23, 2020. https://papers.ssrn.com/sol3/papers.cfm?abstract_id=3250948

Zheng, Tiantian. 2008. "Commodifying Romance and Searching for Love: Rural Migrant Bar Hostesses' Moral Vision in Post-Mao Dalian." *Modern China* 34(4): 442–476.

CHINESE LANGUAGE

All-China Women's Federation. 2012. *Report on the Protection of Rural Women's Land Rights* (维护农村妇女土地权益报告). Beijing: Social Sciences Academic Press.

Chen, Ping. 2008. "A Look at Grassroots Legal Workers Stuck in Awkward Conditions" (浅论尴尬生存的基层法律工作者). Accessed September 29, 2020. http://www.148com.com/html/2310/375384.html

Chen, Wei, and Wenjun He. 2014. "An Empirical Study of Divorce Relief System in China: An Analysis Based on a 2010–2012 Sample of Divorce Cases at a Basic People's Court in Chongqing" (我国离婚救济制度司法实践之实证调查研究: 以重庆市某基层人民法院2010–2012年被抽样调查的离婚案件为对象). *Hebei Law Review* (河北法学) 32(7): 19–32.

China Justice Big Data Service. 2018. "Justice Big Data: Special Report on Divorce Litigation" (司法大数据专题报告: 离婚诉讼). Accessed July 26, 2021. http://www.court.gov.cn/upload/file/2018/03/23/09/33/20180323093343_53196.pdf

China National Knowledge Infrastructure. "A Million of Xiang Army Launching the First Battle of *Paicha*" (百万湘军打响排查治理第一战役). Accessed June 30, 2019. http://www.cnki.com.cn/Article/CJFDTotal-RMTJ199507013.htm

———. "Changing Perceptions, Serving the Overall Interests: A Summary of the Work of People's Mediation in Hubei Province (1)" (转变观念，服务大局—河北省人民调解工作纪实[一]). Accessed June 30, 2019. https://www.cnki.com.cn/Article/CJFDTotal-RMTJ199502002.htm

———. "Further Expanding and Regulating the Delivery of Legal Services" (进一步扩展和规范法律服务工作). Accessed September 7, 2020. http://www.cnki.com.cn/Article/CJFDTotal-ZGLS200302001.htm

Deng, Xiaoping. 1980. "The Reform of the Party and the State Leadership System" (党和国家领导制度的改革). Accessed July 27, 2020. http://cpc.people.com.cn/GB/33839/34943/34944/34946/2617285.html

Dong, Biwu. 1957. "Work Report of the Supreme People's Court" (关于最高人民法院工作的报告). *People's Daily* (人民日报), July 3, 1957.

Fan, Wenhao. 2013. "A Study of the People's Tribunals amid the Three-Anti and Five-Anti Campaigns" (三反、五反运动中的人民法庭刍析). Master's thesis, Southwest University of Political Science and Law.

Feng, Xiaotian. 2006. "Young Migrant Workers' Marriages and Family Lives: A Worthy Subject for Research" (农村外出打工青年的婚姻与家庭：一个值得重视的研究领域). *Population Research* (人口研究) 30(1): 57–60.

Fu, Hualing. 2004. "Law and Development Seen through the Lens of Legal Construction in the Countryside: Dispute Resolution and Economic Development" (从乡村法律制度的建设看法律与发展：纠纷的解决与经济发展). *Journal of Legal and Economic Studies* (洪范评论), edited by Jinlian Wu and Ping Jiang, 117–143. Beijing: China University of Political Science and Law Press.

Fu, Yulin. 2004. "Preliminary Report on the State of Grassroots Legal Services in China: Taking Rural Grassroots Legal Workers' Office as a Window" (中国基层法律服务状况的初步考察报告:以农村基层法律服务所为窗口). *Peking University Law Review* (北大法律评论) 6(1): 86–123.

Gao, Yuncai. 2015. "Agricultural and Rural Development Reaching a Higher Level—The Glorious Twelfth Five-Year" (我国农业农村发展再上台阶[辉煌"十二五"]). *People's Daily*, October 12, 2015.

Han, Yanlong. 1981. "People's Mediation in China in the Past Three Decades" (我国人民调解工作的三十年). *Chinese Journal of Law* (法学研究) (2): 44–50.

He, Wen, and Chenggang Cao. 2014. "A Social Psychological Analysis of 'Temporary Coupling' among Migrant Workers" (农民工"临时夫妻"现象的社会心理学解析). *Social Sciences in Guangxi* (广西社会科学) 229(7): 145–149.

He, Yongjun. 2007. *Fragmentation and Continuity: The Building of the People's Courts, 1978–2005* (断裂与延续:人民法院建设，1978–2005). Beijing: China Social Sciences Press.

———. 2013. "Social Changes in Rural Society and the Evolvement of People's Mediation" (乡村社会嬗变与人民调解制度变迁). *Law and Social Development* (法制与社会发展) 109(1): 76–90.

Hu, Xiabing, and Chunmei Chen. 2011. "The Development of the People's Tribunals in China" (我国人民法庭制度的发展历程). *Law Science Magazine* (法学杂志) 2: 82–85.

Information Office of the State Council. 2008. "Information Office of the State Council Holding Press Conference on Disaster Assessment Regarding the Earthquake in Weichuan,

Sichuan Province" (国新办就四川汶川地震及灾损评估情况举行发布会). Accessed February 6, 2019. http://www.scio.gov.cn/photo/5/Document/795733/795733.htm

Jiang, Dawei. 2020. "Divorce Cooling-off Period: From Experience to Logic, and Comments on Article 1077 in the Civil Code" (离婚冷静期: 由经验到逻辑--《民法典》第1077条评析). *Journal of Huaqiao University (Philosophy and Social Sciences)* (华侨大学学报[哲学社会科学版]) (4): 121–133.

Jiang, Jinliang, and Zhenyuan Zhu. 2014. "How the Judiciary Should Protect Marriage: An Analysis of the Phenomenon of Filing Second-Time Divorce Petitions" (司法如何保护婚姻: 基于离婚案件二次起诉现象的分析). *Shantou University Journal [Humanities & Social Sciences Bimonthly]* (汕头大学学报[人文社会科学版]) 30(2): 81–88.

Jin, Xiaoyi, Feng Ren, and Zhongshan Yue. 2008. "Migrant Workers' Attitudes toward Premarital and Extramarital Sexual Behaviors: A Study Based on Social Networks" (农民工对婚前和婚外性行为的态度:基于社会网络的研究). *Population Research* (人口研究) 32(5): 67–78.

Li, Xufeng 2002. "Minister of Justice, Zhang Fusen, on Adjusting and Regulating the Order of Legal Services" (司法部部长张福森: 要调整规范我国法律服务秩序). Accessed September 7, 2020. http://news.sohu.com/71/34/news202173471.shtml

Li, Yu. 2004. "Red-Headed Document Triggers Repercussions— 'Substandard Lawyers' Ready to Step Off the Stage?" (红头文件引发行业震荡"二律师"要退场?). Accessed September 7, 2020. http://news.sohu.com/2004/06/14/59/news220515992.shtml

Liu, Fang, and Fei Shi. 2016. "Understanding and Applying the Policy Termed 'No Increase in Land Allocation When Households Expand, and No Decrease Otherwise'" ("增人不增地,减人不减地"制度的理解和适用). Accessed December 17, 2019. https://www.chinacourt.org/article/detail/2016/09/id/2087574.shtml

Liu, Guangming. 2012. "Building a Harmonious Socialist Society" (构建社会主义和谐社会). *People's Daily* (人民日报), October 31, 2012.

Liu, Min. 2012. "An Empirical Study of Court Rules on the Judgment of Second-Time Divorce Petitions" (二次离婚诉讼审判规则的实证研究). *Studies in Law and Business* (法商研究) 29(6): 80–84.

Liu, Qing. 2016. "A Study of Institutional Changes Regarding People's Mediation, 1978–2015" (我国人民调解制度变迁研究, 1978–2015). PhD dissertation, Xiangtan University.

Liu, Sida. 2017. *The Logic of Fragmentation: An Ecological Analysis of the Chinese Legal Services Market* (割据的逻辑: 中国法律服务市场的生态分析). Nanjing: Yilin Press.

Luo, Ling. 2016. "An Empirical Study of the Factors Affecting Court Rulings in Divorce Litigation: Drawing on a Sample of Divorce Case Records in Henan Province in 2010–2011" (裁判离婚理由影响因素实证研究:以2010-2011年河南省的部分离婚纠纷案件判决文书为样本). *Journal of China Women's University* (中华女子学院学报) (1): 14–23.

Luo, Mingbai. 2017. "An Empirical Study of Court Procedures Involving Second-Time Divorce Petitions: Taking the Fu'an Basic People's Court in Fujian Province as an Example" (二次离婚诉讼审判规则的司法实证研究: 以福建省福安市法院为例). *Legality Vision* (法制博览) (31): 172–173.

Ma, Qiang. 2008. "Comments on the Importance of Judicial Mediation in Court Practices and Its Improvement" (论法院调解办案方式的完善及其重要地位的重构). Accessed June 3, 2020. https://www.chinacourt.org/article/detail/2008/04/id/296196.shtml

Ma, Xiangying. 2005. "Mediation or Adjudication: An Analysis of Why Divorce Suits at the Miluo Basic People's Court Feature Low Mediation Rates in Case Disposition" (调解还是判决: 关于汨罗市人民法院离婚案件调解结案率低的分析). Master's thesis, Beijing University.

Ouyang, Ying. 2014. "A Reflection on the Notion of 'Crossing the River by Groping the Stepping Stone'" (关于"摸着石头过河"思想的深入思考). *Studies on Mao Zedong and Deng Xiaoping Theories* (毛泽东邓小平理论研究) 11: 81–85.

Qi, Hui. 2018. "2018 *Chunyun* Came to an End Smoothly Nationwide" (2018年全国铁路春运圆满结束). Accessed January 6, 2021. http://www.gov.cn/xinwen/2018-03/16/content_5274558.htm

Research Group of Shanxi Provincial Department of Justice. 2009. "Survey Report on Strengthening the Legal Services in Rural Shanxi Province" (陕西省农村法律服务工作调研报告). *Justice of China* (中国司法) (8): 16–20.

Shu, Renhua. 2007. "An Analysis of 'Chinese-Style Divorce' in Contemporary China: An Examination of 966 Migrant Workers in Anhui Province" (解析当代农民工的"中国式离婚";对安徽省966例农民工的调查). *Journal of Nanjing College for Population Management* (南京人口管理干部学院学报) 23(2): 39–42.

"The SPC President, Xie Juezai, Reporting on the Work of the Supreme People's Court" (谢觉哉院长作最高人民法院工作报告). *People's Daily* (人民日报), January 1, 1965.

Su, Li. 2000. *Sending Law to the Countryside: Research on China's Grassroots Judicial System* (送法下乡：中国基层司法制度研究). Beijing: China University of Political Science and Law Press.

Wang, Bixue. 2000. "Grassroots Legal Workers Attending Qualification Examination" (基层法律服务工作者参加执业资格考试). *People's Daily* (人民日报), December 25, 2000.

Wang, Jue. 2008. "Further Strengthening Judicial Administration at the Grassroots Level to Make New Contributions to the Construction of a Harmonious Socialist Society" (进一步加强司法行政基层工作-为构建社会主义和谐社会做出新贡献). *Justice of China* (中国司法) (7): 35–39.

Wang, Liming. 2014. "*Dingfen zhizheng* versus *dingfen zhizheng*" (定分止争与定纷止争). Accessed March 18, 2019. http://old.civillaw.com.cn/article/default.asp?id=62614&_d_id=3b9b19303ee480dde509f2e1f0c535&security_verify_data=323034382c31313532

Wang, Lungang, and Sida Liu. 2016. "From Substantive Responsibility to the Rule of Procedure: An Empirical Study of the Operation of the Wrongful Case Responsibility System in China" (从实体问责到程序之治-中国法院错案追究制运行的实证考察). *Jurist* (法学家) (2): 27–40.

Weng, Mingjie. 2020. "The Establishment and Improvement of Divorce Cooling-off Period in the Civil Code" (《民法典》中离婚冷静期制度的证成及完善). *Journal of Lüliang Higher College* (吕梁学院学报) 10(5): 67–72.

Wu, Ling. 2008. "Guiding Grassroots Legal Services with a Scientific Outlook of Development" (用科学发展观指导基层法律服务). *Justice of China* (中国司法) (3): 67–69.

Wu, Xia. 2002. "The National Forum for the Heads of Justice Departments (and Bureaus) on Further Regulating the Order of Legal Services" (全国司法厅[局]长座谈会提出进一步规范法律服务秩序). *People's Daily* (人民日报), July 7, 2002.

Xiao, Suowei. 2018. *Desire and Dignity: Class, Gender and Intimacy in Transitional China* (欲望与尊严：转型期中国的阶层、性别与亲密关系). Beijing: Social Sciences Academic Press.

Xu, Anqi. 2007. "A Study of Divorce and Women's Status and Rights" (离婚与女性地位及权益之探讨). *Zhejiang Academic Journal* (浙江学刊) (1): 198–206.

Xu, Anqi, and Wenzhen Ye. 2002. "An Analysis of Regional Variation in Divorce Rates in China" (中国离婚率的地区差异分析). *Population Research* (人口研究) 26(4): 28–35.

Yang, Cuiting. 2018. "The MOJ's Replies to Journalists' Inquiries into the Amended Measures for the Administration of Grassroots Legal Workers' Offices and the Revised Measures for the Administration of Grassroots Legal Workers" (司法部相关负责人就修订后的《基层法律服务所管理办法》、《基层法律服务工作者管理办法》答记者问). Accessed November 26, 2020. http://www.moj.gov.cn/news/content/2018-01/02/zcjd_13061.html

Ye, Xiaogang. 2002. "The Minister of Justice, Zhang Fusen, on Adjusting and Regulating the Order of Chinese Legal Services" (司法部部长张福森:要调整规范中国法律服务秩序). Accessed September 7, 2020. http://www.chinanews.com/2002-07-16/26/203686.html

You, Chenjun. 2005. "Justice Offices Embedded in the Modernization of the Legal System" (嵌入法制现代化进程的乡镇司法所). *Huazhong Law Review* (法学纪元) 2: 78–89.

Yu, Anlong. 2017. "A Historical Analysis of Reform Methodologies: A Perspective Based on the Notion of 'Crossing the River by Groping the Stepping Stones'" (关于改革方法论的历史考察—基于"摸着石头过河"的视角). *CPC History Studies* (中共党史研究) (1): 127–128.

Zhang, Donghua. 1988. "Selflessness and Fearlessness, Turning Danger into Safety" (无私无畏, 化险为夷). *People's Judicature* (人民司法) (9): 28–29.

Zhang, Hongfen. 2018. "A Report on the Handling of Divorce Cases in the People's Court in S County" (S县法院近几年审理离婚案件的调研报告). Master's thesis, Hunan Normal University.

Zhang, Peng. 2008. "100,000 'Substandard Lawyers' Facing a Debate on Their Survival" (10万"二律师"废存之争). *Reporters' Notes* (记者观察) (6): 16–18.

Zhou, Yuansheng. 2004. "Reflection on Further Regulating the Order of the Legal Services Market" (关于进一步规范法律服务市场秩序的思考). *Justice of China* (中国司法) (9): 48–50.

Zhu, Jinwen. 2008. "An Analysis of the Professionalization of Chinese Law Practitioners" (中国法律工作者的职业化分析). *Chinese Journal of Law* (法学研究) (5): 23–35.

Zhu, Ling. 2000. "Gender Inequality in China's Land Tenure System" (农地分配中的性别平等问题). *Economic Research Journal* (经济研究) 9: 34–42.

YEARBOOKS & GOVERNMENT PUBLICATIONS

China Law Society. *China Law Yearbook* (中国法律年鉴). 1987–2019. Beijing: China Law Society.

Ministry of Civil Affairs. *China Civil Affairs' Statistical Yearbook* (中国民政统计年鉴). 2001–2019. Beijing: China Statistics Press.

National Bureau of Statistics. 2010. "The 2009 Monitoring Report on Migrant Workers" (2009年农民工监测调查报告). Accessed November 26, 2020. http://www.stats.gov.cn/ztjc/ztfx/fxbg/201003/t20100319_16135.html

———. 2011. "The 2010 Monitoring Report on Migrant Workers" (2010年农民工监测调查报告). Accessed November 26, 2020. https://www.dydata.io/datastore/detail/1964272941474648064/

———. 2012. "The 2011 Monitoring Report on Migrant Workers" (2011年我国农民工监测调查报告). Accessed November 26, 2020. http://www.stats.gov.cn/ztjc/ztfx/fxbg/201204/t20120427_16154.html

———. 2013. "The 2012 Monitoring Report on Migrant Workers" (2012年我国农民工监测调查报告). Accessed November 26, 2020. http://www.stats.gov.cn/tjsj/zxfb/201305/t20130527_12978.html

———. 2015. "The 2014 Monitoring Report on Migrant Workers" (2014年全国农民工监测调查报告). Accessed November 26, 2020. http://www.stats.gov.cn/tjsj/zxfb/201504/t20150429_797821.html

———. 2016. "The 2015 Monitoring Report on Migrant Workers" (2015年农民工监测调查报告). Accessed November 26, 2020. http://www.stats.gov.cn/tjsj/zxfb/201604/t20160428_1349713.html

———. 2017. "The 2016 Monitoring Report on Migrant Workers" (2016年农民工监测调查报告). Accessed November 26, 2020. http://www.stats.gov.cn/tjsj/zxfb/201704/t20170428_1489334.html

———. 2018. "The 2017 Monitoring Report on Migrant Workers" (2017年农民工监测调查报告). Accessed November 26, 2020. http://www.stats.gov.cn/tjsj/zxfb/201804/t20180427_1596389.html

———. 2019. "National Bureau of Statistics: The 2018 Monitoring Report on Migrant Workers" (国家统计局: 2018年农民工监测调查报告). Accessed November 26, 2020. http://www.cinn.cn/headline/201904/t20190429_211528.html

———. *China Social Statistical Yearbook* (中国社会统计年鉴). 2014–2019. Beijing: China Statistics Press.

———. *China Statistical Yearbook* (中国统计年鉴). 1984–2019. Beijing: China Statistics Press.

China Yearbook of Judicial Administration (中国司法行政年鉴). 1986-1987, 1995, 2002–2004, 2010. Beijing: China Law Press.

Peng, Sen. 2001. *China Economic Systems Reform Yearbook, 2000–2001* (中国经济体制改革年鉴, 2000-2001). Beijing: Chinese Financial & Economic Publishing House.

———. 2018. *China Reform Yearbook* (中国改革年鉴). Beijing: Reform of Economic System Press.

Supreme People's Court. 2000. *Collection of Archival Records on Judicial Statistics of the People's Courts, 1949–1998 (Civil Litigation)* (全国法院历史资料汇编, 1949-1998 [民事部分]). Beijing: People's Courts Press.

———. The 2017 Statistical Communiqué of the People's Courts (2017年全国法院司法统计公报). Accessed November 15, 2020. http://gongbao.court.gov.cn/details/c15ac3fd6bd534567eec8e047941eb.html

———. The 2018 Statistical Communiqué of the People's Courts (2018年全国法院司法统计公报). Accessed November 15, 2020.
http://gongbao.court.gov.cn/details/c70030ba6761ec165c3c2f0bd2a12b.html

———. 2018. *Historical Statistical Books of the People's Courts, 1949–2016* (The First Volume on Civil Litigation, 1950–2004) and (The Second Volume on Civil Litigation, 2005–2016) (人民法院司法统计历史典籍[民事卷一, 1950-2004], [民事卷二, 2005-2016]). Beijing: Press of Chinese Democratic Legal System.

———. The 2019 Statistical Communiqué of the People's Courts (2019年全国法院司法统计公报). Accessed November 15, 2020. http://gongbao.court.gov.cn/details/fcadfe71e8d5a54acd8f840f768e65.html

———. Wang, Zhenchuan. 1981. *China Yearbook of the New Era of Reform and Opening Up* (中国改革开放新时期年鉴). Beijing: Press of Chinese Democratic Legal System.

Index

Note: Page numbers in *italics* refer to tables and figures.

active strategies versus mechanisms, 272n21. *See also*
  mechanisms of power
adjudication, 199–202, 236–242; against
  first-instance divorce suits, 186; as
  mechanism of power to curb divorce,
  153, 164–165, 168, 172, 185–188;
  as mode of case disposition, 162
Administration Council, 92
administrative adjudication, 31, 115–116
administrative reconsideration, 31, 116
adultery and infidelity, 23, 72–74,
  167, 229, 234–235
agenda-setting power, 8, 19, 22,
  47–48, 119–120, 150, 153–154, 225,
  228–229, 257. *See also* power
All-China Women's Federation,
  12, 81–82, 246, 251, 262,
  278n37, 293n27, 294n7
appropriation. *See* cultural appropriation
arbitration, 31, 78, 86, 114–115, 244, 267
arranged marriage, 87
authoritarian legality: historically
  charged, culturalist analysis of,
  4–5, 19, 24, 29; role of culture, 7,
  19, 28–29, 30–41, 136–137, 143;
  scholarship on, 7, 24, 25–29, 33,
  35, 38, 39, 136–137, 139, 270n3;
  social inequality and, 41–42, 123,
  264; use of the term, 4, 24, 29

Banister, Judith, 58
Basic People's Courts, 163, 176,
  179, 181, 183, 198, 287n45
bigamy and polygamy, 87, 167, 235, 242
black-letter laws, 167, 203, 234.
  See also letter of law

Blumberg, Abraham S., 190–191, 224
  –225
Bourdieu, Pierre, 7, 36–37, 271n9, 283n34
breakdown of mutual affection, 166–167,
  171, 185, 286n26. *See also* legal
  grounds for divorce; Marriage Law
bricolage, 32, 33, 272n21
Burawoy, Michael, 15
Bush, George H. W., 99

cadres: party cadres, 36, 86–89, 91,
  93, 97, 115–116, 126, 177, 205,
  210, 220, 273n28; village cadres,
  10–12, 48, 67, 83–85, 103, 110,
  155, 164, 209–211, 237, 241,
  246–247, 250–257, 279n64
Campbell, John L., 7, 38–39, 136–138,
  140–143, 271nn10, 12, 271–
  272nn13, 272nn14, 21, 284n47
Case Quality Assessment System, 163–165, 186. *See also*
  Supreme People's Court
cat theory, 36, 40
CCP. *See* Chinese Communist Party
Center for Integrated Mediation for
  Disputes and Conflicts, 13, 85, 246
Cheesman, Nick, 136
Chen, Heping (judge), 230–234
Chen, Yun, 273n28
child abduction, 217, 222–223, 292n47;
  case of Deng Pingping, 223, 291n46
child custody: allocation in husband-
  initiated suits, 238; allocation in
  wife-initiated suits, 238; case of Wu
  Manli, 190–199, 202, 209–211,
  213–217, 219, 222, 225, 228;
  judges' decision-making power

315

CPSIA information can be obtained
at www.ICGtesting.com
Printed in the USA
JSHW051908050622
26731JS00002B/4